Business Plans Handbook

Business
Plans

**A COMPILATION
OF BUSINESS
PLANS DEVELOPED
BY INDIVIDUALS
THROUGHOUT
NORTH AMERICA**

Handbook

VOLUME

36

**Kristin B. Mallegg,
Project Editor**

GALE
CENGAGE Learning

Farmington Hills, Mich • San Francisco • New York • Waterville, Maine
Meriden, Conn • Mason, Ohio • Chicago

Business Plans Handbook, Volume 36

Project Editor: Kristin B. Mallegg

Content Developer: Michele P. LaMeau

Product Design: Jennifer Wahi

Composition and Electronic Prepress: Evi Seoud

Manufacturing: Rita Wimberley

For product information and technology assistance, contact us at
Gale Customer Support, 1-800-877-4253.
For permission to use material from this text or product,
submit all requests online at **www.cengage.com/permissions.**
Further permissions questions can be emailed to
permissionrequest@cengage.com

While every effort has been made to ensure the reliability of the information presented in this publication, Gale, a part of Cengage Learning, does not guarantee the accuracy of the data contained herein. Gale accepts no payment for listing; and inclusion in the publication of any organization, agency, institution, publication, service, or individual does not imply endorsement of the editors or publisher. Errors brought to the attention of the publisher and verified to the satisfaction of the publisher will be corrected in future editions.

Gale, a part of Cengage Learning
27500 Drake Rd.
Farmington Hills, MI 48331-3535

ISBN-13: 978-1-4103-1108-5
1084-4473

Printed in Mexico
1 2 3 4 5 6 7 20 19 18 17 16

Contents

CONTENTS

Highlights

Business Plans Handbook, Volume 36 (BPH-36) is a collection of business plans compiled by entrepreneurs seeking funding for small businesses throughout North America. For those looking for examples of how to approach, structure, and compose their own business plans, *BPH-36* presents 20 sample plans, including plans for the following businesses:

- Automotive Detailing Business
- Chimney Sweep/Screen Repair Business
- Competitive Intelligence Consulting Business
- Concrete Coating Company
- Crime Scene Cleaning/Bioremediation Business
- Essential Oils Retail Sales
- General Staffing Company
- Healthcare Process Improvement Consultant
- Hot Meal Delivery Service
- Inflatable Party Rentals
- Judicial Interpreter Business
- Mobile Day Spa
- Outdoor Furniture Business
- Package and Mailing Business
- Photo Booth Business
- Scooter Rental Business
- Smart Home Automation Consulting & Installation Business
- Software Training Business
- Sports Fan Experience Business
- Video Game Testing Services Provider

FEATURES AND BENEFITS

BPH-36 offers many features not provided by other business planning references including:

- Twenty business plans, each of which represent an attempt at clarifying (for themselves and others) the reasons that the business should exist or expand and why a lender should fund the enterprise.
- Two fictional plans that are used by business counselors at a prominent small business development organization as examples for their clients. (You will find these in the Business Plan Template Appendix.)
- A directory section that includes listings for venture capital and finance companies, which specialize in funding start-up and second-stage small business ventures, and a comprehensive listing of

Service Corps of Retired Executives (SCORE) offices. In addition, the Appendix also contains updated listings of all Small Business Development Centers (SBDCs); associations of interest to entrepreneurs; Small Business Administration (SBA) Regional Offices; and consultants specializing in small business planning and advice. It is strongly advised that you consult supporting organizations while planning your business, as they can provide a wealth of useful information.

- A Small Business Term Glossary to help you decipher the sometimes confusing terminology used by lenders and others in the financial and small business communities.

- A cumulative index, outlining each plan profiled in the complete Business Plans Handbook series.

- A Business Plan Template which serves as a model to help you construct your own business plan. This generic outline lists all the essential elements of a complete business plan and their components, including the Summary, Business History and Industry Outlook, Market Examination, Competition, Marketing, Administration and Management, Financial Information, and other key sections. Use this guide as a starting point for compiling your plan.

- Extensive financial documentation required to solicit funding from small business lenders. You will find examples of Cash Flows, Balance Sheets, Income Projections, and other financial information included with the textual portions of the plan.

Introduction

Perhaps the most important aspect of business planning is simply doing it. More and more business owners are beginning to compile business plans even if they don't need a bank loan. Others discover the value of planning when they must provide a business plan for the bank. The sheer act of putting thoughts on paper seems to clarify priorities and provide focus. Sometimes business owners completely change strategies when compiling their plan, deciding on a different product mix or advertising scheme after finding that their assumptions were incorrect. This kind of healthy thinking and re-thinking via business planning is becoming the norm. The editors of *Business Plans Handbook, Volume 36 (BPH-36)* sincerely hope that this latest addition to the series is a helpful tool in the successful completion of your business plan, no matter what the reason for creating it.

This thirty-sixth volume, like each volume in the series, offers business plans created by real people. *BPH-36* provides 20 business plans. The business and personal names and addresses and general locations have been changed to protect the privacy of the plan authors.

NEW BUSINESS OPPORTUNITIES

As in other volumes in the series, *BPH-36* finds entrepreneurs engaged in a wide variety of creative endeavors. Examples include an automotive detailing business, a concrete coating company, and an essential oils retail sales. In addition, several other plans are provided, including a hot meal delivery service, a judicial interpreter business, mobile day spa and a photo booth business, among others.

Comprehensive financial documentation has become increasingly important as today's entrepreneurs compete for the finite resources of business lenders. Our plans illustrate the financial data generally required of loan applicants, including Income Statements, Financial Projections, Cash Flows, and Balance Sheets.

ENHANCED APPENDIXES

In an effort to provide the most relevant and valuable information for our readers, we have updated the coverage of small business resources. For instance, you will find a directory section, which includes listings of all of the Service Corps of Retired Executives (SCORE) offices; an informative glossary, which includes small business terms; and a cumulative index, outlining each plan profiled in the complete *Business Plans Handbook* series. In addition we have updated the list of Small Business Development Centers (SBDCs); Small Business Administration Regional Offices; venture capital and finance companies, which specialize in funding start-up and second-stage small business enterprises; associations of interest to entrepreneurs; and consultants, specializing in small business advice and planning. For your reference, we have also reprinted the business plan template, which provides a comprehensive overview of the essential components of a business plan and two fictional plans used by small business counselors.

SERIES INFORMATION

If you already have the first thirty-five volumes of *BPH*, with this thirty-sixth volume, you will now have a collection of over 660 business plans (not including the updated plans); contact information for hundreds of organizations and agencies offering business expertise; a helpful business plan template; more than 1,500 citations to valuable small business development material; and a comprehensive glossary of terms to help the business planner navigate the sometimes confusing language of entrepreneurship.

ACKNOWLEDGEMENTS

The Editors wish to sincerely thank the contributors to *BPH-36*, including:

- Fran Fletcher
- Paul Greenland
- Claire Moore
- Zuzu Enterprises

COMMENTS WELCOME

Your comments on *Business Plans Handbook* are appreciated. Please direct all correspondence, suggestions for future volumes of *BPH*, and other recommendations to the following:

Managing Editor, Business Product
Business Plans Handbook
Gale, a part of Cengage Learning
27500 Drake Rd.
Farmington Hills, MI 48331-3535
Phone: (248)699-4253
Fax: (248)699-8052
Toll-Free: 800-357-GALE
E-mail: BusinessProducts@gale.com

Automotive Detailing Business

Parker Automotive Services LLC

52 Victory Ln.
Windy Ridge, AL 35004

Paul Greenland

Parker Automotive Services is an automotive detailing and hand carwash business.

EXECUTIVE SUMMARY

Joe Parker has always been a perfectionist with a strong eye for detail. A long-time automobile enthusiast, Joe's cars always look their very best, resulting in compliments from friends and neighbors and a steady stream of "side jobs" to detail cars on evenings and weekends. In order to fulfill a lifelong dream of business ownership, Joe has decided to establish Parker Automotive Services, his own auto detailing enterprise, which will allow him to capitalize on his natural abilities. Following regular conversations with vehicle owners throughout the community, he is convinced that there is ample demand for his new business in the local market. Joe will begin the business cost-effectively as a part-time operation from his home. However, a thoughtful organic growth strategy has been developed for Parker Automotive Services that will quickly establish it as a successful full-time enterprise.

INDUSTRY ANALYSIS

The Chicago-based International Carwash Association (http://www.carwash.org) is a leading trade organization representing the carwash industry. Established in 1955, its members include operators, suppliers, and manufacturers. As its name suggests, the organization's reach extends beyond the United States to include approximately 24 different countries, where its members operate about 15,000 carwashes. The association publishes *CAR WASH Magazine* and operates the largest trade show and convention in the world called The Car Wash Show. Members of the auto detailing and carwash industry also benefit from trade publications, including *Professional Carwashing & Detailing*.

The carwash and auto detailing industry dates back more than a century, originating in Detroit in 1914. According to a July 2015 report from the industry information provider, IBISWorld, the carwash and auto detailing industry generates annual revenues of approximately $9 billion, a figure that is growing 2.7 percent annually. The industry, which is dominated by small-business owners, has about 61,000 establishments that collectively employ nearly 195,000 people.

The economy is a significant concern for industry players, because consumers may eliminate carwashes or wash their own vehicles during difficult economic times. Other top challenges faced by the industry include labor and environmental issues. The weather also has a significant impact on business patterns.

For example, inclement weather (snow and rain) can have a negative and sometimes unpredictable impact on demand. The International Carwash Association reports that, in North America, a growing percentage of consumers prefer to have their cars washed professionally. Compared to 1994 (47%), the percentage of drivers that most frequently use professional carwashes has increased, reaching 72 percent in 2014.

MARKET ANALYSIS

Parker Automotive Services is based in Windy Ridge, Alabama, which offers warm weather year-round. Using market research data obtained from the Windy Ridge Public Library, Joe Parker has discovered that the local population included 104,600 people (44,200 households) in 2014. The population is expected to grow slightly (by approximately 2%) through 2019. In 2014 about 45.9 percent of residents had annual household income of more than $40,000, while 27.2 percent had income of more than $60,000, and 18.2 percent had household income of more than $75,000.

There were approximately 80,000 vehicles in Windy Ridge in 2014, with an average of two per household. Specifically, local vehicle ownership within the city is estimated as follows:

Vehicles	Households
1	39%
2	34%
3	9%
4	4%
5	1%

Based on national vehicle registration trends, Joe Parker estimates that vehicle registrations in his business' market area break down as follows:

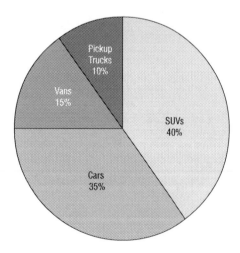

On average, consumers in the local community devote approximately $7,000 to automotive and transportation needs each year. However, it is difficult to determine the amount that is specifically devoted to car washing and auto detailing.

Competition

Windy Ridge already has several carwashes operating in the community. The majority are automated carwashes located at service stations or self-service locations. A locally-owned conveyor-type operation, which offers auto detailing options, will provide the greatest source of competition for Parker Automotive Services. However, Joe Parker will differentiate his business by offering exceptional service and quality at a competitive (but not discounted) price point.

PERSONNEL

Parker Automotive Services is being established by Joe Parker, a Windy Ridge native who has decided to start his own business following a 15-year customer service career with Century Auto Parts. Joe is a perfectionist with a strong eye for detail. A long-time automobile enthusiast, his cars always look their very best, resulting in compliments from friends and neighbors and a steady stream of "side jobs" to detail cars on evenings and weekends.

At Century, Joe has been promoted several times during his tenure with the locally-owned company. Beginning as a clerk, Joe steadily was given more responsibility as the owners recognized his ability to troubleshoot problems and resolve customer service issues. Well-liked by customers, he has done much to help Century build its business. Although Century's owners are reluctant to lose him, they are supportive of his decision to fulfill a lifelong dream of business ownership, and have offered to provide him with some focused training that, along with an online small business management course he is taking, will help him to succeed.

Joe initially will operate his business as a part-time, home-based operation, serving as its only employee. After transitioning the business to a local parking garage, he will continue to serve as Parker Automotive Services' sole employee until he is joined by his son, Brian, during the third year of operation. Ultimately, Joe plans to put his son in charge of two full-time employees and oversee the business' fleet service, which will be established during the fourth year of operation, as outlined in the Growth Strategy section of this plan.

Professional & Advisory Support

Parker Automotive Services has established a business banking account with Windy Ridge Community Bank, including a merchant account for accepting credit card payments. Tax advisement is provided by Stevenson & Associates. Parker has established his limited liability company with the assistance of a local attorney.

SERVICES

Parker Automotive Services has structured services into several convenient packages for customers, along with a menu of á la carte services that can be added to any package for an additional fee.

Service Packages:

Economy: Includes a complete exterior washing and drying: $10

Basic: Includes a complete exterior wash, as well as vacuuming the interior of the vehicle, wiping down the dashboard and door jams, and cleaning all windows: $15

Comprehensive: Includes everything offered as part of the basic package, along with cleaning vehicle rims: $20

Deluxe: Includes everything offered as part of the comprehensive package, along with tire shining: $25

Executive: Includes everything offered as part of the deluxe package, as well as a complete interior detailing package (vinyl/leather/rubber cleaning, trunk cleaning, carpet and upholstery cleaning, and floormat shampooing): $125

Ultimate: Includes everything offered as part of the executive package, along with vehicle waxing: $150

Additional Services:

- Engine Cleaning: $125
- Rubber Matt Cleaning: $5
- Carpet Floormat Cleaning: $10
- Tire Shining: $4
- Foam Wax: $5
- Air Freshener: $2
- Under Flush: $5

A $25 surcharge will be assessed for large vehicles (e.g., SUVs, minivans, over-sized vehicles, etc.)

OPERATIONS

Joe Parker has developed the following list of tools and equipment that are critical to the operation of his business. Although he already owns many of these items, Joe has estimated that he will need to spend $2,000 for additional items, which he will cover from personal savings.

Tools & Equipment:

- Air Compressor
- Brushes (Assortment)
- Extractor
- Orbital Dual-Action Polisher
- Rotary Buffer
- Wet-Dry Vacuum

Supplies & Chemicals:

- Ammonia
- Bug/Tar Remover
- Carwash Shampoo
- Carnauba Wax
- Chrome Polish
- Detailing Clay
- Detailing Spray
- Distilled White Vinegar
- Glass Cleaner
- Glass Polish
- Interior Vinyl Dressing
- Leather & Vinyl Cleaner
- Mitts
- Odor Neutralizer

- Rubber Restorer
- Sponges
- Spot Remover
- Synthetic Wax
- Tire & Wheel Cleaner
- Towels (100% cotton terry cloth)
- WD-40

Location:

Parker Automotive Services will begin operations as a home-based, part-time business. However, Joe Parker has made arrangements to transition the business to a local parking garage, where he will lease space from the garage owner and gain access to a steady stream of regular customers who will appreciate the convenience of having their vehicle washed and/or detailed while they are at work. The parking garage owner has a convenient space that the business can use for automotive washing and detailing, along with a secure area where equipment and supplies can be stored safely.

Hours of Operation

During its first year of operations, Parker Automotive Services will provide services by appointment only, mainly on evenings and weekends. During the second year, services will be provided at the parking garage at the following times:

Monday: 7:30 a.m.—6:00 p.m.

Tuesday: 7:30 a.m.—6:00 p.m.

Wednesday: 7:30 a.m.—6:00 p.m.

Thursday: 7:30 a.m.—6:00 p.m.

Friday: 7:30 a.m.—6:00 p.m.

Saturday: By Appointment

Sunday: Closed

GROWTH STRATEGY

Parker Automotive Services has developed a formal strategy for growing the business during its first four years of operations.

Year One:

Establish Parker Automotive Services as a home-based, part-time operation with one employee, providing service mainly on evenings and weekends. Focus on building an initial customer base and developing awareness of the business in the local community. Make arrangements to establish the business as a full-time, parking garage-based operation in year two.

Year Two:

Transition the business to a full-time operation based in a local parking garage, providing "while you wait" and/or "while you work" services. Continue to offer occasional evening and weekend services to non-parking-garage customers from Joe Parker's home.

Year Three:

Grow the business via the addition of a second employee (Joe Parker's son, Brian), allowing for a significant capacity expansion. Begin pursuing fleet vehicle business, with a goal of establishing at least one contract to begin in year four. Provide Brian Parker with small business management training.

Year Four:

Achieve significant expansion by adding two full-time employees, managed by Brian Parker, who will assist with services provided at the parking garage, and eventually transition to an alternate location where Parker Automotive Services will provide dedicated fleet vehicle services.

After thoughtful analysis, Joe Parker has estimated his monthly volume (by package) as follows:

Monthly volume	2016	2017	2018	2019
Economy	10	160	256	410
Basic	8	80	128	205
Comprehensive	4	60	96	154
Deluxe	3	40	64	102
Executive	2	8	13	20
Ultimate	1	4	6	10
Monthly total	**28**	**352**	**563**	**901**

MARKETING & SALES

A marketing plan has been developed for Parker Automotive Services that includes the following tactics:

1. **Web Site:** A Web site will be developed, providing basic information about services offered, an appointment request function, and a photo gallery of cars that the business has detailed.

2. **Consumer Direct Marketing:** On a monthly basis, postcards will be mailed to households with income of $50,000 and up in Parker Automotive Services' target market area. Mailing lists will be obtained from a local list broker and mail house, which also will prepare and send the mailings.

3. **Business-to-Business Marketing:** Beginning during the third year of operations, Parker Automotive Services will begin marketing to prospective commercial fleet accounts, which have the potential to provide a steady stream of vehicles from area companies.

4. **Fliers:** Parker Automotive Services will produce a quality, four-color flyer that will be distributed to customers of the parking garage beginning in year two. The flyer will include coupons, as an incentive for using the business' services.

5. **Vehicle Graphics:** Joe Parker will have magnetic signage developed for his car, providing a cost-effective source of mobile advertising.

6. **Loyalty Program:** Customers will always receive a coupon good for a 10 percent discount off their next carwash, as long as the coupon is used within 30 days from the date of service.

LEGAL

Joe Parker has decided to establish his business as a limited liability company. He has registered the business' name, secured a Federal tax ID number (Employer Identification Number), and established a bank account at Windy Ridge Community Bank, including a merchant account for accepting credit card payments with a mobile device. Finally, Parker has obtained all of the necessary permits needed to operate Parker Automotive Services in Windy Ridge, Alabama.

FINANCIAL ANALYSIS

The following table provides sales and profit projections for Parker Automotive Services' first four years of operations. Cost of goods sold includes chemicals, supplies, labor, and production-related energy costs. Additional financial statements have been developed, and are available upon request.

	2016	2017	2018	2019
Total sales	**$16,145**	**$154,555**	**$247,293**	**$395,664**
Cost of goods sold	$ 3,229	$ 30,911	$ 49,459	$ 79,133
Labor cost	$ 5,000	$ 60,000	$ 90,000	$140,000
Total cost of goods sold	**$ 8,229**	**$ 90,911**	**$139,459**	**$219,133**
Gross profit	$ 7,916	$ 63,644	$107,834	$176,531
Expenses				
Marketing & advertising	$ 2,000	$ 8,500	$ 8,500	$ 12,500
Sales tax	$ 807	$ 7,728	$ 12,365	$ 19,783
General/administrative	$ 250	$ 500	$ 500	$ 500
Accounting/legal	$ 1,500	$ 1,500	$ 1,500	$ 1,500
Office supplies	$ 250	$ 500	$ 500	$ 700
Facility lease	$ 0	$ 12,500	$ 12,500	$ 12,500
Equipment	$ 750	$ 10,500	$ 10,500	$ 15,000
Business insurance	$ 450	$ 900	$ 1,500	$ 2,500
Payroll taxes	$ 750	$ 9,000	$ 16,175	$ 21,000
Health insurance	$ 0	$ 5,500	$ 10,500	$ 21,000
Postage	$ 250	$ 2,000	$ 2,000	$ 5,000
Maintenance & repairs	$ 250	$ 400	$ 600	$ 1,200
Telecommunications	$ 0	$ 1,000	$ 1,000	$ 2,000
Total expenses	**$ 7,257**	**$ 60,528**	**$ 78,140**	**$115,183**
Net income before taxes	**$ 659**	**$ 3,116**	**$ 29,694**	**$ 61,348**

The following table provides a detailed breakdown of projected business volume and gross revenue for the first four years of operations.

Package	2016		2017		2018		2019	
Economy ($10)	120	$ 1,200	1,920	$ 19,200	3,072	$ 30,720	4,915	$ 49,152
Basic ($15)	96	$ 1,440	960	$ 14,400	1,536	$ 23,040	2,458	$ 36,864
Comprehensive ($20)	48	$ 960	720	$ 14,400	1,152	$ 23,040	1,843	$ 36,864
Deluxe ($25)	36	$ 900	480	$ 12,000	768	$ 19,200	1,229	$ 30,720
Executive ($125)	24	$ 3,000	96	$ 12,000	154	$ 19,200	246	$ 30,720
Ultimate ($175)	12	$ 2,100	48	$ 8,400	77	$ 13,440	123	$ 21,504
Additional services		$ 1,920		$ 16,080		$ 25,728		$ 41,165
Surcharges		$ 4,625		$ 58,075		$ 92,925		$148,675
Gross revenue		**$16,145**		**$154,555**		**$247,293**		**$395,664**
Packages sold	**336**		**4,224**		**6,758**		**10,813**	

On a percentage basis, Joe Parker estimates that the service packages offered by the business will contribute to gross revenues as follows:

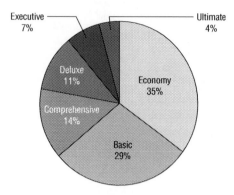

In addition to spending $2,000 for the tools and equipment referenced in the Operations section of this plan, Joe will provide $5,000 from his own savings to cover daily operations.

Chimney Sweep/Screen Repair Business

Rathburn Home Services, Inc.

PO Box 4459
Auburn, CA 95602

Claire Moore

Rathburn Home Services, Inc. (RHSI) is located in Auburn, CA. The corporation provides services in two specialty areas of home maintenance: chimney cleaning and dryer vent cleaning operating under the name Sierra Hills Chimney Sweep & Dryer Vent Cleaning. The other service includes sales, repair and installation of screens for doors and windows operating under the name Sierra Hills Window and Door Screens. We serve residences and businesses in the Sierra and Foothills regions of Northern California.

EXECUTIVE SUMMARY

Rathburn Home Services, Inc. (RHSI) is located in Auburn, CA. The corporation provides services in two specialty areas of home maintenance: chimney cleaning and dryer vent cleaning operating under the name Sierra Hills Chimney Sweep & Dryer Vent Cleaning. The other service includes sales, repair and installation of screens for doors and windows operating under the name Sierra Hills Window and Door Screens.

We serve residences and businesses in the Sierra and Foothills regions of Northern California.

Financing for the business will come from the owners. The funds will be used to purchase equipment, supplies and a van as well as development of a web site and the setup of a storage and workshop location.

Our research has shown that the greater part of our business will come from homeowners who have or desire a wood, gas or pellet stove or fireplace. As our skills, training and equipment lend themselves to providing dryer vent cleaning without significant additional investment, we will offer this service to our customer base as well.

Because servicing heating equipment is a seasonal business, RHSI also plans to operate a business to service window and door screens for the same customer demographic thus securing business the year 'round and giving us the ability to offer value added service to our customers.

Revenues are expected to grow at a rate of 20 percent per year as we establish and develop our brand in the market.

Objectives

RHSI intends to establish its brand as the premier provider of home services related to fire and gas heating, screen repair and installation and dryer vent cleaning. We will begin by placing the focus on our chimney cleaning and related services such as repairs and the sales and installation of stoves and fireplaces. Growth in this area of our business will help to position us to expand into screen and dryer vent services.

- Within one year of launch to achieve at least a 90% or four-star rating on social media services such as Yelp.com

- To increase our list of regular clients by 20 percent each year.

- Within five years to increase business capacity to include three full-time trained and certified employees.

Mission

It is the mission of RHSI to provide home owners and commercial property owners with chimney cleaning and repair, screen repair and installation, and dryer vent cleaning as well as sale and installation of the stove or fireplace to best meet their needs at the right price. Our friendly and knowledgeable staff will help ensure that our customers have the safest and most comfortable environment all year long.

Keys to Success

RHSI's keys to success include:

- Employ only trained and certified technicians who will ensure the safety and proper operation of stoves, fireplaces and dryer vents.

- Integrate our service business software with our web site to streamline scheduling, billing and collections.

- Provide a good customer experience that will encourage word-of-mouth growth, repeat business and the purchase of the full scope of services offered.

COMPANY SUMMARY

RHSI will be a local company serving areas in the Sierra foothills region of Northern California. Established in 2016 as a corporation, RHSI was founded by Al & Cindy Rathburn who operate the business out of their home and a workshop in Auburn, CA.

RHSI does business as Sierra Hills Chimney Sweep & Dryer Vent Cleaning and Sierra Hills Window and Door Screens. The separation of services under two business names will allow for a more focused marketing plan where services can be promoted under a business name that clearly defines what is being sold.

Both businesses will be promoted on the business web site where the public can learn about services provided and will be able to schedule an appointment for any of the services offered by RHSI.

Company Ownership

Al and Cindy Rathburn founded RHSI in January of 2016. Each owns 50 percent of the company.

Start-up Summary

Al and Cindy will invest their personal funds of $23,500 into the business. Al's father, James Rathburn, has agreed to co-sign for a line of credit in the amount of $20,000 to ensure that RHSI has access to working capital as needed.

James Rathburn has also agreed to rent workshop space on his property to RHSI at below-market cost. This will be a temporary arrangement to help the business get established. We intend to move to a commercial warehouse space by the end of year four.

Al has converted a pre-owned industrial van by adding shelving, storage and equipment to use in cleaning chimneys and dryer vents. The van is also equipped with side-mounting to hold brushes and top mounting to hold ladders. For now we will use magnetic signs on the van. We plan to acquire a newer van by year four and install it with a custom wrap that will attract more attention as an advertising device.

Screen work is done at the warehouse.

Start-up expenses

Licenses	$ 150
Advertising	$ 250
Web site development	$ 850
Legal fees incorporation	$1,890
Magnetic truck signs	$ 100
Insurance deposit	$ 400
Office supplies	100
Total start-up expenses	**$3,740**

List of assets needed for startup

Item	Estimated cost
Computer/printer/copier/scanner/fax	$ 1,500
Brushes	$ 700
Storage/filing/shelving	$ 300
Paper shredder	$ 50
Desk/table/chair/lamp	$ 350
Ladders & ladder hooks	$ 1,250
Tarps, drop cloths, tape	$ 325
Misc tools & safety equipment	$ 450
Uniforms & shoes	$ 350
Inspection tools	$ 325
RoVac chimney & dryer vent vacuum	$ 2,700
Misc. supplies	$ 350
Misc. tools	$ 450
Ventilator	$ 120
Draft gauge tester	$ 350
Infrared thermometer	$ 138
Combustible gas leak detector	$ 400
Digital multimeter	$ 130
Digital carbon monoxide analyzer	$ 813
Digital gas pressure manometer	$ 209
Industrial van 2008 GMC Savana Cargo	$ 7,000
Van customization	$ 1,500
Total non-cash assets for startup	**$19,760**

Startup funding

Cash required	$ 5,000
Startup assets to fund	$19,760
Startup expenses to fund	$ 3,740
Total funding required	**$23,500**

SERVICES

In Year One RHSI will emphasize its services related to chimney inspection, cleaning and repair. As our service area experiences colder temperatures during the winter months due to its higher elevation, we feel that this affords us a greater possibility for building a customer base.

During the spring and summer months we will solicit our chimney customers to take advantage of our dryer vent cleaning and screen repairs and installation services.

Services offered include:

- Chimney Sweeping
- Chimney Safety Inspection
- Chimney Repairs
- Gas Fireplace Service/Repairs
- Pellet Stove Cleaning/Repair
- Sealing and tuck-pointing the exterior of chimneys
- Smoke/draft testing
- Repair/replace chimney roof flashing
- Wood Stove and Fireplace sales and installation
- Gas Stove and Fireplace sales and installation
- Measure, make, install new window/door screens
- Measure, make, install new patio door screens
- Dryer Vent Cleaning
- Dryer Vent Installation

On average a thorough chimney cleaning runs from $120 to $250 dollars with an average price of $185.00 per home. Each chimney takes 2-4 hours to complete.

Areas served include communities in Placer, Nevada, Amador and El Dorado counties. Communities served include:

- Roseville
- Newcastle
- Placerville
- Rocklin
- Apple Gate
- Rescue
- Lincoln
- Forest Hill
- Cool
- Auburn
- Grass Valley
- El Dorado Hills

MARKET ANALYSIS

The home services industry currently includes specialties ranging from home remodeling to dog walking. According to a June 16, 2015 article by Neil Howe, "Why Home Services Marketplaces Offer More Than Just Renovations," for Forbes.com estimates of total industry revenue range from $400 billion up to $800 billion.

The market includes both residential and commercial properties.

- **Residences:** homes, apartments, condos including rentals
- **Commercial:** small businesses, restaurants, hotels and resorts

Residences will be by far our larger customer base. While they require a high level of customer care, they also offer the potential for additional sales of services as well as repeat business.

We will focus our marketing and sales efforts in the following counties: Amador, Nevada, El Dorado and Placer. These counties are located in the Sierra Foothills of Northern California. Winter temperatures reach an average low of 30 degrees. Summer temperatures range from the 80s and 90s in the foothills to the 70s and 80s in areas with higher elevation such as Nevada County.

Many businesses and residences have wood, pellet or gas stoves installed not only for heat production but as part of the ambiance of living in sight of the scenic beauty of the Sierra Nevada Mountains.

Number of owners vs. renters	Owner-occupied	Renter-occupied
Amador county	10,859	3,403
Nevada county	29,768	11,223
El Dorado county	50,797	17,088
Placer county	93,656	39,053

Occupied and vacant housing units	Occupied	Vacant
Amador county	79%	21%
Nevada county	78%	22%
El Dorado county	77%	23%
Placer county	86%	14%

Area housing types	One unit detached	Other
Amador county	83%	17%
Nevada county	82%	18%
El Dorado county	82%	18%
Placer county	77%	23%

Fuel used to heat home	Utility gas	Bottled gas	Electricity	Wood	Other
Amador county	25%	28%	21%	22%	4%
Nevada county	33%	34%	14%	16%	3%
El Dorado county	33%	28%	21%	15%	3%
Placer county	60%	9%	24%	5%	2%

	Median age	Median household income	Median home values
Amador county	49.1	$53,684	$270,500
Nevada county	48.5	$57,353	$357,300
El Dorado county	44.1	$69,297	$359,500
Placer county	40.4	$72,725	$342,000

Based on this data we can assume that our typical customer will be a property owner between the ages of 40- to 50, affluent and is willing to pay a premium for professional home maintenance services. This demographic is also likely to use the computer to research and choose service providers.

Data supplied by Town Charts http://www.towncharts.com/California/Housing/Placer-County-CA-Housing-data.html.

Competition

There are several chimney sweeping services in Placer County but not all cover a service area that includes other counties. The Yelp.com listing of, "The Best 10 Chimney Sweeps in Placer County, CA" included four companies with more than 20 reviews.

These competitors included:

Name	Service area	Services
Clean sweep	Sacramento	Fireplace/chimney inspection and clean, dryer vent, gutter clean, roof clean
Ryan brothers	Sacramento & Placer counties	Fireplace/chimney inspection and clean/repairs, gas hearth servicing, dryer vent clean, appliance sales/install
A to Z chimney	Sacramento & Placer counties	Fireplace/chimney inspection and clean/repairs, gas hearth servicing, dryer vent clean, appliance sales/install, screens
A-1 chimney & home	Sacramento	Chimney clean/repair, sales/install fireplace products, gutter clean, power wash, air duct clean

While six chimney sweeps in Nevada County were listed on Yelp.com, none had received more than six reviews.

We feel that our base location in Auburn, CA is ideal in that it places us mid-way between the Sierra foothills with its colder winters and the valley region of Placer County and its hotter summers.

From our location we are positioned to offer chimney and fireplace services to a broad geographic area as well as our screen services to areas where the climate is conducive to open doors and windows in mild weather.

MARKETING PLAN

The median age of residents in our target market area ranges from 40- to 50 years. While this age group is not as active as millennials in utilizing online services, we believe that the Internet will be key factor in our success. According to InterractionsMarketing.com 88 percent of consumers turn to the Internet to research a company or product.

Our marketing efforts will be focused in the following areas:

- **Web site:** pages will cover services offered, service areas, contact information, testimonials, articles on chimney and fire safety and more

- **Blog updated weekly:** short postings of interest to local area residents, periodic focus on sales and specials

- **Social media:** a presence on Facebook, Pinterest and YouTube

- **Yelp listing:** as of March 2015, Yelp received an average of 142 million unique visitors per month

- **Print advertising:** local publications, Yellow Pages ad, post card reminders for annual chimney cleaning to previous customers

Having a web site is crucial to business success today. Our site integrates with our customer management software, ServiceCEO, to help us do a number of essential tasks.

- Set up appointments

- Receive requests for quotes and then follow up

- Scheduling jobs

- Billing and collections

- Send customer reminders

By automating key administrative functions we will be able to provide optimal customer service at an affordable cost.

An independent web specialist has been contracted to design, set up, and maintain our web site and social media accounts. Cindy will create the content for web pages, blog postings and much of the social media activity. Cindy will also monitor emails and online contact submissions and will respond within two business days.

All of our marketing materials will contain our phone number and web site address in order to increase the ability of our target market to learn about us and set up appointments.

MILESTONES

Milestone	Start date	End date	Budget
Incorporation	10/1/2015	1/1/2016	$2,000
Web site design	11/1/2015	1/15/2016	$ 1500
Print advertising	12/1/2015	2/1/2016	$ 500
Social media accounts set up	1/5/2016	2/5/2016	$ 500
Totals			**$4,500**

MANAGEMENT SUMMARY

RHSI is owned by Al and Cindy Rathburn. Al began his professional career after high school in the construction industry working on housing developments in the greater Sacramento, CA area for five years. During this time Al attended Sierra Community college where he took several business courses.

In 2002 Al enlisted in the Army and served for the next four years in the U.S. and Iraq. At the end of his four year commitment Al re-listed for another two years and received an enlistment bonus.

After separation from service in 2009 Al returned to construction work but found that the recession had impacted the industry making regular employment difficult. Al decided to use his veterans' benefits to attend courses at the Chimney Safety Institute of America (CSIA) Technology Center in Plainfield, IN. where he earned certification as a chimney sweep as well as a Certified Dryer Credential.

The CSIA Certified Chimney Sweep and the CSIA Dryer Exhaust Duct Technician credentials are the hallmark of excellence among chimney and venting service professionals. The CSIA has the only national certification program for the chimney and venting service industry.

Al returned to California in 2011 and settled in Auburn, the county seat of Placer County. Known for its California Gold Rush history, Auburn is located in northern California between Sacramento and Lake Tahoe. Al continued to work in construction and often took assignments with chimney sweeps to help him apply and hone his skills.

It was at this time that Al met Cindy Wise, a bookkeeper at an accounting firm in Auburn. Al and Cindy wed in 2013. In 2014 Cindy studied and then passed the exams to become sweep and dryer certified through CSIA.

The Rathburns want to start a family and this desire fueled Al's dream to run his own enterprise. Cindy will work in the office fielding phone calls, helping customers and managing the accounting and paperwork. Because she is certified Cindy will be able to provide expert information and advice in response to customer inquiries.

PERSONNEL PLAN

The following table shows our personnel plan for our first three years.

Personnel plan	Year 1	Year 2	Year 3
Al Rathburn	$32,000	$38,000	$ 40,000
Cindy Rathburn	$18,000	$18,000	$ 20,000
Certified Chimney Sweep 1	$22,000	$30,400	$ 30,400
Certified Chimney Sweep 2			$ 10,000
Totals	**$72,000**	**$86,400**	**$100,400**

FINANCIAL ANALYSIS

Financial Plan

Our financial projections include the following.

Projected Profit and Loss

We are projecting a 20 percent growth rate in revenue each year through year five. Direct costs of labor are estimated at 35 percent of gross revenues.

Pro forma profit and loss

	Year 1	Year 2	Year 3
Sales	$120,000	$144,000	$172,800
Direct costs: labor	$ 42,000	$ 50,400	$ 60,480
Gross profit	**$ 78,000**	**$ 93,600**	**$112,320**
Expenses			
Admin. Payroll	$ 30,000	$ 36,000	$ 40,000
Depreciation	$ 1,574	$ 1,574	$ 1,574
Phone/Internet	$ 2,100	$ 2,400	$ 2,800
Insurance: liability, property, auto, Wcomp	$ 4,200	$ 4,500	$ 5,000
Payroll taxes	$ 7,200	$ 8,640	$ 10,048
Professional dues/memberships	$ 700	$ 850	$ 1,000
Advertising: print	$ 1,500	$ 1,800	$ 2,200
Advertising: Web & Internet	$ 2,000	$ 2,000	$ 2,600
Office supplies	$ 420	$ 420	$ 420
Auto: gas & maintenance	$ 4,000	$ 5,500	$ 6,500
Software	$ 750	$ 750	$ 750
Rent	$ 6,000	$ 6,000	$ 6,000
Utilities	$ 4,800	$ 4,800	$ 4,800
Repairs & maintenance	$ 1,500	$ 1,500	$ 1,800
Accounting & legal	$ 1,800	$ 1,800	$ 2,000
Web site	$ 2,500	$ 2,800	$ 2,800
Other expenses	$ 1,200	$ 1,200	$ 1,500
Total operating expenses	**$ 72,244**	**$ 82,534**	**$ 91,792**
Profit before interest and taxes	$ 5,756	$ 11,066	$ 20,528
Taxes incurred	$ 863	$ 1,660	$ 3,079
Net profit	**$ 4,893**	**$ 9,406**	**$ 17,449**
Net profit/sales	**4%**	**7%**	**10%**
Break-even revenue	$112,473	$129,529	$145,955
Monthly break-even revenue	$ 9,373	$ 10,794	$ 12,163
Estimated monthly fixed cost	$ 3,952	$ 4,677	$ 5,219

Projected Balance Sheet

Projected balance sheet

Assets	Year 1	Year 2	Year 3
Cash in bank	$6,167	$ 2,160	$19,654
Accounts receivable	$ 425	$ 500	$ 550
Other current assets			
Total current assets	**$6,592**	**$ 2,660**	**$20,204**
Fixed assets			
Office furniture & equipment	$2,200	$ 2,200	$ 2,200
Tools & equipment	$5,038	$ 5,038	$ 5,038
Van	$8,500	$ 8,500	$ 8,500
Less: depreciation	($1,574)	($ 1,574)	($ 1,574)
Total assets	**$7,218**	**$16,824**	**$34,368**
Liabilities			
Current liabilities			
Accounts payable	$ 325	$ 525	$ 620
Current maturities loan			
Total current liabilities	**$ 325**	**$ 525**	**$ 620**
Long term liabilities loan	0	0	0
Total liabilities	**$ 325**	**$ 525**	**$ 620**
Paid-in capital	$2,000	$ 2,000	$ 2,000
Retained earnings	$4,893	$14,299	$31,748
Total capital	**$4,893**	**$14,299**	**$31,748**
Total liabilities & capital	**$7,218**	**$16,824**	**$34,368**

Competitive Intelligence Consulting Business

Conwell & Associates LP

44786 N. LaMonde Ave.
Winnetka, IL 60611

Paul Greenland

Conwell & Associates is a newly established competitive intelligence consulting firm.

EXECUTIVE SUMMARY

In today's rapidly changing marketplace, businesses and organizations of all types depend upon a steady stream of reliable information regarding their competitors to be successful. This is especially true in extremely competitive industries, where a company's very livelihood and survival may hinge upon being first to market with a new product or service. While some of this "competitive intelligence" may be obvious, or at least easy to obtain, a comprehensive (and ethical) competitive review calls for detailed research and fact-finding, followed by a thoughtful analysis by an experienced professional.

Based near Chicago, Conwell & Associates is a newly established competitive intelligence consulting firm led by partners John Conwell and Dave Stewart. The firm will help clients by identifying specific competitive intelligence goals and objectives, gathering intelligence on their behalf, performing analyses, and presenting specific recommendations. In addition, the firm also will help customers to establish their own internal competitive intelligence programs and provide related services such as win-loss analyses.

INDUSTRY ANALYSIS

The field of competitive intelligence includes independent consultants, such as Conwell & Associates, as well as professionals who work directly for organizations. Front-line staff may have titles such as competitive intelligence associates, operations analyst, intelligence analyst, or market researcher, while more senior-level positions include competitive/market intelligence manager, director, or vice president.

Those working in the field of competitive intelligence are fortunate to have an industry organization devoted specifically to their profession. Formerly known as the Society of Competitive Intelligence Professionals, San Antonio, Texas-based Strategic and Competitive Intelligence Professionals (SCIP) has been in existence since 1986. SCIP's mission is "to enhance the success of our members through leadership, education, advocacy, and networking." More information is available from: www.scip.org.

MARKET ANALYSIS

Conwell & Associates will leverage the industry-specific expertise of its owners to capitalize on consulting opportunities. Specifically, the firm will focus on consumer packaged goods companies and technology firms working within the aerospace and defense markets. With ample opportunities in the local Chicago market, the firm's partners have used their research and analysis skills to develop a list of first-, second-, and third-tier prospects (available upon request). This was accomplished using a combination of their own market knowledge and a subscription-based information service that enabled them to search for prospects based on criteria such as industry sector, annual revenue, geography, etc. With a database of clearly-defined prospects, the owners will be able to take a highly targeted approach to the tactics outlined in the Marketing & Sales section of this plan.

SERVICES

Process

Typically, Conwell & Associates will take the following approach when working with clients:

1. *Identifying goals and objectives:* Before beginning any project, the firm will meet with clients to identify specific areas of concern, and the specific information that is needed to address these concerns. Concise goals and objectives will be identified, in order to determine the most effective strategy and tactics.

2. *Gathering business intelligence:* At this stage, the firm will gather a wide range of commercial, business, and competitive information, through publicly available sources and networking with a variety of constituents (especially at business conferences and trade shows). Simply listening to conversations between other professionals at trade shows is an incredibly useful source of information. Because Conwell and Stewart's association with their client will not be obvious, they will be in a position to gather information more easily than their client's may be able to do directly. Information from the client's employees (from all areas of the organization) also may be gathered.

3. *Performing intelligence analysis:* Effective competitive intelligence professionals have the ability to take the results of their research and, through a variety of analytic methods, boil down a sometimes overwhelming amount of data and information into concise findings for their clients. At this stage, the client's situation in the marketplace will be clearly defined, and competitive threats and business/market opportunities will be identified.

4. *Presenting strategic recommendations:* Ultimately, the firm will present the results of its research and analysis to the client in the form of concise recommendations and summaries. Conwell & Associates will provide a detailed situational overview and present findings related to competitive threats and business opportunities. In addition, the firm will share trends and forecasts that have been identified as a result of its analysis.

Once Conwell & Associates has a clear understanding of the client's situation, goals, and objectives, the firm will work with the client to identify one or more tactics, such as:

- Establishing internal competitive intelligence programs & departments

- Planning and operating "strategy wargames"

- Performing more detailed/specific competitive threats/opportunities analyses

- Conducting situational and win/loss analyses

- Leading business/brand readiness reviews

- Designing and implementing trend programs

OPERATIONS

Location

With operations located in the Chicago, Illinois, area, and easy access to O'Hare International Airport, Conwell & Associates is strategically positioned to serve clients throughout the continental United States, and travel internationally when necessary. In addition to a healthy local business community that includes many leading corporations, Chicago is located near other major cities such as Milwaukee, Wisconsin; Madison, Wisconsin; and Rockford, Illinois. John Conwell and Dave Stewart will operate their new consulting practice virtually (e.g., from respective home offices) for the first three years of operations, and will consider leasing dedicated office space in year four.

Business Structure

Conwell & Associates is being formed as a limited partnership. John Conwell will serve as the firm's general partner, assuming responsibility for its management and partnership obligations. Dave Stewart will act as a limited partner, with no management responsibilities. However, his limited partner status will entitle him to a pre-determined share of Conwell & Associates's profits, based on his initial investment in the firm.

Fees

When establishing a new consulting practice, fees must be set appropriately. Setting fees too low to undercut the competition and quickly secure new business can be problematic down the road when it becomes necessary to raise fees with existing clients. According to data from the research firm Kilbride & McMahon, entry-level management consultants often charge as much as $175 per hour for their services. Fees generally are highest in coastal regions, and lower in the central states. For this reason, John Conwell has established a rate of $150 per hour for the firm. With all projects, clients will be asked to contract for/agree upon a set number of service hours, and provide advance payment for a mutually agreed-upon number of consulting hours.

PERSONNEL

John Conwell, General Partner

John Conwell will serve as the firm's general partner, assuming responsibility for its management and partnership obligations. He will provide strategic direction for the firm's growth and development, and will concentrate on new business development. Conwell will take the lead with analysis, and also will assist with research and fieldwork. Prior to establishing his own firm, Conwell served as the senior associate director of competitive intelligence for Lanway International, a leading consumer products company. In that role, he led a staff of six professionals, including three competitive intelligence associates and two market researchers.

Dave Stewart, Limited Partner

Dave Stewart will act as a limited partner, with no management responsibilities. However, his limited partner status will entitle him to a share of Conwell & Associates's profits. Stewart will focus almost exclusively on performing research and fieldwork for clients. In addition, he will assist with analysis and present the firm's findings to clients. Prior to joining Conwell & Associates, Stewart spent three years working as an operations analyst for Parker Technologies International, a leading software company. Following this, he was named director of competitive intelligence for Ronway Worldwide, a provider of technology to the aviation and defense industries.

Qualifications & Experience:

Conwell and Stewart have:

- More than 35 years of combined professional business experience

- 20 years of competitive intelligence experience

- Master's degrees (MBA)

Attributes:

In addition, the partners have specific attributes that will position them for success as competitive intelligence consultants, including:

- Proficiency analyzing and manipulating data

- Above average analytical thinking skills

- Persuasive communication skills (verbal and written)

- Strong attention to detail

- Solid project management skills

- Excellent time management capabilities

Professional and Advisory Support

A commercial checking account has been established for Conwell & Associates with BMO Harris Bank. Jennifer Ballard, CPA, has been retained to manage the firm's bookkeeping and tax preparation responsibilities. Finally, John Conwell has retained Chicago business attorney Peter Buscaglia, in the event that legal representation is required. Buscaglia also has assisted in the development of boilerplate agreements (e.g., business partner agreements, confidentiality agreements, contracts, etc.) that Conwell & Associates will use on a regular basis.

GROWTH STRATEGY

Conwell & Associates is fortunate to establish the business with three clients, whose names are not listed due to confidentiality agreements. Together, these clients have contracted with the firm for the equivalent of 35 hours of weekly billable consulting time through the end of 2016. While working on these projects, John Conwell will begin marketing the practice to other potential clients, with a goal of securing at least two new clients by the year's end. Annual gross revenues of nearly $310,000 are expected for 2016, and the partners anticipate that they will recover their $75,000 collective investment that year.

John Conwell has established the following growth targets for the consulting firm's second and third years:

2017: Achieve 55 weekly billable hours and secure at least three additional clients. Generate annual gross revenue of $404,250.

2018: Achieve 65 weekly billable hours and secure at least three additional clients. Generate annual gross revenue of $477,750. With accumulated total net income of $169,750 (less the partners' collective $75,000 investment) from the first three years of operations, consider hiring one or two additional limited partners and leasing dedicated office space in the Chicagoland area.

MARKETING & SALES

Conwell & Associates mainly will focus on growing the business through word-of-mouth (e.g., networking and referrals). However, the following tactics also will be important components of the firm's marketing strategy:

1. The use of social media channels, including LinkedIn, to network with potential customers, as well as professional peers within the competitive intelligence field.

2. A Web site with complete details about the consultancy. This will include a customer inquiry form for prospective clients.

3. Printed collateral describing the consultancy. A high-quality, four-color brochure will be developed for Conwell & Associates, which will include bios of John Conwell and Dave Stewart, a summary of the firm's approach to working with clients, and a brief overview of services offered. In time, testimonials from clients and former colleagues will be added to the brochure.

4. Quarterly direct mailings, consisting of an introductory letter with a strong call to action and the aforementioned brochure, will be sent to key prospects outlined in the Marketing & Sales section of this plan.

5. Conwell and Stewart periodically will submit expert columns regarding competitive intelligence to local, state, and national business publications.

6. Conwell and Stewart occasionally will give presentations at business conferences and take advantage of key opportunities to network with thought leaders, top executives, and other prospective customers.

FINANCIAL ANALYSIS

	2016	2017	2018
Revenue	**$309,750**	**$404,250**	**$477,750**
Expenses			
Salary	$150,000	$250,000	$300,000
Payroll tax	$ 22,500	$ 37,500	$ 45,000
Insurance	$ 6,500	$ 6,500	$ 6,500
Accounting & legal	$ 5,000	$ 7,500	$ 10,000
Office supplies	$ 750	$ 750	$ 750
Equipment	$ 3,500	$ 2,500	$ 2,500
Marketing & advertising	$ 15,000	$ 15,000	$ 15,000
Telecommunications & Internet	$ 2,000	$ 2,250	$ 2,500
Professional development	$ 3,500	$ 3,500	$ 3,500
Unreimbursed travel	$ 6,500	$ 8,000	$ 9,500
Subscriptions & dues	$ 500	$ 500	$ 500
Misc.	$ 500	$ 500	$ 500
Total expenses	**$216,250**	**$334,500**	**$396,250**
Net income	**$ 93,500**	**$ 69,750**	**$ 81,500**

John Conwell will provide $50,000 of his own funds in the form of seed money for Conwell & Associates, while Dave Stewart will contribute $25,000. The partners anticipate that they will recover their collective $75,000 investment by the end of year one. Following its first three years of operations, the firm anticipates having nearly $170,000 to fund growth and expansion in year four.

Concrete Coating Company

TECHNO–COATINGS USA

4653 Hidden Knoll
Oxford, Mississippi 38677

Michele T. Bussone

Using this business plan, the owner of a company that uses concrete to restore, protect and beautify surfaces quickly raised $225,000 of the $375,000 he eventually hopes to secure from investors.

This business plan appeared in a previuoius volume of Business Plans Handbook. It has been updated for this volume.

EXECUTIVE SUMMARY

Mr. Gary Wright, sole shareholder of Techno–Coatings USA (TCU), wants to borrow $375,000 and spend it over a period of 15 months. These funds will be used to grow his business. He will accomplish this growth by adding three additional crews and a manufacturing component for custom concrete work that will enable him to take on more and larger jobs. Growth is expected to hit $4,500,000 by the end of year 2.

Today's climate is extremely favorable to his type of business. New, larger custom homes are popular; remodeling older homes is still a growing industry; and commercial renovations are finding concrete rehabilitation an economical choice while enhancing the appearance of the floors and/or walls.

This growth will require that he fully outfit the new crews, hire supervisors, stock necessary materials and supplies, and have operating funds to cover expenses during the training and ramp–up periods.

In return, Mr. Wright will pay 12% interest annually on the investment for a period of five years. Investors can leave their monies in for the full period or withdraw at any time after two years. Since Mr. Wright basically is the company, insurance will be procured and maintained for the life of the investment to cover all monies involved. This insurance will cover both death and inability to perform the job.

Uses of loan	Time needed	Amount
Payment marketing materials and collaterals	Immediate (1–2 months)	$25,500
Crew #2 set-up	Month 4 of year 1	$90,000
Added materials	Month 4 of year 1	$22,500
Crew #3	Month 10 of year 1	$90,000
Storage building	Month 12 of year 1	$27,000
Crew #4	Year 2	$90,000
Outfit manufacturing forms, equipment, materials for R&D	Year 1	$30,000

COMPANY HISTORY

This is Gary Wright's second year of operation. In that time he has created an excellent reputation for himself and his company based on professional and creative completion of each cement–based overlay project.

His "can–do" attitude has enabled him to set himself apart from the average concrete refinishers or painters in the area. Remodeling was the initial area of work, but new home construction soon followed. Commercial renovation is becoming a popular and economical alternative to tile and carpet. Self–leveling overlays offer tremendous benefits that explain the widespread use in many casinos, hotels, restaurants, shopping malls, resorts, theme parks and office buildings.

NOTE: In situations where a concrete slab has cracked, spalled or aged, cementicious overlayment can provide a solution when compared with the time–consuming and cost alternative off ripping out the old slab and pouring new concrete. Self–leveling overlays, flowable, polymer–modified cementicious toppings have the huge advantage of setting within a few hours. Provided they are properly and regularly maintained, self–leveling overlayments will also last indefinitely, which offers a clear advantage over carpet, tile, vinyl and other more traditional floor coverings. Additionally, overlays are considerable less expensive than pricier alternatives such as granite, terrazzo or marble.

In central south Mississippi, Gary is in the forefront with this technology. With the advent of new paints, polymers and techniques, contractors needed some time to figure out what to do with these new products. Despite this, they're still learning and eager to realize the opportunities. Combine this with the improved willingness to spend on home improvements, and Gary has a winning combination.

OBJECTIVES

Gary's goals are to achieve sales of approximately $1,050,000 in Year 1 and over $4,500,000 in Year 2. He will accomplish this with four crews of experienced contractors primarily from the painting field. By far the majority of his people will be mature workers who realize that this is their last chance to make money and prepare for retirement. It is Gary's intention to retain his employees by creating a two–way commitment that works to everyone's benefit—including but not limited to competitive pay; a simple retirement plan; and recognition/bonuses for work well done.

His long–term goals are to create a niche for TCU in which he can offer new, creative designs and products while his staff performs the daily operations. His artistic designs coupled with the excellent training and execution of staff will ensure business continuity.

The overall objective for TCU is to create a sustainable organization that provides a good living for Gary and allows him to enjoy his family. TCU must also 1) provide a good living for his employees and laborers, and 2) provide a valuable service to home and business owners throughout Mississippi who wish to improve the intrinsic and aesthetic values of their properties.

PRODUCTS & SERVICES

There are three areas for his services: older home remodeling, new home construction, and commercial renovation.

There is a great demand for materials and techniques designed to restore, protect and beautify concrete surfaces that have deteriorated due to normal aging, acid rain, salt attack, and high traffic. Older homes and commercial buildings with cracks, stains, uneven surfaces or simply needing a face–lift are great candidates. He has even been working with counter tops, sinks and bathtubs for interior drama. Then consider new construction that wants the cost and durability of concrete with the look of tile or natural rock. (See the list of TCU services later in this plan.)

What we are discussing here is the implementation of ideas. Gary's forte is listening to what the customer wants—be it patio, living room floor, building entrance, or bathtub—and converting that idea to reality.

His medium is concrete, his palette consists of paints, stains and polymers and his brushes are stamp kits, rakes and brooms. What he creates become integral parts of the buildings and items of pride to their owners.

Gary has taken a conventional business and raised it to an unconventional level; adding beauty and drama to horizontal or vertical surfaces.

MARKET ANALYSIS

Gary currently services a geographical market comprised of central, south Mississippi. His current size limits his range; but so far he has more work than he can handle.

A current list of customers who can keep his current and future crews working regularly is found later in this plan.

Once his crews are trained, jobs can be handled anywhere in Mississippi. A distinct advantage to the services is the fast–track turnaround time on most renovation projects. Even new construction schedules (concrete curing) can be adhered to fairly easily allowing work to be negotiated months out.

Competition

Suppliers of materials are offering paint and concrete contractors training in how to apply their products. Local contractors who used to spend their time repairing concrete in preparation for laying carpet are now being asked to add decorative finishes and skip the carpet.

Suppliers are not moving into the DIY (Do It Yourself) Market as there are too many ways to spoil a job. Warranty issues have always been a concern and even professionals new to the business have problems. Correct substrate preparation is mandatory. Too much moisture content will ruin a job, just as not following specifications exactly!

So competition is limited to the trades, primarily concrete finishing and painting contractors. Except for the largest companies, most contractors are either residential or commercial with little crossover. The larger companies can afford the training charged by suppliers and many will probably have some crews trained for their commercial divisions. Employees of contractors will also be taking jobs on the side. Small contractors may enter with minimal, if any, training. Some of these will "dirty" the business with poor workmanship.

Competition exists—always has, always will. But this is too hot of an area to ignore. Success will depend on two things: marketing and word–of–mouth recommendations.

OPERATIONS

Marketing & Sales

Gary needs to spend more time marketing the business. This is why the first supervisor will be his father–in–law, Sonny. Officially retired from his first career but still full of energy and ideas, Sonny has worked with Gary and understands the business. He also has extensive supervisory experience gained from his previous career. Gary will still design the job and mix the product for it, but will be freed from the routine preparation.

The first resource needed is a color brochure that can be used for general distribution. The second resource is a more complete portfolio of jobs with before and after pictures, especially for the larger commercial and custom jobs. Both will require a professional photographer and a layout designer. The third resource will be actual samples of the possible finishes: field stone, brick, tile, acid–stained (with some color differentiation in all categories). As manufacturing starts, a website will aid in promoting the designs and concepts developed by Gary and his crews.

Word–of–mouth advertising has worked well so far in the residential sector. The brochures left behind with satisfied clients can be given out. Gary's work will be to get the brochures out to new–home builders and general contractors as well as to hotel, mall, and office building owners and managers.

The promotion will focus on the substantial cost savings as well as quick turnaround time. Gary's time spent in sales will prove invaluable here. He knows his products and how to present them and himself. Armed with cost analyses of the various options, his renovation services look really inviting. We must also look at the intangible to be marketed—the skill to create a one–of–a kind solution. The portfolio will assist, but the ability to listen and understand what a client wants and then deliver something a client falls in love with is a real factor here. When we spoke of competition, we also have to look at what separates TCU from the competition, and Gary's ability to work and think "out of the box."

Management Summary

Gary Wright is the only management personnel at this time. He is an experienced Top Sales Achiever with a solid record of performance in setting benchmarks and a proven set of skills that include:

- Excellent Presentation

- Strong Closing

- Sales Process Knowledge

- Relationship Building

- Customer Service

- Staff Training

- Problem Solving

- Market Penetration

His principal personal strengths include a high energy level, an ability to set and attain challenging goals, and a healthy sense of urgency. He is a team leader and team player who can be counted on to attain better than expected results.

From 2006 to 2013, Mr. Wright was employed by Good Deal Enterprises in Jackson, Mississippi. He progressively advanced to positions of increased challenges and responsibilities in support of car sales operations that include: Sales Representative, Sales Manager, and General Sales Manager. In this role, he was selected by senior management to direct the expansion of this dealership from 2 acres to 7 acres and oversaw all aspects of construction. He concurrently hired and trained a staff of 27 personnel that included the sales and support staff. During this time, he consistently met established construction goals while continuing to increase sales of new and used vehicles.

Before this, Mr. Wright was employed as a Food Broker for L&M Foods in Writer, Mississippi. While in this position, he aggressively marketed the company's preprocessed meat products to major accounts in Mississippi including Kroger's, H–E–B Grocery Company, Albertsons, Super K–Mart, Super Wal–Mart, and other grocery companies.

Gary's first supervisor will be his father–in–law, put in place to manage his crew. The second crew will be added within four months and will have its own supervisor. Ten months into Year 1 there will be a third crew and supervisor. Six months into Year 2 will be a fourth crew and supervisor. It is planned that most, if not all, supervisors will come from within the crews.

Gary will continue with the basic office functions, and be helped by his wife the first year. He will also continue to be advised by his accountant. In Year 2, a full–time administrator will need to be hired to free additional time for Gary.

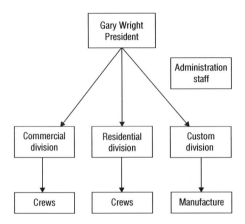

Here is a picture of TCU in five years. Gary is still the primary figure, spokesperson and leader. Each division will have its own manager as well as crews and supervisors. The administration section will have grown to accommodate the accounting and support needs of each division. Crew supervisors, depending on artistic and technical skill levels, will mix their own products for each job. It is not TCU's intention to develop a large organization but to maintain sales in the $10 million range, always with an emphasis on quality production versus quantity.

Financial Analysis

Techno-Coating USA labor estimates worksheet

Position	Wages	Job starts	Conversion to employee
Management (Gary)	$6,750/month	Immediate	Immediate
Crew supervisor 1	$3,000/month	4 months into year 1	Immediate
Crew supervisor 2	$5,250/month	4 months into year 1	Immediate
Crew supervisor 3	$5,250/month	10 months into year 1	Immediate
Crew supervisor 4	$5,250/month	6 months into year 2	Immediate
Replace supervisor (FIL)	$5,250/month	Start year 2	Immediate
Crew #1 (original)	Percent of sales	Immediate	Mid year 1
Crew #2	Percent of sales	4 months into year 1	1 month into year 2
Crew #3	Percent of sales	10 months into year 1	4 months into year 2
Crew #4	Percent of sales	6 months into year 2	3 months into year 3
Crew #5 manufacture	$22.50–25.50/hour	Start year 2	Immediate

Assumptions:
1. Work crews can cover sales of $1,275,000
2. Supervisors will be drawn from crew.
3. Crews start out as contract labor. If they last 9 months, they will have option of employee status with benefits.
4. Crews hired 90 days before needed to allow time for training and ramp up.

These expenses will be incurred as crews are added according to schedule.

Assumptions used in the preparation of proformas include:

Labor

- Labor runs 22 percent of sales.

- It is intended to operate with contract labor initially until an individual proves reliable, thoroughly knowledgeable on the job and requests a more permanent relationship with TCU, estimated to be nine months. At that point, they will become employees.

- TCU has been and will continue to take on more mature labor with a history in concrete construction to reduce the basic training time.

- Training is very important in this business because it is custom work.

- Payroll taxes are calculated for Social Security, Medi, TWC (2.7 percent) and FUTA.

Materials

- Materials currently run 18 percent of sales. Assume 19 percent due to recent increases.

- Even though economies of scale will be available at the higher volumes, we are not figuring this into the calculations. This should cover additional increases in costs.

- Sometime in year 2 a storage facility will be purchased and placed on Wright's land to house materials.

Interest

- Interest on the investment is calculated at 12 percent.

Personnel

- Gary Wright, in the first year, will be a full–time working Supervisor until his father–in–law Sonny can take over.

- Gary's father–in–law will work as the supervisor until the manufacturing operation grows. He will then relinquish that responsibility and will be replaced from within if possible.

- Gary will be spending more time mixing project stains for the crews, creating new products and marketing the business.

- A full–time office administrator will be hired to free Gary's time for the start of Year 2.

Description	Interior	Exterior
Concrete acid staining	X	X
Sealing	X	X
Concrete and wood decorative overlay	X	X
Repair overlay	X	X
Concrete counter tops	X	X
Concrete scoring	X	X
Vertical, horizontal decorative overlay	X	X
Floor preparation	X	X
Floor recovery	X	X
Bath tubs and sinks (custom)		

**Overlays: solid semi gloss, tile, stone, slate, brick

Services

Equipment list per crew

Description	Quantity	$ Amount
Trowels, rake, squeegees, etc.	Misc	$ 750
1/2" drills w/paddles	2	$ 600
300" extension cords	2	$ 225
4 1/2 grinders w/blades	4	$ 900
7 1/2 grinder w/blades	1	$ 675
Bead blaster	1	$ 7,200
Buffer	1	$ 1,500
Compressor	1	$ 4,500
Concrete polishing kit	1	$ 9,000
Crack chaser	1	$ 2,250
6 x 12 enclosed trailer	1	$ 4,200
Ford 250/350 XL	1	$40,500
Generator	1	$ 1,200
Industrial wet vacs	2	$ 600
Light set	2	$ 450
Maintainer and ladders	2	$ 750
Paint gun and air hopper	1	$ 2,550
Parking cover	1	$ 750
Pumps	2	$ 1,800
Rags, buckets, knives, tape, blades, paper	Misc	$ 375
Sanders/discs	3	$ 600
Stamp kits	—	$ 7,200
Sales tax	—	$ 1,425
Total		**$90,000**

*Some equipment many be found second-hand, but only new prices are listed here.

Suppliers

Our suppliers are located in Mississippi and nearby states.

- Limeracoat
- KP Tile Store
- Kerry Contractors Supply
- Morfilled Polymers
- Lowes and Home Depot of Jackson, Mississippi

Customers

Our customers are all located in Mississippi.

- Gregg Custom Homes
- Sabinal Group
- N–Site Architects
- YP Construction
- Joyous Construction
- Marvin Gregg Homes
- Kenneth Quick Homes
- Purte & Larry
- FMT Management

- Leading Edge Flooring
- Insider Looks
- LL Tiling
- Horizon Green Solutions Inc.
- MS Construction

Crime Scene Cleaning/Bioremediation Business

Ballard Enterprises Inc.

87 Market St. W.
Stevens Park, IL 61294

Paul Greenland

Ballard Enterprises Inc. is a new provider of crime scene and bioremediation cleaning services.

EXECUTIVE SUMMARY

Murders, suicides, and violent crimes are regular topics in the news. While certain details regarding these unfortunate acts (e.g., why and where they happened, the people affected, etc.) are frequently discussed, others simply are not top-of-mind with the public. One important, yet often undiscussed, detail is the cleanup that occurs following such an occurrence. Although the public may assume that law enforcement handles this unpleasant task, the fact is that third parties often are brought in to handle the cleanup, either on behalf of government agencies or victims' families, who are financially responsible. Traditional housekeeping and cleaning services often do not handle this highly-specialized form of "bioremediation."

Ballard Enterprises Inc. is a newly established bioremediation service, which provides crime scene cleanup, as well as bioremediation for other situations, including commercial and residential spaces that have been contaminated by dangerous animal or chemical waste. Examples include "unattended deaths," in which an individual may die naturally, but whose body may go undiscovered for a long time; a former meth lab containing dangerous substances; and a home that is contaminated by a freezer of deer meat that thawed and spoiled following a power outage.

The business is being established by David Ballard, a former deputy coroner in Spring City, Alabama, who relocated to Stevens Park, Illinois, for family reasons. With no available employment in his highly-specialized field, Ballard decided to apply his professional knowledge in a new way. He is establishing Ballard Enterprises with Rick Jensen, a recently retired detective with the Stevens Park Police Department, who will benefit the business with his local law-enforcement connections.

MARKET ANALYSIS

One important factor in starting a crime scene/bioremediation business is to locate the operation in an area with (1) a sizable population and (2) a crime level that will result in a steady stream of work. Ballard Enterprises is located in Stevens Park, Illinois, a community that supports both criteria. In 2015 the research firm Sorenson & Langenfeld indicated that, based on an analysis of on national law-enforcement data, Stevens Park was home to several of the nation's most dangerous neighborhoods. In addition, the community ranks in the top five percent of the nation's most dangerous cities.

Stevens Park, Illinois, was home to approximately 150,000 people in 2015. The aforementioned report found that, in 2014, the city experienced 2,075 violent crimes, including 27 murders. Violent crime occurred at a rate of 1,380 incidents per 100,000 people. This is significantly higher than the state average of 379 per 1,000 people, and the national average of 368 per 100,000 people.

In addition to crime scene cleaning, Ballard Enterprises will provide cleaning services that are not typically served by traditional cleaning services. One key market will be cleaning jobs for individuals who suffer from hoarding. According to storage.com, the United States is home to approximately 1.2 million individuals who suffer from hoarding (one in 300 individuals). Based on the statistics, the owners estimate that hundreds of Stevens Park residents suffer from this condition. When these individuals vacate their homes, due to death or other circumstances, proper cleaning can be extremely difficult, resulting in the need for professionals like Ballard Enterprises.

SERVICES

Ballard Enterprises provides highly specialized cleaning services that traditional commercial/residential cleaners do not, pertaining to a variety of incidents, including:

- Animal Waste Contamination
- Biohazards
- Hoarding
- Homicides & Violent Crimes (Crime Scenes)
- Police Vehicle Cleaning
- Food/Meat Spoilage
- Suicides
- Unattended Deaths

Fees

Fees charged by bioremediation services vary considerably, depending on factors such as experience, skill, and location/geography. In smaller markets, a single provider with minimal experience may charge as little as $40 per hour, while more experienced providers in major metropolitan areas may charge as much as $600 per hour. Depending on the type and scope of job, many cleanup projects range in price from $3,000-$15,000. Considering the local market and the owners' skill and experience, Ballard Enterprises typically will bill services at a rate of $250 per hour.

OPERATIONS

Location

David Ballard will handle administrative tasks associated with the business from his home office. Affordable warehouse space has been identified for Ballard Enterprises' operations. The owners have identified a large warehouse that has been subdivided into smaller units for different types of businesses. The warehouse offers 24/7 access and overhead doors at each end, allowing Ballard Enterprises space for vehicle, supplies, and equipment storage. A 500-square-foot section of a warehouse will be leased at a monthly cost of $750.

Transportation

Ballard Enterprises has purchased a used 2010 Chevrolet Express Cargo Van for $16,000. The vehicle has adequate space for transporting supplies, equipment, and biohazardous waste.

Hours

Because crime, death, and other emergencies are not limited to regular business hours, and often occur after dark and on weekends, Ballard Enterprises will provide on-call coverage 24 hours a day, seven days a week. The owners realize that this will present a challenge, personally, during the operation's formative years. A network of reliable, independent contractors will be utilized to minimize some of this burden in the short-term, and the addition of regular employees will provide more support in the long-term. However, the owners acknowledge that this type of business has unpredictable, irregular, and sometimes very long hours.

Equipment

Special equipment is required to perform bioremediation, including:

- Biohazard Disposal Bag/Containers
- Booties
- Chemicals (Enzymes, Deodorizers, Disinfectants, etc.)
- Eye Protection
- Full-Body Decontamination Suits
- Hand Tools
- Masks/Respirators
- Power Tools
- Rubber Gloves

The owners will require $3,500 for their initial inventory of equipment and supplies at the time of start-up.

Process

The amount of time required to clean a particular biohazard site depends on the size and scope of the job. While some cleanups may only require a few hours and involve one technician, others may last for several days and require a large crew.

In most cases, a specific process is followed, which involves (1) establishing a clean room/area where equipment and supplies can be stored safely, (2) a control room/area that allows technicians to enter and exit a biohazard area safely, and finally (3) the job site where the cleaning occurs.

The actual cleaning begins with the removal of larger elements, including human tissue and hazardous waste. Carpeting, furniture, and even hardwood floors may need to be removed as part of the process. Next, traditional cleaning and sanitizing occurs using chemicals and disinfectants. Adenosine triphosphate testing is performed to ensure that the area has been sanitized completely. This is critical to ensure that an area is once again livable/inhabitable. Finally, any resulting biohazardous waste must be disposed of in accordance to local and state regulations.

Payment

Following a homicide or unattended death, property owners and/or families typically are responsible for covering bioremediation costs. For individuals with homeowners insurance, it's comforting to know that most policies cover these costs. Ballard Enterprises will work with customers to submit claims to their insurance companies. In cases where a customer is underinsured or uninsured, Ballard Enterprises will accept payment by cash, check, or credit card. In addition, the business has made arrangements with an area finance company to provide low-interest financing to qualifying customers.

PERSONNEL

Ballard Enterprises is being established by David Ballard and Rick Jensen.

David Ballard, President

Before relocating to Stevens Park, Illinois, for family reasons, David Ballard served as a deputy coroner in Spring City, Alabama. With no available employment in his highly-specialized field, Ballard decided to apply his professional knowledge in a new way. Ballard will be the majority owner of Ballard Enterprises, holding a 65 percent stake in the business. While working as a deputy coroner, Ballard's main responsibilities included investigating and determining causes and manners of death; conducting joint investigations with law enforcement agencies and other institutions; collecting, preserving, and maintaining chains of custody with bodies, physical evidence, specimens, and property; providing photography during autopsies and at death scenes; and communicating with family members, law enforcement personnel, healthcare professionals, and funeral home staff.

Rick Jensen, Vice President

Rick Jensen is a recently retired detective with the Stevens Park Police Department, who will benefit the business with 27 years of experience and connections with the local law enforcement community. Although he has been retired from active law-enforcement for two years, Jensen has continued to work in the private security field. With an entrepreneurial spirit, Jensen was intrigued to learn about and invest in this specialized business, in which he will hold a 35 percent stake. Jensen has maintained his Illinois Law Enforcement Officer credential. In addition, he has pursued many hours of continuing education, including training pertaining to domestic-related homicides.

Training & Certification

Although no formal certification, licensure, or credential exists for crime scene/biohazard cleaners, Ballard and Jensen will each benefit the business with the experience and skill from their former professions. In addition, both business partners have completed Hazardous Waste Operations and Emergency Response Training, providing them with the technical knowledge to clean crime scenes safely and appropriately. The owners of Ballard Enterprises also have received training in the following programs offered by the Occupational Safety and Health Administration (OSHA):

- Asbestos Awareness

- Bloodborne Pathogens

- Fall Protection

- Hazard Communication

- Heat Illness

- Lift Safety

- Lock Out-Tag Out

- Personal Protective Equipment

- Power Tool Safety

Professional and Advisory Support

A commercial checking account has been established for Ballard Enterprises with Stevens Park Community Bank. Local CPA Brian Rangle has been retained to manage the business' bookkeeping and tax preparation responsibilities. Ballard used a local attorney to provide the business with boilerplate agreements that can be used with customers.

GROWTH STRATEGY

Ballard Enterprises has established the following growth targets for its first three years of operations:

Year one: Provide services with two full-time employees (owners) and a network of four independent contractors. Place a strong emphasis on building the Ballard Enterprises brand in the local market, especially with funeral homes and law enforcement professionals. Complete 45 projects and generate gross revenues of $247,500.

Year two: Provide services with two full-time employees (owners), two part-time bioremediation technicians, and a network of six independent contractors. Continue to concentrate on brand building efforts with key target markets. Complete 60 projects and generate gross revenues of $330,000.

Year three: Provide services with three full-time employees (the owners and one bioremediation technician), three part-time bioremediation technicians, and a network of eight independent contractors. Maintain strong marketing initiatives to keep the Ballard Enterprises brand name visible with key target markets. Complete 90 projects and generate gross revenues of $495,000.

MARKETING & SALES

Target Markets

Ballard Enterprises will market its services to:

- Building/Property Managers
- Coroner's Offices
- District Attorney's
- Funeral Homes
- Landlords
- Local Law Enforcement (Homicide Departments)
- Mortuaries
- Private Residents
- Public-Service Agencies

Marketing Tactics

The owners will use the following tactics to promote the business to the aforementioned target markets:

1. A blog, through which Ballard and Jensen will provide observations and insight regarding their profession, including case studies of cleaning jobs that were performed successfully.

2. Social media marketing on Twitter, Facebook, LinkedIn, and YouTube.

3. Advertising in both free and paid industry directories.

4. A media relations strategy that involves the submission of case success stories to local and regional newspapers and network television affiliates.

5. A Web site with complete details about Ballard Enterprises.

6. Business cards that include contact information for the owners, as well as their Web site and social media information.

7. Monthly direct mailings to the business' target markets. The owners will develop their own mailing list using Jensen's specialized knowledge of the local law enforcement community, and also a publicly available database at their local public library, which allows them to create mailing lists based on business type, location, sales, etc.

8. Presentations and networking at local and regional business meetings and conferences catering to the law enforcement and property management fields.

9. Printed collateral describing the services provided by Ballard Enterprises. This also will be used for direct mail purposes.

LEGAL & REGULATORY

Ballard Enterprises has obtained $2 million in aggregate business liability insurance, at a cost of $500 annually. The business will dispose of all biohazardous waste in accordance with state and federal EPA standards.

FINANCIAL ANALYSIS

The owners of prepared the following financial projections for the first three years of Ballard Enterprises' operations:

	2016	2017	2018
Revenue	**$247,500**	**$330,000**	**$495,000**
Expenses			
Salaries	$100,000	$160,000	$260,000
Payroll tax	$ 15,000	$ 24,000	$ 39,000
Supplies	$ 24,750	$ 33,000	$ 49,500
Contract labor	$ 37,125	$ 49,500	$ 74,250
Insurance	$ 500	$ 600	$ 700
Accounting & legal	$ 2,500	$ 2,500	$ 2,500
Office supplies	$ 600	$ 600	$ 600
Equipment	$ 2,000	$ 3,500	$ 4,000
Marketing & advertising	$ 10,000	$ 12,500	$ 15,000
Telecommunications & Internet	$ 2,000	$ 2,250	$ 2,500
Professional development	$ 3,500	$ 3,500	$ 3,500
Warehouse lease	$ 9,000	$ 9,000	$ 9,000
Unreimbursed travel	$ 1,500	$ 2,000	$ 2,500
Misc.	$ 500	$ 500	$ 500
Total expenses	**$208,975**	**$303,450**	**$463,550**
Net income	**$ 38,525**	**$ 26,550**	**$ 31,450**

Start-up Costs

Ballard Enterprises will require $19,500 for the following start-up costs:

- Initial inventory of equipment and supplies ($3,500)

- 2010 Chevrolet Express Cargo Van ($16,000)

In addition, the owners estimate that $25,000 will be needed for ongoing operations.

Using funds from their own savings, they have agreed to split total start-up costs of $44,500 as follows:

- David Ballard (65%): $28,925

- Rick Jensen (35%): $16,020

The owners anticipate that they will recover their respective start-up investments during the second year of operations. By the end of the third year, they estimate that their collective net profit, less their initial start-up investments, will total $52,025.

Essential Oils Retail Sales

Essentially Yours

PO Box 1778
Marysville, MI 48040

Zuzu Enterprises

Essentially Yours will offer a full line of single essential oils, oil blends, diffusers, cleaning products, and beauty products to suit the individual needs of each potential client.

EXECUTIVE SUMMARY

Essential oils are naturally occurring, volatile aromatic compounds are found in the seeds, bark, stems, roots, flowers, and other parts of plants. They can be both beautifully and powerfully fragrant. In addition to giving plants their distinctive smells, essential oils protect plants and play a role in plant pollination. Essential oils are more than nice scents, however; these powerful plant extracts can help you energize your life, disperse stress and negativity, and boost your overall wellness. They are a powerful tool in improving and enhancing the quality of your life.

Essentially Yours will offer a full line of single oils, oil blends, diffusers, cleaning products, and beauty products to suit the individual needs of each potential client.

INDUSTRY ANALYSIS

The Essential Oil manufacturing industry develops and produces concentrated hydrophobic liquids that contain aroma compounds from plants. An oil is "essential" in the sense that it carries a distinctive scent or essence of the plant.

In the United States, favorable shifts in consumer demand and market expansion have helped the Essential Oil Manufacturing industry thrive in the five years to 2015. Disposable income has increased each year since experiencing sharp declines prior to 2010, which has contributed to growth in demand from several key industries, including soap manufacturers, cosmetic and beauty product manufacturers, and cleaning product manufacturers.

Growing consumer preference for natural products has led to the development of novel applications in personal care and beauty products. Rising application scope on account of growing consumer awareness regarding health benefits and negligible side effects associated with essential oil is expected to spur their demand in the homeopathic industry. Growing demand for aromatic flavors and fragrances in cosmetics, perfumes, as well as spa and relaxation applications is expected to fuel the demand over the next six years.

According to IBISWorld estimates, the Essential Oil Manufacturing industry is growing faster than the overall economy. In the ten years to 2020, industry value added, which measures the industry's contribution to the economy, is expected to grow an average of 2.8% annually. Comparatively, the US GDP is projected to grow an annualized 2.5% over the same period. Coupled with factors such as expanding markets and a steadily growing number of enterprises, the Essential Oil manufacturing industry is considered to be in the growth stage of its life cycle.

Conversely, the global essential oil market size is growing as well. The market was estimated at USD 5.51 billion in 2014. Increasing essential oil penetration in aromatherapy coupled with rising demand for fragrances and flavors in food and beverages is expected to remain a key driving factor for the global market. The global essential oil market is expected to reach USD 11.67 billion by 2022, according to a new report by Grand View Research, Inc. Growing consumer awareness regarding health benefits associated with natural and organic personal care products is expected to remain a key driving factor for global essential oil market over the forecast period. Growth of organic product industry has prompted major manufacturers to shift their focus from synthetic to natural additives. Growing use of essential oil in the preparation of natural flavors and fragrances on account of their increasing demand across key end-use industries is also expected to fuel the market growth.

Further key findings from the report include:

- Global essential oil market demand was 165.0 kilo tons in 2014 and is expected to grow at a CAGR of 8.6% from 2015 to 2022.

- Orange oil was the leading product segment and accounted for 29.1% of total market volume in 2014. Environmental friendly characteristics associated with orange oil makes it suitable for use in perfumes and household cleaners in addition to its benefits as an antidepressant, diuretic, anti-inflammatory, aphrodisiac, and antiseptic. Orange oil is also used as a biological pest control agent. Orange oil is also expected to witness the highest growth of 9.7% from 2015 to 2022.

- Other products such as citronella, lime, lemon, basil, chamomile, and lavender are expected to witness high demand due to extensive use in applications including sport equipment disinfection, pet care, air fresheners and odor repellents, insect repellents, and personal care.

- Food & beverages emerged as the most dominant application segment with demand share estimated over 30% in 2014. Growth of food & beverages industry particularly in Asia Pacific is expected to drive this segment over the forecast period. Spa & relaxation is also expected to witness significant gain in its market size on account of growth spa industry in South East Asia and South Asian countries.

- Spa & relaxation accounted for over 29% market share in 2014 owing to rising popularity of aromatherapy and other procedures. The segment is expected to reach USD 3,634.7 million by 2022 growing at a CAGR of 10.0% over the forecast period.

- Other applications such as medical, cleaning & home products where essential oil serves as aromatic compounds and nutritive substitutes for conventional medicines are also expected to witness a sustainable growth.

- Europe was the leading regional market demand share exceeding 40% in 2014. Aware consumers regarding health benefits offered by organic products can be attributed to region's leading position in the global market. Asia Pacific is expected to witness the highest growth of 9.2% from 2015 to 2022.

- Some major companies operating in the global essential oil market includes Biolandes, Sydney Essential Oils, HRF, The Leburmuth Company, Young Living Essential Oils, doTerra, Essential Oils of New Zealand, Sydella Laboratoire, Farotti Essenze, Moksha Lifestyle Products, West India Spices Inc., Falcon and Ungerger Limited among others.

MARKET ANALYSIS

Competition

Some of the dominant companies operating in the global essential oil market include:

- Biolandes
- Sydney Essential Oils
- HRF
- The Leburmuth Company
- Young Living Essential Oils
- doTerra
- Essential Oils of New Zealand
- Sydella Laboratoire
- Farotti Essenze
- Moksha Lifestyle Products
- West India Spices Inc.
- Falcon
- Ungerger Limited

Most essential oils are sold via local distributor. Essentially Yours will offer the same high quality products, but we will also provide our oils in a retail venue so that clients may see and sample the products without having to commit to hosting a party in their own homes. However, we will also be available to provide in-home demonstrations and parties to those who prefer a more personal and private shopping experience.

PRODUCTS

Essentially Yours will offer a full line of single oils, oil blends, diffusers, cleaning products, and beauty products to suit the specific desires of each client. Single oils and oil blends can be helpful when used for mental and physical health including relaxation, stress relief, improved sleep, weight management, improved digestion, and increased energy and stamina.

Single Oils

We will offer more than 30 essential oils, including:

- Basil—helpful in dealing with respiratory ailments, body aches, and as an insect repellent
- Bay—works as a skin toner and can help against razor burns and breakouts on skin. Also considered an analgesic in aromatherapy, relieving muscle and joint pain and neuralgia and is ideal as a massage oil or added to bath water to induce a relaxing effect.
- Bergamot—excellent deodorizer, a natural mosquito repellant, insect-bite salve, deodorant, inhalant, and relaxing massage oil.
- Cardamom—helpful as a digestive aid and as an anti-inflammatory agent; provides relief for pulled muscles and cramps, and can also be used to promote healthy skin, working as a natural cleanser and toner.

- Cassia—as an herbal preparation, cassia bark can be used to improve digestive issues, such as flatulence, colic, dyspepsia, and diarrhea. It can also be used in vapor therapy to alleviate symptoms of the cold and flu.

- Cinnamon—an excellent disinfectant and insect repellent. Also great as a stress reliever, providing an energy boost, and relieving body aches.

- Clary Sage—excellent for calming effects to ease depression and anxiety. Also known to relieve cramps, pain, and stiffness.

- Clove—helpful in dealing with digestive and respiratory issues; excellent as a massage oil to relive pain and stress.

- Coriander—acts as stimulant for people who are feeling low and widely used by athletes because it helps relieve muscle spasm and cramps.

- Cypress—used to calm and relax your mind. Can also help alleviate breathing disorders or used as a massage oil to relieve asthma, arthritis, rheumatism, cramps, varicose veins, and heavy menstrual flow.

- Eucalyptus—commonly used for stimulating mental activity and increasing blood flow to the brain; also used to alleviate pain and inflammation.

- Frankincense—known for its comforting properties in overcoming stress and anxiety.

- Geranium—can uplift mood, lessen fatigue, and promote emotional wellness, as well as reduce pain and inflammation.

- Ginger—helpful as a digestive aid and as an anti-inflammatory agent; also boosts energy.

- Grapefruit—can help curb headaches, mental fatigue, and depression; also used to curb appetite and eliminate unpleasant odors.

- Juniper Berry—fresh and calming aroma widely renowned for relieving stress and anxiety; also used to cleanse and purify the air.

- Lavender—known to relieve aching muscles and stress.

- Lemon—excellent air freshener, insect repellent, spot remover, disinfectant, and headache treatment.

- Lemongrass—clean and calming aroma helps relieve stress, anxiety, irritability, and insomnia, and prevent drowsiness; good as an air freshener and deodorizer.

- Lime—stimulating and refreshing to relieve stress and exhaustion; can also be used to remove grease spots and repel insects.

- Myrrh—excellent in treating skin conditions such as chapped or cracked skin; often used as massage oil or in baths.

- Oregano—helpful in alleviating respiratory symptoms, ease sore throats, relieve muscle and joint pain, ward off insects, and relieve bug bites and rashes

- Patchouli—calming effect is very effective for relaxation and meditation; also valuable as a skin treatment for scrapes, burns, and insect bites.

- Peppermint—effective in relieving anxiety, pain, and vomiting, as well as improving memory and raising alertness.

- Roman Chamomile—used to treat vomiting, nausea, gas, headaches, and heartburn. It can also help relieve anxiety.

- Rosemary—excellent in promoting memory and learning; also used to treat headaches, respiratory symptoms, pain, and stress.

- Sage—excellent aid for digestive issues; can also help address mental fatigue and depression.

- Sandalwood—known for its calming and relaxing effects; also excellent in addressing various skin conditions.

- Spruce—eases anxiety and stress; also useful for treating muscle aches and pains.

- Thyme—stimulates the mind, strengthens memory and concentration, and calms the nerves; also used for respiratory and skin conditions.

- Vanilla—eases stress, anxiety, depression, and insomnia; induces sleep and encourages dreaming; and may relieve nausea.

- Vetiver—calming and soothing properties reduce stress and tension.

- Wild Orange—beneficial in improving digestion and relieving constipation; promotes a feeling of happiness and warmth.

- Wintergreen—excellent in pain relief, including headaches, joint pain, muscle pain, and cramps; also useful in dealing with stress and tension.

- Ylang Ylang—used to alleviate insomnia and fatigue as well as various skin conditions.

Oil Blends

Many different oil blends will also be offered for sale. Some of these include:

Breathing
- Blend includes Peppermint, Eucalyptus, and Lemon along with others

- Promotes feelings of clear airways and easy breathing

- Perfect for nighttime diffusion, allowing for a restful sleep

Calm
- Blend includes spruce and frankincense along with others

- Has a warm, woody aroma that creates a sense of calmness and well-being

- Evokes feelings of tranquility and balance

Energy
- Blend includes wild orange, lemon, grapefruit, and lime

- Cleanses and purifies the air

- Helps reduce stress

- Positively affects mood with energizing and refreshing properties

Women's Health
- Blend includes sage, lavender, ylang ylang, and geranium

- Designed especially for women

- Helps balance mood throughout the month

- Can be applied to abdomen for a soothing massage during menstrual cycle

Sore Muscles
- Blend includes wintergreen, peppermint, and camphor

- Soothes and cools

- Relief that can be felt almost immediately

- Apply before and after exercise

Other Products

A variety of other products will be available as well, including a line of diffusers in varying price points, a line of cleaning products, and a line of beauty aids. The specific items include:

- Diffusers

- Diffuser jewelry such as necklaces and bracelets

- Cleaning products with essential oils, including laundry detergent, stain removal treatments, surface cleaners, and air fresheners

- Beauty products with essential oils, including antiaging treatments, moisturizers, and cleansers

All products, from single essential oils to blends to diffusers, will come with an information sheet and instructions on proper usage.

PRODUCT QUALITY AND SAFETY

All products offered by Essentially Yours are of the highest quality. The essential oils we sell have undergone meticulous practices for planting, cultivating, harvesting, and distilling yield potent, naturally beneficial essential oils that meet or exceed industry-leading standards. Oils are extracted through careful steam distillation and cold pressing; only 100% unadulterated essential oils are used in our oils and oil blends as well as our cleaning and beauty products.

PRICING STRATEGY

All essential oils are sold in 5ml and 15ml bottles. Prices range depending on size and type of oil(s), and a price sheet is available on request. Retail prices are marked up 25-33% to cover costs and make a profit.

PERSONNEL

Owners

Jennifer VanAllen is the owner-operator of Essentially Yours. She is responsible for all ordering and stocking as well as administrative tasks of bookkeeping, taxes, and the like. She will also be the only employee to work private parties and demonstrations. In addition to these tasks, Jennifer will run the retail kiosk on a part-time basis.

Support Staff

Several part-time employees will be hired to operate the sales kiosk so that Jennifer doesn't have to work every day and thus will have the time for private events and demonstrations as well as administrative tasks.

Professional and Advisory Support

A business checking account was opened with First State Bank of Marysville. A merchant account was also established so that Essentially Yours is able to process payments made via cash, check, and all major credit/debit cards.

MARKETING & ADVERTISING

Essentially Yours is located in a desirable, high-traffic area in the Birchwood Mall. Diffusers will be working during all open hours to draw people in and pique their curiosity. Brochures will be available for interested parties so that they may contact us in the future.

A website, Facebook page, Instagram account, Twitter account, and Snapchat account will all be opened for the business. Contact information will be front and center, and tips and tricks will be offered on a timely basis. For example, oils and blends that will help alleviate respiratory symptoms will be featured when allergy season starts; tips on soothing sore muscles and suppressing appetite may be offered in January as people are trying to uphold their New Year's resolutions; and products that are helpful at repelling insects will be featured during the hot summer months.

Word-of-mouth advertising will be extremely important to our business as well. People who attend parties and demonstrations and those just discovering the benefits of essential oils will tell their friends and recommend Essentially Yours as long as we continue to provide quality products and excellent customer service.

All marketing materials and communications will emphasize the benefits of using essential oils, but stress that they are not a replacement for medical treatment.

OPERATIONS

Hours of Operation
The retail kiosk will be open on the following schedule:

Monday-Friday, 10am—8pm

Saturday, 10am—9pm

Sunday, 10am—6pm

Parties and demonstrations will be scheduled to fit the specific needs of the host.

Location
The retail kiosk is located in a desirable, high traffic area inside the Birchwood Mall. Located in nearby Fort Gratiot, this mall is the only one in a 60-mile radius. Parties and demonstrations are available within a 30 minute drive of Marysville, covering the areas of Port Huron, Fort Gratiot, Marysville, Richmond, Romeo, New Baltimore, St. Clair, East China, Algonac, Almont, Imlay City, and Marine City.

Payment Options
Essentially Yours is able to process payments made via cash, check, and all major credit/debit cards.

SWOT ANALYSIS

Strengths
- Essential oils have been around and helping people for thousands of years
- Fragrances provide stimulation in aromatherapy, massages, and other relaxation techniques
- Numerous health benefits associated with essential oils are anticipated to drive the product demand in homeopathic applications
- Essential oils have little to no detrimental side effects when used as directed

Weaknesses

- Sales associates must be as enthusiastic and knowledgeable as the owner to ensure clients are provided excellent customer service

Opportunities

- While independent sales of essential oils are becoming more common, no retail outlets currently exist in the area

Threats

- Limited availability of key raw material

- Many large competitors

- Essential oils can't be patented

- Lack of awareness regarding benefits of essential oils

- Oil production is expensive owing to unique attributes and requires high capital investment with advanced equipment

General Staffing Company

GENRX LLC

7641 Highway 141
Saskatoon, Saskatchewan S7N 1M7

Gerald Rekve

GENRX LLC's mission is to be the best staffing firm in our region. Our focus will be to secure clients who may require our services on an ongoing basis.

This business plan appeared in a previuoius volume of Business Plans Handbook. It has been updated for this volume.

EXECUTIVE SUMMARY

Business Strategy

GENRX LLC is opening a new general staffing company. Our area of focus is to be the best staffing firm in our region.

To begin, GENRX LLC will have six full–time staff, including the owner and five support staff to handle payroll, scheduling, and clients.

GENRX LLC will focus on the business sectors listed below. Other business sectors will be added as GENRX LLC matures and revenue potential for new sectors is increased.

- General labor

- Secretarial

- Specialized labor

- Manual labor

- Hourly or one day at a time

- Drop–in labor force

- Accounting staff

- Human Resource staff

- Technical staff

- Equipment operators

MARKET ANALYSIS

Saskatoon, Saskatchewan is a small market with only 222,000 people living in the city and one million living in the Province. There is another city 200 miles to the south named Regina with a population of 200,000. GENRX LLC will have an office in both locations.

There are 38,000 businesses that operate in the Province that are registered with the Government. Our focus will be to offer these business clients temporary staff as they require. While GENRX LLC will only focus our markets in Saskatoon and Regina, requests from clients outside these two markets will be reviewed to see if there is potential to make profits on an ongoing basis.

Marketing & Demographic Data

All information and charts are provided by the Saskatchewan Economic Development Authority.

Leading growth industries, Saskatoon, 2015

	Count	% of total
Business & professional services	190	27.09%
Personal & household services	109	16.01%
Traditional retail	77	11.31%
Building & construction related services	74	10.87%
Commercial sector services	65	9.43%
Health, wellness & education services	57	8.37%
Repair & maintenance services	39	5.73%
Automotive sales & service	27	3.96%
Manufacturing	18	2.64%
Services related to manufacturing, wholesale & transportation	17	2.50%
Wholesale industries	8	1.17%
Total	**681**	**100.00%**

Competition

Proportion of part time employees by suburban development area

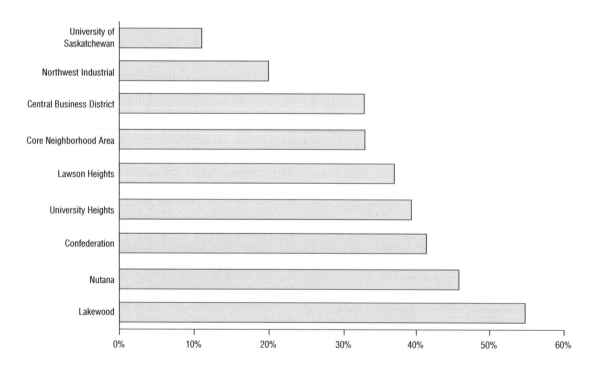

Our direct competitors in the market are Kelly Services, Labour Ready, Adecco, and Employment Network. Listed below are the areas where each one of these companies operate and the prices they charge.

Kelly Services

- Office & Administrative: $16–$20 per hour

- Customer Service: $13–$15 per hour

- Light Industrial: $14–$17 per hour

- Information Technology: $22–$38 per hour

- Scientific personnel: $27–$42 per hour

Labour Ready

- Construction: $16–$22 per hour

- Manufacturing: $14–$18 per hour

- Maintenance: $13–$16 per hour

- Farming: $16–$20 per hour

- Retail: $12–$14 per hour

- Transport: $18–$21 per hour

- Warehouse: $13–$15 per hour

- Hospitality: $12–$14 per hour

- Landscaping: $12–$14 per hour

- Horticulture: $12–$14 per hour

Adecco

- Temporary Staffing: $12–$14 per hour

- Payroll services: Rate quote on request

- Call centre: Rate quote on request

- Contract employment: Rate quote on request

- Permanent Staff Recruiting Service

Employment Network

- Construction: $15–$20 per hour

- Manufacturing: $17–$20 per hour

- Maintenance: $14–$15 per hour

- Farming: $13–$15 per hour

- Retail: $13–$15 per hour

- Transport: $15–$17 per hour

- Warehouse: $15–$16 per hour

- Hospitality: $13–$15 per hour

- Landscaping: $13–$16 per hour

Our Services & Pricing

- Construction: $12–$16 per hour

- Manufacturing: $12–$16 per hour

- Maintenance: $11.50–$13 per hour

- Farming: $13–$15 per hour

- Retail: $12–$13 per hour

- Transport: $16–$18 per hour

- Warehouse: $12–$14 per hour

- Hospitality: $12–$14 per hour

- Landscaping: $12–$14 per hour

- Horticulture: $12–$14 per hour

Growth Strategy

Our goal is to have a steady stream of staff to offer our clients. Our pricing strategy for the first 3 years is to make smaller margins for similar services that competitors offer. While doing this GENRX LLC will be able to win more contracts and build a steady revenue stream.

Our temporary staff will be paid above average wages and benefits. GENRX LLC will also go above the norm in the industry and offer medical and dental benefits to all temp staff who work 25 hours per week or more. While doing this will add to the bottom line cost of our company, it will help us achieve our long-term goal of attracting top-of-the-line workers and therefore offering our clients the best talent.

Marketing our business will take the traditional approach. In addition, we will employ new marketing strategies to build and grow our business. GENRX LLC will place small ads in the yellow pages of both cities in which we operate as well as create an website and online profiles in job search databases. Additionally, we will place sustaining business-card-size ads in local newspapers.

Local Newspapers

Saskatoon Star Phoenix

- Annual Advertising budget of $10,000

- 50,000 paid circulation

- Daily newspaper

- MOPE Nadbank data reflects high business owner/manager readership

Regina Leader Post

- Annual Advertising budget of $7,500

- 62,000 paid circulation

- 219,000 unique visitors to online version of the paper

- Daily newspaper

Prairie Dog Newspaper

- Annual Advertising budget of $5,000

- 50,000 free circulation

- Biweekly newspaper

Planet S

- Annual Advertising budget of $5,000

- 60,000 free circulation

- Biweekly newspaper

Radio Stations

- C95—Annual Advertising budget of $7,500

- CJME—Annual Advertising budget of $7,500

Building our new business will require spending on advertising and marketing. Over the course of the business start–up, however, we are confidant that going into years three and four, our advertising spending will be reduced because we will have built our number of clients and will not be required to continue to spend money to gain awareness.

Business name recognition will be important to our business. We will use a variety of methods to get this awareness in addition to word-of-mouth and media events like charity sponsorships.

Charity sponsorships will be easy to find; all we need to do is offer free staffing in exchange for name coverage via the radio, newspaper or television. This will allow us to get more exposure for less than the cost of traditional advertising.

CUSTOMERS

Our focus will be to secure clients who may require our services on an ongoing basis. This will mean GENRX LLC will ask specific questions once a client calls our firm. These questions will gather key market research information that will help us identify the client's present needs *and* future needs. GENRX LLC will place all this information in the client's file for assessment.

List of Potential Sectors

- Manufacturing

- Retailing

- Construction

- Trucking (both long and short haul)

- Farming

- Office & Administrative

- Sales & Marketing

The industry norm is to charge a minimum of 25 percent for all work required to be done on the site by our staff. What this means is that if a client charged $10.00 per hour, then the worker gets $7.50 per hour and the staffing firm will get $2.50 per hour.

We do not feel this is fair for the worker or the client. Therefore, GENRX LLC will only charge 15 percent. This then will mean that for every $10.00 hour we charge a client, the staff person filling the position will make $8.50 per hour and $1.50 per hour will go to us.

This rate structure will also benefit the client, because we will be able to offer our clients the services of better staff than our competitors.

RISK FACTORS

There are risks in any business that starts from scratch, but having a solid business plan will be key to prepare for these risks.

One of our main risk factors is our competition. They are not likely to sit back and allow us to enter the market; in fact, we are confidant that they will match our pricing once it becomes apparent to them that they are losing business. Based on our review of the market, if we can win 5% of the market in the first year of business and then maintain it, we will be well positioned for future success.

We are very confidant that there is enough business for all of our competitors and us.

FINANCIAL ANALYSIS

Start–Up Expenses

Saskatoon Office

- Office Rental–$1,500 month

- Yellow pages–$150 month

- Telephone line & equipment–$400 month

- Internet–$75 month

- Office supplies–$1,000 (start up)

- Office supplies–$200 month

- Advertising–$16,500 (start up)

- Advertising–$600 month

- Office equipment—Computers, fax, copier, printers, etc–$5,000

- Desks, file cabinets etc.–$2,500

- Utilities–included in rent

- Parking–included in rent

- Leasehold improvements–included in rent

- First 3 months rent–free with 3 year lease

- Payroll and other software–$2,500

Regina Office

- Office Rental–$1,200 month

- Yellow pages–$150 month

- Telephone line & equipment–$400 month

- Internet–$75 month

- Office supplies–$1,000 (start up)

- Office supplies–$200 month

- Advertising–$14,000 (start up)

- Advertising–$400 month

- Office equipment—Computers, fax, copier, printers, etc.–$4,000

- Desks, file cabinets etc.–$1,500

- Utilities–included in rent

- Parking–included in rent

- Leasehold improvements–included in rent

- First 3 months rent–free with 3 year lease

- Payroll and other software–$1,500

We were able to negotiate with the landlord for three free months of rent per year we are in business. Our total start up expenses will amount to $49,500 (not including wages and salaries to our full time staff).

Our ongoing monthly expense will be $5,350 for both locations (not including wages).

Our wages for our full time staff will be expensed at the following rate:

- Manager owner—Monthly salary of $4,500

- 5 staff persons—$1,600 per month for each staff person and 5% of bookings for each client they sign to contracts.

Therefore our monthly staffing expense will be $12,500. Our total monthly company staff and office expense will be $17,850 per month.

Projected Income

We have determined that the in the first year we will set our goal to hire out an average of 30 staff per month for a total of 160 billable hours each at an average of $18.00 per hour.

Based on our estimates, we will average $12,960 per month in revenue. While this is less than our fixed costs, we have budgeted for the loss as a way to manage the risk.

Banking and Finance

Based on the required money to launch this business, the owner has invested $150,000 in cash.

Cash will be used to pay for all start–up expenses and monthly expenses as needed. Additionally this money will be used to secure an operating line of credit.

We have made an arrangement with the bank for an interest rate of five percent on the line of credit because we will maintain at least $50,000 in cash in the reserve.

The bank has also agreed to send us referrals if any of their business clients are in need of staff but cannot afford to hire full– or part–time staff by the traditional methods.

MANAGEMENT SUMMARY

Ben Worth—Owner/Manager

Ben has worked in the Human Resources sector for 20 years with four separate companies. These companies range from 40–employee firms all the way up to a 350–employee firm.

Over the course of the last seven years, Ben started putting aside money for the business start–up because he always wanted to own his own company. His experience in the HR area has given Ben the ability to understand staffing needs and requirements. Furthermore, his direct experience with the general staffing companies in the area has given him a good understanding of our competitors as well the market in general.

Healthcare Process Improvement Consultant

Johnson Healthcare Consulting LLC

2904 Timber Ln.
Ft. Landon, AR 72100

Paul Greenland

Johnson Healthcare Consulting LLC is an independent healthcare consultancy specializing in process improvement.

EXECUTIVE SUMMARY

The healthcare industry is changing rapidly. The Accountable Care Act has shifted the focus for hospitals, healthcare systems, and physicians in several key ways. Instead of focusing on increasing utilization (e.g., doing a larger number of procedures to generate more revenue), healthcare reform has resulted in greater attention on quality. Minimizing inappropriate emergency room use, avoiding readmissions (especially as the result of improper care), and managing patients' chronic health problems effectively to avoid hospitalizations have become key focal points throughout the industry. Financial penalties for readmissions, and the need to manage large patient populations for a pre-determined fee, have made cost-containment, productivity, efficiency, and quality more important than ever before.

In this challenging climate, healthcare industry players are using process improvement initiatives to succeed, and in some cases, to survive. While some organizations already have robust process improvement initiatives (in some cases, entire process improvement departments), others are only beginning to consider the possibilities. Some organizations refer to their process improvement initiatives with terms such as process redesign, change management, lean, Six Sigma, and kaizen (Japanese for "change for the better"). Although they are now being applied in a wide range of industries, including healthcare, "lean" initiatives have their roots in manufacturing, especially automotive production.

Johnson Healthcare Consulting LLC is an independent healthcare consultancy specializing in process improvement. Established by Stephanie Johnson, the practice is focused on helping independent physician practices, larger physician groups, outpatient surgery centers, hospitals, and healthcare systems plan, implement, and measure process improvement initiatives, ranging from individual/small projects to the establishment of dedicated/in-house process improvement teams. Stephanie Johnson has eight years of specialized experience in the areas of performance improvement and project management. She has a strong command of methodologies, concepts, and performance improvement techniques as they pertain to healthcare organizations and is a Certified Lean Six Sigma Black Belt.

INDUSTRY ANALYSIS

Johnson Healthcare Consulting is focused on serving clients in the healthcare industry, especially hospitals and physician practices of all sizes. According to the American Hospital Association (www.aha.org), there are approximately 5,700 hospitals in the United States. The AHA's membership base includes nearly 5,000 organizations, including hospitals and healthcare systems, as well as 43,000 individual members. With roots dating back to 1898, the association represents the needs of its members on the legislative and regulatory fronts, and also provides healthcare leaders with education and information regarding industry trends.

The industry also is represented by the American Medical Group Association (www.amga.org), which serves as "a leading voice in advocating for efficient, team-based, and accountable care." According to the AMGA, its members include hospital-affiliated medical groups; physician-owned, independent group practices; accountable care organizations; academic and faculty practices; independent practice associations; and health systems. Collectively, its members include approximately 160,000 physicians who care for some 120 million patients.

Another key industry organization for process improvement professionals is the Milwaukee, Wisconsin-based American Society for Quality (http://asq.org). The ASQ's mission is: "To increase the use and impact of quality in response to the diverse needs of the world." The organization benefits members cross the globe via a network of National Service Centers in countries such as China, Mexico, and India, along with a regional service center in the United Arab Emirates. Membership benefits include access to professional certifications (including Six Sigma).

MARKET ANALYSIS

Johnson Healthcare Consulting will market its services nationally, targeting the following markets:

- Hospitals (specifically quality management departments, process improvement engineers, and directors of performance improvement)

- Outpatient Care Centers

- Independent Physician Practices

According to the *AHA Annual Survey*, published by the American Hospital Association's affiliate, Health Forum, the United States was home to 5,686 registered hospitals in 2013, which broke down by category as follows:

- Community Hospitals (4,974)

- Nongovernment Not-for-Profit Community Hospitals (2,904)

- Investor-Owned (For-Profit) Community Hospitals (1,060)

- State and Local Government Community Hospitals (1,010)

- Federal Government Hospitals (213)

- Nonfederal Psychiatric Hospitals (406)

- Nonfederal Long Term Care Hospitals (81)

- Institutions (12)

PERSONNEL

Stephanie Johnson has eight years of specialized experience in the areas of performance improvement and project management. She has a strong command of methodologies, concepts, and performance improvement techniques as they pertain to healthcare organizations. In addition to holding a master's degree in business administration, she is a Certified Lean Six Sigma Black Belt. (Six Sigma is a widely recognized quality-focused management philosophy with different levels of certifications.

Before establishing her own consulting practice, Johnson worked as a process improvement engineer for Blackstone Health System in Ridgway, Oregon. In that role she interacted with all areas of the organization while working on change management and process improvement projects. After three years Johnson was promoted to director of performance improvement, overseeing a staff of seven people, including four process improvement engineers. As the department leader, she was tasked with overseeing the redesign of existing processes and workflows throughout the health system, with a goal of improving performance in areas such as patient care, customer service, finance, and operations.

Johnson is well-suited for work as a process improvement consultant. She has exceptional time management and organizational skills, and is a strong oral and written communicator. In addition, she is a proven leader and has demonstrated her success in leading interdisciplinary work groups and teams that include individuals from varying organizational levels. Finally, Johnson has a keen analytical mind and the ability to perform complex data analysis and break down information into reports and presentations that can be easily understood by a wide range of audiences.

Professional & Advisory Support

Johnson Healthcare Consulting has established a business banking account with Main Street Bank, including a merchant account for accepting credit card payments. Legal representation is provided by Forreston, Lewis & Cerrado, and tax advisory services are provided by Mid-States Accounting LLC. Johnson has retained a business attorney to prepare the documents needed to establish her limited liability company and establish agreements with clients.

SERVICES

Johnson Healthcare Consulting will concentrate on helping clients to establish their own process improvement initiatives, programs, or departments. In addition, the practice also will help clients with specific process improvement initiatives. In the latter case, Stephanie Johnson will follow a kaizen approach to process improvement, which involves individual improvement events that last between three and five days and include approximately 4-5 key individuals. Johnson typically will employ the following process when working with clients.

1. *Identifying improvement areas:* This initial phase involves meeting with clients to discuss specific areas where processes can potentially be improved. Depending on the organization and the nature of the project, Johnson may meet with a range of different professionals, including quality managers, process improvement directors, physician leaders, CEOs, chief nursing officers, and clinic managers. Improvement areas can vary significantly, ranging from a desire to shorten the admission process for patients to eliminating waste in a hospital department. Johnson will work with her clients to identify specific improvement goals, which may include:

- Preventing/reducing avoidable hospital admissions/readmissions

- Increasing efficiency

- Employee empowerment/development

- Cost reduction/containment

- Optimizing workflows

- Reducing and/or eliminating waste (inventory, motion, defects, over-production, over-processing, waiting, etc.)

- Reducing inappropriate emergency room utilization

- Simplifying processes

- Optimizing patient care

- Eliminating barriers

2. *Defining project scope:* Some projects can be completed in their entirety within a short timeframe, while larger initiatives may involve a series of smaller improvement events. Johnson will help her client to make this determination in advance.

3. *Establishing objectives:* Once the improvement area and project scope have been clearly defined, Stephanie Johnson will work with her client to establish concise, measurable improvement objectives.

4. *Improvement event:* Next, Johnson will schedule an on-site improvement event that involves the improvement team, along with necessary management and information technology personnel (when needed). During the event, Johnson will seek to create an environment where staff members from all levels work cooperatively with mutual respect for one another, guiding them through the following steps:

- Observing the current process/work environment.

- Using root-cause analysis to visually map the current process and identify waste/problems.

- Developing and visually mapping an improved future state in which waste is minimized and value is maximized.

5. *Final presentation:* Following the conclusion of the improvement event, Johnson and/or her clients' designated staff will develop and give a presentation, outlining results to company leaders and describing how the new process will be implemented.

6. *Evaluation and adjustment:* Johnson will work with her clients to identify specific milestones/timeframes for measuring and reporting progress/success.

GROWTH STRATEGY

Stephanie Johnson is fortunate to establish her consulting practice with several customers. During her time with Blackstone Health System, she made it a point to network with colleagues in similar positions at hospitals and healthcare systems throughout the country. In addition to attending conferences, she was a frequent poster and responder on process improvement-related message boards utilized by industry players. Through these relationships, she has established connections with two community hospitals (in Indianapolis and Pittsburgh) that are in need of guidance in establishing their own process improvement departments.

Together, these clients have contracted with Johnson for approximately 20 hours of weekly billable consulting time through the middle of 2016. These new consulting relationships will provide her with a solid base from which to begin. However, Johnson recognizes that she will need to market her services continuously in order to maintain a steady stream of business.

From her strong starting position, Johnson has established targets for the number of billable hours she would like to work during Johnson Healthcare Consulting's first three years of operations. As she becomes acclimated to working for herself and managing clients, Johnson has set a target of generating 20 billable hours per week during the first year of operations (1,000 hours per year). She will increase this target to 25 hours per week (1,250 hours annually) during year two and 30 hours per week (1,500 annually) during year three. Johnson is confident that these targets will allow her to grow her practice gradually without sacrificing quality, and devote non-billable time to administrative and marketing-related tasks.

After her first three years in practice, Johnson will be "at capacity." At that time, she will consider establishing an office outside of her home and taking on additional consultants in order to maintain her practice's growth.

OPERATIONS

To minimize overhead during the formative years of the practice, Stephanie Johnson initially will operate her consultancy from office space within her Ft. Landon, Arkansas, home. She already has the tools needed to work as an independent consultant, including a laptop, tablet computer, and smartphone. In addition, she has access to a major airport, making travel by air easy to all points throughout the United States.

Fees

One challenge faced by new consultants is establishing a rate that is competitive, but not too low. Thoughtful consideration, and research involving a number of different sources, must be used to arrive at a base rate. This rate can then be used for providing clients with hourly or project-based estimates. Consultants who set their fees too low will find it challenging to increase them later on, while a base rate that is too high will be equally problematic when attempting to secure clients. Based on feedback from people in the industry, and her own independent research, Johnson has established an hourly consulting rate of $125.

MARKETING & SALES

Johnson Healthcare Consulting has developed a marketing plan that involves the following primary tactics:

1. *Social Media:* Johnson Healthcare Consulting will maintain a process improvement-related blog, and also leverage business-related social networks such as LinkedIn to network with potential clients.

2. *Printed Collateral:* A high-quality, four-color brochure will be developed, which can be used as sales collateral when approaching prospective clients.

3. *Web Site:* A local Web developer has been retained to create a simple but effective Web site, which will offer information about Stephanie Johnson, her approach to process improvement, a link to her blog and social media platforms, testimonials, and a contact form that prospective clients can use to contact her.

4. *Quarterly Direct Mailings:* Johnson has developed an introductory letter with a strong call to action, which will be used with the aforementioned brochure as part of a quarterly direct mail campaign to her target markets. Johnson has secured a mailing list of the top 100 U.S. hospitals/healthcare systems, along with key independent medical groups nationwide. A local mail house will be retained to produce and manage the mailings, with a goal of generating a steady stream of referrals.

5. *Public Relations:* Johnson will share her expertise by attempting to write expert columns for healthcare trade magazines such as *Group Practice Journal* and *Hospitals & Health Networks.*

6. *Professional Presentations:* Johnson will attend and give presentations at healthcare industry conferences, and will then pursue opportunities to network with attendees and share her contact information.

FINANCIAL ANALYSIS

Following are Johnson Healthcare Consultin's projected sales, expenses, and net profits for the first three years of operations:

	2016	2017	2018
Revenue	**$125,000**	**$156,250**	**$187,500**
Expenses			
Salaries	$ 75,000	$ 90,000	$105,000
Payroll taxes	$ 11,250	$ 13,500	$ 15,750
Insurance	$ 863	$ 920	$ 978
Office supplies	$ 1,438	$ 1,725	$ 2,013
Equipment	$ 4,025	$ 2,300	$ 2,300
Marketing & advertising	$ 8,625	$ 9,775	$ 10,925
Telecommunications & Internet	$ 2,818	$ 2,818	$ 2,818
Professional development	$ 1,725	$ 2,875	$ 2,875
Travel & entertainment	$ 15,525	$ 17,250	$ 18,975
Subscriptions & dues	$ 403	$ 403	$ 403
Total expenses	**$121,670**	**$141,565**	**$162,035**
Net income	**$ 3,330**	**$ 14,685**	**$ 25,465**

SWOT ANALYSIS

Strengths: Stephanie Johnson has highly specialized knowledge and expertise, resulting in strong demand for her services.

Weaknesses: As a one-person operation, Johnson has limited capacity. This will limit the number and scope of consulting assignments that she can take on without hiring additional employees.

Opportunities: Because of changes in the healthcare industry (namely healthcare reform), the market for process improvement consulting is virtually unlimited.

Threats: Like any business that relies solely on one individual, Stephanie Johnson's practice could be in jeopardy in the event of a serious illness or injury that makes it impossible for her to work.

Hot Meal Delivery Service

Stanley Delivery Services Inc.

2837 Guilford Ave.
Parker, AL 21987

Paul Greenland

Stanley Delivery Services Inc. is a hot meal delivery services provider focused on getting healthy meal options to senior citizens living in multi-unit residential housing complexes and adult day centers.

EXECUTIVE SUMMARY

According to the report, *Spotlight on Senior Hunger,* published by Feeding America and the National Foundation to End Senior Hunger, approximately 4.8 million senior citizens (one in every 12 people above age 60) are "food insecure" in the United States. This number doubled between 2001 and 2011. By 2016 the figure had likely increased, considering that more than 10,000 baby boomers were reaching age 65 on a daily basis—a trend that was expected to continue through the year 2030.

Because the population of senior citizens in need of access to healthy meals was expected to skyrocket, Martin and Becky Stanley have established Stanley Delivery Services Inc., which partners with a community kitchen operated by Bright Horizons, a consortium of local social service agencies, to deliver healthy meal options to senior citizens living in multi-unit residential housing complexes. The owners are positioning their business as a key solution for seniors who wish to "age in place" and remain independent in their own apartment.

Stanley Delivery Services is a unique transportation service that makes deliveries throughout the Parker, Alabama market area. Parker is served by a Meals on Wheels program, which has limited resources, a long waiting list, and no further capacity. In addition, the Meals on Wheels program does not make deliveries on weekends. For this reason, Stanley Delivery Services and Bright Horizons will play a key role in fulfilling a significant community need. Stanley Delivery Services knows all about transportation and delivery, while its social service agency partner is experienced at preparing meals and understanding the needs of area seniors.

This business plan also could apply to other types of hot meal delivery programs, including school lunch programs (private, public, or college/university), head-start/preschool programs, day care facilities, homeless shelters, etc.

MARKET ANALYSIS

Primary Market

Stanley Delivery Services is located in Parker, Alabama.

The local population included 64,567 people in 2015. Individuals over the age of 55 accounted for 32 percent of the population (higher than the national average of 26.2 percent). By 2020 the population is projected to reach 67,795 people, at which time individuals over 55 will account for 34 percent of the population, still above the national average. The following tables provide detailed actual and projected breakdowns of the over-55 population:

I. 2015 actual population

Age	Percentage	Population
55–64	15%	9,685
65–74	8%	5,165
75–84	5%	3,228
85+	4%	2,583
Total	**32%**	**20,661**

Projected annual deliveries (year two)

Facility	Weekday	Weekend	Holiday	Total
Parker Village Center	$ 19,350	$ 8,585	$ 600	$ 28,535
Lawrence West Senior Center	$ 19,350	$ 8,585	$ 600	$ 28,535
Sunlight Terrace Apartments	$ 19,350	$ 8,585	$ 600	$ 28,535
Mason Heights Independent Living	$ 19,350	$ 8,585	$ 600	$ 28,535
Peterson Willows	$ 19,350	$ 8,585	$ 600	$ 28,535
Weston Willows	$ 19,350	$ 8,585	$ 600	$ 28,535
Oak Ridge High-Rise	$ 19,350	$ 8,585	$ 600	$ 28,535
Golden Valley Adult Day Support Center	$ 19,350	$ 0	$ 0	$ 19,350
Peachtree Adult Center	$ 19,350	$ 0	$ 0	$ 19,350
Cherryvale Adult Day Support Center	$ 19,350	$ 0	$ 0	$ 19,350
	$193,500	**$60,095**	**$4,200**	**$257,795**

In 2015, the average household income in Parker was $61,464. More specifically, the market broke down as follows:

$ 0—$9,999 9.9%

$ 10,000—$19,999 13.3%

$ 20,000—$29,999 12.0%

$ 30,000—$39,999 10.7%

$ 40,000—$49,999 9.4%

$ 50,000—$59,999 8.1%

$ 60,000—$74,999 9.8%

$ 75,000—$99,999 11.0%

$100,000—$124,999 6.6%

$125,000—$149,999 3.3%

$150,000 + 5.4%

Competitive Analysis

In early 2016 there were no delivery services focusing exclusively on the senior market in Parker, with the exception of the local Meals on Wheels program.

Primary Market

Approximately 90 percent of Stanley Delivery Services' business will come from regular lunchtime and dinnertime routes between the community kitchen and senior housing communities or apartment complexes, including:

- Parker Village Center

- Lawrence West Senior Center

- Sunlight Terrace Apartments

- Weston willows

- Oak Ridge High-Rise

As the population ages, the number of adult day programs is projected to increase, resulting in growing demand for meal solutions. The remaining 10 percent of Stanley Delivery Services' business will come from meal deliveries to adult day programs for senior citizens, including:

- Golden Valley Adult Day Support Center

- Cherryvale Adult Day Support Center

Secondary Markets

Beyond Parker, there are sizable populations of senior citizens in several smaller nearby communities, including Denton, Wheeling, and Orangeville. Collectively, these markets are served by a number of senior living complexes and adult day programs, outlined in the Growth Strategy section of this plan. Bright Horizons is in the process of seeking funding for the introduction of senior meal programs in these communities. Stanley Delivery Services has been included in the strategic planning process, and the Stanleys are committed to expanding their delivery services if the appropriate resources become available.

INDUSTRY ANALYSIS

According to the U.S. Department of Health and Human Services' Administration for Community Living, the portion of the U.S. population over the age of 65 will more than double between 2013 and 2060, increasing from 44.7 million to approximately 98 million, respectively. By 2040 individuals over age 65 will account for 21.7 percent of the population. Businesses like Stanley Delivery Services, which play a role in improving the quality of life for older citizens, are projected to achieve healthy growth for the foreseeable future.

Operated by the U.S. Department of Health and Human Services, the Administration for Community Living has a mission to "Maximize the independence, well-being, and health of older adults, people with disabilities across the lifespan, and their families and caregivers." The agency "brings together the efforts and achievements of the Administration on Aging, the Administration on Intellectual and Developmental Disabilities, and the HHS Office on Disability to serve as the Federal agency responsible for increasing access to community supports, while focusing attention and resources on the unique needs of older Americans and people with disabilities across the lifespan."

According to the United States Department of Labor, Bureau of Labor Statistics' *Occupational Outlook Handbook,* 1.33 million delivery truck drivers and driver/sales workers were employed in 2014, earning an average of $13.22 per hour. By 2024 the industry was expected to employ an additional 48,100 workers.

PERSONNEL

Martin Stanley, President

Martin Stanley "grew up" in the transportation industry. The son of an independent semi-truck owner/operator, he spent many weekends and summers helping out with his father's trucking business. After high school, Martin joined FedEx, beginning a 15-year career as a delivery driver for the transportation leader. Ultimately, Martin transitioned to a route management position for Sawchuck Logistics, a regional transportation provider. After serving in this role for seven years, Martin is ready to utilize his broad knowledge base and establish a transportation business that makes an important difference in the lives of the community's older population every day. To position himself for success, Martin has completed a small business management training program at a local community college.

Becky Stanley, CPA, Vice President & Treasurer

Martin is joined in the business by his wife, Becky, a local accountant who will serve the business on a part-time basis as vice president and treasurer. A Parker native, Becky has a big heart for the local community. Her passion for serving the elderly was a major source of inspiration for the establishment of Stanley Delivery Services. Becky has served as a volunteer at several local senior centers over the past 10 years, as a board member for a local social service agency, and also helps to care for aging parents and her grandmother. Becky earned her accounting degree from the University of Alabama and worked for several leading accounting firms before establishing her own practice in 2006. Becky played an instrumental role in winning a delivery contract from the newly established Bright Horizons consortium (through a competitive bidding process).

The Stanleys will be joined in their business by a staff that includes the following positions:

- Full-Time Driver/Route Coordinator

- Part-Time Driver 1

- Part-Time Driver 2

- Part-Time Driver 3

- Part-Time Driver 4

Position	2016	2017	2018
Martin Stanley, President	$ 50,000	$ 55,000	$ 60,000
Becky Stanley, Vice President & Treasurer	$ 15,000	$ 20,000	$ 25,000
Full-time driver/route coordinator	$ 25,000	$ 30,000	$ 35,000
Part-time driver 1	$ 12,500	$ 13,000	$ 13,500
Part-time driver 2	$ 12,500	$ 13,000	$ 13,500
Part-time driver 3	$ 0	$ 12,500	$ 13,000
Part-time driver 4	$ 0	$ 0	$ 12,500
Total	**$115,000**	**$143,500**	**$172,500**

Professional & Advisory Support

Stanley Delivery Services has established a business banking account with Parker Community Bank. Tax advisement is provided by Ridgway Tax Advisors LLC.

GROWTH STRATEGY

The Stanleys have developed the following growth strategy for their new business:

Year One: Provide deliveries to an initial network of five multi-unit complexes for senior citizens (Parker Village Center, Lawrence West Senior Center, Sunlight Terrace Apartments, Weston Willows, and Oak Ridge High-Rise) and two senior adult day centers (Golden Valley Adult Day Support Center and Cherryvale Adult Day Support Center). Begin operations with two delivery vans, one full-time driver/route coordinator, and two part-time drivers. Generate net income of $18,875 on gross revenue of $181,375.

Year Two: Expand services to include an additional two residential complexes (Mason Heights Independent Living and Peterson Willows) and one adult day program (Peachtree Adult Center).

The owners have determined that, at maximum capacity, it is theoretically possible to service all of their routes with one vehicle during year one. However, two vehicles will allow them to deliver meals more quickly, and also maintain operations in the event of a vehicle breakdown or accident. For this reason, the business has purchased two used (2013) modified vans at a cost of $25,000 each. The owners will purchase a third van in year two, and a fourth in year three to accommodate projected growth.

The owners will provide the necessary start-up capital to purchase one van, but will finance the second vehicle needed for operations during year one. Financing has been obtained from a local bank at 3.11% interest for 60 months (total cost with interest $27,026).

Prior to purchasing the vans, Stanley Delivery Services made sure that they were in compliance with all requirements from the state health board.

Features of the vehicles include:

- Thermostatically-controlled hot compartment
- Thermostatically-controlled refrigerated compartment
- Thermostatically controlled frozen compartment
- Convenient access doors
- Temperature alarm
- Configurable interior racks
- Heavy-duty handles and security locks on all compartments

LEGAL

Stanley Delivery Services will maintain appropriate liability and automotive insurance policies (available upon request). In addition, criminal background checks, drug and alcohol testing, and CPR/first aid certification will be required for all employees.

MARKETING & SALES

Stanley Delivery Services is somewhat unique in that it is a service provider for one entity. Although there are opportunities to expand the business' operations, it engages in limited marketing and sales activities at the present time. The following tactics are used to communicate Stanley Delivery Services' capabilities:

1. A four-color brochure with profiles of the owners, an overview of the business' fleet/capabilities, and a statement regarding insurance.

2. Monthly lunch meetings with the president of Bright Horizons, to ensure that services are being provided to the consortium's satisfaction and to stay abreast of the agency's growth plans.

3. Monthly strategic planning meetings with Bright Horizons' board of directors.

4. Quarterly drop-ins with administrators/facility managers at delivery sites to address any concerns and maximize quality/service.

5. Relationship building tactics with local officials (e.g., city council members, aldermen, etc.).

6. Membership in the Parker Chamber of Commerce.

7. A Web site with complete details about Stanley Delivery Services and its services/capabilities.

FINANCIAL ANALYSIS

Stanley Delivery Services has prepared a full set of conservative financial projections in partnership with an accountant, which are available upon request. Following is an overview of projected sales and expenses for the first three years of operations.

Sales	$181,375	$257,795	$334,215
Expenses			
Advertising & marketing	$ 1,000	$ 1,000	$ 1,000
General/administrative	$ 500	$ 500	$ 500
Legal	$ 1,250	$ 500	$ 500
Accounting	$ 2,000	$ 1,250	$ 1,250
Office supplies	$ 500	$ 500	$ 500
Computers/peripherals	$ 1,000	$ 250	$ 250
Software	$ 550	$ 550	$ 550
Business insurance	$ 2,500	$ 3,000	$ 3,500
Payroll	$115,000	$143,500	$172,500
Payroll taxes	$ 17,250	$ 21,525	$ 25,875
Facility lease	$ 4,800	$ 4,800	$ 4,800
Postage	$ 500	$ 1,000	$ 1,000
Telecommunications	$ 1,250	$ 1,250	$ 1,250
Maintenance & repairs	$ 3,000	$ 4,500	$ 6,000
Vehicle purchases	$ 0	$ 25,000	$ 25,000
Vehicle loans	$ 5,400	$ 5,400	$ 5,400
Fuel	$ 6,000	$ 9,000	$ 12,000
Total expenses	**$162,500**	**$223,525**	**$261,875**
Net income (before taxes)	**$ 18,875**	**$ 34,270**	**$ 72,340**

In addition, the owners have prepared the following annual delivery projections for the first three years of operations.

Projected annual deliveries (year one)

Facility	Weekday	Weekend	Holiday	Total
Parker Village Center	$ 19,350	$ 8,585	$ 600	$ 28,535
Lawrence West Senior Center	$ 19,350	$ 8,585	$ 600	$ 28,535
Sunlight Terrace Apartments	$ 19,350	$ 8,585	$ 600	$ 28,535
Weston Willows	$ 19,350	$ 8,585	$ 600	$ 28,535
Oak Ridge High-Rise	$ 19,350	$ 8,585	$ 600	$ 28,535
Golden Valley Adult Day Support Center	$ 19,350	$ 0	$ 0	$ 19,350
Cherryvale Adult Day Support Center	$ 19,350	$ 0	$ 0	$ 19,350
	$135,450	**$42,925**	**$3,000**	**$181,375**

Projected annual deliveries (year two)

Facility	Weekday	Weekend	Holiday	Total
Parker Village Center	$ 19,350	$ 8,585	$ 600	$ 28,535
Lawrence West Senior Center	$ 19,350	$ 8,585	$ 600	$ 28,535
Sunlight Terrace Apartments	$ 19,350	$ 8,585	$ 600	$ 28,535
Mason Heights Independent Living	$ 19,350	$ 8,585	$ 600	$ 28,535
Peterson Willows	$ 19,350	$ 8,585	$ 600	$ 28,535
Weston Willows	$ 19,350	$ 8,585	$ 600	$ 28,535
Oak Ridge High-Rise	$ 19,350	$ 8,585	$ 600	$ 28,535
Golden Valley Adult Day Support Center	$ 19,350	$ 0	$ 0	$ 19,350
Peachtree Adult Center	$ 19,350	$ 0	$ 0	$ 19,350
Cherryvale Adult Day Support Center	$ 19,350	$ 0	$ 0	$ 19,350
	$193,500	**$60,095**	**$4,200**	**$257,795**

Projected annual deliveries (year three)

Facility	Weekday	Weekend	Holiday	Total
Parker Village Center	$ 19,350	$ 8,585	$ 600	$ 28,535
Lawrence West Senior Center	$ 19,350	$ 8,585	$ 600	$ 28,535
Sunlight Terrace Apartments	$ 19,350	$ 8,585	$ 600	$ 28,535
Mason Heights Independent Living	$ 19,350	$ 8,585	$ 600	$ 28,535
Peterson Willows	$ 19,350	$ 8,585	$ 600	$ 28,535
Weston Willows	$ 19,350	$ 8,585	$ 600	$ 28,535
Oak Ridge High-Rise	$ 19,350	$ 8,585	$ 600	$ 28,535
Orangeville Apartments	$ 19,350	$ 8,585	$ 600	$ 28,535
The Villas of Wheeling	$ 19,350	$ 8,585	$ 600	$ 28,535
Golden Valley Adult Day Support Center	$ 19,350	$ 0	$ 0	$ 19,350
Peachtree Adult Center	$ 19,350	$ 0	$ 0	$ 19,350
Denton Center	$ 19,350	$ 0	$ 0	$ 19,350
Cherryvale Adult Day Support Center	$ 19,350	$ 0	$ 0	$ 19,350
	$251,550	**$77,265**	**$5,400**	**$334,215**

Start-up costs

Modified vans:

$50,000 (year one)

$25,000 (year two)

The Stanleys will provide the necessary start-up capital to purchase one van, but will finance the second vehicle needed for operations during year one. Financing has been obtained from a local bank at 3.11% interest for 60 months (total cost with interest $27,026).

Funding

The owners are seeking an investment of $25,000, in the form of a private investment or small business loan, to provide initial capital for operations.

Inflatable Party Rentals

Party Masters

8779 South Ammon Rd.
Idaho Falls, ID 83406

Zuzu Enterprises

Party Masters is a party rental business specializing in inflatables and interactive games. Low overhead costs and the possibility of a flexible schedule led Mr. Steve Bartels to start the business 2 years ago. As business has increased through successful bookings and word-of-mouth, Mr. Bartels has decided to expand into a full-time operation.

EXECUTIVE SUMMARY

Party Masters is a party rental business specializing in inflatables and interactive games. Low overhead costs and the possibility of a flexible schedule led Mr. Steve Bartels to start the business two years ago. As business has increased through successful bookings and word-of-mouth, Mr. Bartels has decided to expand into a full-time operation.

This business plan will serve to outline where the business is and where we see it headed in the next five years. It is crucial to know our target market, have a consistent pricing strategy, and know our competitors if we are to survive and even thrive in the long term.

Vital to our success will be the introduction of new games and inflatables each year, making our business current, fresh, and in-demand. To this end, Party Masters has decided to add the following new games to our portfolio:

- Human Billiards
- Giant Connect 4
- Foam Pit
- Jousting
- Sumo wrestling suits
- Rock wall

INDUSTRY ANALYSIS

The Party Supply Rental industry is expected to grow at an annualized rate of 2.3% to $4.7 billion over the five years to 2020. Renewed confidence in the economy has encouraged business and consumers to host events that require products from the Party Supply Rental industry. Continued economic recovery will likely aid growth through 2025. Armed with higher personal and corporate income, households and businesses are projected to expand their party budgets, which will allow them to spend more on rentals beyond basic necessities to full-service product lines including inflatables, games, and other fun activities.

MARKET ANALYSIS

Idaho Falls has one of the largest percentages of the population under the age of 18 in the entire United States, with 32.2% of the overall population under falling under this number. The total population in 2013 was estimated at more than 58,000, with a 10-year growth rate of nearly 15%.

The surrounding areas of Ammon, Lincoln, Iona, Ucon, Shelley, Rigby, Basalt, Lewisville, Blackfoot, and Rexburg will provide an additional source of potential customers. The metropolitan area has a combined population of nearly 140,000 people, of which about 31% are under the age of 18. This provides an excellent customer base for our growing business.

Within this geographical area, potential clients come from a variety of different places, ranging from the family planning a special birthday party to a school scheduling a carnival, and even to a church organizing Bible school or a corporation planning a family picnic.

Weekends will obviously be the busiest times for party rentals, but school and library events are also popular during the week, as are rentals to preschools and day care centers. Summer months also tend to be busier than the winter, but indoor events are also possible and provide a safe, fun atmosphere for kids to run off steam when they are less likely to play outdoors.

Competition

There are three major competitors to Party Masters in the Idaho Falls market. They include:

Bounce Your World

823 Coachman Dr, Idaho Falls, ID 83402

Limited inventory; only own 8 inflatables of various kinds

I.F. Inflatables

3446 Greenwillow Ln, Idaho Falls, ID 83401

Good reputation; has 12 different kinds of inflatables, including boxing, bungee run, jousting, sumo suits, and bubble soccer. They will be our biggest competition.

Signature Party Rental

598 W Broadway St, Idaho Falls, ID 83402

Mainly tents and wedding equipment, including dance floor, tents, tables, linens, wedding décor. Only have 7 inflatables for rent.

Pricing among the three businesses is competitive. What will set Party Masters apart from the rest is our breadth of rentals and our commitment to continually updating our offerings. Safety, cleanliness, and professionalism will also be a main focus of Party Masters, so that all customers are confident in their choice to hire Party Masters and always 100% satisfied.

Personnel

Running a successful party rental business is not a one-man show. It takes the help of a team to achieve our goals and provide optimal service and availability to our customers. Mr. Bartels will be the only full-time employee, but several part-time employees will be on the payroll as well. Mrs. Judy Bartels,

Steve's wife, will provide accounting and scheduling support. With summer months the busiest, several college students will be added to the staff during that time to help with delivery, set-up, and operation of the games and equipment.

All employees must have a clean driving and criminal record. They will be properly vetted with local law enforcement with periodic checks being done to ensure the best staff around. Extensive training of all staff will also be done and feedback from clients will be sought to ensure all employees are adhering to the high expectations that Party Masters has for its employees.

All employees will be considered independent contractors with no set schedule or guaranteed hours. Taxes and insurance will be the responsibility of the employee.

Professional & Advisory Support

Party Masters has established business accounts with Citizens Community Bank. The Alpine Insurance Agency has insured the business and will issue additional, temporary insurance to all venues that book with Party Masters.

SERVICES

Party Masters is a party rental business specializing in inflatables and interactive games. Possible venues include:

- Churches
- Schools
- Community colleges and colleges
- Businesses
- City recreation centers
- Parks
- Private homes
- Libraries
- Preschools
- Daycare centers
- Summer camps
- Pumpkin patches/cider mills
- Car dealerships

The types of events that utilize inflatables and party games include, but aren't limited to:

- Bible school
- Birthday parties
- Building dedications
- Church picnics
- Company holiday parties
- Company picnics
- End-of-school year parties

- Family holiday parties
- Family picnics
- Family reunions
- Graduation parties
- Grand opening events
- High school reunion picnics
- Library events
- Post-prom parties
- Sales promotions
- School carnivals
- Senior all night parties
- Tailgate parties
- Team building activities

Party Packages

Party packages will be available and encouraged. Beyond the first item rented, additional rentals will receive up to a 10% discount. These packages inspire clients to offer additional activities, and are beneficial to Party Masters in many ways. Additional rentals mean additional revenue and maximize the delivery time invested. It also makes for a more exciting even that people are likely to remember and want to replicate.

Discounts

In addition to party packages, further discounts may be available to customers. A determination of the possibility of the discount will be based on:

- Type of customer (nonprofit versus profit)
- Seasonality (winter versus summer)
- Day of the week (weekday versus weekend)
- Delivery status (delivered versus picked up)

OPERATIONS

Equipment

All of our inflatables, games and other equipment will be of the highest quality and inspected and maintained on a monthly basis. Safety and appearance of our units is of utmost importance to ensure the safety and satisfaction of our clients.

Our inflatables boast:

- 18 ounce heavy duty American-made vinyl (second hand materials are never used)
- Patented "locking" entry door designs, which keeps the participants from falling out
- The most comprehensive ASTM certified safety rules in the industry sewn on the front of unit
- Optional custom designed safety ramp with child-safe side bumpers
- Exclusive safety feature which keeps bounces inflated up to 60 seconds in the event of a power failure

- Four anchor straps (one in each corner) for added installation safety

- Double stitching on all seams, with quadruple-stitched, double reinforced, top mattress seams

- No visible exterior seams running up the columns of the main structure

- Felded seams (which require special tooling) on the main structure, giving the unit 50% more resistance to failure

- Permanent waterproof roof structure to keep the hot sun and the rain out, with rain Flaps sewn on bottom of units to allow for quick drainage

- Dust cover on top mattress seams to prevent dirt or other debris from entering top floor seams

In addition to having these safety and quality features, equipment and games from Party Masters will also be unique and offer a wide variety from which to choose. Clients will be drawn to our large selection and our exclusive designs.

Setup time for inflatables averages 10 minutes, with take down time averaging 15 minutes.

Interactive Games and Equipment
Party Masters has an extensive inventory of available party rentals, including:

- 12' water slide

- 17' slide (dry)

- 20' water slide

- 22' water slide

- 52' obstacle course

- Arcade Games—including foosball, ping pong, pool, air hockey, darts, etc.

- Baseball Radar Speed Pitch

- Bounce house

- Bounce house/slide combo

- Boxing ring

- Bubble soccer

- Bungee run

- Carnival Games

- Cash cube

- Casino Games and Table Rental, including Roulette Wheel, poker table, craps table

- Dodge Ball Arena

- Dunk tank

- Flip Book Photo Booth

- Foam Pit

- Giant Connect 4

- Giant Twister Game

- Human Billiards

- Human Foosball Court

- Inflatable Movie Screen

- Jousting

- Karaoke

- Laser Tag

- Log Slammer Ride

- Mechanical Bull

- Mechanical Surfboard

- Photo Booth

- Rock wall

- Sumo wrestling suits

- Velcro Sticky Wall

- Video games and consoles, including DDR, Guitar Hero, etc.

Other Rental Equipment
Other equipment that is available for rent includes:

- Cotton candy machine

- Popcorn machine

- Snocone maker

- Tables–60" round

- Tables–6' long

- Chairs, folding

- Tents–10 x 10 Canopy (10 people)

- Tents—16' x 16' frame tent (26 people)

- Tents—20' x 20' frame tent (40 people)

- Tents—20' x 30' frame tent (60 people)

- Tents—20' x 40' frame tent (80 people)

- Linens, skirting, chair covers, and other decorations

- Sound system

- Tent Sidewalls

- Tent Heater

- Dance Floor (4' x 4' section)

Office Equipment & Transportation
In addition to the inventory of games, inflatables and other equipment to rent, Party Masters will require some office equipment and storage.

Equipment that will be required includes:

- Office phone for bookings, payments, and other communications

- Cell phone for delivery drivers and on-site personnel to facilitate communication and for emergencies

- Dedicated storage space for all of the rental equipment to keep it organized and protected from the elements

All of the rental equipment will be stored in a heated pole barn on Mr. and Mrs. Bartels' property. Each bouncer looks like a big sleeping bag standing on end and only takes up a 2' x 2' square foot area, and the tents are compact as well. The chairs and tables are easily stacked. A storage unit has been constructed for easy vertical placement of all machines and linens. The entire barn is organized and labeled so that each item has a home, which will facilitate easy, quick access.

Party Masters will not own a delivery vehicle. Any SUV, truck, van or small trailer will work fine. You can usually fit 5 to 6 inflatables in a truck, 4 to 5 in a minivan and up to 3 in a SUV.

Location
Party Masters will be located at the home of Mr. and Mrs. Bartels, 8779 South Ammon Rd. in Idaho Falls. The property features a heated pole barn that will house all of the rental equipment as well as a small office for bookings, scheduling, and billing.

Hours of Operation
Party Masters will be available to clients via phone and email at all times. Delivery of equipment will vary depending on the event and the specific needs of each client.

Payment
Payment will be accepted via cash, check, and credit card.

SAFETY AND LIABILITY

Safety and liability issues will be mitigated by our commitment to purchasing high-quality equipment that is regularly inspected and maintained. Older models will be retired and replaced with new, more trendy inflatables and games, which will attract clients and also eliminate problems of old, worn-out gear.

Waivers and rental agreements were drafted by an attorney to protect Party Masters as well as Mr. and Mrs. Baretls; they correspond with all state regulations. Party Masters is incorporated as an LLC to protect their personal assets. In addition, all contracts, waivers and rental agreement MUST be signed by the same person who is accepting and signing off on the delivery of the equipment. Copies of all documents are given along with safety sheets for all units; brief but thorough safety checks and tutorials are provided at drop-off and must be completed before Party Masters' staff can leave.

Written training guides and instructions are also provided to all employees after their physical training is complete. All delivery personnel must have a copy of these training guides and instructions with them at all times and they must complete a safety checklist before leaving a venue. Photos of the devices to show proper placement, appropriate weighting, clean and damage-free equipment, etc. are also mandatory at drop off.

Weather reports are monitored closely for challenging wind and rain conditions. If there is any concern, clients are notified and alternative arrangements are made.

A very high level of liability insurance has also been purchased; additional, temporary policies are available for the venues to purchase as well.

It is our belief that these precautions and standard practices will greatly diminish any problems with the safety of our rental equipment or liability to the company.

MARKETING & ADVERTISING

Several advertising methods will be employed.

To begin, the website will be updated with photos of all available rentals and promoted on search engines. This will be one of the most important tools for marketing Party Masters because potential customers will likely begin their search for an inflatable rental company online. The website will include contact information and other relevant information so that potential customers can get an idea of what is available and how to proceed. The website will be featured on all business cards, advertisements, and communications. Other social media venues will also be explored, including Twitter, Facebook, and Instagram.

A full set of marketing brochures will be printed. The brochures and business cards will be left at venues for clients and their guests. Advertising signs will also be prominently placed at each venue so that guests as well as passersby will know who to contact for similar events and parties.

Print and online advertisements will be placed both *East Idaho Family Fun Guide* and *Discover Idaho Falls: Parks & Recreation Guide*; both are well-known and established publications geared towards parents and families.

Word-of-mouth advertising will be essential to our success as 60-70% of our bookings are expected to result from referrals. It is imperative that each dealing is professional, safe, and successful so that we can maintain our reputation for quality and ensure that we are recommended to friends and colleagues.

Target Markets

The target market for Party Masters will be within the Idaho Falls metropolitan area. Specifically, potential customers in the following area will be pursued:

- Idaho Falls
- Ammon
- Lincoln
- Iona
- Ucon
- Shelley
- Rigby
- Basalt
- Lewisville
- Blackfoot
- Rexburg

FINANCIAL ANALYSIS

Fees

Party Masters' prices are fair and competitive while still allowing the company to make a profit. Price lists are shown below.

Price list—games and inflatables

Equipment	Price (delivered)	Price (picked up)	Price (weekend)
12' water slide	$175		$225
17' slide (dry)	$150		$200
20' water slide	$275		$350
22' water slide	$300		$375
52' obstacle course	$250		$325
Arcade games—including foosball, ping pong, pool, air hockey, darts, etc.	$ 50/game		$ 75/game
Baseball radar speed pitch	$ 50		$ 75
Bounce house	$100		$150
Bounce house/slide combo	$150		$200
Boxing ring	$150		$200
Bubble soccer	$ 20/ball	$ 15/ball	
Bungee run	$175		$225
Carnival games	$ 50/game		$ 75/game
Cash cube	$100		$150
Casino games and table rental, including roulette wheel, poker table, craps table	$ 50/game		$ 75/game
Dodge ball arena	$200		$250
Dunk tank	$250		$300
Flip book photo booth	$500		$750
Foam pit	$150		$175
Giant connect 4	$200		$250
Giant twister game	$200		$250
Human billiards	$200		$250
Human foosball court	$200		$250
Inflatable movie screen	$225		$300
Jousting	$150		$200
Karaoke	$100	$ 75	
Laser tag	$250		$300
Log slammer ride	$300		$350
Mechanical bull	$300		$350
Mechanical surfboard	$300		$350
Photo booth	$400		$550
Rock wall	$200		$250
Sumo wrestling suits		$125	$200
Velcro sticky wall	$200		$250
Video games and consoles, including DDR, guitar hero, etc.	$ 50/game		$ 75/game

Price list—other

Equipment	Price (delivered)	Price (picked up)	Price (weekend)
Cotton candy machine	$ 75	$50	
Popcorn machine	$ 75	$50	
Snocone maker	$ 75	$50	
Tables—60" round	$ 12		$ 15
Tables—6' long	$ 7		$ 10
Chairs, folding	$ 1/chair		$1.50
Tent—10 x 10 Canopy (10 people)	$125		$ 150
Tent—16' x 16' frame tent (26 people)	$175		$ 200
Tent—20' x 20' frame tent (40 people)	$225		$ 250
Tent—20' x 30' frame tent (60 people)	$275		$ 300
Tent—20' x 40' frame tent (80 people)	$325		$ 350
Linens, skirting, chair covers, and other decorations	Varies	Varies	Varies
Sound system	$100	$75	
Tent sidewalls	$ 30		$ 30
Tent heater	$150		$ 150
Dance floor (4' x 4' section)	$ 25		$ 25

Delivery Charges

Nominal deliver charges will be applied to any delivery made beyond the city of Idaho Falls to cover fuel costs as well as wear and tear on the delivery vehicle. The charge for other cities is as follows:

- Ammon, $20 delivery charge

- Lincoln, $20 delivery charge

- Iona, $20 delivery charge

- Ucon, $20 delivery charge

- Shelley, $20 delivery charge

- Rigby, $20 delivery charge

- Basalt, $20 delivery charge

- Lewisville, $20 delivery charge

- Blackfoot, $35 delivery charge

- Rexburg, $35 delivery charge

Revenue

Based on conservative numbers, the revenue potential for games and inflatables is shown below. This chart assumes each game or inflatable is rented two times per week at $100.00 per rental.

Revenue

Revenue for games/inflatables rented 2 times per week at $100.00 per rental.

Total game/inflatable	Week	Month	Year
1 game/inflatable	$ 200.00	$ 800.00	$ 9,600.00
2 games/inflatables	$ 400.00	$ 1,600.00	$ 19,200.00
3 games/inflatables	$ 600.00	$ 2,400.00	$ 28,800.00
5 games/inflatables	$ 1,000.00	$ 4,000.00	$ 48,000.00
10 games/inflatables	$ 2,000.00	$ 8,000.00	$ 96,000.00
25 games/inflatables	$ 5,000.00	$20,000.00	$240,000.00
50 games/inflatables	$10,000.00	$40,000.00	$480,000.00

SWOT ANALYSIS

Strengths

- Unique, trendy inflatables and games

- New models of old standbys (i.e. bouncers)

- Limited overhead

- Healthy market with a large percentage of people under the age of 18

- Competitive pricing

- Established business with quality reputation

Weaknesses

- Seasonality of the business

- Pricing against lowballers

Opportunities

- Recent acquisition of new games/inflatables

- New website including photos of each game/inflatable

- Expanded service hours since expansion to full-time

Threats

- Downturn in the economy will result in less disposable income

- Safety and liability concerns

Judicial Interpreter Business

Marquez & Peterson Inc.

23419 Green St.
Chicago, IL 60612

Paul Greenland

Marquez & Peterson Inc. provides interpretation services in judicial and legal settings to both the hearing impaired and Hispanic individuals with limited English proficiency.

EXECUTIVE SUMMARY

Marquez & Peterson Inc. is a judicial interpretation business established by paralegals Julia Marquez and Stacy Peterson. The owners have combined their legal knowledge with additional training and personal experience to offer a service that is in demand and has excellent growth prospects. Judicial interpreters provide services in a variety of legal settings, including federal, state, municipal, and juvenile courts; law enforcement facilities; and attorneys' offices. Marquez & Peterson is qualified to provide services in all of these settings, but will specialize in serving the federal court system.

Marquez & Peterson provides impartial and ethical interpretation services to both the hearing impaired and Hispanic individuals with limited English proficiency, playing an important role in the judicial process. In the case of individuals with limited English proficiency, the Civil Rights Act often requires the provision of interpretation services in state and federal courts. Marquez & Peterson is located in the city of Chicago, which not only has a large population overall, but one of the highest concentrations of Hispanic people in the United States. The city also is home to a sizable hearing-impaired population.

INDUSTRY ANALYSIS

According to the U.S. Bureau of Labor Statistics' *Occupational Outlook Handbook,* approximately 61,000 interpreters and translators were employed in 2014. This figure includes many different types of interpreters, the majority of whom worked in the professional, scientific, and technical services category (29%). Another 26 percent worked in educational services, followed by healthcare and social assistance (16%), and government (7%). One of every five interpreters and translators was self-employed. Through the year 2024, an additional 17,500 positions were expected to open in the field, fueled by an above-average growth rate of 29 percent. Interpreters with specialized knowledge and certifications, like Julia Marquez and Stacy Peterson, were expected to have the best prospects.

Translators may join a number of industry associations, including the American Translators Association, which offers certification in 27 different language combinations. Certification for hearing-impaired translators is available through a joint program offered by the National Association of the Deaf and the Registry of Interpreters for the Deaf. Specialized interpreters like Marquez and Peterson also benefit from membership in organizations such as the National Association of Judiciary Interpreters and Translators.

MARKET ANALYSIS

Marquez & Peterson is located in Chicago, Illinois, and will specialize in providing interpretation services in the federal courts, and to attorneys working on federal court cases. Beyond Chicago proper, the business will provide services throughout the region of northern Illinois.

In 2015 Chicago had a population of nearly 9.8 million people. At 21.4 percent (compared to 17.3 percent nationally), the local Hispanic population is among the largest in the United States. According to demographic information from the Bureau of the Census' American Community Survey, compiled by the Gallaudet Research Institute, in Illinois there were approximately 126,710 individuals between the ages of 18 and 64 with a hearing disability in 2012. Although this figure represented less than two percent of the overall population, it is logical to assume that a larger than average number of hearing-impaired individuals will be located in the Chicago area, due to the size of the population.

Chicago has a thriving legal community, employing more than 66,000 people at nearly 100 law firms. Statewide, more than 91,000 lawyers practice in Illinois, providing judicial interpreters with ample opportunity beyond judicial and law enforcement-related settings.

The principal court locations where Marquez & Peterson will provide services are:

U.S. District Court

Federal Courthouse

219 S. Dearborn St.

Chicago, IL 60604

Stanley J. Roszkowski

United States Courthouse

327 South Church Street

Rockford, IL 61101

In addition to these two locations, bankruptcy cases also are held in several other locations throughout northern Illinois, including:

Joliet City Hall

150 West Jefferson Street

Joliet, IL 60432

North Branch Court

1792 Nicole Lane

Round Lake Beach, IL 60073

Kane County Courthouse

100 South Third Street

Geneva, IL 60134

Although Julia Marquez and Stacy Peterson will specialize in federal cases, the owners also will provide interpretation services in county and state courts, which have dedicated offices for interpretation services. In Chicago, for example, the Circuit Court of Cook County provides interpreters through the Office of Interpreter Services.

SERVICES

Overview

Marquez & Peterson provides impartial and ethical interpretation services to both the hearing impaired and Hispanic individuals with limited English proficiency, playing an important role in the judicial process. Because the owners have significant experience (as paralegals) working on federal court cases, Marquez & Peterson will specialize in providing interpretation services in the federal courts. Several different types of cases are heard in federal courts, including appeals, bankruptcy, civil, and criminal cases.

According to the Administrative Office of the U.S. Courts, the U.S. Courts have jurisdiction over "cases that raise a 'federal question' involving the United States Government, the U.S. Constitution, or other federal laws; and cases involving 'diversity of citizenship,' which are disputes between two parties not from the same state or country, and where the claim meets a set dollar threshold for damages."

The federal courts recognize three categories of interpreters (language-skilled, professionally-qualified, and certified). Marquez & Peterson's owners have both successfully passed the Federal Court Interpreter Certification Examination, qualifying them for listing in the National Court Interpreter Database, which is used by the federal court system to find interpreters.

Rates

In 2016 the federal courts compensated both professionally-qualified and certified interpreters at the following rates:

Half-day: $226

Full-day: $418

Overtime: $59 per-hour

Additionally, Marquez & Peterson will provide interpretation services to attorneys. Although rates are negotiable, the owners will attempt to build their services at an hourly rate of $65.

Specialization

As interpreters, Marquez & Peterson will:

1. Provide Spanish to English interpretation.

2. Provide English to Spanish interpretation.

3. Provide interpretation between American Sign Language and spoken language.

4. Perform "sight translations, " which involves reading English and Spanish documents aloud in the opposite language.

The owners will provide interpretation services either simultaneously or consecutively, depending on the needs of their clients. Because simultaneous interpretation requires significant mental energy and concentration, both Marquez and Peterson will be required for that type of interpretation, if the assignment is longer than 30 minutes in duration.

Venues

Marquez & Peterson typically will provide their services in the following settings:

- Courtrooms
- Law Offices
- Juvenile Facilities
- Jails
- Prisons

during the following types of proceedings:

- Trials
- Depositions
- Arraignments
- Hearings

OPERATIONS

Location

To keep overhead low, Marquez & Peterson will operate as a virtual business. Julia Marquez and Stacy Peterson will both maintain dedicated home offices. They have established an inexpensive toll-free number that can be routed to one or both of their mobile phones, allowing them to stay in contact with customers throughout northern Illinois at all times. This telephone service also provides them with an option to translate voicemail messages to text, allowing them to view messages more conveniently and discreetly in courtroom settings.

Business structure

Marques & Peterson is an Illinois S-Corporation, allowing owners to take a portion of their profits in the form of dividends, and a portion as regular income. This business structure provides certain tax and liability benefits to the owners.

PERSONNEL

Both Julia Marquez and Stacy Peterson have the qualities needed for success in the field of interpreting. In addition to having excellent written and verbal and oral communication skills, they have strong concentration abilities. Additionally, they are excellent listeners and have the ability to work objectively with individuals from diverse situations and backgrounds.

Julia Marquez

A Minneapolis native of Hispanic descent, Julia Marquez earned her paralegal associate's degree from Central Technical College in Minnesota. Her training prepared her for working in all areas of the legal system, including law firms and courts. After graduating from a two-year program, Marquez successfully passed the National Certified Legal Assistant/Paralegal Examination (CLA/CP Exam), gaining status as a certified paralegal. After working for Smith & Hewitt, a small law firm in Minnesota, she then went to work for Clark, Stone, & Merrill, a leading law firm in Chicago, gaining invaluable experience with federal court cases. Marquez has successfully passed the Federal Court Interpreter Certification

Examination, qualifying her for listing in the National Court Interpreter Database, which is used by the federal court system to find interpreters.

Stacy Peterson

Chicago native Stacy Peterson earned her paralegal associates degree from Central Illinois Community College, and also has passed the passed the CLA/CP Exam. Although she has worked as a paralegal for several area law firms over the last 15 years, Peterson obtained certification as a sign language interpreter from the National Association of the Deaf and the Registry of Interpreters five years ago. She has known sign language almost her entire life, because her younger brother is hearing-impaired. This personal experience inspired her to gain formal certification, which made her an invaluable employee at Benson & Hamel, the law firm where she was last employed. Like Marquez, Peterson has significant experience in the federal court system, positioning her for success in the new business.

Marquez & Peterson plans to add one additional interpreter to the business during years two and three.

Professional & Advisory Support

Marquez & Peterson has established a business banking account with the Bank of Chicago, including a merchant account for accepting credit card payments. Tax advisement is provided by the accounting firm of Lewis and Zukowski LLC.

GROWTH STRATEGY

Year One: Concentrate on establishing Marquez & Peterson and generating awareness of the business within the legal community. Generate net income of $48,784 on gross revenues of $231,984. Achieve the following business volume:

Year 1

Category	Week	Month	Year
Federal half-day	1.5	18	216
Federal full-day	2	24	288
Overtime (per-hour)	4	48	576
Private (per-hour)	8	32	384

Year Two: Continue building awareness about the business within the Chicago-area legal community. Add an additional interpreter to the business. Increase service volume by 50 percent from year one. Generate net income of $31,526 on gross revenues of $347,976. Achieve the following business volume:

Year 2

Category	Week	Month	Year
Federal half-day	2	27	324
Federal full-day	3	36	432
Overtime (per-hour)	6	72	864
Private (per-hour)	12	48	576

Year Three: Increase service volume by 33 percent from year two. Add an additional interpreter to the business. Evaluate expansion strategy for years four and five and consider adding (1) virtual interpretation services (allowing the business to expand into new geographic markets by conducting interpretation sessions via video) and (2) translation services. Generate net income of $23,268 on gross revenues of $463,968. Achieve the following business volume:

Year 3

Category	Week	Month	Year
Federal half-day	3	36	432
Federal full-day	4	48	576
Overtime (per-hour)	8	96	1,152
Private (per-hour)	16	64	768

MARKETING & SALES

Marquez & Peterson has developed a marketing plan that involves the following primary tactics:

- A unique logo/brand identity.

- Stationery (e.g., business cards, envelopes, letterhead).

- The use of social media channels, including LinkedIn, to network with potential customers and peers within the judicial interpretation field.

- A high-quality, four-color brochure providing brief bios of Julia Marquez and Stacy Peterson, along with a list of interpretation services offered.

- A Web site with complete details about Marquez & Peterson.

- Quarterly direct mailings, consisting of an introductory letter and the aforementioned brochure, to law firms in Chicago and northern Illinois. The owners will obtain a mailing list from a national mailing list broker and hire a local mail house to prepare and send the mailings.

- Writing expert blog entries and articles for local, state, and national newsletters, Web sites and publications serving the judicial, law enforcement, and legal communities, providing valuable exposure for the business.

- Periodic presentations at industry conferences attended by prospects in the judicial, law enforcement, and legal communities.

FINANCIAL ANALYSIS

Marquez & Peterson has prepared a full set of conservative financial projections in partnership with a local accountant, which are available upon request. Following is an overview of projected sales and expenses for the first three years of operations.

	2016	2017	2018
Sales	$231,984	$347,976	$463,968
Expenses			
Advertising & marketing	$ 5,000	$ 5,000	$ 5,000
General/administrative	$ 500	$ 500	$ 500
Legal	$ 2,500	$ 2,500	$ 2,500
Accounting	$ 1,500	$ 1,500	$ 1,500
Office supplies	$ 500	$ 500	$ 500
Computers/peripherals	$ 3,000	$ 1,500	$ 1,500
Software	$ 700	$ 700	$ 700
Business insurance	$ 3,000	$ 3,500	$ 4,000
Payroll	$140,000	$255,000	$360,000
Payroll taxes	$ 21,000	$ 38,250	$ 54,000
Postage	$ 500	$ 500	$ 500
Telecommunications	$ 1,500	$ 2,000	$ 2,500
Continuing education	$ 3,500	$ 5,000	$ 7,500
Total expenses	$183,200	$316,450	$440,700
Net income	$ 48,784	$ 31,526	$ 23,268

In addition, the owners have prepared the following annual volume projections for the first three years of operations:

Year one

Category	Rate	Week	Month	Year
Federal half-day	$226	$ 339	$ 4,068	$ 48,816
Federal full-day	$418	$ 836	$10,032	$120,384
Overtime (per-hour)	$ 59	$ 236	$ 2,832	$ 33,984
Private (per-hour)	$ 75	$ 600	$ 2,400	$ 28,800
		$2,011	$19,332	$231,984

Year two

Category	Rate	Week	Month	Year
Federal half-day	$226	$ 452	$ 6,102	$ 73,224
Federal full-day	$418	$1,254	$15,048	$180,576
Overtime (per-hour)	$ 59	$ 354	$ 4,248	$ 50,976
Private (per-hour)	$ 75	$ 900	$ 3,600	$ 43,200
		$2,960	$28,998	$347,976

Year three

Category	Rate	Week	Month	Year
Federal half-day	$226	$ 678	$ 8,136	$ 97,632
Federal full-day	$418	$1,672	$20,064	$240,768
Overtime (per-hour)	$ 59	$ 472	$ 5,664	$ 67,968
Private (per-hour)	$ 75	$1,200	$ 4,800	$ 57,600
		$4,022	$38,664	$463,968

Mobile Day Spa

Heaven on Wheels Mobile Day Spa, Inc.

2554 Vernon Street
Roseville, CA 95678

Claire Moore

Heaven on Wheels (HoW) is a mobile day spa operating in Roseville, CA. offering a variety of facials, hand and foot treatments, body wraps, waxing and custom makeup.

EXECUTIVE SUMMARY

Heaven on Wheels (HoW) is a mobile day spa operating in Roseville, CA. It is owned and operated by MaryAnn Powell. We cater to primarily to mothers and working women who find it a challenge to make time to go to the spa. We are also actively developing relationships with local corporations that will utilize our services as part of their employee incentive and wellness programs.

We offer a variety of facials, hand and foot treatments, body wraps, waxing and custom makeup. The products we use contain safe ingredients that are gentle on the skin and revitalizing to the spirit. We do not currently offer full body massages, hair services, manicures or pedicures.

This business plan has been developed to aid in planning for business development and the possible expansion of services provided in the future. While we are not currently seeking funding this plan can serve as preliminary research for the use of funds for expansion.

Objectives

Our objectives for the first three years of operation include:

- Achieve average gross sales of $5,500 per month by the end of the first full year

- Increase gross sales by at least 10 percent each year during the first five years

- Cultivate clientele from corporate accounts that employ our services as part of their employee incentive and wellness programs

- Establish a reputation as the premiere mobile day spa in Placer County

- Secure a studio location in a commercial building

- Add estheticians to our staff who are skilled in hair styling, nails and massage

Mission

Our mission is to achieve profit and growth by providing excellent spa services to our clients in the comfort of their home or workplace. We will use the highest quality products, the latest techniques and employ only licensed estheticians in order to ensure our clients the best possible service.

Keys to Success

- We employ only licensed and experienced estheticians who have met the standards of the California Board of Cosmetology.

- Customers can create their own spa experience by choosing from our menu of services.

- We use the latest skin care techniques and engage in continuous improvement.

- Owner's contact list of past clients who are favorably disposed to do business with her.

COMPANY SUMMARY

HoW is a mobile day spa offering a wide variety of skin care services to mothers, businesses and working women in Placer County California. We operate primarily in the city of Roseville but we travel to our clients' home or work site for an additional travel fee.

According to City–Data.com, Roseville has a population of 127,035 that is 100 percent urban. It is one of the fastest growing cities in the county with a growth rate of 59 percent since the year 2000. The population is 52 percent female and the median resident age is 37.4 years. Median household income in 2013 (the most recent compiled figures) is $75,153. We are confident that by basing our operations in Roseville that we are well positioned to build a strong foundation upon which to expand into other cities in Placer County.

Our office is located in the home of MaryAnn Powell in Roseville, CA. The office houses our supplies, files, computer equipment and our company van which is rented. Services are provided to our clients at their home or office location. We use our fully stocked van to transport all needed supplies and equipment to our service locations.

Company Ownership

HoW is a California corporation wholly owned by MaryAnn Powell. Ms. Powell is the Chief Esthetician and provides all services to clients. She is licensed through the California Board of Barbering and Cosmetology having completed the required 600 school hours of training and passing the state board written and practical exams administered by the National–Interstate Council of State Boards of Cosmetology (NIC).

Her training covered the following skills:

- Skin analysis and treatments

- Hair removal and chemical skin treatments

- Makeup application

- Skin disorders and conditions

- Reflexology

- Aromatherapy and body treatments

- Human physiology and anatomy

- Safety and sanitation techniques

Ms. Powell is a member of the Professional Beauty Association (PBA) and the Aesthetics International Association (AIA) and as such has access to continuing education and resources to help her operate and grow her business.

MaryAnn came to the esthetician field after successful careers as travel agent and event planner. The organization and communications skills developed in these careers will prove invaluable in developing a loyal customer base and steady referrals. Moreover, Ms. Powell has many business contacts in the greater Sacramento area and Placer County. She has contacted this client list and has several appointments scheduled for the year 2016.

In November 2015 Ms. Powell concluded negotiations on the sale of her event planning business. Part of the contract included the stipulation that she stay on for a year in the capacity of assistant manager. She will attend to the event business two days a week in the office and will be available for scheduled meetings as required. She received a down payment for the business in November 2015 and under the terms of the sale will continue to receive payments of principal and interest on the contract sales price until November 2020. MaryAnn is using the funds from the sale of her event planning business as well as savings to start and grow the mobile day spa. In year two she will take over the lease at a studio location and sublease studio space to other practitioners.

Start–up Summary

The following tables summarize the startup costs that have been incurred. These costs have been funded entirely through owner investment.

List of equipment needed for startup

Item	Estimated cost
Computer/printer/copier/scanner/fax	$1,500
Storage/filing/shelving	$ 300
Adding machine	$ 50
Paper shredder	$ 50
Desk/table/chair/lamp	$ 350
Misc. supplies	$ 350
Portable Diamond Microdermabrasion multifunction Facial Machine	$1,000
Prostool	$ 150
Reclining reflexology chair/carrying bag	$ 230
Portable massage chair/carry case	$ 225
Paraffin warmer	$ 160
Makeup carrying case	$ 175
Makeup supplies	$ 150
Waxing supplies	$ 100
Facial supplies	$ 250
Misc supplies	$ 300
Total	**$5,340**

The Portable Multifunction Facial Machine does the following:

- Spray diffuser

- Vacuum extractor

- Exfoliating rotary brush

- High frequency

- Galvanic current

- Diamond Microdermabrasion

- Ultrasonic sound wave massage (sonphoresis)

Start-up expenses

Licenses	$ 200
Van rent deposit	$3,000
Advertising	$ 250
Web site development	$ 750
Legal fees incorporation	$1,500
Magnetic vam signs	$ 200
Insurance	$ 300
Cards & brochures	$ 200
Accountant	$ 300
Total start-up expenses	**$6,700**

Startup funding

Cash required	$ 5,500
Startup assets to fund	$ 5,340
Startup expenses to fund	$ 6,700
Total funding required	**$17,540**

The startup funding of $17,540 is being provided by MaryAnn Powell from her own funds. Ms. Powell also has access to a business line of credit.

SERVICES

HoW will offer a variety of facial treatments, hand and foot treatments, body wraps, waxing and custom makeup. The products we use contain safe ingredients that are gentle on the skin and revitalizing to the spirit. We do not currently offer full body massages, hair services, manicures or pedicures.

Services

European facial	$75
Acne facial	$90
Anti-aging facial	$90
Diamond micro-dermabrasion	$90
Mini facials for group events	$80 per hour
Hand/foot treatments	$40–$70
Aloe body wrap with facial	$130–$230
Clay and aloe body wrap	$139–$239
Waxing	Call for quote
Makeup	Call for quote
Men's facial	$50
Teen facial	$55

Service add-ons

Vitamin C treatment	$30
Clay masque treatment	$12
Eye treatment with replenishing eye crème	$12
Hydration masque	$12
Essential oils	$ 5
Reflexology foot treatment	$15

Spa packages

Quick refresh	Mini facial and hand treatment	$55–$100
Men's refresh	Men's facial and hand treatment	$55–$100
Couples indulgence	Cleanse, tone, exfoliate, face/neck massage, cooling masque, aromatherapy and essential oils	$240 for 60 minutes, $290 for 90 minutes

MARKET ANALYSIS

According to the International Spa Association (ISPA) U.S. Spa Industry Study "Big 5" statistics revealed positive trends in 2015 that are expected to continue to stimulate the economy and generate revenue in the U.S. in months ahead. The total number of spa visits climbed to an all–time high in 2014, reaching 176 million (6.7 percent increase on the previous year). Combined with a 5.3 percent increase in total revenue per visit, total revenues generated by spas in 2014 rose to $15.5 billion, an increase of over five percent on the 2013 level. Nearly 360,000 individuals are employed by the spa industry nationwide, close to a two percent rise from the previous year. The global skin care industry alone is estimated to reach $121 billion in 2016 and by 2018 the U.S. market will reach almost $11 billion.

In its study the ISPA also listed the top ten trends projected for 2016 which included:

• An increase in workplace wellness programs

• Subscription membership services to encourage clients to schedule services as a regular part of their lives

• Further emphasis on the use of "natural" products

While Sacramento and Placer counties are home to dozens of day spas, the area has only a handful of mobile day spas. These appear to be operations run by a sole practitioner who wears all the hats and so is limited in the ability to scale operations to a more expanded level. We intend to scale our business reach by adding mobile staff each year. We will also acquire a studio location in a commercial building by taking over the lease on a salon during our second year.

Each new staff member will add to our ability to not only reach more clients but to add more services such as body massage, nail and hair services. We are currently targeting potential clients within 30 miles of Roseville, CA. Our primary demographic is women ages 30 to 50 with income in excess of $45,000. Our research has shown that the population of Roseville is 52 percent female and the median resident age is 37.4 years. Median household income in 2013 (the most recent compiled figures) is $75,153. Research has also revealed that stay–at–home mothers desire to schedule services between the hours of 9 a.m. and 2 p.m., the hours when children are in school. Working women prefer to schedule services in the early evening and on weekends.

MARKETING PLAN

In marketing to our target market we will stress the following:

• skin health: steaming, cleansing, exfoliation and massage aid in refining your complexion.

• anti–aging: regular facials promote cell turnover and boost collagen production.

• stress management: massage of face, neck and décolletage promotes lymphatic drainage, rids the body of toxins and reduces fluid retention. Massage of hands and feet using reflexology techniques also promotes relaxation and well–being.

- expert advice: skin analysis and advice on matching the proper products to skin type.

- flexibility and convenience in scheduling for services.

We will encourage new customers with the use of coupons, gift certificates, Groupon discounts and local advertising. Skin care benefits are enhanced by regular treatments rather than a one–time visit. Follow–up strategy with customers will include sending information through mail and email about the benefits of regular treatment. We will keep them informed about sales and specials thus encouraging them to purchase a subscription package at discount.

Savings specials

Save 5%	Purchase 3 facials
Save 12%	Purchase 6 facials
Save 15%	Purchase 12 facials

Our marketing strategy will include the following channels:

- Local advertising: newspapers, fliers, mailers to customers.

- Social media: Facebook page with regular postings containing beauty tips and promotions

- Networking: forming and maintaining connections with other business owners for purposes of cross–promotion; includes: wedding planners, event planners, human resource managers, hotel concierges, women's groups.

- Web site & blog: We have engaged a web design company that is working with us to create our web site. By using the Word Press design tools we will be able to modify and update our site at any time. The site design includes a blog, contact form, and links to our social media sites. Our design professionals will also work with us on maintaining our social media marketing campaigns.

MILESTONES

Milestone	Start	End
Business plan	October 2015	December 2015
Web design	November 2015	February 2016
Brochures & cards	January 2016	January 2016
Logo design	December 2015	December 2015
Studio lease	July 2017	July 2017
Additional esthetician	August 2017	August 2017

PERSONNEL PLAN

We intend to take on an additional esthetician in the fall of year two. This time frame coincides with our move into a studio location in a commercial building. MaryAnn will be available full–time having completed her obligation to the buyer of her event planning business. She will split her time between the studio and mobile customers.

In year three because MaryAnn will be spending more time in the studio, sublease income will decrease.

	Year 1	Year 2	Year 3
Owner	$19,600	$24,000	$24,000
Estheticians		$ 3,700	$10,700
Total people	1	2	2
Total payroll	**$19,600**	**$27,700**	**$34,700**

FINANCIAL ANALYSIS

Financial Plan

Our financial projections include the following.

Projected Profit and Loss

Pro forma profit and loss

	Year 1	Year 2	Year 3
Sales			
Services	$56,000	$62,000	$82,000
Studio sublease		$ 6,000	$10,500
Total gross sales	**$56,000**	**$68,000**	**$92,500**
Direct costs			
Material, supplies	$ 4,480	$ 4,960	$ 6,560
Commissions	$19,600	$21,700	$28,700
Gross profit	$31,920	$41,340	$57,240
Expenses			
Payroll		$ 6,000	$ 6,000
Depreciation	$ 280	$ 280	$ 280
Phone/Internet	$ 1,600	$ 1,600	$ 1,600
Insurance: liability, property, auto	$ 3,000	$ 3,000	$ 3,000
Payroll taxes	$ 2,940	$ 4,155	$ 5,205
Professional dues/memberships	$ 500	$ 500	$ 500
Advertising: print	$ 1,500	$ 1,800	$ 2,200
Advertising: web site and internet marketing	$ 200	$ 375	$ 850
Office supplies	$ 420	$ 420	$ 420
Auto: gas & maintenance	$ 3,000	$ 3,800	$ 5,500
Web site maintenance/social media	$ 840	$ 840	$ 840
Software: quickbooks online	$ 480	$ 480	$ 480
Quickbooks mobile payments	$ 360	$ 360	$ 360
Van rental	$ 3,600	$ 3,600	$ 3,600
Repairs & maintenance	$ 750	$ 1,200	$ 1,500
Accounting & legal	$ 1,800	$ 1,800	$ 2,000
Studio rent		$ 6,000	$12,000
Other expenses	$ 1,200	$ 1,200	$ 1,500
Total operating expenses	**$22,470**	**$31,410**	**$41,835**
Profit before interest and taxes	$ 9,450	$ 9,930	$15,405
Taxes incurred	$ 1,418	$ 1,490	$ 2,311
Net profit	**$ 8,033**	**$ 8,441**	**$13,094**
Net profit/sales	**14%**	**14%**	**16%**
Break-even revenue	$38,930	$54,614	$72,904
Monthly break-even revenue	$ 3,244	$ 4,551	$ 6,075
Estimated monthly fixed cost	$ 1,479	$ 1,946	$ 2,597

Projected Balance Sheet

Pro forma balance sheet

Assets	Year 1	Year 2	Year 3
Cash in bank	$1,299	$10,133	$23,357
Accounts receivable			
Inventory	$ 514	$ 400	$ 550
Other current assets			
Total current assets	**$1,813**	**$10,533**	**$23,907**
Fixed assets			
Office furniture & equipment	$2,800	$ 2,800	$ 2,800
Less: depreciation	($ 280)	($ 560)	($ 840)
Total assets	**$4,333**	**$12,773**	**$25,867**
Liabilities			
Current liabilities			
Accounts payable			
Current maturities loan			
Total current liabilities	**$ —**	**$ —**	**$ —**
Long term liabilities loan	0	0	0
Total liabilities	**$ —**	**$ —**	**$ —**
Paid-in capital	$3,000	$ 3,000	$ 3,000
Retained earnings	($6,700)	$ 1,333	$ 9,773
Earnings	$8,033	$ 8,441	$13,094
Total capital	**$4,333**	**$12,773**	**$25,867**
Total liabilities & capital	**$4,333**	**$12,773**	**$25,867**

Outdoor Furniture Business

Noble's Custom Creations Inc.

3477 Central Circle Dr.
Sedona Hills, CA 90446

Paul Greenland

Noble's Custom Creations Inc. makes high-quality, handcrafted outdoor furniture.

EXECUTIVE SUMMARY

Ed Noble is a high school history teacher who has plans to retire in two years. A long-time woodworker, he has received strong word-of-mouth recognition over the past five years for his ability to make handcrafted outdoor furniture. After making beautiful cedar tables, planters, and chairs for his own patio, he soon began receiving requests from family and friends to make similar items. Ultimately, his efforts evolved into a successful hobby and he began making items for sale. This success has prompted Noble to establish Noble's Custom Creations Inc., a part-time outdoor furniture business that will allow him to generate extra income. Following retirement, Noble plans to expand the business to a near-full-time operation.

MARKET ANALYSIS

Noble's Custom Creations is located in the central California town of Sedona Hills, which offers clear skies and pleasant year-round temperatures. Sedona Hills is the perfect location for an outdoor furniture business, because people enjoy their patios and outdoor spaces every month of the year. In addition to a relatively affluent local population, the town draws tourists and visitors from the surrounding region and other states because of its scenic surroundings, antique stores, gift shops, art galleries, and bed-and-breakfasts.

The local economy has been growing during the middle of the decade. According to a recent survey conducted by the Sedona Hills Visitors Association, retail sales increased 2.5 percent in 2013, 2.7 percent in 2014, and are projected to grow nearly 3.1 percent in 2015. According to economic data from Leslie County, there are 5,351 households in Sedona Hills with an average household income of $135,431. Within a 15-mile radius there are 21,443 households with an average household income of $129,399.

Finally, data from Statistica show that retail sales in the U.S. miscellaneous outdoor furniture market have been growing steadily, rising from $229 million in 2011 to $242 million in 2012 and $246 million in 2013.

PRODUCTS

Noble's Custom Creations will offer the following outdoor furniture items in both treated lumber and Cedar:

- Garden Bench (no back): $150/$400

- Classic Bench: $200/$500

- Classic Planter: $65/$150

- Bench/Planter Combo (two square planters connected by a backless sitting bench) $175/$450

- Octagon Picnic Table (seats 8): $650/$1,450

- Trestle-Style Picnic Table & Two Benches (seats 8): $650/$1,450

- Adirondack Chair: $185/$350

- Double Lounger (two chairs connected by a center console with an umbrella hole): $350/$750

Pre-made items are sold unfinished. A variety of finishes (e.g., stains, oils, paints, lacquers, etc.) are available are available for custom orders (additional 15% charge).

OPERATIONS

Manufacturing Process

Most of the items sold by Noble's Custom Creations will be pre-made. In order to be successful, Ed has developed a process whereby he will produce all of the various parts needed for his furniture selections in sizable quantities. To do this efficiently, he has identified equipment settings and obtained or produced a variety of jigs that will allow him to expedite the process of cutting and drilling large number of the same pieces. Noble's Custom Creations' pre-made products will be assembled and sanded, but unfinished.

Noble's Custom Creations also will accept custom orders. When the business receives a custom order, Ed Noble will contact the customer and provide them with a written summary of their requirements, which will be signed by both parties. Ed will require a deposit of 50 percent, with the balance due upon delivery. His production process will include:

1. **Material Selection:** This involves choosing the specific type of wood (e.g., treated lumber or Cedar) that will be used.

2. **Production:** Utilizing various hand and power tools, Ed Noble will manufacture the desired item according to the customer's specifications.

3. **Finishing:** If requested by the customer, Ed Noble will apply the appropriate finish (e.g., paint, stain, oil, varnish, etc.).

4. **Assembly & Delivery:** Finally, the furniture item will be assembled and delivered to the customer.

Equipment

Ed Noble is fortunate to begin his business with all of the tools and equipment that he will need for production. His inventory of tools includes the following items:

- Air Compressor

- Band Saw

- Bench Grinder

- Biscuit Joiner

- Block Plane
- Caliper
- Chisel Assortment
- Circular Saw
- Clamps Assortment
- Claw Hammer
- Compound Miter Saw
- Drill Press
- Feather Board
- Hand Saw
- Jigs
- Jointer
- Layout Square
- Level
- Metal Detector
- Miter Gauge
- Moisture Meter
- Nail Gun
- Nail Set
- Orbital Sander
- Palm Sander
- Power Drill
- Router
- Router Table
- Sabre Saw
- Safety Equipment
- Saw Horse
- Screwdriver
- Shop Vac
- Sliding Bevel
- Surface Planer
- Table Saw
- Tape Measure
- Tool Storage System
- Utility Knife
- Workbench

Realizing that commercial production levels will increase wear and tear on his equipment, Ed will budget funds to purchase new tools and equipment as needed.

Supplies

- Finishes
- Glue
- Sandpaper
- Dust Masks
- Nails
- Screws
- Tack Cloth

Location and Facilities

Noble's Custom Creations will operate as a home-based business. Ed Noble already has a dedicated workshop, which is located in an out building on his property. His workshop is equipped with dust collection and air filtration systems, as well as an area for lumber storage and staging. The building includes two garage doors, providing convenient access to load/unload lumber and furniture items. Additionally, the building includes a partitioned area with adequate ventilation, where various finishes can be safely applied when needed. Ed Noble will perform administrative tasks related to the business from dedicated home office space within his house, which includes a desk, filing cabinet, personal computer, multifunction device (e.g., copier/printer/fax), telephone, and Internet access.

Major Suppliers

Noble's Custom Creations will use a variety of suppliers for lumber and hardware, including both "big box stress" and the following regional companies:

- Johnston Hardware Co.
- Renfro Lumber Company Inc.
- Western Lumber & Supply Co.

OWNER PROFILE

Ed Noble is a high school history teacher who has plans to retire in two years. A long-time woodworker, he has received strong word-of-mouth recognition over the past five years for his ability to make handcrafted outdoor furniture. After making beautiful cedar tables, planters, and chairs for his own patio, he soon began receiving requests from family and friends to make similar items. Ultimately, his efforts evolved into a successful hobby and he began making items for sale. This success has prompted Noble to establish Noble's Custom Creations.

Ed earned his undergraduate and graduate education degrees from Colorado College in 1975 and 1978, respectively. He has been an avid woodworker since his teenage years. In addition to teaching history, Ed also has taught several woodworking courses for the industrial arts program at Sedona Hills High School.

Noble has attended several seminars hosted by the nonprofit association, SCORE, which utilizes education and mentorship to help small businesses get started successfully. SCORE is supported by the U.S. Small Business Administration. Ed also has taken an introductory small business management class at Sedona Hills Community College.

Professional & Advisory Support

A business checking account for Noble's Custom Creation has been established at Sedona Hills Community Bank, including a merchant account for accepting credit card payments. Ed Noble will handle bookkeeping and tax preparation on his own, using leading off-the-shelf software programs.

BUSINESS STRATEGY

The following table shows anticipated monthly production for the first 12 months of 2016:

	January	February	March	April	May	June
Classic bench	4	4	4	4	4	6
Garden bench	2	2	2	2	2	4
Classic planter	6	6	6	6	6	18
Bench/planter combo	2	2	2	2	2	6
Octagon picnic table	0	0	0	0	0	1
Trestle-style picnic table & benches	0	0	0	0	0	1
Adirondack chairs	4	4	4	4	4	6
Double lounger	0	0	0	0	0	1

	July	August	September	October	November	December
Classic bench	10	6	4	6	6	5
Garden bench	8	6	2	4	4	3
Classic planter	22	16	6	18	10	8
Bench/planter combo	12	10	2	6	5	4
Octagon picnic table	2	2	0	1	1	0
Trestle-style picnic table & benches	3	2	0	1	1	0
Adirondack chairs	10	8	4	6	5	4
Double lounger	3	2	0	2	1	0

Ed Noble has established the following growth targets for the first three years of Noble's Custom Creations' operations:

Year One: Achieve gross sales of $60,150, and net sales of $42,105.

Year Two: Achieve gross sales of $66,165, and net sales of $46,315.

Year Three: Achieve gross sales of $82,706 and net sales of $57,894.

MARKETING & SALES

Prior to establishing Noble's Custom Creations, Ed Noble relied only on word-of-mouth to let others know about his abilities to make high-quality outdoor furniture. This resulted in sufficient demand, based on his availability. However, Ed realizes that he will need to take additional steps to generate awareness about his business as he prepares to increase capacity.

In addition to word-of-mouth, Ed has reached out to several reputable landscaping contractors and greenhouses (that do not already sell outdoor furniture). In exchange for making literature about Noble's Custom Creations available and, when possible, allowing him to display his work, Ed has agreed to give them 10 percent of the sale price on any item that is made by referral.

Ed's daughter, Maria, is an accomplished Web developer who has agreed to develop a Web site for Noble's Custom Creations. The site will feature a photograph of each item that Ed offers for sale. Customers will have the ability to view the item of their choice in unfinished cedar or treated wood. In addition, they will have the ability to select from a variety of "virtual" stains and finishes, in order to help visualize what the finished product might look like. Finally, the site will allow customers to place and customize their order.

The semi-annual Sedona Hills Lawn & Garden Expo is a prime opportunity for Noble's Custom Creations to showcase its offerings to prospective buyers, who attend the annual event to review product and service offerings from a variety of vendors, including landscape architects, landscapers, pool & patio companies, and more.

With the help of a local graphic designer, Ed has developed a large, glossy, four-color brochure that showcases each of the different items made by Noble's Custom Creations. Ed will utilize the services of a digital printer, so that he does not need to produce large quantities of his brochure. This way, it also will be easy to make changes as needed.

Finally, Ed will showcase examples of the furniture he makes by displaying items on the corner of his property, which is located at an intersection that receives a steady flow of traffic. This has been a main source of new business in the past.

FINANCIAL ANALYSIS

Sales and expenses for Noble's Custom Creations are projected as follows:

	2016	2017	2018
Gross product sales	$60,150	$66,165	$82,706
Cost of goods sold	$18,045	$19,850	$24,812
Net sales	**$42,105**	**$46,315**	**$57,894**
Expenses			
Salary	$28,500	$29,500	$35,500
Equipment	$ 1,000	$ 1,250	$ 1,500
Marketing	$ 3,500	$ 4,500	$ 5,500
Licenses & fees	$ 1,250	$ 1,250	$ 1,250
Business insurance	$ 1,000	$ 1,000	$ 1,000
Telecommunications	$ 900	$ 900	$ 900
Office supplies	$ 300	$ 400	$ 500
Payroll taxes	$ 5,250	$ 7,500	$ 9,000
Total expenses	**$41,700**	**$46,300**	**$55,150**
Net profit	**$ 405**	**$ 15**	**$ 2,744**

	January	February	March	April	May	June
Classic bench	$ 600	$ 600	$ 600	$ 600	$ 600	$ 900
Garden bench	$ 400	$ 400	$ 400	$ 400	$ 400	$ 800
Classic planter	$ 390	$ 390	$ 390	$ 390	$ 390	$1,170
Bench/planter combo	$ 350	$ 350	$ 350	$ 350	$ 350	$1,050
Octagon picnic table	$ 0	$ 0	$ 0	$ 0	$ 0	$ 650
Trestle-style picnic table & benches	$ 0	$ 0	$ 0	$ 0	$ 0	$ 650
Adirondack chairs	$ 740	$ 740	$ 740	$ 740	$ 740	$1,110
Double lounger	$ 0	$ 0	$ 0	$ 0	$ 0	$ 350
	$2,480	**$2,480**	**$2,480**	**$2,480**	**$2,480**	**$6,680**

	July	August	September	October	November	December
Classic bench	$ 1,500	$ 900	$ 600	$ 900	$ 900	$ 750
Garden bench	$ 1,600	$1,200	$ 400	$ 800	$ 800	$ 600
Classic planter	$ 1,430	$1,040	$ 390	$1,170	$ 650	$ 520
Bench/planter combo	$ 2,100	$1,750	$ 350	$1,050	$ 875	$ 700
Octagon picnic table	$ 1,300	$1,300	$ 0	$ 650	$ 650	$ 0
Trestle-style picnic table & benches	$ 1,950	$1,300	$ 0	$ 650	$ 650	$ 0
Adirondack chairs	$ 1,850	$1,480	$ 740	$1,110	$ 925	$ 740
Double lounger	$ 1,050	$ 700	$ 0	$ 700	$ 350	$ 0
	$12,780	**$9,670**	**$2,480**	**$7,030**	**$5,800**	**$3,310**

A complete set of pro forma financial statements has been prepared and is available upon request.

SWOT ANALYSIS

Strengths: Noble's Custom Creations will differentiate itself by offering outdoor furniture that is of higher quality than selections offered in "big-box" stores. In addition, the business is located in one of the nation's most temperate climates, assuring a steady stream of orders year-round.

Weaknesses: Responsiveness to customer service inquiries may be slow, since Ed Noble will devote the majority of his time to production. In addition, because Ed is the only employee, responding to a large influx of demand (e.g., especially around the holidays) could prove to be difficult, requiring greater efficiency and preparation.

Opportunities: There is steady demand and growth potential in the local and regional markets for quality outdoor furniture, reflecting national trends.

Threats: Woodworking can be a dangerous business. In the event of an injury or illness, Noble's Custom Creations could be in jeopardy, requiring Ed to offer refunds or rely on other local woodworkers for assistance in completing unfulfilled orders in the event that he is unable to work.

Package and Mailing Business

Package Keepers

9235 North Main Street, Ste. 2500
Bainbridge, GA 31719

Fran Fletcher

Package Keepers is a Bainbridge, Georgia based business that will offer customers a variety of products and services to meet their shipping needs.

BUSINESS OVERVIEW

Package Keepers is a Bainbridge, Georgia based business that will offer customers a variety of products and services to meet their shipping needs. The idea for this business was conceived after owner Maggie Jones heard reports of massive package swiping during the holidays. This disturbed Ms. Jones and she wanted to provide Bainbridge residents with a safe place to have their packages delivered.

The majority of homeowners are not at home during delivery hours and have to hope that a thief will not grab their package while they are at work. Package Keepers will be a place where customers can rent boxes and have their packages delivered there to keep them secure. Employees of Package Keepers will also be available to sign for any packages requiring a signature. Additionally, Package Keepers will assist customers in packing boxes for shipment, offer a large selection of shipping supplies, and serve as a pickup location for all major package carriers.

Package Keepers has secured a space to rent that is conveniently located on Main Street. Business hours are Monday through Friday 8:00 a.m. to 6:00 p.m. The business will offer customers 24–hour access to mailboxes using a key card.

According to the Bureau of Labor Statistics, the shipping industry is expected to increase by 16% over the next ten years. This growth is partly due to rising online sales and the need for a secure place to have these products delivered. Current statistics reveal that the city of Bainbridge is home to more than 3,600 households and 89% of its population is employed. That adds up to thousands of packages being left on doorsteps while homeowners are away at work.

Home–based Internet businesses are also on the rise in Bainbridge. Local Chamber of Commerce reports that there are currently 38 home–based Internet businesses in the area. Many of these businesses would benefit from employing the services of a local shipping business.

The target market for Package Keepers will be individuals needing a secure place to have their packages delivered and home–based businesses in the Bainbridge area needing the services offered by the company.

The overall strategy of Package Keepers is to provide individualized services to both its private and business customers. Additionally, it is the goal of Package Keepers to obtain and retain a loyal customer base and to achieve strong financial growth during the first year of operation.

Package Keepers plans to expand and add mailboxes as demand for its services increases. The company also plans to offer package pick–up services in the near future.

The owners are seeking financing in the amount of $34,200 to cover start–up costs. Conservative estimates predict small profits the first and second months, then modest profits for the next four months that should remain steady over the years. If predictions are correct, the owner should earn enough profits to effortlessly pay back the financing within three years.

COMPANY DESCRIPTION

Location

Package Keepers will be conveniently located on Main Street, which is one of the major streets in the city. The owners strategically picked this location for its high visibility and large parking lot.

Hours of Operation

Package and shipping services

Monday–Friday 8 AM — 6 PM

24/7 mailbox access

Personnel

Maggie Jones (owner, office manager)

B.S. Business Management from Florida State University

Ms. Jones has five years of experience working in retail. She will use the skills she learned at the university and the skills she learned working in retail to start and run Package Keepers.

Employee

One part time employee will be hired to assist with daily duties. This job may become full time as profits allow.

Products and Services

Services

- 24/7 accessible mailboxes
- Secure package delivery
- Accept packages requiring signatures
- Pickup location for all major package delivery companies
- Mail/Package assistance
- Notary services
- Oversized package receiving area (for packages that will not fit in X Large mailboxes)

Products

- Boxes of all sizes
- Mailing tubes
- Envelopes
- Bags

- Styrofoam

- Bubble wrap

- Packing paper

- Packing tape

- Mailing labels

MARKET ANALYSIS

Industry Overview

According to the Bureau of Labor Statistics, the shipping industry is expected to increase by 16% over the next ten years. This growth is partly due to rising online sales and the need for a secure place to have these products delivered.

Current census data reveals that the city of Bainbridge is home to more than 3,600 households and 89% of its population is employed. That adds up to thousands of packages being left on doorsteps while homeowners are away at work, just waiting to be stolen, especially around the holidays.

Home–based Internet businesses are also on the rise in Bainbridge. The Chamber of Commerce reports there are currently 38 home–based Internet businesses in the area. Many of these businesses would benefit from utilizing a local shipping service.

Target Market

The target market for Package Keepers will be individuals needing a secure place to have their packages delivered and home–based businesses in the Bainbridge area needing the services offered by the company.

Competition

Mail It, 3577 Old River Road, Bainbridge, GA – offers mailing supplies, carrier pick–up, packaging services

Package Keepers will set itself apart from other similar businesses by offering 24–hour key card access to mailboxes and by offering its services to local home7–based businesses.

GROWTH STRATEGY

The overall strategy of Package Keepers is to provide individualized services to both its private and business customers. Additionally, it is the goal of Package Keepers to obtain and retain a loyal customer base and to achieve strong financial growth during the first year of operation.

Package Keepers plans to expand and add mailboxes as demand for its services increases. The company also plans to offer package pick–up services in the near future.

Sales and Marketing

The owner has identified key tactics to support the business's growth strategy.

Initial advertising/marketing will include:

- Newspaper ads in the Decatur County News.

- Discounted services to employees of area industries, including the county school system and hospital.

- Word of mouth – the owner expects her exceptional customer service to bring in additional customers.

Ongoing advertising/marketing will include:

- Using social media to advertise products, services, and promotions.

- Offering coupons in the Decatur County News.

FINANCIAL ANALYSIS

Start–up Costs

Package Keepers has found a storefront to lease in a highly visible area that is conveniently located in the center of town. The owner will need approximately $34,200 to purchase furniture, equipment, and supplies for the business.

Start-up costs

Mailboxes	$25,000
Business license	$ 200
Initial advertising	$ 2,000
Office furniture	$ 5,000
Shipping supplies	$ 2,000
Total	**$34,200**

Estimated Monthly Expenses

Generally, the cost of monthly expenses is fixed. Monthly rent is $1,000 and includes electricity and water. The owner will sign a three–year lease and rent will not increase during this period. A monthly advertising budget of $100 will be used for ongoing advertising needs.

The owner will initially be paid $15 per hour. The employee will be paid $10 per hour initially. The wages of workers will be re–evaluated at six–month intervals and again after the business loan is repaid.

Monthly expenses

Rent	$1,000
Phone/Internet	$ 100
Advertising	$ 100
Insurance	$ 100
Wages	$3,200
Loan repayment	$ 950
Total	**$5,450**

Estimated Monthly Income

Estimated Income for Package Keepers will be determined by the amount of services provided. The owner plans to start with 50 extra large, 50 large, and 50 small mailboxes. Conservative estimates predict that one half of the mailboxes will be rented out during the first month, three quarters of the mailboxes will be rented out during the second month, and all mailboxes will be rented out during the third month. The owner estimates that customers will require 20 package signatures per week.

Price Schedule

Prices for services

Mailbox (X Large)	$50/month
Mailbox (Large)	$40/month
Mailbox (Small)	$30/month
24-hr mailbox access	$20/month
Signature services	$5
Packaging services	$5
Oversized package services	$5/day
Shipping surcharge	Based on weight
Notary public services	$2/signature

The owner will add $25 to the prices listed above during the months of November and December. This increase does not apply to customers who have rented a mailbox for at least one month prior to the holidays.

Package Keepers will also offer service bundles.

Service bundles

Bundle 1 $150/month	Bundle 2 $250/month
X Large mailbox	X Large mailbox
24-hour keycard	24-hour keycard
Up to 15 signatures	Up to 30 signatures
Up to 50 packaging services	Up to 90 packaging services
50% off notary services	Free notary services

Profit/Loss

The chart titled "Monthly Profit/Loss" demonstrates the business's estimated monthly income. The owner hopes to rent out one half of its mailboxes the first month, three quarters of its mailboxes the second month, and all mailboxes the third month. The business also expects to provide 20 signature services per week and about 20 package services per week. Additionally, the owner plans to notarize 25 s per week. The chart shows monthly profits increasing from $150 in Month 1 to $3,150 in Month 3. The chart estimates that monthly expenses will be fixed at $3,150 for the first six months and that profits will remain steady during this time.

Monthly profit/loss

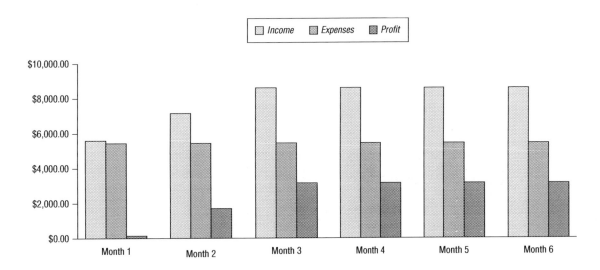

Financing

The owner of Package Keepers wishes to obtain financing in the form of a business loan or line of credit for the amount needed to cover the start–up costs. This loan would be in the amount of $34,200. According to the estimated Expenses vs. Income, Package Keepers will be able to pay back the loan by the end of the third year.

Loan repayment plan

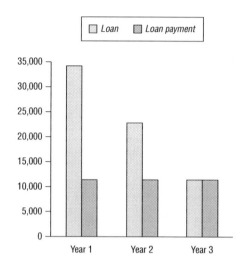

Photo Booth Business

In a Snap

24 Tower Ave., #4
Petersman, CO 81503

Paul Greenland

In a Snap is a photo booth business that uses creative props and themes to differentiate itself in a competitive marketplace.

EXECUTIVE SUMMARY

Business Overview

In a Snap is a photo booth business that uses creative props and themes to differentiate itself in a competitive marketplace. The business is a partnership between Rebecca Newhouse and Jessica Tillman, who are both sophomores at Central College. Newhouse is pursuing a business degree and Tillman is double majoring in theater and education. The owners have entrepreneurial spirits and, instead of pursuing traditional part-time jobs, have decided to establish a photo booth business because it is fun, scalable, and has tremendous earning potential. Although the owners both attend college, they live at home with their parents in Petersman, allowing them to operate In a Snap year-round, and giving them the opportunity to either maintain ownership or sell the business following the conclusion of their time at Central College. Newhouse and Tillman have developed a compelling strategy for growing In a Snap organically over the next three years.

MARKET ANALYSIS

In a Snap will serve both individual consumers and organizations/groups in Petersman. Area organizations include, but are not limited to:

- Large Corporations (6 establishments)

- Mid-sized Companies (145 establishments)

- Childcare Services (21 establishments)

- Colleges & Universities (5 establishments)

- Entertainment & Recreation Services (61 establishments)

- Hospitals (2 establishments)

- Health & Medical Services (127 establishments)

- Membership Organizations (45 establishments)

- Museums & Zoos (4 establishments)

- Primary & Secondary Education (48 establishments)

- Churches & Religious Organizations (37 establishments)

Specifically, In a Snap will target organizations/groups that are looking to enhance the following types of events:

- Award Galas/Ceremonies

- Bar-B-Ques

- Bowling Banquets

- Business Dinners

- Charity Balls

- Concerts

- Conferences

- Conventions & Expos

- Fairs & Festivals

- Fundraisers

- Golf Outings

- Holiday Parties

- Luncheons

- Networking Events

- Political Rallies

- Product Launches

- Receptions

- Sporting Events

- Theme Parties

- Trade Shows

Consumers

The average household income in Petersman was $56,973 in 2015. This figure is expected to grow 8.5 percent by 2020, reaching $61,834. In a Snap will target its consumer marketing initiatives toward households with income of $50,000 or more. In 2015 approximately 19.6 percent of households (the largest market area segment) had income between $50,000 and $74,999. Next were households with income between $75,000 and $99,999 (10.4%), $100,000 and $149,999 (7.4%), and more than $150,000 (4.4%).

When targeting individual consumers, In a Snap will market services for events and occasions such as:

- Anniversary Parties

- Baby Showers

- Baptisms

- Bar/Bat Mitzvahs

- Birthday Parties
- Engagement Parties
- Graduation Parties
- Holiday Celebrations
- Retirement Parties
- Reunions
- Weddings & Rehearsal Dinners

Competition

In a Snap is prepared to face strong competition, because a growing number of entrepreneurs have established photo booth businesses in recent years. However, Newhouse and Tillman will differentiate their business through the availability of unique backdrops and props, drawing on Tillman's specialized tech theater background. The owners believe that this will truly set their business apart from the competition. Because most photo booth providers generate the vast majority of their earnings from weddings, In a Snap will put a special emphasis on marketing to organizations and special events, in a further effort to differentiate itself in the marketplace. Additionally, Newhouse and Tillman know that a successful photo booth business requires staff members who are extremely friendly, outgoing, and fun. In a Snap will make sure to deliver in this regard every time.

INDUSTRY ANALYSIS

Although there is no specific industry data available regarding photo booth providers, information from the Moline, Illinois-based American Rental Association (ARA), which includes representation for businesses that rent items for events, revenues within the North American equipment rental industry were projected to reach $38.5 billion in 2015. Specifically, the party/event/wedding category was expected to total about $2.7 billion, up nearly five percent from the previous year.

Established in 1955, the ARA is "the international nonprofit trade association for equipment rental businesses and manufacturers and suppliers of rental equipment." As of 2015, the organization's members hailed from all 50 states and 30 different countries throughout the world. For companies in the party/event/wedding category, the ARA offers benefits such as liability insurance, as well as resources for education and business lead generation.

PERSONNEL

In a Snap is a partnership between Rebecca Newhouse and Jessica Tillman, who are both sophomores at Central College. The owners have entrepreneurial spirits and, instead of pursuing traditional part-time jobs, have decided to establish their own photo booth business. Although the owners both attend college, they live at home with their parents in Petersman, allowing them to operate In a Snap year-round (evenings and weekends), and giving them the opportunity to either maintain ownership or sell the business following the conclusion of their time at Central College.

Rebecca Newhouse

Newhouse graduated with high honors from Petersman High School, where she was president of the Economics Club and helped to plan many school activities and events as part of the Student Council. She is pursuing a business degree at Central College. Newhouse has learned a great deal about business operations from her father, Jonathan Newhouse, who owns a plumbing supply company. For the past two years she has worked as a part-time employee in the front office of Newhouse Plumbing Supply Co. In addition to operating photo booths at events with Tillman, Newhouse will focus on new business development, marketing, and administrative responsibilities.

Jessica Tillman

Tillman is double majoring in theater and education. She is the creative force behind In a Snap. Since becoming involved with theater in junior high, Tillman has participated in nearly 20 different plays and musicals as a theater technician, specializing in the purchase and creation of a wide variety of scenic and hand props. Tillman is an outgoing individual who is passionate about education and learning. She will use these qualities to ensure the success of In a Snap. In addition to operating photo booths at events with Newhouse, Tillman will focus on operations, customer relations, and the creative side of the business.

Professional and Advisory Support

In a Snap has selected Petersman Professional Accounting to provide bookkeeping and tax assistance beginning in year two when operations become more complex. A commercial checking account has been established with Community Bank & Trust, along with a merchant account for accepting credit card and debit card payments.

BUSINESS STRATEGY

Newhouse and Tillman have developed a strategy for growing In a Snap organically over the next three years.

Year One: Operate In a Snap as a part-time business on evenings and weekends, with one photo booth and two employees (Newhouse and Tillman).

Year Two: Expand the business with the addition of a second photo booth and two part-time employees. Hire a bookkeeper to keep In a Snap's finances and administrative paperwork (e.g., tax, payroll forms, etc.) in order. Change the business from a partnership to a limited liability company or corporation, providing more liability coverage.

Year Three: Continue to expand In a Snap by adding a third photo booth and two additional part-time employees, for a total of six part-time employees.

The following table shows projected business volume by month for the first three years of operations:

	January	February	March	April	May	June
2016	3	3	4	4	5	10
2017	6	6	8	8	11	21
2018	10	10	13	13	17	33

	July	August	September	October	November	December
2016	12	16	8	6	6	10
2017	25	34	17	13	13	21
2018	40	53	26	20	20	33

By year, the owners anticipate that event volume will break down as follows:

Year	Events
2016	87
2017	183
2018	287

SERVICES

In a Snap offers a variety of options for customers seeking the very best photo booth experience. The owners will meet with customers prior to their event to determine their expectations and develop a package to meet their unique needs. Packages can include a combination of the following:

Classic Booth ($499)

This option is best for one or several people interested in the classic experience.

Open Booth ($549)

This provides a more spacious setting that is suitable for larger groups and offers a wider range of options for customized backgrounds.

Custom Backgrounds ($175)

In a Snap can develop unique backgrounds that feature the name of a couple, company, group, organization, or event.

Standard Backgrounds (No additional charge)

- Solid Color
- Color Mosaic
- Black
- White
- Sequin (Gold & Silver)

Thematic Backgrounds ($100)

With this option, customers can choose from one of several pre-defined themes, including:

- Beach (ocean, palm trees, sand, and sun)
- Sports (football, basketball, baseball, golf, and tennis)
- Cityscape (silhouettes of skyscrapers with small twinkling lights)
- Country (barns & hay bales)

Props (No additional charge)

All options will provide customers with a variety of interesting props, including:

- Funny Hats
- Glasses
- Mustaches
- Letters (that photo subjects can hold up to make a word or phrase)

In a Snap will provide customers with the following standard services:

- Early photo booth delivery and setup (minimum of 60 min. before event begins)
- Three hours of service (classic or open booth/standard background or theme)
- Online password-protected photo gallery with social media sharing options (e.g., Facebook, InstaGram, Twitter, etc.)
- Photo CD (following event conclusion)
- Unlimited personalized photo strips and prints

- Prop selection

- Two on-site attendants

- Photo booth teardown & removal (within 45 min. of event conclusion)

An additional fee will be charged for:

- Extra service hours ($100/hour)

- Extra photo CDs ($5/each)

- Photo books (Will provide quote/many options)

MARKETING & SALES

A marketing plan has been developed for In a Snap that includes these main tactics:

1. **Direct Marketing:** Newhouse and Tillman will develop and execute an ongoing direct-mail initiative to area organizations and groups who are prospective customers. A mailing list has been obtained from a local list broker, and an area mail house has been identified to handle the mailings.

2. **Community Events:** In partnership with local community groups and the Petersman Chamber of Commerce, the owners have compiled their own list of recurring annual events and festivals. Newhouse or Tillman will personally contact the organizers of each event in order to provide information about In a Snap.

3. **Web Site:** In a Snap has developed a Web site that provides information about the business, including various photo booth options. In addition, the site will feature an online gallery for customers, where they can view, share, and download their images for up to one year. The site will feature an online calendar, allowing prospective customers to check availability, as well as an online contact form that can be completed to request a quote.

4. **Social Media:** In a Snap will maintain a presence on social media outlets including InstaGram, Facebook, and Twitter.

5. **Mobile Marketing:** Magnetic signage, featuring the business name and contact information, will be produced to promote In a Snap on Newhouse's and Tillman's vehicles. In addition, affordable vinyl graphics will be produced for a trailer that the business will use to transport photo booths to and from events.

6. **Promotional Fliers:** Two different full-color fliers will be produced to promote the business. One will be targeted toward consumers and the other will focus on organizations interested in entertainment options for various functions. These printed pieces can be used for direct mailings or posted at various public places. A local printer with a digital press can produce these in small quantities as needed.

7. **Word-of-Mouth Marketing:** In a Snap will strongly emphasize word-of-mouth to promote the business. To encourage referrals and repeat business, Newhouse and Tillman will offer $25 gift cards to a local restaurant for customers who make referrals that lead to new clients.

The owners will evaluate their marketing plan on a quarterly basis during the first year of operations, and semi-annually thereafter.

OPERATIONS

Hours

In a Snap typically will provide evening and weekend service during the school year. During the summer months, services will be available during daytime weekday hours as well.

Customer Communication

In a Snap has established a dedicated phone number with a leading Internet-based phone service. The phone number will go to voicemail, and messages will be automatically routed to Rebecca Newhouse's mobile phone. Rebecca or Jessica will respond to customer inquiries within one business day.

Payment

After determining a customer's expectations, the owners will then develop a detailed time and cost estimate. Once this has been accepted, In a Snap will require a 50 percent deposit from the customer to reserve a specific date. A written agreement outlining the services to be provided (using information from the time and cost estimate), will be signed by both parties. The owners have worked with a local attorney to draft a basic agreement that will meet their needs. Customers will be required to pay the balance due the day of the event, prior to photo booth set up. In a Snap will accept on-site credit/debit card payments utilizing a payment service that works with mobile devices.

Facility and Location

In a Snap will require space to store equipment. Rebecca Newhouse's father, Jonathan Newhouse, has agreed to allow the business to use storage space within Newhouse Plumbing Supply Co.'s warehouse. The space should be sufficient to store the equipment and trailer(s) that will be used to transport attractions to and from customer locations.

Equipment

Open Booth: Instead of purchasing an open-booth system from a supplier, Jessica Tillman has developed a custom solution at minimal cost, using her knowledge as a theater technician.

Classic Booth: In a Snap decided to purchase a classic photo booth from a reputable vendor for $2,500.

Trailer: The owners have purchased a low-profile Pulmor trailer for $3,500. The trailer is available in a variety of bright colors, and with some additional graphics can double as a form of mobile advertising. The trailer is lightweight, easy to maneuver, weatherproof, lockable, and capable of carrying up to 1,000 pounds. Additional trailers will be purchased after the first year of operation, providing a complete transportation solution for each photo booth team.

Props: Tillman and Newhouse have a $1,100 budget to purchase props. Although some of the items are disposable (e.g., mustaches, etc.), other props can be reused at multiple events. The owners will purchase items from thrift shops and produce things on their own whenever possible to make their budget go as far as possible.

FINANCIAL ANALYSIS

First-year Start-up Costs

Acquisition of the following equipment will be required for In a Snap's operations during the first year:

Start-up costs

Photo booth shell	$ 2,500
DSLR camera	$ 550
Camera AC adaptor	$ 55
Laptop	$ 375
Photo printer	$ 1,200
Software	$ 165
Printer paper	$ 660
Props	$ 1,100
Printer ink	$ 450
Trailer	$ 3,500
Total	**$10,555**

As partners, Tillman and Newhouse have agreed to split the start-up costs. Each owner will contribute $3,500 from their own personal savings. Tillman's father has agreed to provide a no interest loan for the remaining $3,555, which will be repaid during the first year.

Newhouse and Tillman estimate that, on average, their earnings per-event will break down in this way:

Revenue per event

Gross fee	$650
Paper	$ 8
Ink	$ 17
Labor	$240
Props	$ 10
Fuel	$ 10
Net profit	**$350**

The owners anticipate that projected monthly gross revenue will break down as follows during the first three years of operations:

	January	February	March	April	May	June
2016	$1,950	$1,950	$2,600	$2,600	$ 3,250	$ 6,500
2017	$4,095	$4,095	$5,460	$5,460	$ 6,825	$13,650
2018	$6,435	$6,435	$8,580	$8,580	$10,725	$21,450

	July	August	September	October	November	December
2016	$ 7,800	$10,400	$ 5,200	$ 3,900	$ 3,900	$ 6,500
2017	$16,380	$21,840	$10,920	$ 8,190	$ 8,190	$13,650
2018	$25,740	$34,320	$17,160	$12,870	$12,870	$21,450

Following is a detailed breakdown of projected sales and expenses for the first three years of In a Snap's operation:

	2016	2017	2018
Sales	**$56,550**	**$118,755**	**$180,180**
Expenses			
Marketing & advertising	$ 8,500	$ 17,500	$ 27,000
General/administrative	$ 500	$ 500	$ 500
Accounting/legal	$ 1,200	$ 2,500	$ 1,800
Office supplies	$ 350	$ 350	$ 350
Props	$ 870	$ 1,830	$ 2,870
Computer/technology	$ 250	$ 500	$ 750
Insurance	$ 350	$ 600	$ 850
Payroll	$20,880	$ 43,920	$ 68,880
Payroll taxes	$ 3,132	$ 6,588	$ 10,332
Postage	$ 750	$ 750	$ 750
Photo paper	$ 696	$ 1,464	$ 2,296
Printer ink	$ 1,479	$ 3,111	$ 4,879
Fuel	$ 1,000	$ 1,250	$ 1,500
Maintenance & repairs	$ 350	$ 500	$ 650
Total expenses	**$40,307**	**$ 81,363**	**$123,407**
Net income	**$16,243**	**$ 37,392**	**$ 56,773**

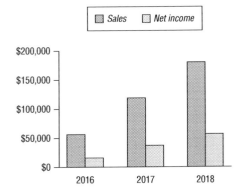

Funding

In addition to their contributions toward start-up costs, Tillman and Newhouse will each contribute $2,500 from personal savings to use for ongoing operations (namely marketing). The owners expect to recover all of their cash investments after the first year.

Scooter Rental Business

Rob's Scooter Rentals Inc.

23 Vista Ave.
Longmont Lake, OH 43921

Paul Greenland

Rob's Scooter Rentals Inc. is a newly established scooter rental business located in the tourist town of Longmont Lake, Ohio.

EXECUTIVE

Rob's Scooter Rentals Inc. is a newly established scooter rental business located in the tourist town of Longmont Lake, Ohio. Longmont Lake is a popular tourist destination, with attractions that include a 10.25-square-mile lake, four public beaches, a forest preserve, bed and breakfasts, hotels, wineries, antique stores, restaurants, bakeries, art galleries, eclectic stores and more. Most of Rob's Scooter Rentals inventory consists of 50cc scooters, but the business also rents several 150cc scooters for larger guests and those looking for a bike that can accommodate two passengers. Scooters rentals are available in several options, including hourly, two-hours, half-day, daily, and weekly.

Rob's Scooter Rentals, which has a tremendous advantage as the area's first scooter rental business, is being established by Rob Moore (a long-time scooter owner and enthusiast who also is an experienced scooter/motorcycle mechanic) and his father-in-law Bill Kelly, a Longmont Lake native and owner-operator of several area cottages. Operating from May through October, this seasonal business expects to generate first-year net income of about $230,000 on gross revenues of approximately $450,000. Moore and Kelly are collectively contributing $35,000 to establish the business, about $25,000 of which will be used to cover startup costs. They are seeking an outside investment or short-term small business loan in the amount of $20,000 for operations purposes.

The owners have prepared the following business plan, which outlines a thoughtful growth strategy for Rob's Scooter Rentals and showcases the operation's tremendous potential.

INDUSTRY ANALYSIS

According to the Moline, Illinois-based American Rental Association (ARA), a trade association for equipment rental businesses, manufacturers, and other industry players, revenues within the North American equipment rental industry were projected to reach approximately $48.7 billion by 2019, fueled by annual growth of about 6 percent.

Established in 1955, the ARA bills itself as "the source for information, advocacy, risk management, business development tools, education and training, networking and marketplace opportunities for the equipment rental industry throughout the world." The association counted some 9,500 rental businesses, as well as approximately 1,000 manufacturers and suppliers, among its membership base in 2016.

MARKET ANALYSIS

Located in southern Ohio, the town of Longmont Lake is a popular tourist destination. In 2015 the local population included 8,692 people, with an average household income of $64,123. At that time the population was expected to achieve 2.5 percent growth by the year 2020. Longmont Lake's business community included 572 establishments, which collectively employed 4,832 people. Rob's Scooter Rentals falls within the amusement and recreation services category, which included 23 competitors. Of these, five were focused on tourism-related transportation. Rob's Scooter Rentals has the advantage of being the very first scooter rental operation in the Longmont Lake area.

With four public beaches, Longmont Lake is the town's main attraction. The lake covers a total area of 10.25 square miles and has a maximum depth of 132 feet. The lake is a popular destination for swimming, boating, and fishing. Hikers enjoy access to trails in nearby Longmont Lake Forest Preserve, with many trails bordering the lake itself. The community includes several bed and breakfasts, hotels, wineries, antique stores, restaurants, bakeries, art galleries, eclectic stores and other attractions.

SERVICES

Most of Rob's Scooter Rentals inventory consists of 50cc scooters, but the business also rents several 150cc scooters for larger guests and those looking for a bike that can accommodate two passengers. Scooters rentals are available in several options, including:

- Hourly ($35)

- Two Hours ($45)

- Half-Day/5 Hours ($55)

- All-Day/24 Hours ($95)

- Weekly ($289)

Customers are required to sign liability waivers and pay for their rental with a major credit card. A $150 deposit is needed for all-day and longer rentals.

Fuel tanks will be full at the time of rental. Customers are required to pay for their own fuel (a gas station is conveniently located across the street) or pay a $20 surcharge.

OPERATIONS

Facility, Location, and Hours

Rob's Scooter Rentals has leased a former gas station/auto-repair shop on a high-profile street with exposure to approximately 10,400 vehicles per day. The facility has three service bays (for scooter storage and maintenance), a waiting area, and a restroom. There is enough space for the owners to sell snacks, beverages, and souvenirs, and display literature from local points of interest. The business will operate from 7 AM to 7 PM, Monday through Sunday, from May through October.

Scooter Fleet

Generally speaking, scooters are manufactured in several different engine sizes, based on cubic centimeters, including 50cc, 150cc, and 250cc. A motorcycle license often is required to operate scooters with larger engine sizes. Rob's Scooter Rentals mainly will rent 50cc scooters, which typically travel at speeds of 35 to 40 miles per hour. However, the business will offer a small selection of 150cc scooters, capable of speeds of 50 to 60 miles per hour, for larger guests and those looking for a bike that can accommodate two passengers.

One of the attractive things about 50cc scooters is that a motorcycle license is not required. However, the owners understand that first-time riders may be apprehensive. For this reason, Rob's Scooter Rentals will offer both reassurance and guidance to those who need it. The business has a generous-sized parking lot where customers can easily learn how to handle a scooter before venturing out into the town of Longmont Lake to see the sights.

Rob's Scooter Rentals will begin operations with a fleet of 13 50cc scooters and four 150cc scooters.

Maintenance

Rob's Scooter Rentals has established the following maintenance schedule to maximize the lifespan of its fleet. In addition to inspecting many different scooter components, the owners will perform cleaning, lubrication, adjustments, and maintenance as needed.

The owners estimate that customers will travel 15-20 miles per hour on average, factoring in stops for sightseeing, etc.

Every 250 miles, the owners will check the following:

- Battery
- Horn
- Lights
- Tire Pressure
- Engine Oil Level

Every 1,000 miles, the owners will change the engine oil in every scooter and check:

- Tires
- Valve Stems
- Brakes
- Throttle
- Muffler & Exhaust Fasteners
- Front & Rear Axles

Every 2,000 miles, the owners will change the oil and transmission fluid in every scooter and check:

- Air cleaner
- Spark Plugs
- Brake Linings
- Brake and Throttle Cables
- Wheel and Steering Bearings
- CVT Drive Belt
- Valve Clearance

Tools & Equipment

The owners have purchased the following tools for maintaining Rob's Scooter Rentals' scooter fleet:

- 1/2" Drive Air Impact Gun
- 10" Vice Grip Pliers
- 12" Channel Locks
- 16oz Ball Peen Hammer
- 16oz Soft Faced Dead Blow Hammer
- 3/8" Drive Air Ratchet
- 6" Needle Nose Pliers
- 6" Slip Joint Pliers
- 7" Diagonal Cutters
- Air Compressor
- Brass Punch—3/4"
- Cape Chisel—5/16"
- Center Punch
- Cold Chisels—3/8"—3/4"
- Combination Wrenches
- Compression Gauge
- Creeper
- External Retaining Ring Pliers
- Feeler Gauge
- Feeler Gauge (Blade type)
- Funnels
- Gasoline Containers (2)
- Grease Gun
- Hack Saw
- Halogen Work Lights (2)
- Hearing Protectors
- Hex (Allen) Wrenches
- Internal Retaining Ring Pliers
- Micrometer
- Oil Can
- Oil Disposal Containers (2)
- Pin Punch—1/8", 3/16", 1/4", 5/16"
- Pocket Flash Light
- Pocket Knife

- Portable Generator
- Portable Grinder
- Pry Bar Screwdriver
- Rotary Tool
- Round 8"—10" File
- Safety Glasses
- Screw Drivers (Phillips & Flat-Head)
- Snap Ring Pliers
- Socket Set—1/2" Drive
- Socket Set—1/4" Drive
- Socket Set—3/8" Drive
- Spark Plug Gap Tool
- Tape Measure 12"
- Taper Punch 3/8", 1/2", 5/8"
- Three-cornered File
- Torque Wrench—1/2" Drive
- Torx Bits (Screwdriver & Sockets)
- Tubing Cutter
- Wire Stripper/Cutter Pliers 8"

Supplies & Parts

In addition, Rob's Scooter Rentals' will maintain a limited inventory of supplies and parts, including:

- Air Filters
- Degreaser
- Fuel Filters
- Gasoline
- Grease
- Hand Cleaner
- Hardware (common standard and metric bolts, nuts, washers, etc.)
- Lubricants
- Motor Oil
- Rags
- Razor Blades
- Sandpaper
- Spark Plugs
- Tubing
- Zip Ties

PERSONNEL

Rob's Scooter Rentals is being established by Rob Moore, a long-time scooter owner and enthusiast. For 15 years, Rob worked as a scooter/motorcycle mechanic for a number of businesses throughout southern Ohio. However, his entrepreneurial spirit prompted him to take several small business ownership courses at his local community college. After saving and investing for five years, Rob is prepared to fill his lifelong dream of small business ownership by establishing Rob's Scooter Rentals in partnership with his father-in-law, Bill Kelly, a Longmont Lake native and owner-operator of several area cottages.

Rob will serve as president of the business, contributing his mechanical knowledge and personally maintaining the business' fleet. This will be a significant advantage, considering that many customers inflict above-average wear-and-tear on scooters and repair shops typically charge $75 per hour for labor. Rob will share administrative responsibilities with Bill (vice president & treasurer) who will take a lead role in new business development/marketing, utilizing his extensive knowledge of the local market to promote the business to area tourists (including his cottage rental customers).

In addition to Rob and Bill, Rob's Scooter Rentals will employ four part-time employees to help operate the seasonal business, which will be open 12 hours per day, seven days per week. The owners have developed the following salary schedule for their first year of operations:

Salaries

*   Rob Moore (President): $50,000

*   Bill Kelly (Vice President & Treasurer): $35,000

*   Part-Time Associate 1: $5,400

*   Part-Time Associate 2: $5,400

*   Part-Time Associate 3: $5,400

*   Part-Time Associate 4: $5,400

GROWTH STRATEGY

The owners have developed a thoughtful growth strategy for Rob's Scooter Rentals, which is based on the assumption that scooter rentals will break down as follows:

Projected rentals by type

Hourly	20%
Two hours	45%
Half-day/6 hours	15%
All-day/24 hours	10%
Weekly	10%

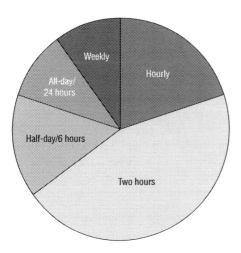

In addition, the owners have calculated the business' maximum rental capacity for the first year as a basis for their growth projections:

Maximum rental unit capacity (year one)

Rental type	Scooters	Daily	Weekly	Monthly	Season
Hourly	3	36	252	1,008	6,048
Two hours	6	36	252	1,008	6,048
Half-day/6 hours	4	8	56	224	1,344
All-day/24 hours	2	2	14	56	336
Weekly	2	0	2	8	48

Rob's Scooter Rentals has established the following utilization targets for the business:

• **Year One:** 75% capacity

• **Year Two:** 80% capacity

• **Year Three:** 85% capacity

The owners' objective is to increase rental utilization by 5 percent annually, while concurrently increasing the size/maximum capacity of their scooter fleet by 15 percent annually. Based on these assumptions, the owners are confident that the business can achieve the following financial targets:

• **Year One:** Generate net income of $229,924 on gross revenues of $452,664.

• **Year Two:** Generate net income of $337,460 on gross revenues of $555,268.

• **Year Three:** Generate net income of $425,569 and gross revenues of $678,468.

MARKETING & SALES

Target Markets

Rob's Scooter Rentals will cater to tourists who seek to experience Longmont Lake in a unique and enjoyable way. In particular, its scooter rentals will be especially popular for customers who are celebrating special occasions, including:

• Birthdays

• Family Reunions

- Bachelorette Parties

- Romantic Getaways

- Family Vacations

- Anniversaries

- Engagements

Beyond the consumer market, the business' scooter rentals also will be an attractive option for organizations in search of unique teambuilding exercises in connection with business meetings, conferences and other corporate events.

Marketing Tactics

The following tactics will be used to market Rob's Scooter Rentals:

1. A social media strategy involving the establishment of a Facebook page, as well as a presence on both Instagram and Twitter.

2. A four-color brochure that can be distributed at restaurants, hotels, and tourist locations throughout southern Ohio.

3. Regional print advertising in lifestyle publications and newspapers serving Longmont Lake in the southern Ohio counties of Webster, Breckenridge, and Fenton.

4. A monthly advertisement in the magazine, *Southern Ohio Business* , to reach organizational prospects.

5. Online tourism directory/Web site listings.

6. A Web site with complete details about Rob's Scooter Rentals, including a listing of scooter rental options, pricing, and terms/conditions, as well as online reservation and payment options

7. Co-marketing initiatives with the Longmont Lake Convention and Visitors Bureau.

8. Participation in the annual Longmont Lake Memorial Day Festival & Parade, which provides strong exposure at the beginning of the rental season, as well as other public events and celebrations, including the annual Fourth of July and Labor Day parades. In particular, the parades provide the business with an opportunity to show off its scooter fleet for promotional purposes.

9. Mobile marketing (displaying the Rob's Scooter Rentals name and Web site address on the outside of the owners' vehicles using affordable magnetic signage).

10. Participation in regional tourism and bridal shows throughout southern Ohio.

11. A customer loyalty program that provides a 15 percent discount to those referring a friend or family member to the business.

FINANCIAL ANALYSIS

Rob's Scooter Rentals has prepared a full set of conservative financial projections in partnership with an accountant, which are available upon request. Following are projected sales and expense projections for the first three years of operations:

	2016	2017	2018
Sales	**$452,664**	**$555,268**	**$678,468**
Expenses			
Marketing & advertising	$ 50,000	$ 50,000	$ 50,000
Facility lease	$ 12,500	$ 12,500	$ 12,500
General/administrative	$ 500	$ 500	$ 500
Accounting/legal	$ 1,100	$ 750	$ 750
Office supplies	$ 350	$ 350	$ 350
Scooters	$ 20,150	$ 10,000	$ 10,000
Helmets	$ 1,000	$ 500	$ 500
Tools & equipment	$ 3,500	$ 1,500	$ 15,500
Supplies & parts	$ 750	$ 2,000	$ 2,500
Computer/technology	$ 750	$ 250	$ 250
Insurance	$ 3,750	$ 4,250	$ 4,750
Payroll	$106,600	$111,930	$128,720
Payroll taxes	$ 15,990	$ 16,790	$ 19,308
Postage	$ 350	$ 350	$ 350
Utilities	$ 450	$ 500	$ 550
Maintenance & repairs	$ 4,250	$ 4,888	$ 5,621
Telecommunications	$ 750	$ 750	$ 750
Total expenses	**$222,740**	**$217,808**	**$252,899**
Net income	**$229,924**	**$337,460**	**$425,569**

Startup Costs

Rob's Scooter Rentals will begin operations with a fleet that includes 13 50cc scooters. Although the list price per unit is $1,500, the owners have negotiated volume pricing of $950 per unit. In addition, the business' initial inventory also will include four 150cc scooters. While these have a list price of $2,500, the owners have negotiated pricing of $1,950 each. In addition, startup costs for the aforementioned lists of tools/equipment ($3,500) and supplies/parts ($750) will cost a total of $4,250. The business' total projected startup costs are $24,400.

Financing

The owners are collectively contributing $35,000 of their own funds to establish the business and cover startup costs. They are seeking an outside investment or short-term small business loan in the amount of $20,000, which will be used to provide initial cash flow for operations.

Smart Home Automation Consulting & Installation Business

The Smarter Home LLC

2876 Sedona Hills Dr.
Ridgway, MN 77895

Paul Greenland

The Smarter Home LLC is a newly established smart home automation consulting and installation business.

EXECUTIVE SUMMARY

The ability to remotely unlock doors, operate appliances, or use video cameras to see who just rang the doorbell was once science fiction. Later, such "smart home automation" capabilities became options for only the wealthiest of homeowners. By 2015 the "Internet of Things" had arrived, giving everyday consumers the ability to manage their home or apartment through apps on their mobile device.

From individual devices like thermostats, to off-the-shelf systems sold at home improvement stores and big-box retailers, to systems offered by leading telecommunications and cable companies, consumers had a wide range of options for automating different aspects of their home environment in areas such as security, climate control, and entertainment. Independent consultants/installers also fulfilled an important niche in the smart home automation technology market, which was expected to reach $71 billion by the year 2018, up from $25 billion in 2012, according to Icontrol Networks Inc.'s *2014 State of the Smart Home Report.*

Located in Ridgway, Minnesota, The Smarter Home LLC is a newly established smart home automation consulting and installation business, formed by retired electrical engineer Larry Colberg and his nephew, electrician Pete Fenton. The inspiration to establish the business occurred three years ago when Fenton successfully installed an automation system in his own home. This led to several projects for family and friends, and ultimately a steady stream of side jobs that provided much-needed income during the economic slowdown. With more demand than his part-time schedule can accommodate, and considering the rapid growth occurring in the smart home automation market, Fenton decided to establish a dedicated business in partnership with his uncle.

MARKET ANALYSIS

Overview

According to the *State of the Smart Home Report,* published by Icontrol Networks Inc. in 2014, the firm Juniper Research projected that the market for smart home automation technology will total approximately

$71 billion by the year 2018, an significant increase from $25 billion in 2012. Icontrol Networks' report further indicated that "smart" devices were being adopted at a rapid pace. Compared to an estimated 1.9 billion devices in use as of 2014, the number of smart devices was expected to total 9 billion four years later. One of the report's main findings is that family security is an important consideration among consumers when choosing a home automation solution. In addition, it revealed that about one-third of Americans would spend as much as $3,000 for a comprehensive system.

Local Market

The Smarter Home will target upper-middle-class consumers who account for nearly 65 percent of the local population in Ridgway. Specifically, the business will focus its marketing efforts on busy working professionals (e.g., doctors, attorneys, nurses, engineers, and professors), who constitute a significant portion of the local workforce. Ridgway is home to a large medical center, four colleges and universities, and several leading corporations in the technology and aviation industries. Healthcare, in particular, is a major employer in Ridgway and the surrounding region, with about 1,700 facilities categorized under health & medical services (including immediate care clinics, family medicine clinics, and specialty care centers). In all, healthcare workers account for 16.5 percent of the region's service employees.

Competition

At the lower end of the market, The Smarter Home will face competition from off-the-shelf systems available at leading retailers, such as the home improvement store chain, Lowe's. Companies marketing do-it-yourself systems include Wink Inc.; iSmart Alarm Inc.; Samsung Electronics; and Icontrol Networks Inc. In addition, telecommunications and cable companies also are offering a variety of security and home automation systems for consumers, in connection with their strategies to generate additional revenue and secure more significant consumer wallet share through bundling. In addition to alarm companies such as ADT, competitors in this category include AT&T, Comcast, and Cox Communications.

The Smarter Home will differentiate itself against these types of competitors by offering consulting services that will help consumers choose the very best options to meet their needs, based on their specific budget and life circumstances. In addition, the company will offer high-quality systems that are modular, scalable, and cost-effective, providing customers with the ability to automate a single room/ space to an entire property.

Significant competition also will come from companies that are similar to The Smarter Home. In particular, there are three independent installers currently operating in the Ridgway market, including:

- Noble Electric LLC—A local group of licensed electricians with extensive experience performing low-voltage wiring projects, for whom smart home automation simply is an additional service offering.

- Awesome Entertainment Inc.—A company whose primary focus is entertainment/audio-visual systems.

- Ridgway Security Corp.—A well-established local security/alarm installation firm.

The Smarter Home's differential will be its exclusive focus on all aspects of smart home automation. With smart home automation as its core competency, the business will seek to establish itself as a regional expert. Importantly, the company will emphasize its ability to provide integrated systems that meet all of a customer's needs.

SERVICES

Home Automation Systems

The Smarter Home's systems, which include a mix of both hardwired and wireless options, include software and mobile apps, as well as a variety of hardware. In addition to automation hubs, which provide connectivity to various digital devices, installation projects will include a variety of components, such as:

- Central Controllers
- Control Boxes
- Power Distribution Units
- Switchers
- Touch Panels
- Transmitters & Receivers

One of the differentiating features of the systems offered by The Smarter Home is that they are compatible with multiple communication protocols. Although consumers may have existing devices in their homes that are compatible with smart home automation, they may not all use the same language to communicate. The Smarter Home's systems maximize configuration options for the customer because they are compatible with protocols such as ZigBee, Wi-Fi, and Bluetooth LE.

Packages

The Smarter Home will market three levels of base packages for customers seeking a whole-home automation solution. These modular packages can then be customized (or expanded at a later time) based on the customer's specific needs or situation:

- Bronze ($3,500): Ideal for smaller homes/living spaces, or customers who want only the most fundamental level of automation. Includes basic safety/security and climate control options.

- Silver ($5,000): Ideal for medium-sized homes/living spaces, this package provides a more extensive offering of everything included in the Bronze package, along with automation features for appliances and some home entertainment.

- Gold ($15,000): This package is ideal for larger homes/living spaces and customers seeking a very robust home automation experience. It includes more extensive home entertainment options, as well as features such as automated window treatments/shading, irrigation, etc.

OPERATIONS

Process

The Smarter Home will begin every new client relationship with a discovery process, in order to learn more about a customer's house, condominium, or apartment and identify specific smart home automation goals and objectives. Customers may wish to automate many different aspects of their living space, including:

- Appliances (electrical plugs and switches)
- Audio-Visual Systems
- Climate Control/HVAC (thermostats)
- Irrigation (sprinkler systems)
- Lighting (light switches and lightbulbs)
- Pet Monitoring/Management
- Safety (smoke alarms, fire alarms, gas leak detectors, carbon monoxide detectors, water sensors, etc.)

- Security (alarms, cameras, window and door locks, etc.)

- Shading (window treatments)

Once specific goals and objectives have been identified, The Smarter Home will develop a detailed project estimate that includes specific milestones and timelines. This information will then become part of a formal written agreement with the customer.

Payment

The Smarter Home will require customers to pay for all hardware in advance, along with 50 percent of installation labor costs. The remaining 50 percent will be due upon completion, or at mutually agreed upon milestones. The Smarter Home will accept payments via check or credit card.

Suppliers

The Smarter Home will obtain control systems from two leading vendors (Pine Technologies and Fenway Integration Co.), which offer systems that are somewhat advanced, but not too technical for the business to install. Some smart home automation installers work with systems that require computer programming knowledge. In addition to the vendors that The Smarter Home will work with, other leading industry suppliers include companies such as Creston, AMX, and Elan Home Systems.

Location

The Smarter Home will begin operations from affordable leased space in downtown Ridgway, Minnesota. Formerly a small retail storefront, the location provides space for several home automation displays and a meeting area where customers can have conversations with the owners. The back portion of the storefront includes a small office and an area with overhead door access for storing hardware, wiring, and other supplies. Because The Smarter Home will follow a "just-in-time" approach (e.g., only storing hardware components that have been ordered for specific jobs, versus keeping them in inventory), the owners believe that the space will meet the business' needs for its first several years of operations.

Insurance

The Smarter Home is bonded and insured. Copies of the business' insurance policies and other documentation are available upon request.

PERSONNEL

The Smarter Home is being established by retired electrical engineer Larry Colberg and his nephew, Pete Fenton.

Larry Colberg

With more than 35 years of technical and management experience, Larry will provide key leadership for the business. In addition to handling administrative functions, he will serve as the main contact for The Smarter Home's customers, helping them to identify their home automation goals and plan their systems. Prior to his early retirement, Larry enjoyed a successful career with Parkway Aviation, most recently serving as vice president of electrical engineering.

Pete Fenton

Pete will serve as the main installer, and also will be responsible for overseeing independent contractors when additional labor is required for larger projects. A licensed electrician, he brings more than 15 years of practical experience to the business, having worked for a local electric firm and two residential construction companies. In addition, Pete also worked as a part-time as an installer for a leading security company. He will be responsible for handling all electrical-related work, when required.

Independent Contractors

To keep their labor costs low and have the flexibility to scale their workforce up and down based on project volume, Larry and Pete will rely upon a pool of skilled independent contractors who have previous installation experience with telecommunications, cable, or alarm companies. The owners have obtained an independent contractor agreement from a leading online legal document service, which they have modified to meet their specific needs. The agreement addresses the finer points of matters such as taxes, compensation, and liability.

Training & Continuing Education

Both Larry and Pete will take full advantage of technical training opportunities offered by their suppliers, in order to stay current on the technologies they are installing, as well as emerging industry trends.

Professional and Advisory Support

The Smarter Home will use the local accounting firm, Parkview Financial Services Inc., for assistance with tax preparation and bookkeeping. In addition, the owners have established a commercial checking account with Ridgway Community Bank, and will utilize a popular mobile point-of-sale service to accept credit card and debit card payments from customers.

GROWTH STRATEGY

The Smarter Home has established the following growth targets for its first three years of operations. Projections are based on a total of 49 work weeks, allowing for holidays and vacation-related downtime.

Year One: Focus on establishing The Smarter Home in the local market and promoting general awareness of the benefits associated with smart home automation. Perform 49 installations in each package category (bronze, silver, and gold). Generate net income of $59,522 on adjusted gross revenue of $209,622.

Year Two: Continue to establish local brand recognition for The Smarter Home. Perform 74 installations in each package category (bronze, silver, and gold). Generate net income of $108,952 on adjusted gross revenue of $317,052. Secure at least one contract with a custom homebuilder.

Year Three: Perform 98 installations in each package category (bronze, silver, and gold). Generate net income of $153,144 on adjusted gross revenue of $419,244. Secure at least two contracts with custom homebuilders. Develop regional expansion plans for The Smarter Home, capitalizing on growth opportunities in the nearby communities of Creston and Applewood.

MARKETING & SALES

The Smarter Home has developed the following marketing tactics to grow the business:

- A four-color brochure will be developed to promote the business and the smart home automation systems that it sells. The brochure will be ideal for direct marketing campaigns.

- A referral program that offers a 15 percent discount for friends and family.

- A social media strategy involving highly targeted advertising on popular social networking sites, such as Facebook.

- A sustained commercial direct marketing program targeting homebuilders and remodeling companies.

- A sustained consumer direct marketing program targeting homeowners with household incomes of $75,000 and up.

- A Web site with complete details about The Smarter Home and its smart home automation systems.

- Active membership in the Ridgway Chamber of Commerce.

- Affordable vinyl vehicle signage to promote the business via mobile advertising.

- Development of a smart home automation blog, providing homeowners with information regarding the advantages associated with automating different aspects of their home.

- Magnetic business cards that will double as advertising specialties.

- The use of media relations to promote the owners' position as regional smart home automation experts (e.g., guest columns and interviews with local radio, TV, newspaper outlets).

- Trade show marketing at home building and remodeling shows.

FINANCIAL ANALYSIS

A complete set of projected financial statements have been prepared with the owners' accountants, which are available upon request. The following graph shows projected gross and net revenues for The Smarter Home's first three years of operations:

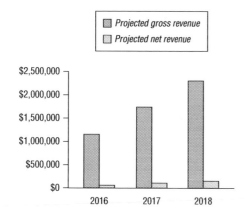

The owners anticipate that revenues will break down, on a package basis, as follows:

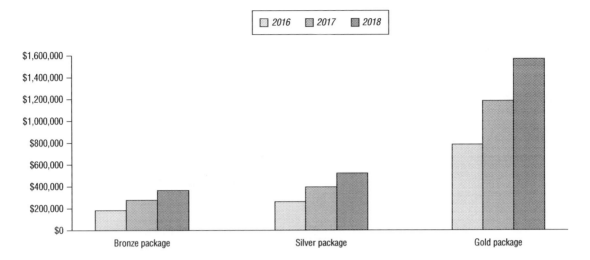

Following are revenue and expense projections for the first three years of The Smarter Home's operations:

Revenue	2016	2017	2018
Projected gross revenue	$1,151,500	$1,739,000	$2,303,000
Hardware costs	($ 894,838)	($1,351,388)	($1,789,676)
Independent contractor labor	($ 47,040)	($ 70,560)	($ 94,080)
Adjusted gross revenue	**$ 209,622**	**$ 317,052**	**$ 419,244**
Expenses			
Salaries	$ 80,000	$ 120,000	$ 160,000
Payroll taxes	$ 12,000	$ 18,000	$ 24,000
Utilities	$ 2,500	$ 2,750	$ 3,000
Rent	$ 9,350	$ 9,350	$ 9,350
Insurance	$ 3,500	$ 4,500	$ 5,500
Office supplies	$ 750	$ 1,250	$ 1,750
Equipment	$ 2,500	$ 2,500	$ 2,500
Business loan	$ 10,000	$ 10,000	$ 10,000
Marketing & advertising	$ 25,000	$ 35,000	$ 45,000
Telecommunications & Internet	$ 2,000	$ 2,250	$ 2,500
Professional development	$ 1,500	$ 1,500	$ 1,500
Licenses & fees	$ 1,000	$ 1,000	$ 1,000
Total expenses	**$ 150,100**	**$ 208,100**	**$ 266,100**
Net income/loss	**$ 59,522**	**$ 108,952**	**$ 153,144**

Financing

The owners will begin operations with $20,000 in capital, which Pete Fenton has saved from doing smart home automation installations on an independent basis over the past few years. In addition, Larry Colberg will borrow $25,000 from his savings and contribute the funds to the business in the form of a personal loan, which the business will repay (with interest) within its first three years of operations.

EVALUATION & ADJUSTMENT

This plan will be evaluated quarterly during The Smarter Home's first year of operations, and semi-annually thereafter.

Software Training Business

Trevani Training Solutions LLC

9512 Ocean Ave., SW
Marble Junction, CO 81503

Paul Greenland

Trevani Training Solutions LLC is a software training business that offers training for many common applications, as well as customized training for proprietary applications, training program development, and project management.

EXECUTIVE SUMMARY

Business Overview

Trevani Training Solutions LLC is a software training business that offers training for many common applications, including popular programs from companies such as Adobe and Microsoft, as well as customized training for proprietary applications. The business is being established by Parker Trevani, who has 15 years of experience in the field of technology training, several specialized certifications, and qualities that will ensure his success as an independent trainer and small business owner. A thoughtful growth strategy has been established for Trevani Training Solutions, which in addition to software training, will offer services such as project management and training program development.

MARKET ANALYSIS

There always is a market for skilled software trainers, thanks to the continuous evolution of technology. New software applications are being developed continuously, and new versions of existing applications are introduced every day. As users are faced with the need to learn new features and become accustomed to new interfaces, individuals and organizations alike turn to software trainers for assistance.

Based on an analysis of the local market, Parker Trevani believes that his greatest opportunity exists with mid-sized companies, which are more likely to contract with an independent trainer and also have revenue streams that are substantial enough to fund a robust training program.

The community of Marble Junction was home to 1,051 establishments in 2015. Trevani has determined that, based on the local business climate, his revenue by customer industry/type will likely break down as follows during the first year:

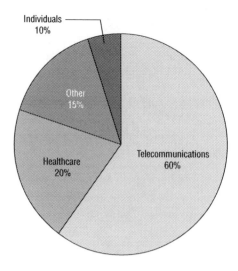

INDUSTRY ANALYSIS

According to the U.S. Bureau of Labor Statistics, strong growth is expected for the training and development industry in general. Approximately 228,800 training and development specialists were employed in 2012. By 2022 employment is expected to increase 15 percent (much faster than average), resulting in an additional 35,400 jobs.

Many trainers are members of the Association for Talent Development (www.td.org), which is known as ATD for short. Previously known as the American Society for Training & Development (ASTD), this membership organization is the largest of its kind dedicated to the learning and talent development field. ATD's members hail from approximately 120 different countries and virtually every industry. The association offers a wide range of benefits, including 125 local chapters, conferences and events, and publications and e-newsletters. To help its members succeed professionally, ATD offers the Certified Professional in Learning and Performance (CPLP) credential, as well as a number of other specialized certifications, including ones in the areas of training, instructional design, management, and human resources/organizational development.

PERSONNEL

Trevani Training Solutions is owned by Parker Trevani. After earning a Bachelor of Science degree in computer information systems from Webster University, Trevani began his career as an assistant software trainer with a large healthcare system in Bradfield, Colorado. In that role, his responsibilities included providing application training to doctors, nurses, management, and staff. He performed extensive training pertaining to the organization's electronic medical record (EMR) and time-and-attendance systems. Over the course of 10 years, Trevani provided training to thousands of people, and ultimately was promoted to the roles of software trainer and training manager. Following his experience in healthcare, Trevani joined a private information technology consulting firm, Brampton & Anfield, where he worked as a consultant to clients in a wide range of industries. There, over the course of five years, he gained invaluable experience helping customers develop customized (in-classroom and Web-based) training programs for proprietary applications, many of which involved the use of cloud computing technologies. After sensing a tremendous opportunity to establish his own business, Trevani decided to branch off on his own and form Trevani Training Solutions.

Trevani possesses skills and traits that are essential for success as a software trainer and small business owner. He is passionate about technology, people, and learning, and possesses excellent writing, critical thinking, time management, prioritization, problem-solving, and project management skills. In addition, Trevani has a knack for communicating technical information in non-technical terms, making things easy to understand for a general audience. He also is highly adaptable, and can quickly modify his training methods to meet the needs of specific audiences and groups when needed.

Trevani holds a number of specialized training and technology-related certifications, including:

- Certified Professional in Learning and Performance (CPLP)

- ATD Master Instructional Designer

- ATD Master Trainer

- Adobe Certified (Photoshop, Illustrator, InDesign)

- Microsoft Office Specialist (MOS)

Professional and Advisory Support

Trevani has established a commercial checking account with his local bank, including a merchant account for accepting credit card payments. He will rely on a local CPA for accounting and tax advisory services. Trevani has used a popular online legal document service to establish his LLC cost effectively and obtain templates for customer contracts.

BUSINESS STRATEGY

A thoughtful growth strategy has been established for Trevani Training Solutions, which includes the following annual milestones:

Year One: Average 25 hours of billable hours per week (1,250 hours annually). Achieve gross revenues of $114,274 and generate net income of $3,724.

Year Two: Increase weekly billable hours per to 30 (1,500 annually). Increase gross revenues approximately 15 percent, to $130,536, and generate net income of $6,136.

Year Three: Achieve 35 hours weekly billable hours (1,750 hours annually). Increase gross revenues approximately 14 percent, to $149,287, and generate net income of $10,537.

In the above scenarios, Trevani acknowledges that he will need to devote additional (e.g., non-billable) hours for administrative tasks such as marketing and operations.

SERVICES

Trevani Training Solutions will provide the following key services to its customers:

Training—Providing end-users with application and software program use instruction on a group or one-on-one basis. Training may be delivered via a variety of different approaches, including on-site training and/or e-learning or Web-based methods. Trevani will leverage a variety of approaches including lab-based programs, social media, video, group discussions, lectures, team exercises, mobile learning methods, and visual simulations.

Project Management—Working with organizations to conduct needs assessments (using survey instruments and other tools) and identify specific training needs; working with IT departments or management to secure proper internal or external training resources (including choosing existing training materials from publishers/vendors and selecting or hiring other training vendors/staff); coordinating the selection of effective on-site or off-site training locations; conducting "train the trainer" programs; and performing post-training evaluations.

Training Program Development—Developing curricula, lesson plans, and custom instructional materials (online learning modules, training manuals, etc.) for group software training once specific needs have been identified. In the case of custom or proprietary applications, this may involve Trevani working with the client's software development staff to test new product releases and assist with problem-solving during the development phase. In addition, Trevani will include time to gain a thorough understanding of the custom application from a user standpoint.

MARKETING & SALES

A marketing plan has been developed for Trevani Training Solutions that includes the following principal tactics:

1. *Web Site:* Using a popular Web site service, Parker Trevani has developed an effective Web site that provides essential information about his business, including Parker's background, services offered, and more. The site includes plug-ins that enable easy integration with popular social media platforms.

2. *Direct Marketing:* Parker Trevani has developed a custom list of mid-sized organizations in a 100-mile radius surrounding Marble Junction. The list was developed using a business information database available through a local university library. Trevani will use the list to send regular direct mailings, which will include a letter, business card, and four-color brochure with information about Trevani Training Solutions. In addition, Trevani has contracted with a local mailing services firm to produce and manage sustained direct marketing (U.S. Mail and e-mail) throughout the year, with a goal of providing a steady stream of inquiries.

3. *Social Media:* Trevani Training Solutions will utilize popular social media channels, namely LinkedIn and Twitter, to reach key business prospects. Additionally, Parker Trevani will maintain a technology training blog, with postings scheduled on a weekly basis. Trevani will cross-promote the blog via his Web site and other social media platforms.

4. *Advertising:* Trevani Training Solutions will maintain a regular advertising presence (print and digital) in The Marble Junction Chamber Times, a newspaper published by the local Chamber of Commerce, as well as Business Today, a monthly publication serving the business community in Trevani's target market.

5. *Sales Presentations:* Parker Trevani will attempt to make at least five sales calls to key prospects in his target market every month. Working from the aforementioned list of mid-sized organizations, Trevani will identify a segment of "hot prospects, " with whom he will follow up with by phone approximately 1-2 weeks after a direct mailing, with a goal of securing an in-person meeting.

6. *Networking:* Parker Trevani will become a member of the Marble Junction Chamber Of Commerce and attend various functions and networking events, in order to build connections with area business leaders.

Trevani Training Solutions will evaluate its marketing plan on a semi-annual basis during the first year of operations, and annually thereafter.

OPERATIONS

Location

Trevani Training Solutions has found affordable office space in Marble Junction. Parker Trevani has leased space in the Sterling Office Park, in a building that offers individual offices for lease, along with shared conference room space. The building includes a copy center, as well as convenient service pickups for shipping services such as FedEx and UPS. Trevani's lease includes affordable business-class Internet service. Trevani Training Solutions will not perform any actual training within its offices; services will always be provided within a computer laboratory, training facility, conference room, or classroom at the client's location, or at a designated outside training site.

Fees

Based on his knowledge of the regional market, Trevani has established a baseline hourly rate ($90) that he will use for calculating project estimates, although this will vary depending on negotiations with customers. Trevani typically will require his customers to pay for existing or custom training materials separately (e.g., he will not fund the purchase or production of materials on behalf of his clients).

Payment

Although he will attempt to be as flexible as possible with clients, Parker Trevani typically will require 50 percent of his fees in advance, based on his written time and cost estimate.

FINANCIAL ANALYSIS

Following are Trevani Training Solutions' projected sales, expenses, and net profits for the first three years of operations:

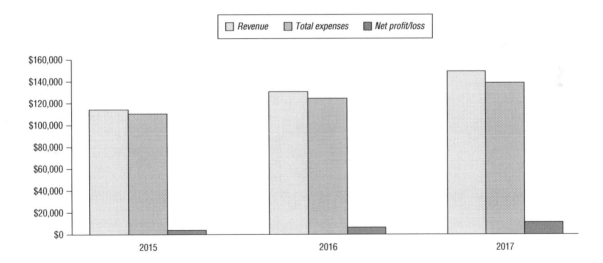

Revenue	2016	2017	2018
Individual training	$ 27,280	$ 32,735	$ 39,283
Group training	$ 42,143	$ 48,463	$ 55,733
Training program development	$ 44,852	$ 49,338	$ 54,271
Total revenue	**$114,274**	**$130,536**	**$149,287**
Expenses			
Salaries	$ 65,000	$ 75,000	$ 85,000
Payroll taxes	$ 10,500	$ 12,000	$ 13,500
Utilities	$ 650	$ 700	$ 750
Rent	$ 3,600	$ 3,600	$ 3,600
Insurance	$ 750	$ 800	$ 850
Office supplies	$ 1,250	$ 1,500	$ 1,750
Equipment	$ 3,500	$ 2,000	$ 2,000
Marketing & advertising	$ 7,500	$ 8,500	$ 9,500
Telecommunications & internet	$ 2,450	$ 2,450	$ 2,450
Professional development	$ 1,500	$ 2,500	$ 2,500
Travel & entertainment	$ 13,500	$ 15,000	$ 16,500
Subscriptions & dues	$ 350	$ 350	$ 350
Total expenses	**$110,550**	**$124,400**	**$138,750**
Net income	**$ 3,724**	**$ 6,136**	**$ 10,537**

Sports Fan Experience Business

Legendary Experiences Inc.

23 Lake Ave. West
Mountain Pointe, MN 55400

Paul Greenland

Legendary Experiences Inc. is a newly established sports fan experience business, with a special focus on sports history.

EXECUTIVE SUMMARY

In a September 10, 2010 post on *Blog Maverick,* Dallas Mavericks owner Mark Cuban offered his perspective on sports marketing when he said: "We in the sports business don't sell the game, we sell unique, emotional experiences. We are not in the business of selling basketball. We're in the business of selling fun and unique experiences." When fans reflect on their favorite sports memories, they often extend well beyond a particular game, evoking positive emotions associated with specific players, coaches, stadiums, restaurants, bars, family members, and friends.

Located in the city of Mountain Pointe, Minnesota, Legendary Experiences Inc. is a newly established sports fan experience business, with a special focus on sports history. The business works with individual consumers, as well as groups and organizations, to create ultimate, unforgettable, nostalgic sports experiences. Legendary Experiences is being established by Jake Remington, former director of public relations for the Mountain Pointe Marauders professional hockey team, and travel agent Patricia Fenton. One of the most popular teams in the history of the Professional Hockey League (Central Division), the Marauders have a history dating back 75 years and a sizable, loyal fan base extending well beyond the state of Minnesota.

The owners of Legendary Experiences have developed a thoughtful business plan outlining the operation and growth of their new enterprise. They have adopted a business model that is flexible, scalable, and adaptable. It could be applied successfully on a local, regional, national, or international basis. The business could concentrate on a single team, sport, or league, or on a much broader scale based on the owners' connections, skills, expertise, and available resources.

Legendary Experiences will begin operations by focusing exclusively on the development of sports fan experience packages for fans of the Mountain Pointe Marauders. However, a national growth strategy has been developed which reflects the virtually unlimited and largely untapped potential of this new business. Because the owners' connections and knowledge are strongest in the sport of hockey, Legendary Experiences' growth strategy initially will concentrate on this sport in general, and the Professional Hockey League (18 teams in three regional divisions) in particular.

MARKET ANALYSIS

According to demographic data obtained from the firm, Clearview Analytics, the city's population included 405,623 people in 2015. As previously mentioned, Mountain Pointe's residents are among the most loyal, devoted fans in the Professional Hockey League—and with average household income of $81,823, many of them have the disposable income to spend on entertainment in general, and sports-related experiences in particular. When the Marauders won the national championship in 2014, an estimated 9,000 fans stood in line for their chance to see the Victory Cup at a local shopping mall, helping to drive total team merchandise sales of $42 million that year.

Beyond Mountain Pointe, the Professional Hockey League is very successful in all of the 18 markets in which it operates. For example, merchandise sales alone totaled $1.32 billion in 2015, and were projected to increase at a compound annual rate of 5.3 percent through the year 2020, according to the sports marketing research firm, Parker & Associates. Although sports history is a niche category, its popularity is evident by the fact that many professional sports teams (in all types of sports leagues) sell "classic" or "heritage" apparel and memorabilia.

By 2011 sports-related travel and tourism already had become a more than $7.68 billion business, according to a report from the National Association of Sports Commissioners. Although this figure includes individual and team travel for watching and/or participating in a variety of sporting activities, it also includes travel for nostalgic reasons, including visiting sports halls of fame, taking stadium tours, and participating in sports "fantasy" camps.

Target Markets

Legendary Experiences will market its services to both consumers (individuals and groups) and organizations.

Consumers

Legendary Experiences will market to individuals who may want to buy unforgettable experiences as gifts in conjunction with special occasions, or as a prize associated with a special event. Examples include:

- Anniversaries
- Birthdays
- Engagements
- Fundraisers
- Golf Outings
- Graduations
- Retirements
- Reunions
- Theme Parties

Organizations

Legendary Experiences also will market its offerings to organizations, which may wish to use unforgettable experiences as special awards, recognition gifts, incentives for salespeople, or in association with a themed event. Examples include:

- Award Ceremonies
- Business Dinners
- Conferences

- Conventions & Expos

- Networking Events

- Receptions

- Seminars

- Team-building Exercises

- Trade Shows

Based on data from Clearview Analytics, organizational prospects in Mountain Pointe break down as follows:

- Colleges & Universities (56 establishments)

- Large Companies (19 establishments)

- Mid-sized Companies (157 establishments)

- Hospitals (38 establishments)

- Health & Medical Services (1,935 establishments)

- Membership Organizations (1,134 establishments)

- Museums & Zoos (32 establishments)

- Churches & Religious Organizations (1,633 establishments)

Competition

Although many companies engage in specific aspects of what Legendary Experiences provides, the business' owners believe that their business model is somewhat unique, and that their historical/nostalgic focus serves as an important market differential.

Legendary Experiences' closest competitor is the emerging sports fan experience business, Fandeavor. Founded by former Zappos executives Tom Ellingson and Dean Curtis, Fandeavor also packages together unforgettable sports experiences for customers, including travel arrangements, game tickets, and special "behind the scenes" experiences like field access and meet-and-greets with coaches and players. However, its business model focuses on contemporary sports experiences, as opposed to the more nostalgic ones offered by Legendary Experiences.

SERVICES

Legendary Experiences helps customers dream of the ultimate nostalgic sports experience. Owners Jake Remington and Patricia Fenton then use their contacts to turn this dream into reality, handling every detail to create an experience for their customers that is unique, unforgettable, and in some cases, once-in-a-lifetime.

Because sports are a people business, the ideal sports fan experience varies from person to person and budget to budget. However, Legendary Experiences will include many of the following services/elements when creating an experience for customers:

- Scheduling/planning

- Site logistics

- Event booking

- Autographed memorabilia

- Box seats at professional sports events, allowing fans to watch modern-day games with yesterday's legends.

- Private "fantasy" clinics with retired players

- Private parties/dinners with legendary sports alumni

- Golf outings with former professional players

- Motivational speaking

- Special group events/parties

- Historical sports presentations/videos

- Stadium tours

- Sports hall of fame tours

- Trip/travel planning

- Photography

Due to the variability involved (including fees charged by former athletes), developing specific package fees in advance is virtually impossible. Legendary Experiences will work within the parameters of its customers' budget to create the very best experience possible. Based on conversations with potential business partners, the owners feel that they will be able to offer three general levels of sports fan experiences at the following levels:

- Bronze ($100-$350 per person)

- Silver ($200-$700 per person)

- Gold ($300-$1,050 per person)

Examples of a possible bronze-level experience could include dinner in a private room at Casey's Restaurant & Grill (a favorite Mountain Pointe Marauders hangout for more than 30 years) with legendary goaltender Lefty Nelson and Pete Stanton (who led the marauders to more wins than any other coach in team history). A silver level package could also include a private tour of Marauders Stadium with Nelson and Stanton. A gold level package could include all of the aforementioned things along with private box seats at a Marauders game with Nelson and Stanton and locker room access after the game, or a travel package to the Hockey Hall Of Fame in Toronto, Ontario, Canada.

Legendary Experiences provides customers with a detailed written agreement, summarizing everything provided as part of their package. Because travel and tourism experiences carry certain risks (for example, a former player is suddenly unavailable due to a health problem), Legendary Experiences will offer optional insurance to its customers. In all cases, Legendary Experiences will take every measure to ensure its customers' satisfaction.

OPERATIONS

Location

Legendary Experiences has leased office space in the Mountain Pointe Corporate Center, located in Mountain Pointe, Minnesota. The lease includes a small reception area, two private offices, a small kitchenette, phones with mobility/voicemail capabilities, and access to shared conference room space with videoconferencing. In addition, the facility provides room for future expansion if needed.

The owners will need to make several capital purchases, including two tablet computers, a portable projector, and a selection of office furniture. These start-up expenses will total approximately $10,000. An itemized list is available upon request.

PERSONNEL

Jake Remington, President

After earning an undergraduate degree in public relations, as well as an MBA in sports management, Jake Remington began a successful career in public relations with the Mountain Pointe Marauders. With a desire to establish his own business, Remington has parted ways with the team, but maintains excellent relationships with the owners and management. He will capitalize on his 18 years of experience with the Marauders, and his strong connections with the Mountain Pointe Marauders Alumni Association, to develop unforgettable sports experiences for the customers of Legendary Experiences.

Patricia Fenton, Executive Vice President

Patricia Fenton will benefit the business by drawing on her 21 years of experience as a travel agent to help Legendary Experiences developed unique travel and tourism packages for its customers when needed. In addition, Fenton also has more than a decade of small business ownership experience, which she will use to benefit the operational aspects of Legendary Experiences.

GROWTH STRATEGY

Legendary Experiences will begin operations by developing sports fan experience packages exclusively for fans of the Mountain Pointe Marauders. However, the owners have developed a thoughtful national growth strategy that reflects the virtually unlimited and largely untapped potential of this new business. Because the owners' connections and knowledge are strongest in the sport of hockey, Legendary Experiences' growth strategy initially will concentrate on this sport in general, and the Professional Hockey League (18 teams in three regional divisions) in particular.

The key to a successful sports fan experience business is developing partnerships and building relationships with a variety of constituents. In the case of Legendary Experiences, these include:

- Former Professional Athletes
- Hotels
- Player Agents/Representatives
- Restaurants
- Speakers Bureaus
- Sports Alumni Associations
- Sports Halls of Fame
- Sports Teams
- Tourist Attractions

During its first five years of operations, Legendary Experiences' growth strategy is as follows:

Year One: Begin operations with owners' capital of $50,000. Focus on building awareness about Legendary Experiences among fans of the Mountain Pointe Marauders and developing unique sports fan experience packages. Maintain and strengthen existing relationships with members of the Mountain Pointe Marauders Alumni Association, as well as the Mountain Pointe Marauders Professional Hockey Team Inc.

Year Two: Continue to build awareness about Legendary Experiences among fans of the Mountain Pointe Marauders. Increase gross profits by 30 percent. Continue to maintain and strengthen existing relationships with members of the Mountain Pointe Marauders Alumni Association, as well as the Mountain Pointe Marauders Professional Hockey Team. Make initial contacts with all other Professional Hockey League clubs and their respective alumni associations, and begin relationship building activities with the five remaining Central Division teams.

Year Three: Secure $100,000 in venture capital funding. Hire a Director of New Business Development, Central Region. Begin marketing and offering sports fan experience packages for all Central Division Professional Hockey League teams. Begin relationship building activities with all six Eastern Division teams.

Year Four: Secure $100,000 in additional venture capital funding. Hire a Director of New Business Development, Eastern Region. Begin marketing and offering sports fan experience packages for all Eastern Division Professional Hockey League teams. Begin relationship building activities with all six Western Division teams.

Year Five: Secure $100,000 in additional venture capital funding. Hire a Director of New Business Development, Western Region. Begin marketing and offering sports fan experience packages for all Western Division Professional Hockey League teams. Initiate strategic planning process focused on the expansion into the second sport of football and restructuring into a two-division format (Professional Hockey and Professional Football). Hire a new VP-level executive with extensive connections in professional football to oversee the new division and its growth and development beginning in year six.

MARKETING & SALES

The following marketing plan has been developed for Legendary Experiences.

1. **Social Media:** The business will rely heavily upon LinkedIn, Facebook, Instagram, and Twitter to promote its offerings to prospective customers. In addition to engaging with customers through these channels, the business also will pursue highly targeted advertising opportunities to reach sports fans. For example, customers can be identified by geography, and also their affinity for the Mountain Pointe (whether or not they live in the Mountain Pointe area).

2. **Public/Media Relations:** A major emphasis will be placed upon securing free publicity from the news media. When clients are agreeable, we will submit occasional customer stories to television stations and newspapers in the Mountain Pointe market.

3. **Web Site:** Legendary Experiences will develop a Web site with complete details about the business and the services it offers, including customer photos, video clips, testimonials, and contact information.

4. **Brochure:** A four-color brochure will be developed that can be used in conjunction with direct marketing efforts, and also for promotions at Marauders Stadium and other venues.

5. **Advertising:** The business will be a regular advertiser in game programs at Marauders Stadium, on the Mountain Pointe Marauders' Web site, and in *Minnesota Hockey Weekly* (a free newspaper that is distributed at hockey rinks throughout the state of Minnesota).

6. **Sales Promotion:** Each month, the owners will make at least four lunch presentations to local organizations promoting Legendary Experiences, in an effort to secure corporate business.

7. **Direct Marketing:** Legendary Experiences has made arrangements to conduct several direct marketing initiatives. These include a semi-annual mailing to Mountain Pointe Marauders season-ticket holders, as well as semi-annual mailings to members of the Mountain Pointe Marauders Fan Club and subscribers to *Minnesota Hockey Weekly*. Arrangements have been made with a local mail house to prepare and execute the mailings.

FINANCIAL ANALYSIS

The owners of Legendary Experiences have conducted extensive market research to determine the potential of the new business. Based on a survey of local sports fans and a series of focus groups (both of which were done in partnership with a local business professor), the following package levels have been developed:

- Bronze ($200-$450 per person)

- Silver ($450-$900 per person)

- Gold ($900-$1,250 per person)

The owners estimate that, on average, packages will generate per-unit revenue as follows:

- Bronze ($325)

- Silver ($675)

- Gold ($1,075)

Legendary Experiences anticipates that its gross profit margin, after factoring in the cost of goods sold, will be 25 percent, resulting in projected gross revenue of $164,250 during the first year of operations. On average, the owners anticipate that gross profits will increase by approximately $150,000 each time the company enters a new geographic market, and that sales in that market well increase by about 30 percent the second year, followed by increases of 20 percent, 15 percent, and 10 percent during the third, fourth, and fifth years, respectively, as market potential is maximized. Considering the growth strategy outlined in this plan, gross profits are projected as follows for the first five years of operations:

- 2016: $164,250

- 2017: $213,525

- 2018: $406,230

- 2019: $639,665

- 2020: $903,131

A detailed breakdown of projected expenses (including salaries, taxes, office lease, etc.) is available upon request. However, the owners anticipate that expenses will account for 75 percent of gross profits, resulting in net annual profits as follows:

- 2016: $41,063

- 2017: $53,381

- 2018: $101,558

- 2019: $159,916

- 2020: $225,783

Video Game Testing Services Provider

Game Development Solutions Inc.

2938 Campus Drive, 858A
Rainier, TX 55512

Paul Greenland

Game Development Solutions Inc. is a newly established provider of video game testing solutions.

EXECUTIVE SUMMARY

Video games are a key component of the global entertainment industry. Worldwide, gaming-related revenues were expected to reach $91.5 billion in 2015, according to the research firm, Newzoo, which specializes in the gaming market. Video game developers have long used individuals to perform testing on both new and existing games, in order to discover flaws and make related improvements and enhancements.

Based in Rainier, Texas, Game Development Solutions Inc. is a newly established provider of video game testing solutions. The business is the brainchild of Garrett Hansen, a recent graduate of Lone Star Technical Institute. Hansen worked his way through college as an independent video game tester, gaining valuable experience and developing professional relationships while earning his bachelor's degree in computer science.

Although his long-term plan was to find work as a software developer, Hansen discovered that he has a strong entrepreneurial spirit and a desire to work independently. For this reason, he decided to establish his own testing services firm. Using a staff of independent contractors (undergraduate computer science students), Game Development Solutions will differentiate itself in the market by providing video game developers with pre-qualified testers with specialized capabilities (many independent testers are unskilled) on a per-project basis.

Opportunities for video game testing are greatest in cities where there are large concentrations of technology firms. More than 75 technology companies that engage in video game development have operations in Rainier, Texas. These include leaders such as Atari and Nintendo, as well as many smaller and mid-sized start-ups. Within this promising market, Game Development Solutions expects to become profitable during its second year of operations.

INDUSTRY ANALYSIS

Video games are a key component of the global entertainment industry. Worldwide, gaming-related revenues were expected to reach $91.5 billion in 2015, according to the research firm, Newzoo, which specializes in the gaming market. This represented a 9.5 percent increase from 2014. Moving forward, revenues were expected to total $107 billion by 2017. In the United States, specifically, the video game market was growing at a compound annual rate of 5.5 percent, according to the accounting firm, PwC. From $15 billion in 2014, revenues were projected to reach $19.6 billion by 2019.

Video game developers have long used individuals to perform testing on both new and existing games, in order to discover flaws and make related improvements and enhancements. Many developers utilize independent contractors for this task, providing them with three to six months of work at a time. Although a college degree typically is not required (many independent testers are unskilled), companies look for individuals who not only are passionate and knowledgeable about video games, but who are patient, analytical, professional, and have good communication skills. Testers who do a good job usually will be hired for other projects, and in some cases, regular employment.

Video game developers hire testers directly, and also through employment agencies. Although video game testing provides opportunities for individuals to get paid for playing games and being part of the development process, opportunities for advancement are limited. Entry-level testers often make between $8 and $10 per hour, while more experienced testers command hourly rates that are closer to $20 per hour. Although some testing opportunities are offered on a work-from-home basis, testers usually are required to work on-site. Therefore, opportunities are greatest in cities where there are large concentrations of technology firms, such as Silicon Valley.

MARKET ANALYSIS

Because so many new video games are developed every year, across multiple platforms, there is a strong market for video game testers—especially in cities that are major technology hubs, and for testers with the type of advanced skills that Game Development Solutions will provide.

More than 75 technology companies that engage in video game development have operations in Rainier, Texas, including leading companies like Atari, Sierra Entertainment, Broderbund, Capcom, EA, Epic Games, Konami, Microsoft, Midway, Namco, Nintendo, Sierra Entertainment, and Westwood Studios, as well as many smaller and mid-sized start-ups.

A healthy amount of venture capital flows into the local market on a regular basis, ensuring continued innovation and development. Rainier's local video game developers offer considerable variety in the types and categories of games they produce, including arcade, PC/Mac, casino, social, mobile, and console games. Collectively, these firms employed roughly about 27,000 people in 2016.

An analysis conducted by Dr. Stephen Ridgway and the Lone Star Technical Institute revealed that local game development breaks down by category as follows:

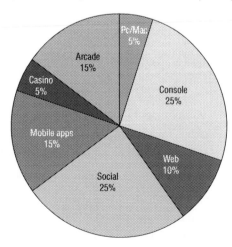

SERVICES

Game Development Solutions will provide testing for many different types of games and platforms, including:

- Arcade
- Console-Based Games (Xbox, Playstation, Wii, etc.)
- Web Applications
- Social Games
- Mobile Apps/Games (Android, iOS, Windows Phone, etc.)
- Client/Server-Based Games

The business will provide several different types of testing, such as:

1. Functionality testing: Assessing the features of games based on design specifications.
2. Regression testing: Ensuring that previously identified problems have been corrected by programmers.
3. Open testing: Free-form gameplay to assess overall playability.

Game Development Solutions' testers will perform a variety of specific tasks, including:

- Helping to develop test plans
- Identifying and tracking bugs, defects, and inconsistencies
- Maintaining database of bugs
- Performing crash analyses
- Producing documentation/standardized reports
- Providing developers/engineers with regular feedback
- Testing new game features
- Verifying externally identified bugs
- Verifying video game functionality, features, and performance

Game Development Solutions' testers will have experience with a variety of analysis and testing tools, such as:

- Android DMS
- Bugzilla
- Mantis
- Trac
- VS Debugger
- Xcode Instruments

The testers hired by Game Development Solutions will be evaluated for the skills, attributes, and capabilities that are essential for success in this profession, including:

- Analytical Thinking
- Goal/Deadline-Focused
- Multi-Tasking

- Passion for Gaming
- Problem-Solving
- Written/Verbal Communication

Because its independent contractors will be among the very best students in undergraduate computer science programs, Game Development Solutions will differentiate itself by providing its customers with testers whose capabilities are more advanced and specialized than ordinary testers. The majority of the company's contractors will be able to function near the level of a software development engineer, test (SDET), meaning that they will have the ability to actually work with the code that is used to create the video games being tested. Most will have skills with test automation and programming languages such as C, C++, .Net, Microsoft SQ Server, and Java.

OPERATIONS

Location

In order to keep overhead low, Game Development Solutions will operate from a home office during the first several years of operations. Garrett Hansen has devoted space within his home to be used specifically for business purposes. Although some business travel may be necessary, Hansen typically will conduct Web-based meetings with clients who require him to communicate with offices in other states or countries.

Process

Garrett Hansen will serve as the face of Game Development Solutions to customers and will take a consistent approach to every project. Specifically, he will begin by defining project objectives and expectations in as much detail as possible. This will enable him to identify the specific testing resources (e.g., skills, availability, etc.) needed for every project. Once objectives and timeframes have been clearly identified, Hansen will provide clients with a written agreement that details the scope of work to be performed.

PERSONNEL

Garrett Hanson, President

Game Development Solutions is the brainchild of Garrett Hansen, a recent graduate of Lone Star Technical Institute. Hansen worked his way through college as a video game tester. This allowed him to gain valuable experience and develop professional relationships while earning his bachelor's degree in computer science. Many of Hansen's classes were scheduled in the evening or taken online, providing him with the ability to maximize his availability during regular business hours. While working as a tester, many of Hansen's employers looked to him for referrals when other testers were needed. Hansen began to recognize that many of his employers were in search of testers with specialized expertise that unskilled testers simply could not provide.

Because of his strong connections at Lone Star Technical Institute, Hansen usually was able to connect his employers with students whose skill sets were a perfect match. Although his long-term plan was to find work as a software developer, Hansen discovered that he has a strong entrepreneurial spirit, and a desire to work independently. For this reason, he has established his own video game testing services firm. As the president of Game Development Solutions, Hansen will focus on maintaining and building relationships with area technology firms, and also recruiting and screening prospective video game testers from the local college community.

Dr. Stephen Ridgway, Vice President

Hansen will work alongside Dr. Stephen Ridgway, a computer science professor at Lone Star Technical Institute who will join the company as a minority stakeholder and advisor. Dr. Ridgway sits on the boards of several technology firms and video game development companies, which will benefit Game Development Solutions' efforts to develop new business.

Testers

Game Development Solutions will develop and maintain a staff of independent contractors to serve its clients. This will enable the business to maintain a continuous pool of fresh, top IT talent without the expense of maintaining actual employees. Dr. Ridgway will benefit Game Development Solutions by maintaining a pipeline to top student workers at Lone Star Technical Institute. Game Development Solutions will begin operations with a staff of five testers during its first year. Based on growth projections, it is anticipated that an additional five testers will be needed in both years two and three.

Working in partnership with Dr. Ridgway, the business has selected a set of assessment tools that will be used to pre-screened/pre-qualify all of its independent contractors, assuring that they possess a minimum foundation of knowledge and skill. In addition, other tools will be used to assess contractors in specific/specialized skill areas. Results of these assessments will be provided to clients upon request, giving them peace of mind that the contractor is qualified for a particular assignment.

In addition to providing skilled testers on a per-project basis, Game Development Solutions also will be an attractive option for clients, because it will provide them with an opportunity to work with top IT students who eventually could transition into regular full-time employment as software developers and engineers after graduation.

Projected Independent Contract Labor Costs

Year	January	February	March	April	May	June
2016	$10,820	$ 5,826	$ 4,162	$2,497	$2,081	$2,081
2017	$21,640	$11,652	$ 8,323	$4,994	$4,162	$4,162
2018	$32,460	$17,479	$12,485	$7,491	$6,242	$6,242

	July	August	September	October	November	December	Total
2016	$2,081	$2,081	$ 8,323	$12,485	$16,646	$21,557	**$108,766**
2017	$4,162	$4,162	$16,646	$24,969	$33,292	$43,114	**$217,532**
2018	$6,242	$6,242	$24,969	$37,454	$49,939	$64,670	**$326,299**

Professional & Advisory Support

Because video game development is a highly competitive industry, Game Development Solutions has retained a law firm with experience in intellectual property and technology. The firm has provided Game Development Solutions with general and specialized boilerplate agreements (non-disclosure, non-compete, etc.) that can be used with its independent contractors and customers. This same firm can provide adequate representation in the event that counsel is needed. In addition, Game Development Solutions has established a business banking account with Central Community Bank, as well as a merchant account for accepting credit card payments.

GROWTH STRATEGY

Game Development Solutions has prepared the following growth strategy for its first three years of operations:

Year One: Generate gross revenues of $190,341 and sustain a projected net loss of $18,775. Focus on developing relationships with developers and software engineers within the local market, capitalizing on

Dr. Stephen Ridgway's relationships within the technology community. Begin operations with a staff of five independent contractors.

Year Two: Generate gross revenues of $380,682 and break even after achieving a net profit of $24,200. Double testing capacity via the addition of five independent contractors. Begin utilizing a part-time virtual assistant service to help with project scheduling and coordination.

Year Three: Generate gross revenues of $571,023 and a net profit of $72,174. Continue to expand testing capacity through the addition of another five independent contractors. Expand the use of the virtual assistant service to provide additional administrative support. Establish growth targets for the next three years of the business. Identify physical office space to lease beginning in year four.

The following table provides a detailed overview of Game Development Solutions' projected billable testing hours for the first three years of operations:

Year	January	February	March	April	May	June
2016	541	291	208	125	104	104
2017	1,082	583	416	250	208	208
2018	1,623	874	624	375	312	312

	July	August	September	October	November	December	Total
2016	104	104	416	624	832	1,078	**5,438**
2017	208	208	832	1,248	1,665	2,156	**10,877**
2018	312	312	1,248	1,873	2,497	3,234	**16,315**

MARKETING & SALES

Game Development Solutions will grow the business by employing the following marketing tactics:

1. A Web site promoting Game Development Solutions' testing capabilities. The site will include bios of Garrett Hansen and Dr. Stephen Ridgway, case study examples of successful testing projects, testimonials, and links to social media channels including Facebook and Twitter.

2. Search engine optimization (SEO). Game Development Solutions will continuously monitor and modify its site to ensure top placement in results for leading search engines.

3. A word-of-mouth marketing strategy that will place a heavy emphasis on networking with developers and software engineers at video game publishers. In particular, the business will leverage and capitalize on Dr. Stephen Ridgway's contacts with area technology firms—especially during its formative years.

4. A media relations strategy that will involve the submitting case studies to technology trade publications, such as *Computerworld* and *InformationWeek*.

5. Attendance at leading industry trade shows and seminars. In addition to networking opportunities, Garrett Hansen and Dr. Stephen Ridgway will make presentations to key industry players regarding video game testing best practices.

FINANCIAL ANALYSIS

The following projections have been prepared in cooperation with Game Development Solutions' accountant. A complete set of pro forma financials are available upon request.

Gross Revenue Projections

Year	January	February	March	April	May	June	
2016	$18,935	$10,196	$ 7,283	$ 4,370	$ 3,641	$ 3,641	
2017	$37,870	$20,392	$14,565	$ 8,739	$ 7,283	$ 7,283	
2018	$56,805	$30,587	$21,848	$13,109	$10,924	$10,924	

Year	July	August	September	October	November	December	Total
2016	$ 3,641	$ 3,641	$14,565	$21,848	$29,131	$ 37,724	**$190,341**
2017	$ 7,283	$ 7,283	$29,131	$43,696	$58,262	$ 75,449	**$380,682**
2018	$10,924	$10,924	$43,696	$65,544	$87,393	$113,173	**$571,023**

Gross revenue

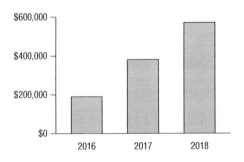

Projected Revenue & Expenses

Revenue	2016	2017	2018
Projected gross revenue	$190,341	$380,682	$571,023
Independent contractor labor	($108,766)	($217,532)	($326,299)
Adjusted gross revenue	$ 81,575	$163,150	$244,724
Expenses			
Ridgway investments	$ 9,500	$ 19,000	$ 28,500
Salary	$ 70,000	$ 80,000	$ 90,000
Payroll tax	$ 10,500	$ 12,000	$ 13,500
Virtual assistant	$ 0	$ 15,000	$ 25,000
Insurance	$ 750	$ 800	$ 850
Accounting & legal	$ 1,500	$ 1,500	$ 1,500
Office supplies	$ 450	$ 450	$ 450
Equipment	$ 1,000	$ 1,000	$ 1,000
Marketing & advertising	$ 5,000	$ 7,500	$ 10,000
Telecommunications & Internet	$ 1,000	$ 1,000	$ 1,000
Subscriptions & dues	$ 150	$ 200	$ 250
Misc.	$ 500	$ 500	$ 500
Total expenses	**$100,350**	**$138,950**	**$172,550**
Net income	**($ 18,775)**	**$ 24,200**	**$ 72,174**

Startup Capital

Game Development Solutions will begin operations with capital of $50,000, provided by Dr. Stephen Ridgway (Ridgway Investments) in exchange for a five percent ownership stake in the business.

BUSINESS PLAN TEMPLATE

USING THIS TEMPLATE

A business plan carefully spells out a company's projected course of action over a period of time, usually the first two to three years after the start-up. In addition, banks, lenders, and other investors examine the information and financial documentation before deciding whether or not to finance a new business venture. Therefore, a business plan is an essential tool in obtaining financing and should describe the business itself in detail as well as all important factors influencing the company, including the market, industry, competition, operations and management policies, problem solving strategies, financial resources and needs, and other vital information. The plan enables the business owner to anticipate costs, plan for difficulties, and take advantage of opportunities, as well as design and implement strategies that keep the company running as smoothly as possible.

This template has been provided as a model to help you construct your own business plan. Please keep in mind that there is no single acceptable format for a business plan, and that this template is in no way comprehensive, but serves as an example.

The business plans provided in this section are fictional and have been used by small business agencies as models for clients to use in compiling their own business plans.

GENERIC BUSINESS PLAN

Main headings included below are topics that should be covered in a comprehensive business plan. They include:

Business Summary

Purpose
Provides a brief overview of your business, succinctly highlighting the main ideas of your plan.

Includes

- Name and Type of Business
- Description of Product/Service
- Business History and Development
- Location
- Market
- Competition
- Management
- Financial Information
- Business Strengths and Weaknesses
- Business Growth

Table of Contents

Purpose
Organized in an Outline Format, the Table of Contents illustrates the selection and arrangement of information contained in your plan.

Includes

- Topic Headings and Subheadings
- Page Number References

Business History and Industry Outlook

Purpose

Examines the conception and subsequent development of your business within an industry specific context.

Includes

- Start-up Information
- Owner/Key Personnel Experience
- Location
- Development Problems and Solutions
- Investment/Funding Information
- Future Plans and Goals
- Market Trends and Statistics
- Major Competitors
- Product/Service Advantages
- National, Regional, and Local Economic Impact

Product/Service

Purpose

Introduces, defines, and details the product and/or service that inspired the information of your business.

Includes

- Unique Features
- Niche Served
- Market Comparison
- Stage of Product/Service Development
- Production
- Facilities, Equipment, and Labor
- Financial Requirements
- Product/Service Life Cycle
- Future Growth

Market Examination

Purpose

Assessment of product/service applications in relation to consumer buying cycles.

Includes

- Target Market
- Consumer Buying Habits
- Product/Service Applications
- Consumer Reactions
- Market Factors and Trends
- Penetration of the Market
- Market Share
- Research and Studies
- Cost
- Sales Volume and Goals

Competition

Purpose

Analysis of Competitors in the Marketplace.

Includes

- Competitor Information
- Product/Service Comparison
- Market Niche
- Product/Service Strengths and Weaknesses
- Future Product/Service Development

Marketing

Purpose

Identifies promotion and sales strategies for your product/service.

Includes

- Product/Service Sales Appeal
- Special and Unique Features
- Identification of Customers
- Sales and Marketing Staff
- Sales Cycles
- Type of Advertising/ Promotion
- Pricing
- Competition
- Customer Services

Operations

Purpose

Traces product/service development from production/inception to the market environment.

Includes

- Cost Effective Production Methods
- Facility
- Location
- Equipment
- Labor
- Future Expansion

Administration and Management

Purpose

Offers a statement of your management philosophy with an in-depth focus on processes and procedures.

Includes

- Management Philosophy
- Structure of Organization
- Reporting System
- Methods of Communication
- Employee Skills and Training
- Employee Needs and Compensation
- Work Environment
- Management Policies and Procedures
- Roles and Responsibilities

Key Personnel

Purpose

Describes the unique backgrounds of principle employees involved in business.

Includes

- Owner(s)/Employee Education and Experience
- Positions and Roles
- Benefits and Salary
- Duties and Responsibilities
- Objectives and Goals

Potential Problems and Solutions

Purpose

Discussion of problem solving strategies that change issues into opportunities.

Includes

- Risks
- Litigation
- Future Competition
- Economic Impact
- Problem Solving Skills

Financial Information

Purpose

Secures needed funding and assistance through worksheets and projections detailing financial plans, methods of repayment, and future growth opportunities.

Includes

- Financial Statements
- Bank Loans
- Methods of Repayment
- Tax Returns
- Start-up Costs
- Projected Income (3 years)
- Projected Cash Flow (3 Years)
- Projected Balance Statements (3 years)

Appendices

Purpose

Supporting documents used to enhance your business proposal.

Includes

- Photographs of product, equipment, facilities, etc.
- Copyright/Trademark Documents
- Legal Agreements
- Marketing Materials
- Research and or Studies
- Operation Schedules
- Organizational Charts
- Job Descriptions
- Resumes
- Additional Financial Documentation

Fictional Food Distributor

Commercial Foods, Inc.

3003 Avondale Ave.
Knoxville, TN 37920

This plan demonstrates how a partnership can have a positive impact on a new business. It demonstrates how two individuals can carve a niche in the specialty foods market by offering gourmet foods to upscale restaurants and fine hotels. This plan is fictional and has not been used to gain funding from a bank or other lending institution.

STATEMENT OF PURPOSE

Commercial Foods, Inc. seeks a loan of $75,000 to establish a new business. This sum, together with $5,000 equity investment by the principals, will be used as follows:

- Merchandise inventory $25,000
- Office fixture/equipment $12,000
- Warehouse equipment $14,000
- One delivery truck $10,000
- Working capital $39,000
- Total $100,000

DESCRIPTION OF THE BUSINESS

Commercial Foods, Inc. will be a distributor of specialty food service products to hotels and upscale restaurants in the geographical area of a 50 mile radius of Knoxville. Richard Roberts will direct the sales effort and John Williams will manage the warehouse operation and the office. One delivery truck will be used initially with a second truck added in the third year. We expect to begin operation of the business within 30 days after securing the requested financing.

MANAGEMENT

A. Richard Roberts is a native of Memphis, Tennessee. He is a graduate of Memphis State University with a Bachelor's degree from the School of Business. After graduation, he worked for a major manufacturer of specialty food service products as a detail sales person for five years, and, for the past three years, he has served as a product sales manager for this firm.

B. John Williams is a native of Nashville, Tennessee. He holds a B.S. Degree in Food Technology from the University of Tennessee. His career includes five years as a product development chemist in gourmet food products and five years as operations manager for a food service distributor.

Both men are healthy and energetic. Their backgrounds complement each other, which will ensure the success of Commercial Foods, Inc. They will set policies together and personnel decisions will be made jointly. Initial salaries for the owners will be $1,000 per month for the first few years. The spouses of both principals are successful in the business world and earn enough to support the families.

They have engaged the services of Foster Jones, CPA, and William Hale, Attorney, to assist them in an advisory capacity.

PERSONNEL

The firm will employ one delivery truck driver at a wage of $8.00 per hour. One office worker will be employed at $7.50 per hour. One part-time employee will be used in the office at $5.00 per hour. The driver will load and unload his own trucks. Mr. Williams will assist in the warehouse operation as needed to assist one stock person at $7.00 per hour. An additional delivery truck and driver will be added the third year.

LOCATION

The firm will lease a 20,000 square foot building at 3003 Avondale Ave., in Knoxville, which contains warehouse and office areas equipped with two-door truck docks. The annual rental is $9,000. The building was previously used as a food service warehouse and very little modification to the building will be required.

PRODUCTS AND SERVICES

The firm will offer specialty food service products such as soup bases, dessert mixes, sauce bases, pastry mixes, spices, and flavors, normally used by upscale restaurants and nice hotels. We are going after a niche in the market with high quality gourmet products. There is much less competition in this market than in standard run of the mill food service products. Through their work experiences, the principals have contacts with supply sources and with local chefs.

THE MARKET

We know from our market survey that there are over 200 hotels and upscale restaurants in the area we plan to serve. Customers will be attracted by a direct sales approach. We will offer samples of our products and product application data on use of our products in the finished prepared foods. We will cultivate the chefs in these establishments. The technical background of John Williams will be especially useful here.

COMPETITION

We find that we will be only distributor in the area offering a full line of gourmet food service products. Other foodservice distributors offer only a few such items in conjunction with their standard product line. Our survey shows that many of the chefs are ordering products from Atlanta and Memphis because of a lack of adequate local supply.

SUMMARY

Commercial Foods, Inc. will be established as a foodservice distributor of specialty food in Knoxville. The principals, with excellent experience in the industry, are seeking a $75,000 loan to establish the business. The principals are investing $25,000 as equity capital.

The business will be set up as an S Corporation with each principal owning 50% of the common stock in the corporation.

FICTIONAL HARDWARE STORE

OSHKOSH HARDWARE, INC.

123 Main St.
Oshkosh, WI 54901

The following plan outlines how a small hardware store can survive competition from large discount chains by offering products and providing expert advice in the use of any product it sells. This plan is fictional and has not been used to gain funding from a bank or other lending institution.

EXECUTIVE SUMMARY

Oshkosh Hardware, Inc. is a new corporation that is going to establish a retail hardware store in a strip mall in Oshkosh, Wisconsin. The store will sell hardware of all kinds, quality tools, paint, and housewares. The business will make revenue and a profit by servicing its customers not only with needed hardware but also with expert advice in the use of any product it sells.

Oshkosh Hardware, Inc. will be operated by its sole shareholder, James Smith. The company will have a total of four employees. It will sell its products in the local market. Customers will buy our products because we will provide free advice on the use of all of our products and will also furnish a full refund warranty.

Oshkosh Hardware, Inc. will sell its products in the Oshkosh store staffed by three sales representatives. No additional employees will be needed to achieve its short and long range goals. The primary short range goal is to open the store by October 1, 1994. In order to achieve this goal a lease must be signed by July 1, 1994 and the complete inventory ordered by August 1, 1994.

Mr. James Smith will invest $30,000 in the business. In addition, the company will have to borrow $150,000 during the first year to cover the investment in inventory, accounts receivable, and furniture and equipment. The company will be profitable after six months of operation and should be able to start repayment of the loan in the second year.

THE BUSINESS

The business will sell hardware of all kinds, quality tools, paint, and housewares. We will purchase our products from three large wholesale buying groups.

In general our customers are homeowners who do their own repair and maintenance, hobbyists, and housewives. Our business is unique in that we will have a complete line of all hardware items and will be able to get special orders by overnight delivery. The business makes revenue and profits by servicing our customers not only with needed hardware but also with expert advice in the use of any product we sell. Our major costs for bringing our products to market are cost of merchandise of 36%, salaries of $45,000, and occupancy costs of $60,000.

173

Oshkosh Hardware, Inc.'s retail outlet will be located at 1524 Frontage Road, which is in a newly developed retail center of Oshkosh. Our location helps facilitate accessibility from all parts of town and reduces our delivery costs. The store will occupy 7500 square feet of space. The major equipment involved in our business is counters and shelving, a computer, a paint mixing machine, and a truck.

THE MARKET

Oshkosh Hardware, Inc. will operate in the local market. There are 15,000 potential customers in this market area. We have three competitors who control approximately 98% of the market at present. We feel we can capture 25% of the market within the next four years. Our major reason for believing this is that our staff is technically competent to advise our customers in the correct use of all products we sell.

After a careful market analysis, we have determined that approximately 60% of our customers are men and 40% are women. The percentage of customers that fall into the following age categories are:

Under 16: 0%
17-21: 5%
22-30: 30%
31-40: 30%
41-50: 20%
51-60: 10%
61-70: 5%
Over 70: 0%

The reasons our customers prefer our products is our complete knowledge of their use and our full refund warranty.

We get our information about what products our customers want by talking to existing customers. There seems to be an increasing demand for our product. The demand for our product is increasing in size based on the change in population characteristics.

SALES

At Oshkosh Hardware, Inc. we will employ three sales people and will not need any additional personnel to achieve our sales goals. These salespeople will need several years experience in home repair and power tool usage. We expect to attract 30% of our customers from newspaper ads, 5% of our customers from local directories, 5% of our customers from the yellow pages, 10% of our customers from family and friends, and 50% of our customers from current customers. The most cost effect source will be current customers. In general our industry is growing.

MANAGEMENT

We would evaluate the quality of our management staff as being excellent. Our manager is experienced and very motivated to achieve the various sales and quality assurance objectives we have set. We will use a management information system that produces key inventory, quality assurance, and sales data on a weekly basis. All data is compared to previously established goals for that week, and deviations are the primary focus of the management staff.

GOALS IMPLEMENTATION

The short term goals of our business are:

1. Open the store by October 1, 1994
2. Reach our breakeven point in two months
3. Have sales of $100,000 in the first six months

In order to achieve our first short term goal we must:

1. Sign the lease by July 1, 1994
2. Order a complete inventory by August 1, 1994

In order to achieve our second short term goal we must:

1. Advertise extensively in Sept. and Oct.
2. Keep expenses to a minimum

In order to achieve our third short term goal we must:

1. Promote power tool sales for the Christmas season
2. Keep good customer traffic in Jan. and Feb.

The long term goals for our business are:

1. Obtain sales volume of $600,000 in three years
2. Become the largest hardware dealer in the city
3. Open a second store in Fond du Lac

The most important thing we must do in order to achieve the long term goals for our business is to develop a highly profitable business with excellent cash flow.

FINANCE

Oshkosh Hardware, Inc. Faces some potential threats or risks to our business. They are discount house competition. We believe we can avoid or compensate for this by providing quality products complimented by quality advice on the use of every product we sell. The financial projections we have prepared are located at the end of this document.

JOB DESCRIPTION-GENERAL MANAGER

The General Manager of the business of the corporation will be the president of the corporation. He will be responsible for the complete operation of the retail hardware store which is owned by the corporation. A detailed description of his duties and responsibilities is as follows.

Sales

Train and supervise the three sales people. Develop programs to motivate and compensate these employees. Coordinate advertising and sales promotion effects to achieve sales totals as outlined in budget. Oversee purchasing function and inventory control procedures to insure adequate merchandise at all times at a reasonable cost.

Finance

Prepare monthly and annual budgets. Secure adequate line of credit from local banks. Supervise office personnel to insure timely preparation of records, statements, all government reports, control of receivables and payables, and monthly financial statements.

Administration

Perform duties as required in the areas of personnel, building leasing and maintenance, licenses and permits, and public relations.

Organizations, Agencies, & Consultants

A listing of Associations and Consultants of interest to entrepreneurs, followed by the Small Business Administration Regional Offices, Small Business Development Centers, Service Corps of Retired Executives offices, and Venture Capital and Finance Companies.

Associations

This section contains a listing of associations and other agencies of interest to the small business owner. Entries are listed alphabetically by organization name.

American Business Women's Association
9100 Ward Pkwy.
PO Box 8728
Kansas City, MO 64114-0728
(800)228-0007
E-mail: abwa@abwa.org
Website: http://www.abwa.org
Jeanne Banks, National President

American Franchisee Association
53 W Jackson Blvd., Ste. 1157
Chicago, IL 60604
(312)431-0545
E-mail: info@franchisee.org
Website: http://www.franchisee.org
Susan P. Kezios, President

American Independent Business Alliance
222 S Black Ave.
Bozeman, MT 59715
(406)582-1255
E-mail: info@amiba.net
Website: http://www.amiba.net
Jennifer Rockne, Director

American Small Businesses Association
206 E College St., Ste. 201
Grapevine, TX 76051
800-942-2722
E-mail: info@asbaonline.org
Website: http://www.asbaonline.org/

American Women's Economic Development Corporation
216 East 45th St., 10th Floor
New York, NY 10017

(917)368-6100
Fax: (212)986-7114
E-mail: info@awed.org
Website: http://www.awed.org
Roseanne Antonucci, Exec. Dir.

Association for Enterprise Opportunity
1601 N Kent St., Ste. 1101
Arlington, VA 22209
(703)841-7760
Fax: (703)841-7748
E-mail: aeo@assoceo.org
Website: http://www.microenterprise
works.org
Bill Edwards, Exec.Dir.

Association of Small Business Development Centers
c/o Don Wilson
8990 Burke Lake Rd.
Burke, VA 22015
(703)764-9850
Fax: (703)764-1234
E-mail: info@asbdc-us.org
Website: http://www.asbdc-us.org
Don Wilson, Pres./CEO

BEST Employers Association
2505 McCabe Way
Irvine, CA 92614
(949)253-4080
800-433-0088
Fax: (714)553-0883
E-mail: info@bestlife.com
Website: http://www.bestlife.com
Donald R. Lawrenz, CEO

Center for Family Business
PO Box 24219
Cleveland, OH 44124
(440)460-5409
E-mail: grummi@aol.com
Dr. Leon A. Danco, Chm.

Coalition for Government Procurement
1990 M St. NW, Ste. 400
Washington, DC 20036
(202)331-0975
E-mail: info@thecgp.org
Website: http://www.coalgovpro.org
Paul Caggiano, Pres.

Employers of America
PO Box 1874
Mason City, IA 50402-1874
(641)424-3187
800-728-3187
Fax: (641)424-1673
E-mail: employer@employerhelp.org
Website: http://www.employerhelp.org
Jim Collison, Pres.

Family Firm Institute
200 Lincoln St., Ste. 201
Boston, MA 02111
(617)482-3045
Fax: (617)482-3049
E-mail: ffi@ffi.org
Website: http://www.ffi.org
Judy L. Green, Ph.D., Exec.Dir.

Independent Visually Impaired Enterprisers
500 S 3rd St., Apt. H
Burbank, CA 91502
(818)238-9321
E-mail: abazyn@bazyncommunications
.com
Website: http://www.acb.org/affiliates
Adris Bazyn, Pres.

International Association for Business Organizations
3 Woodthorn Ct., Ste. 12
Owings Mills, MD 21117
(410)581-1373
E-mail: nahbb@msn.com
Rudolph Lewis, Exec. Officer

177

ORGANIZATIONS, AGENCIES, & CONSULTANTS

International Council for Small Business
The George Washington University
School of Business and Public
Management
2115 G St. NW, Ste. 403
Washington, DC 20052
(202)994-0704
Fax: (202)994-4930
E-mail: icsb@gwu.edu
Website: http://www.icsb.org
Susan G. Duffy. Admin.

International Small Business Consortium
3309 Windjammer St.
Norman, OK 73072
E-mail: sb@isbc.com
Website: http://www.isbc.com

Kauffman Center for Entrepreneurial Leadership
4801 Rockhill Rd.
Kansas City, MO 64110-2046
(816)932-1000
E-mail: info@kauffman.org
Website: http://www.entreworld.org

National Alliance for Fair Competition
3 Bethesda Metro Center, Ste. 1100
Bethesda, MD 20814
(410)235-7116
Fax: (410)235-7116
E-mail: ampesq@aol.com
Tony Ponticelli, Exec.Dir.

National Association for the Self-Employed
PO Box 612067
DFW Airport
Dallas, TX 75261-2067
(800)232-6273
E-mail: mpetron@nase.org
Website: http://www.nase.org
Robert Hughes, Pres.

National Association of Business Leaders
4132 Shoreline Dr., Ste. J & H
Earth City, MO 63045
Fax: (314)298-9110
E-mail: nabl@nabl.com
Website: http://www.nabl.com/
Gene Blumenthal, Contact

National Association of Private Enterprise
PO Box 15550
Long Beach, CA 90815
888-224-0953
Fax: (714)844-4942

Website: http://www.napeonline.net
Laura Squiers, Exec.Dir.

National Association of Small Business Investment Companies
666 11th St. NW, Ste. 750
Washington, DC 20001
(202)628-5055
Fax: (202)628-5080
E-mail: nasbic@nasbic.org
Website: http://www.nasbic.org
Lee W. Mercer, Pres.

National Business Association
PO Box 700728
5151 Beltline Rd., Ste. 1150
Dallas, TX 75370
(972)458-0900
800-456-0440
Fax: (972)960-9149
E-mail: info@nationalbusiness.org
Website: http://www.nationalbusiness
.org
Raj Nisankarao, Pres.

National Business Owners Association
PO Box 111
Stuart, VA 24171
(276)251-7500
(866)251-7505
Fax: (276)251-2217
E-mail: membershipservices@nboa.org
Website: http://www.rvmdb.com.nboa
Paul LaBarr, Pres.

National Center for Fair Competition
PO Box 220
Annandale, VA 22003
(703)280-4622
Fax: (703)280-0942
E-mail: kentonp1@aol.com
Kenton Pattie, Pres.

National Family Business Council
1640 W. Kennedy Rd.
Lake Forest, IL 60045
(847)295-1040
Fax: (847)295-1898
E-mail: lmsnfbc@email.msn.com
Jogn E. Messervey, Pres.

National Federation of Independent Business
53 Century Blvd., Ste. 250
Nashville, TN 37214
(615)872-5800
800-NFIBNOW
Fax: (615)872-5353
Website: http://www.nfib.org
Jack Faris, Pres. and CEO

National Small Business Association
1156 15th St. NW, Ste. 1100
Washington, DC 20005
(202)293-8830
800-345-6728
Fax: (202)872-8543
E-mail: press@nsba.biz
Website: http://www.nsba.biz
Rob Yunich, Dir. of Communications

PUSH Commercial Division
930 E 50th St.
Chicago, IL 60615-2702
(773)373-3366
Fax: (773)373-3571
E-mail: info@rainbowpush.org
Website: http://www.rainbowpush.org
Rev. Willie T. Barrow, Co-Chm.

Research Institute for Small and Emerging Business
722 12th St. NW
Washington, DC 20005
(202)628-8382
Fax: (202)628-8392
E-mail: info@riseb.org
Website: http://www.riseb.org
Allan Neece, Jr., Chm.

Sales Professionals USA
PO Box 149
Arvada, CO 80001
(303)534-4937
888-736-7767
E-mail: salespro@salesprofessionals-usa.com
Website: http://www.salesprofessionals-usa.com
Sharon Herbert, Natl. Pres.

Score Association - Service Corps of Retired Executives
409 3rd St. SW, 6th Fl.
Washington, DC 20024
(202)205-6762
800-634-0245
Fax: (202)205-7636
E-mail: media@score.org
Website: http://www.score.org
W. Kenneth Yancey, Jr., CEO

Small Business and Entrepreneurship Council
1920 L St. NW, Ste. 200
Washington, DC 20036
(202)785-0238
Fax: (202)822-8118
E-mail: membership@sbec.org
Website: http://www.sbecouncil.org
Karen Kerrigan, Pres./CEO

Small Business in Telecommunications
1331 H St. NW, Ste. 500
Washington, DC 20005
(202)347-4511
Fax: (202)347-8607
E-mail: sbt@sbthome.org
Website: http://www.sbthome.org
Lonnie Danchik, Chm.

Small Business Legislative Council
1010 Massachusetts Ave. NW, Ste. 540
Washington, DC 20005
(202)639-8500
Fax: (202)296-5333
E-mail: email@sblc.org
Website: http://www.sblc.org
John Satagaj, Pres.

Small Business Service Bureau
554 Main St.
PO Box 15014
Worcester, MA 01615-0014
(508)756-3513
800-343-0939
Fax: (508)770-0528
E-mail: membership@sbsb.com
Website: http://www.sbsb.com
Francis R. Carroll, Pres.

Small Publishers Association of North America
1618 W Colorado Ave.
Colorado Springs, CO 80904
(719)475-1726
Fax: (719)471-2182
E-mail: span@spannet.org
Website: http://www.spannet.org
Scott Flora, Exec. Dir.

SOHO America
PO Box 941
Hurst, TX 76053-0941
800-495-SOHO
E-mail: soho@1sas.com
Website: http://www.soho.org

Structured Employment Economic Development Corporation
915 Broadway, 17th Fl.
New York, NY 10010
(212)473-0255
Fax: (212)473-0357
E-mail: info@seedco.org
Website: http://www.seedco.org
William Grinker, CEO

Support Services Alliance
107 Prospect St.
Schoharie, NY 12157
800-836-4772
E-mail: info@ssamembers.com

Website: http://www.ssainfo.com
Steve COle, Pres.

United States Association for Small Business and Entrepreneurship
975 University Ave., No. 3260
Madison, WI 53706
(608)262-9982
Fax: (608)263-0818
E-mail: jgillman@wisc.edu
Website: http://www.ususbe.org
Joan Gillman, Exec. Dir.

Consultants

This section contains a listing of consultants specializing in small business development. It is arranged alphabetically by country, then by state or province, then by city, then by firm name.

Canada

Alberta

Tenato
1229A 9th Ave. SE
Calgary, AB, Canada T2G 0S9
(403)242-1127
Fax: (403)261-5693
E-mail: jdrew@tenato.com
Website: http://www.tenato.com

Varsity Consulting Group
School of Business
University of Alberta
Edmonton, AB, Canada T6G 2R6
(780)492-2994
Fax: (780)492-5400

British Columbia

Andrew R. De Boda Consulting
1523 Milford Ave.
Coquitlam, BC, Canada V3J 2V9
(604)936-4527
Fax: (604)936-4527
E-mail: deboda@intergate.bc.ca

Reality Marketing Associates
3049 Sienna Ct.
Coquitlam, BC, Canada V3E 3N7
(604)944-8603
Fax: (604)944-4708
E-mail: info@realityassociates.com
Website: http://www.realityassociates.com

Pinpoint Tactics Business Consulting
5525 West Blvd., Ste. 330
Vancouver, BC, Canada V6M 3W6
(604)263-4698

E-mail: info@pinpointtactics.com
Website: http://www.pinpointtactics.com

Ketch Consulting Inc.
6890 Winnifred Pl.
Victoria, BC, Canada V8M 1N1
(250)661-1208
E-mail: info@ketch.ca
Website: http://www.ketch.ca

Mahigan Consulting Services
334 Skawshen Rd.
West Vancouver, BC, Canada V7P 3T1
(604)210-3833
Fax: (778)285-2736
E-mail: info@mahiganconsulting.com
Website: http://www.mahiganconsulting.com

Nova Scotia

The Marketing Clinic
1384 Bedford Hwy.
Bedford, NS, Canada B4A 1E2
(902)835-4122
Fax: (902)832-9389
E-mail: office@themarketingclinic.ca
Website: http://www.themarketingclinic.ca

Ontario

The Cynton Co.
17 Massey St.
Brampton, ON, Canada L6S 2V6
(905)792-7769
Fax: (905)792-8116
E-mail: cynton@home.com
Website: http://www.cynton.com

CRO Engineering Ltd.
1895 William Hodgins Ln.
Carp, ON, Canada K0A 1L0
(613)839-1108
Fax: (613)839-1406
E-mail: J.Grefford@ieee.ca

Business Plan World
PO Box 1322, Sta. B
Mississauga, ON, Canada L4Y 4B6
(709)643-8544
E-mail: theboss@businessplanworld.com
Website: http://www.businessplanworld.com

JPL Consulting
236 Millard Ave.
Newmarket, ON, Canada L3Y 1Z2
(416)606-9124
E-mail: sales@jplbiz.ca
Website: http://www.jplbiz.ca

Black Eagle Consulting 2000 Inc.
451 Barclay Cres.
Oakville, ON, Canada L6J 6H8
(905)842-3010
Fax: (905)842-9586
E-mail: info@blackeagle.ca
Website: http://www.blackeagle.ca

Care Concepts & Communications
21 Spruce Hill Rd.
Toronto, ON, Canada M4E 3G2
(416)420-8840
E-mail: info@cccbizconsultants.com
Website: http://www.cccbizconsultants
.com

FHG International Inc.
14 Glengrove Ave. W
Toronto, ON, Canada M4R 1N4
(416)402-8000
E-mail: info@fhgi.com
Website: http://www.fhgi.com

Harrison Pricing Strategy Group Inc.
1235 Bay St., Ste. 400
Toronto, ON, Canada M5R 3K4
(416)218-1103
Fax: (416) 827-8595

Ken Wyman & Associates Inc.
64 Lamb Ave.
Toronto, ON, Canada V
(416)362-2926
Fax: (416)362-3039
E-mail: kenwyman@compuserve.com

Quebec

PGP Consulting
17 Linton
Dollard-des-Ormeaux, QC, Canada H9B
1P2
(514)796-7613
Fax: (866)750-0947
E-mail: pierre@pgpconsulting.com
Website: http://www.pgpconsulting.com

Komand Consulting
1250 Rene Levesque Blvd.,W
22nd Fl., Ste. 2200
Montreal, QC, Canada H3B 4W8
(514)934-9281
Fax: (514)934-0770
E-mail: info@komand.ca
Website: http://www.komand.ca

Saskatchewan

Banda Marketing Group
410 - 22nd St. E, Ste. 810
Saskatoon, SK, Canada S7K 5T6
(306) 343-6100

Fax: (306) 652-1340
E-mail: admin@bandagroup.com
Website: http://www.bandagroup.com

Oracle Planning
106 28th St. W
Saskatoon, SK, Canada, S7L 0K2
(306) 717-5001
Fax: (650)618-2742

United states

Alabama

Business Planning Inc.
2090 Columbiana Rd., Ste. 2950
Vestavia Hills, AL 35216
(205)824-8969
Fax: (205)824-8939
E-mail: kmiller@businessplanninginc.com
Website: http://www. business
planninginc.com

Tradebank of Eastern Alabama
400 S St. E
Talladega, AL 35160
(256)761-9051
Fax: (256)761-9227

Alaska

**Alaska Business Development
Center**
840 K St., Ste. 202
Anchorage, AK 99501
(907)562-0335
Free: 800-478-3474
Fax: (907)562-6988
E-mail: info@abdc.org
Website: http://www.abdc.org

Arizona

Carefree Direct Marketing Corp.
8001 E Serene St.
PO Box 3737
Carefree, AZ 85377-3737
(480)488-4227
Fax: (480)488-2841

Management 2000
39342 S Winding Trl.
Oro Valley, AZ 85737
(520)818-9988
Fax: (520)818-3277
E-mail: m2000@mgmt2000.com
Website: http://www.mgmt2000.com

CMAS
5125 N 16th St.
Phoenix, AZ 85016

(602)395-1001
Fax: (602)604-8180

Moneysoft Inc.
1 E Camelback Rd. #550
Phoenix, AZ 85012
Free: 800-966-7797
E-mail: mbray@moneysoft.com
Website: http://www.moneysoft.com

Harvey C. Skoog
7151 E Addis Ave.
Prescott Valley, AZ 86314
(928)772-1448

The De Angelis Group Inc.
9815 E Bell Rd., Ste. 120
Scottsdale, AZ 85260
(480)609-4868
Fax: (480)452-0401
E-mail: info@thedeangelisgroup.com
Website: http://www.thedeangelisgroup.com

Incendo Marketing L.L.C.
7687 E Thunderhawk Rd., Ste. 100
Scottsdale, AZ 85255
(480)513-4208
Fax: (509)561-9011

Sauerbrun Technology Group Ltd.
7979 E Princess Dr., Ste. 5
Scottsdale, AZ 85255-5878
(602)502-4950
Fax: (602)502-4292
E-mail: info@sauerbrun.com
Website: http://www.sauerbrun.com

Van Cleve Associates
6932 E 2nd St.
Tucson, AZ 85710
(520)296-2587
Fax: (520)296-3358

Variantia
6161 N Canon del Pajaro
Tucson, AZ 85750
(520)577-7680

Louws Management Corp.
PO Box 130
Vail, AZ 85641
(520)664-1881
Fax: (928)222-0086
E-mail: info@louwstraining.com
Website: http://www.louwsmanagement
.com

California

Thomas E. Church & Associates Inc.
PO Box 2439
Aptos, CA 95001
(831) 662-7950

Fax:(831) 684-0173
E-mail: thomase2@trueyellow.net
Website: http://www.thomas_church
.ypgs.net

AB Manley Partners Worldwide L.L.C.
1428 S Marengo Ave.
Alhambra, CA 91803-3096
(626) 457-8841

**Lindquist Consultants-Venture
Planning**
225 Arlington Ave.
Berkeley, CA 94707
(510)524-6685
Fax: (510)527-6604

One Page Business Plan Co.
1798 Fifth St.
Berkeley, CA 94710
(510)705-8400
Fax: (510)705-8403
E-mail: info@onepagebusinessplan.com
Website: http://www.onepagebusiness
plan.com

WordCraft Creative Services
2687 Shasta Rd.
Berkeley, CA 94708
(510) 848-5177
Fax:(510) 868-1006
E-mail: info@wordcraftcreative.com
Website: http://www.wordcraft
creative.com

Growth Partners
1566 La Pradera Dr., Ste. 5
Campbell, CA 95008
(408) 871-7925
Fax: (408) 871-7924
E-mail: mark@growth-partners.com
Website: http://www.growth-partners
.com

The Success Resource
25773 Flanders Pl.
Carmel, CA 93923
(831) 236-0732

W and J PARTNERSHIP
PO Box 2499
18876 Edwin Markham Dr.
Castro Valley, CA 94546
(510)583-7751
Fax: (510)583-7645
E-mail: wamorgan@wjpartnership.com
Website: http://www.wjpartnership.com

JB Associates
21118 Gardena Dr.
Cupertino, CA 95014
(408)257-0214

Fax: (408)257-0216
E-mail: semarang@sirius.com

House Agricultural Consultants
1105 Kennedy Pl., Ste. 1
Davis, CA 95616
(916)753-3361
Fax: (916)753-0464
E-mail: infoag@houseag.com
Website: http://www.houseag.com/

3C Systems Co.
16161 Ventura Blvd., Ste. 815
Encino, CA 91436
(818)907-1302
Fax: (818)907-1357
E-mail: mark@3CSysCo.com
Website: http://www.3CSysCo.com

Technical Management Consultants
3624 Westfall Dr.
Encino, CA 91436-4154
(818)784-0626
Fax: (818)501-5575
E-mail: tmcrs@aol.com

Rainwater-Gish & Associates
317 3rd St., Ste. 3
Eureka, CA 95501
(707)443-0030
Fax: (707)443-5683

MedMarket Diligence L.L.C.
51 Fairfield
Foothill Ranch, CA 92610-1856
(949) 859-3401
Fax: (949) 837-4558
E-mail: info@mediligence.com
Website: http://www.mediligence.com

Global Tradelinks
451 Pebble Beach Pl.
Fullerton, CA 92835
(714)441-2280
Fax: (714)441-2281
E-mail: info@globaltradelinks.com
Website: http://www.globaltradelinks.com

Larson Associates
1440 Harbor Blvd., Ste. 800
Fullerton, CA 92835
(714)529-4121
Fax: (714)572-3606
E-mail: ray@consultlarson.com
Website: http://www.consultlarson.com

Strategic Business Group
800 Cienaga Dr.
Fullerton, CA 92835-1248
(714)449-1040
Fax: (714)525-1631

Burnes Consulting
20537 Wolf Creek Rd.
Grass Valley, CA 95949
(530)346-8188
Free: 800-949-9021
Fax: (530)346-7704
E-mail: kent@burnesconsulting.com
Website: http://www.burnesconsulting
.com

International Health Resources
PO Box 2738
Grass Valley, CA 95945
Website: http://www.futureofhealthcare
.com

Pioneer Business Consultants
9042 Garfield Ave., Ste. 211
Huntington Beach, CA 92646
(714)964-7600

Fluor Daniel Inc.
3353 Michelson Dr.
Irvine, CA 92612-0650
(949)975-2000
Fax: (949)975-5271
E-mail: sales.consulting@fluordaniel.com
Website: http://www.fluor.com

MCS Associates
18881 Von Karman, Ste. 1175
Irvine, CA 92612
(949)263-8700
Fax: (949)263-0770
E-mail: info@mcsassociates.com
Website: http://www.mcsassociates.com

Savvy Communications
9730 Soda Bay Rd., Ste. 5035
Kelseyville, CA 95451-9576
(707) 277-8078
Fax:(707) 277-8079

Sky Blue Consulting Inc.
4165 Executive Dr.
Lafayette, CA 94549
(925) 283-8272

Comprehensive Business Services
3201 Lucas Cir.
Lafayette, CA 94549
(925)283-8272
Fax: (925)283-8272

The Ribble Group
27601 Forbes Rd., Ste. 52
Laguna Niguel, CA 92677
(714)582-1085
Fax: (714)582-6420
E-mail: ribble@deltanet.com

Norris Bernstein, CMC
9309 Marina Pacifica Dr. N
Long Beach, CA 90803

(562)493-5458
Fax: (562)493-5459
E-mail: norris@ctecomputer.com
Website: http://foodconsultants.com/
bernstein/

Horizon Consulting Services
1315 Garthwick Dr.
Los Altos, CA 94024
(415)967-0906
Fax: (650)967-0906

Blue Garnet Associates L.L.C.
8055 W Manchester Ave., Ste. 430
Los Angeles, CA 90293
(310) 439-1930
Fax: (310) 388-1657
E-mail: hello@bluegarnet.net
Website: http://www.bluegarnet.net

CAST Management Consultants Inc.
700 S Flower St., Ste. 1900
Los Angeles, CA 90017
(213) 614-8066
Fax: (213) 614-0760
E-mail: info@castconsultants.com
Website: http://www.castconsultants.com

Rubenstein/Justman Management Consultants
11620 Wilshire Blvd., Ste. 750
Los Angeles, CA 90025
(310)445-5300
Fax: (310)496-1450
E-mail: info@rjmc.net
Website: http://www.rjmc.net

F.J. Schroeder & Associates
1926 Westholme Ave.
Los Angeles, CA 90025
(310)470-2655
Fax: (310)470-6378
E-mail: fjsacons@aol.com
Website: http://www.mcninet.com/
GlobalLook/Fjschroe.html

Western Management Associates
5777 W Century Blvd., Ste. 1220
Los Angeles, CA 90045
(310)645-1091
Free: (888)788-6534
Fax: (310)645-1092
E-mail: gene@cfoforrent.com
Website: http://www.cfoforrent.com

Inspiration Quest Inc.
PO Box 90
Mendocino, CA 95460
(415) 235-6002
E-mail: info@inspirationquest.com
Website: http://www.inspirationquest
.com

Heron Advisory Group
9 Heron Dr.
Mill Valley, CA 94941
(415) 380-8611
Fax: (415) 381-9044
E-mail: janetmca@pacbell.net
Website: http://www.hagroup.biz

Emacula Consulting Group
131 Draeger Dr., Ste. A
Moraga, CA 94556
(925) 388-6083
Fax: (267) 589-3151
E-mail: drochlin@emacula.com
Website: http://www.emacula.com

BizplanSource
1048 Irvine Ave., Ste. 621
Newport Beach, CA 92660
Free: 888-253-0974
Fax: 800-859-8254
E-mail: info@bizplansource.com
Website: http://www.bizplansource.com
Adam Greengrass, President

The Market Connection
20051 SW Birch St., Ste 310
Newport Beach, CA 92660
(949)851-6313
Fax: (949)833-0283

Intelequest Corp.
722 Gailen Ave.
Palo Alto, CA 94303
(415)968-3443
Fax: (415)493-6954
E-mail: frits@iqix.com

Beblie, Brandt & Jacobs Inc.
19 Brista del Lago
Rancho Santa Margarita, CA 92618
(949)589-5120
Fax: (949)203-6225
E-mail: darcy@bbjinc.com

California Business Incubation Network
225 Broadway, Ste. 2250
San Diego, CA 92101
(619)237-0559
Fax: (619)237-0521

The Drake Group
824 Santa Clara Pl.
San Diego, CA 92109-7224
(858) 488-3911
Fax: (810) 454-4593
E-mail: cdrake@drakegroup.com
Website: http://www.drakegroup.com

G.R. Gordetsky Consultants Inc.
11414 Windy Summit Pl.
San Diego, CA 92127

(858)487-4939
E-mail: gordet@pacbell.net

Noorany Marketing Resources
3830 Valley Centre Dr., Ste. 705
San Diego, CA 92130
(858) 792-9559
Fax: (858) 259-2320
E-mail: heidi@noorany.com
Website: http://www.noorany.com

Freeman, Sullivan & Co.
1101 Montgomery St., 15th Fl.
San Francisco, CA 94104
Website: http://www.fscgroup.com

PKF Consulting Corp.
50 California St., 19th Fl.
San Francisco, CA 94111
(415)788-3102
Fax: (415)433-7844
E-mail: callahan@pkfc.com
Website: http://www.pkfc.com

Welling & Woodard Inc.
1067 Broadway
San Francisco, CA 94133
(415)776-4500
Fax: (415)776-5067

Highland Associates
16174 Highland Dr.
San Jose, CA 95127
(408)272-7008
Fax: (408)272-4040

Leckrone Law Corp.
4010 Moorpark Ave., Ste. 215
San Jose, CA 95117-1843
(408) 243-9898
Fax: (408) 296-6637

ORDIS Inc.
6815 Trinidad Dr.
San Jose, CA 95120-2056
(408)268-3321
Free: 800-446-7347
Fax: (408)268-3582
E-mail: ordis@ordis.com
Website: http://www.ordis.com

Bay Area Tax Consultants and Bayhill Financial Consultants
1840 Gateway Dr.
San Mateo, CA 94404
(650)378-1373
Fax: (650)585-5444
E-mail: admin@baytax.com
Website: http://www.baytax.com/

Helfert Associates
111 St. Matthews, Ste. 307
San Mateo, CA 94401

(650)377-0540
Fax: (650)377-0472

Mykytyn Consulting Group Inc.
185 N Redwood Dr., Ste. 200
San Rafael, CA 94903
(415)491-1770
Fax: (415)491-1251
E-mail: info@mcgi.com

Omega Management Systems Inc.
3 Mount Darwin Ct.
San Rafael, CA 94903-1109
(415)499-1300
Fax: (415)492-9490
E-mail: information@omegamgt.com

Manex Consulting
2010 Crow Canyon Pl., Ste. 320
San Ramon, CA 94583
(925) 807-5100
Website: http://
www.manexconsulting.com

Brincko Associates Inc.
530 Wilshire Blvd., Ste. 201
Santa Monica, CA 90401
(310)553-4523
Fax: (310)553-6782

hE Myth
131B Stony Cir., Ste. 2000
Santa Rosa, CA 95401
(541)552-4600
Free: 800-300-3531
E-mail: info@emyth.com
Website: http://www.emyth.com

Figueroa Farms L.L.C.
PO Box 206
Santa Ynez, CA 93460
(805) 686-4890
Fax: (805) 686-2887
E-mail: info@figueroafarms.com
Website: http://www.FigueroaFarms.com

Reilly, Connors & Ray
1743 Canyon Rd.
Spring Valley, CA 91977
(619)698-4808
Fax: (619)460-3892
E-mail: davidray@adnc.com

RJR Associates
1639 Lewiston Dr.
Sunnyvale, CA 94087
(408)737-7720
E-mail: bobroy@rjrassoc.com
Website: http://www.rjrassoc.com

Schwafel Associates
333 Cobalt Way, Ste. 107
Sunnyvale, CA 94085

(408)720-0649
Fax: (408)720-1796
E-mail: schwafel@ricochet.net
Website: http://www.patca.org

The International Coverting Institute
5200 Badger Rd
Terrebonne, CA 97760
(503) 548-1447
Fax: (503) 548-1618

GlobalReady
1521 Kirk Ave.
Thousand Oaks, CA 91360
(805) 427-4131
E-mail: info@globalready.com
Website: http://www.globalready.com

Staubs Business Services
23320 S Vermont Ave.
Torrance, CA 90502-2940
(310)830-9128
Fax: (310)830-9128
E-mail: Harry_L_Staubs@Lamg.com

Enterprise Management Corp.
17461 Irvine Blvd., Ste. M
Tustin, CA 92780
(714) 505-1925
Fax: (714) 505-9691
E-mail: cfotogo@companycfo.com
Website: http://www.companycfo.com

Out of Your Mind . . . and Into the Marketplace
13381 White Sands Dr.
Tustin, CA 92780-4565
(714)544-0248
Free: 800-419-1513
Fax: (714)730-1414
Website: http://www.business-plan.com

Ingman Company Inc.
7949 Woodley Ave., Ste. 120
Van Nuys, CA 91406-1232
(805)650-9353
Fax: (805)984-2979

Innovative Technology Associates
3639 E Harbor Blvd., Ste. 203E
Ventura, CA 93001
(805)650-9353

Grid Technology Associates
20404 Tufts Cir.
Walnut, CA 91789
(909)444-0922
Fax: (909)444-0922

Bell Springs Publishing
PO Box 1240
Willits, CA 95490
(707)459-6372

E-mail: bellsprings@sabernet
Website: http://www.bellsprings.com

Hutchinson Consulting and Appraisal
23245 Sylvan St., Ste. 103
Woodland Hills, CA 91367
(818)888-8175
Free: 800-977-7548
Fax: (818)888-8220
E-mail: r.f.hutchinson-cpa@worldnet
.att.net

Colorado

Sam Boyer & Associates
4255 S Buckley Rd., No. 136
Aurora, CO 80013
(303)766-1557
Free: 800-785-0485
Fax: (303)766-8740
E-mail: samboyer@samboyer.com
Website: http://www.samboyer.com/

Associated Enterprises Ltd.
183 Pauls Ln.
Bailey, CO 80421

Comer & Associates LLC
5255 Holmes Pl.
Boulder, CO 80303
(303) 786-7986
Fax: (303)895-2347
E-mail: jerry@comerassociates.com
Website: http://www.comerassociates
.com

Ameriwest Business Consultants Inc.
3725 E. Wade Ln.
Colorado Springs, CO 80917
(719)380-7096
Fax: (719)380-7096
E-mail: email@abchelp.com
Website: http://www.abchelp.com

GVNW Consulting Inc.
2270 La Montana Way
Colorado Springs, CO 80936
(719)594-5800
Fax: (719)594-5803
Website: http://www.gvnw.com

M-Squared Inc.
755 San Gabriel Pl.
Colorado Springs, CO 80906
(719)576-2554
Fax: (719)576-2554

Foxhall Consulting Services
2532 Dahlia St.
Denver, CO 80207
(303)355-7995
Fax: (303)377-0716

E-mail: michael@foxhallconsulting.com
Website: http://www.foxhallconsulting
.com

KLA Associates
2352 Humboldt St.
Denver, CO 80205-5332
(303)830-8042

Wilson Hughes Consulting LLC
2100 Humboldt St., Ste. 302
Denver, CO 80205
Website: http://www.wilsonhughes
consultingllc.com

Co-Active Communications Corp.
400 Inverness Pkwy., Ste. 200
Englewood, CO 80112-6415
(303)771-6181
Fax: (303)771-0080

Thornton Financial FNIC
1024 Centre Ave., Bldg. E
Fort Collins, CO 80526-1849
(970)221-2089
Fax: (970)484-5206

Extelligent Inc.
8400 E Crescent Pky., Ste. 600
Greenwood Village, CO 80111
(720)201-5672
E-mail: info@extelligent.com
Website: http://www.extelligent.com

Western Capital Holdings Inc.
10050 E Applwood Dr.
Parker, CO 80138
(303)841-1022
Fax: (303)770-1945

Connecticut

Christiansen Consulting
56 Scarborough St.
Hartford, CT 06105
(860)586-8265
Fax: (860)233-3420
Website: http://www.Christiansen
Consulting.com

Follow-up News
185 Pine St., Ste. 818
Manchester, CT 06040
(860)647-7542
Free: 800-708-0696
Fax: (860)646-6544
E-mail: Followupnews@aol.com

Musevue360
555 Millbrook Rd.
Middletown, CT 06457
(860)463-7722
Fax: (860)346-3013

E-mail: jennifer.eifrig@musevue360.com
Website: http://www.musevue360.com

Alltis Corp.
747 Farmington Ave., Ste. 6
New Britain, CT 06053
(860)224-1300
Fax: (860)224-1700
E-mail: info@alltis.com
Website: http://www.alltis.com

Kalba International Inc.
116 McKinley Ave.
New Haven, CT 06515
(203)397-2199
Fax: (781)240-2657
E-mail: kalba@comcast.net
Website: http://www.kalbainternational
.com

Lovins & Associates Consulting
357 Whitney Ave.
New Haven, CT 06511
(203)787-3367
Fax: (203)624-7599
E-mail: Alovinsphd@aol.com
Website: http://www.lovinsgroup.com

JC Ventures Inc.
4 Arnold St.
Old Greenwich, CT 06870-1203
(203)698-1990
Free: 800-698-1997
Fax: (203)698-2638

Charles L. Hornung Associates
52 Ned's Mountain Rd.
Ridgefield, CT 06877
(203)431-0297

Greenwich Associates
6 High Ridge Park
Stamford, CT 06905
(203)629-1200
Fax: (203)629-1229
E-mail: lisa@greenwich.com
Website: http://www.greenwich.com

Management Practice Inc.
216 W Hill Rd.
Stamford, CT 06902
(203)973-0535
Fax: (203)978-9034
E-mail: mpayne@mpiweb.com
Website: http://www.mpiweb.com

RealBusinessPlans.com
156 Westport Rd.
Wilton, CT 06897
(914)837-2886

E-mail: ct@realbusinessplans.com
Website: http://www.RealBusinessPlans
.com

Wellspring Consulting LLC
198 Amity Rd., 2nd Fl.
Woodbridge, CT 06525
(203)387-7192
Fax: (203)387-1345
E-mail: info@wellspringconsulting.net
Website: http://www.wellspring
consulting.net

Delaware

Focus Marketing
61-7 Habor Dr.
Claymont, DE 19703
(302)793-3064

Daedalus Ventures Ltd.
PO Box 1474
Hockessin, DE 19707
(302)239-6758
Fax: (302)239-9991
E-mail: daedalus@mail.del.net

The Formula Group
PO Box 866
Hockessin, DE 19707
(302)456-0952
Fax: (302)456-1354
E-mail: formula@netaxs.com

Selden Enterprises Inc.
2502 Silverside Rd., Ste. 1
Wilmington, DE 19810-3740
(302)529-7113
Fax: (302)529-7442
E-mail: selden2@bellatlantic.net
Website: http://
www.seldenenterprises.com

District of Columbia

The Breen Consulting Group LLC
1101 Pennsylvania Ave, NW, 7th Fl.
Washington, DC 20004
(877)881-4688
E-mail: sales@joebreen.com
Website: http://www.joebreen.com

Catalysr IpF
1514Upshur St. NW
Washington, DC 20011
(202)230-2662
E-mail: contact@catalystipf.com
Website: http://www.catalystipf.com

Smith, Dawson & Andrews Inc.
1150 Connecticut Ave., Ste. 1025
Washington, DC 20036
(202)835-0740

Fax: (202)775-8526
E-mail: webmaster@sda-inc.com
Website: http://www.sda-inc.com

1000 Cranes LLC
1425 K St. NW, Ste. 350
Washington, DC 20005
(202)587-2737
E-mail: info@1000cranes.com
Website: http://www.1000cranes.com

Florida

BackBone, Inc.
20404 Hacienda Court
Boca Raton, FL 33498
(561)470-0965
Fax: 516-908-4038
E-mail: BPlans@backboneinc.com
Website: http://www.backboneinc.com

Dr. Eric H Shaw and Associates
500 South Ocean Blvd., Ste. 2105
Boca Raton, FL 33432
(561)338-5151
E-mail: ericshaw@bellsouth.net
Website: http://www.ericshaw.com

E.N. Rysso & Associates
180 Bermuda Petrel Ct.
Daytona Beach, FL 32119
(386)760-3028
E-mail: erysso@aol.com

Eric Sands Consulting Services
6750 N. Andrews Ave., Ste. 200
Fort Lauderdale, FL 33309
(954)721-4767
Fax: (954)720-2815
E-mail: easands@aol.com
Website: http://
www.ericsandsconsultig.com

F.A. McGee Inc.
800 Claughton Island Dr., Ste. 401
Miami, FL 33131
(305)377-9123

Strategic Business Planning Co.
12000 Biscayne Blvd., Ste. 203
Miami, FL 33181
(954)704-9100
E-mail: info@bizplan.com
Website: http://www.bizplan.com

Professional Planning Associates, Inc.
1440 NE 35th St.
Oakland Park, FL 33334
(954)829-2523
Fax:(954)537-7945
E-mail: Mgoldstein@proplana.com
Website: http://proplana.com
Michael Goldstein, President

Hunter G. Jackson Jr.
3409 Canoga Dr.
Orlando, FL 32861-8272
(407)245-7682
E-mail: hunterjackson@juno.com

F. Newton Parks
210 El Brillo Way
Palm Beach, FL 33480
(561)833-1727
Fax: (561)833-4541

Hughes Consulting Services LLC
522 Alternate 19
Palm Harbor, FL 34683
(727)631-2536
Fax: (727)474-9818
Website: http://consultinghughes.com

Avery Business Development Services
2506 St. Michel Ct.
Ponte Vedra Beach, FL 32082
(904)280-8840
Fax: (904)285-6033

Dufresne Consulting Group Inc.
10014 N Dale Mabry, Ste. 101
Tampa, FL 33618-4426
(813)264-4775
Fax: (813)264-9300
Website: http://www.dcgconsult.com

Tunstall Consulting LLC
13153 N. Dale Mabry Hwy., Ste. 200
Tampa, FL 33618
(813)968-4461
Fax: (813)961-2315
Website: http://www.tunstallconsulting
.com

The Business Planning Institute, LLC.
580 Village Blvd., Ste. 150
West Palm Beach, FL 33409
(561)236-5533
Fax: (561)689-5546
Website: http://www.bpiplans.com

Georgia

Fountainhead Consulting Group, Inc.
3970 Old Milton Pkwy, Ste. 210
Atlanta, GA 30005
(770)642-4220
Website: http://www.fountainhead
consultinggroup.com/

CHScottEnterprises
227 Sandy Springs P., NE, Ste. 720702
Atlanta, GA 30358
(770)356-4808
E-mail: info@chscottenterprises.com
Website: http://www.chscottenterprises
.com

US Business Plan Inc.
1200 Barrett Pky., Ste. 4-400
Kennesaw, GA 30144
(770)794-8000
Website: http://www.usbusinessplan.com

Business Ventures Corp.
1650 Oakbrook Dr., Ste. 405
Norcross, GA 30093
(770)729-8000
Fax: (770)729-8028

Tom C. Davis CPA LLC
1808-A Plum St.
Valdosta, GA 31601
(229)247-9801
Fax:(229) 244-7704
E-mail: mail@tcdcpa.com
Website: http://www.tcdcpa.com/

Illinois

TWD and Associates
431 S Patton
Arlington Heights, IL 60005
(847)398-6410
Fax: (847)255-5095
E-mail: tdoo@aol.com

Management Planning Associates Inc.
2275 Half Day Rd., Ste. 350
Bannockburn, IL 60015-1277
(847)945-2421
Fax: (847)945-2425

Phil Faris Associates
86 Old Mill Ct.
Barrington, IL 60010
(847)382-4888
Fax: (847)382-4890
E-mail: pfaris@meginsnet.net

Seven Continents Technology
787 Stonebridge
Buffalo Grove, IL 60089
(708)577-9653
Fax: (708)870-1220

Grubb & Blue Inc.
2404 Windsor Pl.
Champaign, IL 61820
(217)366-0052
Fax: (217)356-0117

ACE Accounting Service Inc.
3128 N Bernard St.
Chicago, IL 60618
(773)463-7854
Fax: (773)463-7854

AON Consulting Worldwide
200 E Randolph St., 10th Fl.
Chicago, IL 60601

(312)381-4800
Free: 800-438-6487
Fax: (312)381-0240
Website: http://www.aon.com

FMS Consultants
5801 N Sheridan Rd., Ste. 3D
Chicago, IL 60660
(773)561-7362
Fax: (773)561-6274

Grant Thornton
800 1 Prudential Plz.
130 E Randolph St.
Chicago, IL 60601
(312)856-0001
Fax: (312)861-1340
E-mail: gtinfo@gt.com
Website: http://www.grantthornton.com

Kingsbury International Ltd.
5341 N Glenwood Ave.
Chicago, IL 60640
(773)271-3030
Fax: (773)728-7080
E-mail: jetlag@mcs.com
Website: http://www.kingbiz.com

MacDougall & Blake Inc.
1414 N Wells St., Ste. 311
Chicago, IL 60610-1306
(312)587-3330
Fax: (312)587-3699
E-mail: jblake@compuserve.com

James C. Osburn Ltd.
6445 N. Western Ave., Ste. 304
Chicago, IL 60645
(773)262-4428
Fax: (773)262-6755
E-mail: osburnltd@aol.com

Tarifero & Tazewell Inc.
211 S Clark
Chicago, IL 60690
(312)665-9714
Fax: (312)665-9716

Human Energy Design Systems
620 Roosevelt Dr.
Edwardsville, IL 62025
(618)692-0258
Fax: (618)692-0819

China Business Consultants Group
931 Dakota Cir.
Naperville, IL 60563
(630)778-7992
Fax: (630)778-7915
E-mail: cbcq@aol.com

Center for Workforce Effectiveness
500 Skokie Blvd., Ste. 222
Northbrook, IL 60062
(847)559-8777

Fax: (847)559-8778
E-mail: office@cwelink.com
Website: http://www.cwelink.com

Smith Associates
1320 White Mountain Dr.
Northbrook, IL 60062
(847)480-7200
Fax: (847)480-9828

Francorp Inc.
20200 Governors Dr.
Olympia Fields, IL 60461
(708)481-2900
Free: 800-372-6244
Fax: (708)481-5885
E-mail: francorp@aol.com
Website: http://www.francorpinc.com

Camber Business Strategy Consultants
1010 S Plum Tree Ct
Palatine, IL 60078-0986
(847)202-0101
Fax: (847)705-7510
E-mail: camber@ameritech.net

Partec Enterprise Group
5202 Keith Dr.
Richton Park, IL 60471
(708)503-4047
Fax: (708)503-9468

Rockford Consulting Group Ltd.
Century Plz., Ste. 206
7210 E State St.
Rockford, IL 61108
(815)229-2900
Free: 800-667-7495
Fax: (815)229-2612
E-mail: rligus@RockfordConsulting.com
Website: http://www.Rockford
Consulting.com

RSM McGladrey Inc.
1699 E Woodfield Rd., Ste. 300
Schaumburg, IL 60173-4969
(847)413-6900
Fax: (847)517-7067
Website: http://www.rsmmcgladrey.com

A.D. Star Consulting
320 Euclid
Winnetka, IL 60093
(847)446-7827
Fax: (847)446-7827
E-mail: startwo@worldnet.att.net

Indiana

Bingham Economic Development Advisors
8900 Keystone Xing
Indianapolis, IN 46240
(317)968-5576

Ketchum Consulting Group
7575 Copperfield Way
Indianapolis, IN 46256
(317)845-5411
Fax: (317)842-9941

Cox and Company
3930 Mezzanine Dr. Ste A
Lafayette, IN, 47905
(765)449-4495
Fax: (765)449-1218
E-mail: stan@coxpa.com

Iowa

McCord Consulting Group Inc.
3425 Sycamore Ct. NE
Cedar Rapids, IA 52402
(319)378-0077
Fax: (319)378-1577
E-mail: sam@mccordgroup.com

Management Solutions L.L.C.
3815 Lincoln Pl. Dr.
Des Moines, IA 50312
(515)277-6408
Fax: (515)277-3506

Kansas

Aspire Business Development
10955 Lowell Ave., Ste. 400
Overland Park, KS 66210
(913)660-9400
Free: (888)548-1504
Website: http://www.aspirekc.com

Maine

Pan Atlantic SMS Group Inc.
6 City Ctr., Ste. 200
Portland, ME 04101
(207)871-8622
Fax: (207)772-4842
E-mail: pmurphy@panatlanticsmsgroup
.com
Website: http://www.panatlanticsms
group.com

Maryland

Clemons & Associates Inc.
5024-R Campbell Blvd.
Baltimore, MD 21236
(410)931-8100
Fax: (410)931-8111
E-mail: info@clemonsmgmt.com
Website: http://www.clemonsmgmt.com

Employee Benefits Group Inc.
4405 E West Hwy., Ste. 202
Bethesda, MD 20814
(301) 718-4637

Fax: (301) 907-0176
E-mail: info@ebg.com
Website: http://www.ebg.com

Burdeshaw Associates Ltd.
4701 Sangamore Rd.
Bethesda, MD 20816-2508
(301)229-5800
Fax: (301)229-5045
E-mail: jstacy@burdeshaw.com
Website: http://www.burdeshaw.com

Michael E. Cohen
5225 Pooks Hill Rd., Ste. 1119 S
Bethesda, MD 20814
(301)530-5738
Fax: (301)530-2988
E-mail: mecohen@crosslink.net

World Development Group Inc.
5800 Madaket Rd., Ste. 100
Bethesda, MD 20816
(301) 320-0971
Fax: (301) 320-0978
E-mail: wdg@worlddg.com
Website: http://www.worlddg.com

Creative Edge Consulting
6047 Wild Ginger Ct.
Columbia, MD 21044
(443) 545-5863
Website: http://
www.creativeedgeconsulting.org

Paul Yelder Consulting
9581 Standon Pl.
Columbia, MD 21045
(410) 740-8417
E-mail: consulting@yelder.com
Website: http://www.yelder.com

Hammer Marketing Resources
19118 Silver Maple Ct.
Hagerstown, MD 21742
(301) 733-8891
Fax: (305) 675-3277

Strategies
8 Park Center Ct., Ste. 200
Owings Mills, MD 21117
(410)363-6669
Fax: (410)363-1231
E-mail: info@strategiescorp.net
Website: http://www.strategiescorp.net

Managance Consulting and Coaching
1708 Chester Mill Rd.
Silver Spring, MD 20906
(301) 260-9503
E-mail: info@managance.com
Website: http://www.managance.com

Andrew Sussman & Associates
13731 Kretsinger
Smithsburg, MD 21783
(301)824-2943
Fax: (301)824-2943

Massachusetts

Geibel Marketing and Public Relations
PO Box 611
Belmont, MA 02478-0005
(617)484-8285
Fax: (617)489-3567
E-mail: jgeibel@geibelpr.com
Website: http://www.geibelpr.com

Bain & Co.
131 Dartmouth St.
Boston, MA 02116
(617)572-2000
Fax: (617)572-2427
E-mail: corporate.inquiries@bain.com
Website: http://www.bain.com

Fairmont Consulting Group
470 Atlantic Ave., 4th Fl.
Boston, MA 02210
(617)217-2401
Fax: (617)939-0262
E-mail: info@fairmontcg.com
Website: http://www.fairmontcg.com

Information & Research Associates
PO Box 3121
Framingham, MA 01701
(508)788-0784

Walden Consultants Ltd.
252 Pond St.
Hopkinton, MA 01748
(508)435-4882
Fax: (508)435-3971
Website: http://www.waldenconsultants.com

Consulting Resources Corp.
6 Northbrook Park
Lexington, MA 02420
(781)863-1222
Fax: (781)863-1441
E-mail: res@consultingresources.net
Website: http://www.consultingresources.net

Mehr & Co.
31 Woodcliffe Rd.
Lexington, MA 02421
(781)372-1055

Real Resources
27 Indian Hill Rd.
Medfield, MA 02052
(508)359-6780

VMB Associates Inc.
115 Ashland St.
Melrose, MA 02176
(781)665-0623
Fax: (425)732-7142
E-mail: vmbinc@aol.com

The Company Doctor
14 Pudding Stone Ln.
Mendon, MA 01756
(508)478-1747
Fax: (508)478-0520

Data and Strategies Group Inc.
190 N Main St.
Natick, MA 01760
(508)653-9990
Fax: (508)653-7799
E-mail: dsginc@dsggroup.com
Website: http://www.dsggroup.com

The Enterprise Group
73 Parker Rd.
Needham, MA 02494
(617)444-6631
Fax: (617)433-9991
E-mail: lsacco@world.std.com
Website: http://www.enterprise-group.com

PSMJ Resources Inc.
10 Midland Ave.
Newton, MA 02458
(617)965-0055
Free: 800-537-7765
Fax: (617)965-5152
E-mail: psmj@tiac.net
Website: http://www.psmj.com

Non Profit Capital Management
41 Main St.
Sterling, MA 01564
(781)933-6726
Fax: (781)933-6734

Michigan

BBC Entrepreneurial Training & Consulting LLC
803 N Main St.
Ann Arbor, MI 48104
(734)930-9741
Fax: (734)930-6629
E-mail: info@bioconsultants.com
Website: http://www.bioconsultants.com

Center for Simplified Strategic Planning Inc.
2219 Packard Rd., Ste. 13
Ann Arbor, MI 48104
(734)995-3465
E-mail: tidd@cssp.com
Website: http://www.cssp.com

Walter Frederick Consulting
1719 South Blvd.
Ann Arbor, MI 48104
(313)662-4336
Fax: (313)769-7505

Aimattech Consulting LLC
568 Woodway Ct., Ste. 1
Bloomfield Hills, MI 48302
(248) 540-3758
Fax: (248) 540-3011
E-mail: dpwconsult@aol.com
Website: http://www.aimattech.com

QualSAT International Inc.
30777 NW Highway., Ste. 101
Farmington Hills, MI 48334
866-899-0020
Fax: (248)932-3801
E-mail: info@qualsat.com
Website: http://www.qualsat.com

Fox Enterprises
6220 W Freeland Rd.
Freeland, MI 48623
(989)695-9170
Fax: (989)695-9174

T. L. Cramer Associates LLC
1788 Broadstone Rd.
Grosse Pointe Woods, MI 48236
(313)332-0182
E-mail: info@tlcramerassociates.com
Website: http://www.tlcramerassociates
.com

G.G.W. and Associates
1213 Hampton
Jackson, MI 49203
(517)782-2255
Fax: (517)782-2255

BHM Associates Inc.
2817 Canterbury Dr.
Midland, MI 48642
(989) 631-7109
E-mail: smiller@bhmassociates.net
Website: http://www.bhmassociates.net

MarketingHelp Inc.
6647 Riverwoods Ct. NE
Rockford, MI 49341
(616) 866-1198
Website: http://www.mktghelp.com

Rehmann, Robson PC
5800 Gratiot
Saginaw, MI 48605
(989)799-9580
Fax: (989)799-0227
E-mail: info@rehmann.com
Website: http://www.rehmann.com

Private Ventures Inc.
16000 W 9 Mile Rd., Ste. 504
Southfield, MI 48075
(248)569-1977
Free: 800-448-7614
Fax: (248)569-1838
E-mail: pventuresi@aol.com

JGK Associates
14464 Kerner Dr.
Sterling Heights, MI 48313
(810)247-9055
Fax: (248)822-4977
E-mail: kozlowski@home.com

Cool & Associates Inc.
921 Village Green Ln., Ste. 1068
Waterford, MI 48328
(248)683-1130
E-mail: jcool@cool-associates.com
Website: http://www.cool-associates.com

Griffioen Consulting Group Inc.
6689 Orchard Lake Rd., Ste. 295
West Bloomfield, MI 48322
(888)262-5850
Fax: (248)855-4084
Website: http://www.griffioenconsulting.com

Minnesota

Health Fitness Corp.
31700 W 82nd St., Ste. 200
Minneapolis, MN 55431
(952)831-6830
E-mail: info@hfit.com
Website: http://www.hfit.com

Consatech Inc.
PO Box 1047
Burnsville, MN 55337
(612)953-1088
Fax: (612)435-2966

Kaes Analytics Inc.
14960 Ironwood Ct.
Eden Prairie, MN 55346
(952)942-2912

DRI Consulting
2 Otter Ln.
Saint Paul, MN 55127
(651)415-1400
Fax: (651)415-9968
E-mail: dric@dric.com
Website: http://www.dric.com

Markin Consulting
12072 87th Pl. N
Maple Grove, MN 55369
(763)493-3568
Fax: (763)322-5013
E-mail: markin@markinconsulting.com

Website: http://www.markinconsulting
.com

**Minnesota Cooperation Office for
Small Business & Job Creation Inc.**
5001 W 80th St., Ste. 825
Minneapolis, MN 55437
(612)830-1230
Fax: (612)830-1232
E-mail: mncoop@msn.com
Website: http://www.mnco.org

Power Systems Research
1365 Corporate Center Curve, 2nd Fl.
St. Paul, MN 55121
(612)905-8400
Free: (888)625-8612
Fax: (612)454-0760
E-mail: Barb@Powersys.com
Website: http://www.powersys.com

Missouri

**Business Planning and Development
Corp.**
4030 Charlotte St.
Kansas City, MO 64110
(816)753-0495
E-mail: humph@bpdev.demon.co.uk
Website: http://www.bpdev.demon.co.uk

CFO Service
10336 Donoho
St. Louis, MO 63131
(314)750-2940
E-mail: jskae@cfoservice.com
Website: http://www.cfoservice.com

Nebraska

**International Management Consulting
Group Inc.**
1309 Harlan Dr., Ste. 205
Bellevue, NE 68005
(402)291-4545
Free: 800-665-IMCG
Fax: (402)291-4343
E-mail: imcg@neonramp.com
Website: http://www.mgtconsulting.com

**Heartland Management Consulting
Group**
1904 Barrington Pky.
Papillion, NE 68046
(402)952-5339
Fax: (402)339-1319

Nevada

The DuBois Group
865 Tahoe Blvd., Ste. 108
Incline Village, NV 89451

(775)832-0550
Free: 800-375-2935
Fax: (775)832-0556
E-mail: DuBoisGrp@aol.com

New Hampshire

Wolff Consultants
10 Buck Rd.
Hanover, NH 03755
(603)643-6015

BPT Consulting Associates Ltd.
12 Parmenter Rd., Ste. B-6
Londonderry, NH 03053
(603)437-8484
Free: (888)278-0030
Fax: (603)434-5388
E-mail: bptcons@tiac.net
Website: http://www.bptconsulting.com

New Jersey

Delta Planning Inc.
138 Hillcrest Dr.
Denville, NJ 07834
(913)625-1742
Free: 800-672-0762
Fax: (973)625-3531
E-mail: DeltaP@worldnet.att.net
Website: http://deltaplanning.com

Kumar Associates Inc.
1004 Cumbermeade Rd.
Fort Lee, NJ 07024
(201)224-9480
Fax: (201)585-2343
E-mail: mail@kumarassociates.com
Website: http://kumarassociates.com

John Hall & Company Inc.
14 Houston Rd.
Little Falls, NJ 07424
(973)680-4449
Fax: (973)680-4581
E-mail: jhcompany@aol.com

Market Focus
12 Maryland Rd.
Maplewood, NJ 07040
(973)378-2470
Fax: (973)378-2470
E-mail: mcss66@marketfocus.com

Distinctive Marketing Inc.
516 Bloomfield Ave., Ste. 7
Montclair, NJ 07042
(973)746-9114
Fax: (973)783-5555
Website: http://www.distinctivemktg
.com

Vanguard Communications Corp.
45 S Park Pl., Ste. 210
Morristown, NJ 07960
(973)605-8000
Fax: (973)605-8329
Website: http://www.vanguard.net/

Bedminster Group Inc.
16 Arrowhead Dr.
Neshanic Station, NJ 08853
 (908)347-0006
Fax: (908)369-4767
E-mail: info@bedminstergroup.com
Website: http://www.bedminstergroup
.com

ConMar International Ltd.
1405 Rte. 18, Ste. 200
Old Bridge, NJ 08857
(732)607-6415
Fax: (732)607-6480
Website: http://www.conmar-intl.com

PA Consulting Group
600 Alexander Pk., Ste. 209A
Princeton, NJ 08540
(609)806-0800
Fax: (609)936-8811
E-mail: info@paconsulting.com
Website: http://www.pa-consulting.com

Aurora Marketing Management Inc.
66 Witherspoon St., Ste. 600
Princeton, NJ 08542
(908)904-1125
Fax: (908)359-1108
E-mail: aurora2@voicenet.com
Website: http://www.auroramarketing
.net

Schkeeper Inc.
130-6 Bodman Pl.
Red Bank, NJ 07701
(732)219-1965
Fax: (732)530-3703
Website: http://www.schkeeper.com

Henry Branch Associates
2502 Harmon Cove Twr.
Secaucus, NJ 07094
(201)866-2008
Fax: (201)601-0101
E-mail: hbranch161@home.com

Robert Gibbons & Company Inc.
46 Knoll Rd.
Tenafly, NJ 07670-1050
(201)871-3933
Fax: (201)871-2173

PMC Management Consultants Inc.
6 Thistle Ln.
Three Bridges, NJ 08887-0332

(908)788-1014
Free: 800-PMC-0250
Fax: (908)806-7287
E-mail: inguiry@pmc-management.com
Website: http://www.pmc-management
.com

R.W. Bankart & Associates
20 Valley Ave., Ste. D-2
Westwood, NJ 07675-3607
(201)664-7672

New Mexico

Vondle & Associates Inc.
4926 Calle de Tierra, NE
Albuquerque, NM 87111
(505)292-8961
Fax: (505)296-2790
E-mail: vondle@aol.com

InfoNewMexico
2207 Black Hills Rd., NE
Rio Rancho, NM 87124
(505)891-2462
Fax: (505)896-8971

New York

Powers Research and Training Institute
PO Box 78
Bayville, NY 11709
(516)628-2250
Fax: (516)628-2252
E-mail: powercocch@compuserve.com
Website: http://www.nancypowers.com

Consortium House
296 Wittenberg Rd.
Bearsville, NY 12409
(845)679-8867
Fax: (845)679-9248
E-mail: eugenegs@aol.com
Website: http://www.chpub.com

Progressive Finance Corp.
3549 Tiemann Ave.
Bronx, NY 10469
(718)405-9029
Free: 800-225-8381
Fax: (718)405-1170

Wave Hill Associates Inc.
2621 Palisade Ave., Ste. 15-C
Bronx, NY 10463
(718)549-7368
Fax: (718)601-9670
E-mail: pepper@compuserve.com

Management Insight
96 Arlington Rd.
Buffalo, NY 14221
(716)631-3319

Organizations, Agencies, & Consultants

Fax: (716)631-0203
E-mail: michalski@foodserviceinsight.com
Website: http://www.foodserviceinsight
.com

**Samani International Enterprises,
Marions Panyaught Consultancy**
2028 Parsons
Flushing, NY 11357-3436
(917)287-8087
Fax: 800-873-8939
E-mail: vjp2@biostrategist.com
Website: http://www.biostrategist.com

Marketing Resources Group
71-58 Austin St.
Forest Hills, NY 11375
(718)261-8882

**Mangabay Business Plans &
Development**

Subsidiary of Innis Asset Allocation
125-10 Queens Blvd., Ste. 2202
Kew Gardens, NY 11415
(905)527-1947
Fax: 509-472-1935
E-mail: mangabay@mangabay.com
Website: http://www.mangabay.com
Lee Toh, Managing Partner

ComputerEase Co.
1301 Monmouth Ave.
Lakewood, NY 08701
(212)406-9464
Fax: (914)277-5317
E-mail: crawfordc@juno.com

Boice Dunham Group
30 W 13th St.
New York, NY 10011
(212)924-2200
Fax: (212)924-1108

Elizabeth Capen
27 E 95th St.
New York, NY 10128
(212)427-7654
Fax: (212)876-3190

Haver Analytics
60 E 42nd St., Ste. 2424
New York, NY 10017
(212)986-9300
Fax: (212)986-5857
E-mail: data@haver.com
Website: http://www.haver.com

The Jordan, Edmiston Group Inc.
150 E 52nd Ave., 18th Fl.
New York, NY 10022
(212)754-0710
Fax: (212)754-0337

KPMG International
345 Park Ave.
New York, NY 10154-0102
(212)758-9700
Fax: (212)758-9819
Website: http://www.kpmg.com

Mahoney Cohen Consulting Corp.
111 W 40th St., 12th Fl.
New York, NY 10018
(212)490-8000
Fax: (212)790-5913

Management Practice Inc.
342 Madison Ave.
New York, NY 10173-1230
(212)867-7948
Fax: (212)972-5188
Website: http://www.mpiweb.com

Moseley Associates Inc.
342 Madison Ave., Ste. 1414
New York, NY 10016
(212)213-6673
Fax: (212)687-1520

Practice Development Counsel
60 Sutton Pl. S
New York, NY 10022
(212)593-1549
Fax: (212)980-7940
E-mail: pwhaserot@pdcounsel.com
Website: http://www.pdcounsel.com

Unique Value International Inc.
575 Madison Ave., 10th Fl.
New York, NY 10022-1304
(212)605-0590
Fax: (212)605-0589

The Van Tulleken Co.
126 E 56th St.
New York, NY 10022
(212)355-1390
Fax: (212)755-3061
E-mail: newyork@vantulleken.com

Vencon Management Inc.
301 W 53rd St.
New York, NY 10019
(212)581-8787
Fax: (212)397-4126
Website: http://www.venconinc.com

Werner International Inc.
55 E 52nd, 29th Fl.
New York, NY 10055
(212)909-1260
Fax: (212)909-1273
E-mail: richard.downing@rgh.com
Website: http://www.wernertex.com

Zimmerman Business Consulting Inc.
44 E 92nd St., Ste. 5-B
New York, NY 10128
(212)860-3107
Fax: (212)860-7730
E-mail: ljzzbci@aol.com
Website: http://www.zbcinc.com

Overton Financial
7 Allen Rd.
Peekskill, NY 10566
(914)737-4649
Fax: (914)737-4696

Stromberg Consulting
2500 Westchester Ave.
Purchase, NY 10577
(914)251-1515
Fax: (914)251-1562
E-mail: strategy@stromberg_
consulting.com
Website: http://www.stromberg_
consulting.com

**Innovation Management
Consulting Inc.**
209 Dewitt Rd.
Syracuse, NY 13214-2006
(315)425-5144
Fax: (315)445-8989
E-mail: missonneb@axess.net

M. Clifford Agress
891 Fulton St.
Valley Stream, NY 11580
(516)825-8955
Fax: (516)825-8955

Destiny Kinal Marketing Consultancy
105 Chemung St.
Waverly, NY 14892
(607)565-8317
Fax: (607)565-4083

Valutis Consulting Inc.
5350 Main St., Ste. 7
Williamsville, NY 14221-5338
(716)634-2553
Fax: (716)634-2554
E-mail: valutis@localnet.com
Website: http://www.valutisconsulting
.com

North Carolina

Best Practices L.L.C.
6320 Quadrangle Dr., Ste. 200
Chapel Hill, NC 27514
(919)403-0251
Fax: (919)403-0144
E-mail: best@best:in/class
Website: http://www.best-in-class.com

Norelli & Co.
1340 Harding Pl.
Charlotte, NC 28204
(704)376-5484
Fax: (704)376-5485
E-mail: consult@norelli.com
Website: http://www.norelli.com

North Dakota

Center for Innovation
Ina Mae Rude Entrepreneur Ctr.
4200 James Ray Dr.
Grand Forks, ND 58203
(701)777-3132
Fax: (701)777-2339
E-mail: info@innovators.net
Website: http://www.innovators.net

Ohio

Transportation Technology Services
208 Harmon Rd.
Aurora, OH 44202
(330)562-3596

Empro Systems Inc.
4777 Red Bank Expy., Ste. 1
Cincinnati, OH 45227-1542
(513)271-2042
Fax: (513)271-2042

Alliance Management International Ltd.
1440 Windrow Ln.
Cleveland, OH 44147-3200
(440)838-1922
Fax: (440)838-0979
E-mail: bgruss@amiltd.com
Website: http://www.amiltd.com

Bozell Kamstra Public Relations
1301 E 9th St., Ste. 3400
Cleveland, OH 44114
(216)623-1511
Fax: (216)623-1501
E-mail: jfeniger@cleveland.bozellkamstra
.com
Website: http://www.bozellkamstra.com

Cory Dillon Associates
111 Schreyer Pl. E
Columbus, OH 43214
(614)262-8211
Fax: (614)262-3806

Holcomb Gallagher Adams
300 Marconi, Ste. 303
Columbus, OH 43215
(614)221-3343
Fax: (614)221-3367
E-mail: riadams@acme.freenet.oh.us

Young & Associates
PO Box 711
Kent, OH 44240
(330)678-0524
Free: 800-525-9775
Fax: (330)678-6219
E-mail: online@younginc.com
Website: http://www.younginc.com

Robert A. Westman & Associates
8981 Inversary Dr. SE
Warren, OH 44484-2551
(330)856-4149
Fax: (330)856-2564

Oklahoma

Innovative Partners L.L.C.
4900 Richmond Sq., Ste. 100
Oklahoma City, OK 73118
(405)840-0033
Fax: (405)843-8359
E-mail: ipartners@juno.com

Oregon

INTERCON - The International Converting Institute
5200 Badger Rd.
Crooked River Ranch, OR 97760
(541)548-1447
Fax: (541)548-1618
E-mail: johnbowler@crookedriverranch
.com

Talbott ARM
HC 60, Box 5620
Lakeview, OR 97630
(541)635-8587
Fax: (503)947-3482

Management Technology Associates Ltd.
2768 SW Sherwood Dr, Ste. 105
Portland, OR 97201-2251
(503)224-5220
Fax: (503)224-5334
E-mail: lcuster@mta-ltd.com
Website: http://www.mgmt-tech.com

Pennsylvania

Healthscope Inc.
400 Lancaster Ave.
Devon, PA 19333
(610)687-6199
Fax: (610)687-6376
E-mail: health@voicenet.com
Website: http://www.healthscope.net/

Elayne Howard & Associates Inc.
3501 Masons Mill Rd., Ste. 501
Huntingdon Valley, PA 19006-3509
(215)657-9550

GRA Inc.
115 West Ave., Ste. 201
Jenkintown, PA 19046
(215)884-7500
Fax: (215)884-1385
E-mail: gramail@gra-inc.com
Website: http://www.gra-inc.com

Mifflin County Industrial Development Corp.
Mifflin County Industrial Plz.
6395 SR 103 N
Bldg. 50
Lewistown, PA 17044
(717)242-0393
Fax: (717)242-1842
E-mail: mcide@acsworld.net

Autech Products
1289 Revere Rd.
Morrisville, PA 19067
(215)493-3759
Fax: (215)493-9791
E-mail: autech4@yahoo.com

Advantage Associates
434 Avon Dr.
Pittsburgh, PA 15228
(412)343-1558
Fax: (412)362-1684
E-mail: ecocba1@aol.com

Regis J. Sheehan & Associates
Pittsburgh, PA 15220
(412)279-1207

James W. Davidson Company Inc.
23 Forest View Rd.
Wallingford, PA 19086
(610)566-1462

Puerto Rico

Diego Chevere & Co.
Metro Parque 7, Ste. 204
Metro Office
Caparra Heights, PR 00920
(787)774-9595
Fax: (787)774-9566
E-mail: dcco@coqui.net

Manuel L. Porrata and Associates
898 Munoz Rivera Ave., Ste. 201
San Juan, PR 00927
(787)765-2140
Fax: (787)754-3285
E-mail: m_porrata@manuelporrata.com
Website: http://manualporrata.com

South Carolina

Aquafood Business Associates
PO Box 13267
Charleston, SC 29422

(843)795-9506
Fax: (843)795-9477
E-mail: rraba@aol.com

Profit Associates Inc.
PO Box 38026
Charleston, SC 29414
(803)763-5718
Fax: (803)763-5719
E-mail: bobrog@awod.com
Website: http://www.awod.com/gallery/
business/proasc

Strategic Innovations International
12 Executive Ct.
Lake Wylie, SC 29710
(803)831-1225
Fax: (803)831-1177
E-mail: stratinnov@aol.com
Website: http://www.strategicinnovations
.com

Minus Stage
Box 4436
Rock Hill, SC 29731
(803)328-0705
Fax: (803)329-9948

Tennessee

Daniel Petchers & Associates
8820 Fernwood CV
Germantown, TN 38138
(901)755-9896

Business Choices
1114 Forest Harbor, Ste. 300
Hendersonville, TN 37075-9646
(615)822-8692
Free: 800-737-8382
Fax: (615)822-8692
E-mail: bz-ch@juno.com

**RCFA Healthcare Management
Services L.L.C.**
9648 Kingston Pke., Ste. 8
Knoxville, TN 37922
(865)531-0176
Free: 800-635-4040
Fax: (865)531-0722
E-mail: info@rcfa.com
Website: http://www.rcfa.com

Growth Consultants of America
3917 Trimble Rd.
Nashville, TN 37215
(615)383-0550
Fax: (615)269-8940
E-mail: 70244.451@compuserve.com

Texas

**Integrated Cost Management Systems
Inc.**
6001 W I-20, Ste. 209
Arlington, TX 76094-0206
(817)475-2945
E-mail: abm@icms.net
Website: http://www.icms.net

Business Resource Software Inc.
1779 Wells Branch Pky.
Austin, TX 78728
Free: 800-423-1228
Fax: (512)251-4401
E-mail: info@brs-inc.com
Website: http://www.brs-inc.com

Erisa Adminstrative Services Inc.
12325 Hymeadow Dr., Bldg. 4
Austin, TX 78750-1847
(512)250-9020
Fax: (512)250-9487
Website: http://www.cserisa.com

R. Miller Hicks & Co.
1011 W 11th St.
Austin, TX 78703
(512)477-7000
Fax: (512)477-9697
E-mail: millerhicks@rmhicks.com
Website: http://www.rmhicks.com

Pragmatic Tactics Inc.
3303 Westchester Ave.
College Station, TX 77845
(409)696-5294
Free: 800-570-5294
Fax: (409)696-4994
E-mail: ptactics@aol.com
Website: http://www.ptatics.com

Zaetric Business Solutions LLC
27350 Blueberry Hill, Ste. 14
Conroe, TX 77385
(713)621-4885
Fax: (713)824-1654
E-mail: inquiries@zaetric.com
Website: http://www.zaetric.com

Perot Systems
12404 Park Central Dr.
Dallas, TX 75251
(972)340-5000
Free: 800-688-4333
Fax: (972)455-4100
E-mail: corp.comm@ps.net
Website: http://www.perotsystems.com

ReGENERATION Partners
3811 Turtle Creek Blvd., Ste. 300
Dallas, TX 75219

(214)559-3999
Free: 800-406-1112
E-mail: info@regeneration-partner.com
Website: http://www.regeneration-
partners.com

High Technology Associates
5739 Longmont Ln.
Houston, TX 77057
(713)963-9300
Fax: (713)963-8341
E-mail: baker@hta-usa.com
Website: http://www.high-technology-
associates.com

SynerImages LLC
1 Riverway, Ste. 1700
Houston, TX 77056
(713)840-6442
Fax: (713)963-8341
Website: http://www.synerimages.com

PROTEC
4607 Linden Pl.
Pearland, TX 77584
(281)997-9872
Fax: (281)997-9895
E-mail: p.oman@ix.netcom.com

Bastian Public Relations
614 San Dizier
San Antonio, TX 78232
(210)404-1839
E-mail: lisa@bastianpr.com
Website: http://www.bastianpr.com
Lisa Bastian CBC

**Business Strategy Development
Consultants**
PO Box 690365
San Antonio, TX 78269
(210)696-8000
Free: 800-927-BSDC
Fax: (210)696-8000

Utah

Vector Resources
7651 S Main St., Ste. 106
Midvale, UT 84047-7158
(801) 352-8500
Fax: (801) 352-8506
E-mail: info@vectorresources.com
Website: http://www.vectorresources
.com

StreetMaker Inc.
524 West 440 South
Orem, UT 84058-6115
(801)607-2246
Fax: (800)561-4928
E-mail: contact@streetmaker.com
Website: http://www.streetmaker.com

Biomedical Management Resources
PO Box 521125
Salt Lake City, UT 84152-1125
(801)272-4668
Fax: (801)277-3290
E-mail: SeniorManagement@Biomedical
Management.com
Website: http://
www.biomedicalmanagement.com

Marriott Consulting Inc.
6945 S Knudsen Ridge Cir.
Salt Lake City, UT 84121
(801)944-5000
Fax: (801)947-9022
E-mail: info@marriottconsulting.com
Website: http://www.marriott
consulting.com

Virginia

Crown Consulting Inc.
1400 Key Blvd., Ste. 1100
Arlington, VA 22209
(703)650-0663
Fax: (703)243-1280
E-mail: info@crownci.com
Website: http://www.crownci.com

Dare Mighty Things
901 N Glebe Rd., Ste. 1005
Arlington, VA 22203
(703)752-4331
Fax: (703)752-4332
E-mail: info@daremightythings.com
Website: http://www.daremightythings
.com

Elliott B. Jaffa
2530-B S Walter Reed Dr.
Arlington, VA 22206
(703)931-0040

Koach Enterprises - USA
5529 N 18th St.
Arlington, VA 22205
(703)241-8361
Fax: (703)241-8623

AMX International Inc.
9016 Triple Ridge Rd.
Fairfax Station, VA 22039-3003
(703)864-7046
Fax: (703)690-9994
E-mail: info@amxi.com
Website: http://www.amxi.com

Joel Greenstein & Associates
6212 Nethercombe Ct.
McLean, VA 22101
(703) 893-1888

John C. Randall and Associates Inc.
10197 Georgetown Rd.
Mechanicsville, VA 23116
(804)746-4450

Charles Scott Pugh (Investor)
4101 Pittaway Dr.
Richmond, VA 23235-1022
(804)560-0979
Fax: (804)560-4670

Robert Martens & Co.
2226 Floyd Ave.
Richmond, VA 23220
(804) 342-8850
Fax: (804)342-8860
E-mail: rm@robertmartens.com
Website: http://www.robertmartens.com

William W. Garry Inc.
PO Box 61662
Virginia Beach, VA 23466
(757) 467-7874
E-mail: drbillgarry@freeyellow.com

Regis J. Sheehan & Associates
500 Belmont Bay Dr.
Woodbridge, VA 22191-5445
(703)491-7377

Washington

Burlington Consultants
10900 NE 8th St., Ste. 900
Bellevue, WA 98004
(425)688-3060
Fax: (425)454-4383
E-mail: partners@burlington
consultants.com
Website: http://www.burlington
consultants.com

Perry L. Smith Consulting
800 Bellevue Way NE, Ste. 400
Bellevue, WA 98004-4208
(425)462-2072
Fax: (425)462-5638

St. Charles Consulting Group
1420 NW Gilman Blvd.
Issaquah, WA 98027
(425)557-8708
Fax: (425)557-8731
E-mail: info@stcharlesconsulting.com
Website: http://www.stcharlesconsulting
.com

Independent Automotive Training Services
PO Box 334
Kirkland, WA 98083
(425)822-5715
E-mail: ltunney@autosvccon.com
Website: http://www.autosvccon.com

Kahle Associate Inc.
6203 204th Dr. NE
Redmond, WA 98053
(425)836-8763
Fax: (425)868-3770
E-mail: randykahle@kahleassociates.com
Website: http://www.kahleassociates.com

Dan Collin
3419 Wallingord Ave N, No. 2
Seattle, WA 98103
(206)634-9469
E-mail: dc@dancollin.com
Website: http://members.home.net/
dcollin/

ECG Management Consultants Inc.
1111 3rd Ave., Ste. 2700
Seattle, WA 98101-3201
(206)689-2200
Fax: (206)689-2209
E-mail: ecg@ecgmc.com
Website: http://www.ecgmc.com

Northwest Trade Adjustment Assistance Center
900 4th Ave., Ste. 2430
Seattle, WA 98164-1001
(206)622-2730
Free: 800-667-8087
Fax: (206)622-1105
E-mail: matchingfunds@nwtaac.org
Website: http://www.taacenters.org

Business Planning Consultants
S 3510 Ridgeview Dr.
Spokane, WA 99206
(509)928-0332
Fax: (509)921-0842
E-mail: bpci@nextdim.com

West Virginia

**Stanley & Associates Inc./
BusinessandMarketingPlans.com**
1687 Robert C. Byrd Dr.
Beckley, WV 25801
(304)252-0324
Free: 888-752-6720
Fax: (304)252-0470
E-mail: cclay@charterinternet.com
Website: http://
www.BusinessandMarketingPlans.com
Christopher Clay

Wisconsin

White & Associates Inc.
5349 Somerset Ln. S
Greenfield, WI 53221
(414)281-7373
Fax: (414)281-7006
E-mail: wnaconsult@aol.com

Organizations, Agencies, & Consultants

Small business administration regional offices

This section contains a listing of Small Business Administration offices arranged numerically by region. Service areas are provided. Contact the appropriate office for a referral to the nearest field office, or visit the Small Business Administration online at www.sba.gov.

Region 1

U.S. Small Business Administration
Region I Office
10 Causeway St., Ste. 812
Boston, MA 02222-1093
Phone: (617)565-8415
Fax: (617)565-8420
Serves Connecticut, Maine, Massachusetts, New Hampshire, Rhode Island, and Vermont.

Region 2

U.S. Small Business Administration
Region II Office
26 Federal Plaza, Ste. 3108
New York, NY 10278
Phone: (212)264-1450
Fax: (212)264-0038
Serves New Jersey, New York, Puerto Rico, and the Virgin Islands.

Region 3

U.S. Small Business Administration
Region III Office
1150 First Avenue Suite 1001
King of Prussia, PA 19406
(610)382-3092
Serves Delaware, the District of Columbia, Maryland, Pennsylvania, Virginia, and West Virginia.

Region 4

U.S. Small Business Administration
Region IV Office
233 Peachtree St. NE
Harris Tower 1800
Atlanta, GA 30303
Phone: (404)331-4999
Fax: (404)331-2354
Serves Alabama, Florida, Georgia, Kentucky, Mississippi, North Carolina, South Carolina, and Tennessee.

Region 5

U.S. Small Business Administration
Region V Office
500 W. Madison St.
Citicorp Center, Ste. 1150
Chicago, IL 60661
Phone: (312)353-0357
Fax: (312)353-3426
Serves Illinois, Indiana, Michigan, Minnesota, Ohio, and Wisconsin.

Region 6

U.S. Small Business Administration
Region VI Office
4300 Amon Carter Blvd., Ste. 108
Fort Worth, TX 76155
Phone: (817)684-5581
Fax: (817)684-5588
Serves Arkansas, Louisiana, New Mexico, Oklahoma, and Texas.

Region 7

U.S. Small Business Administration
Region VII Office
1000 Walnut Suite 530
Kansas City, MO 64106
Phone: (816)426-4840
Fax: (816)426-4848
Serves Iowa, Kansas, Missouri, and Nebraska.

Region 8

U.S. Small Business Administration
Region VIII Office
721 19th St., Ste. 400
Denver, CO 80202
Phone: (303)844-0500
Fax: (303)844-0506
Serves Colorado, Montana, North Dakota, South Dakota, Utah, and Wyoming.

Region 9

U.S. Small Business Administration
Region IX Office
330 N Brand Blvd., Ste. 1200
Glendale, CA 91203
Phone: (818)552-3437
Fax: (818)552-0344
Serves American Samoa, Arizona, California, Guam, Hawaii, Nevada, and the Trust Territory of the Pacific Islands.

Region 10

U.S. Small Business Administration
Region X Office
2401 Fourth Ave., Ste. 400
Seattle, WA 98121
Phone: (206)553-5676
Fax: (206)553-4155
Serves Alaska, Idaho, Oregon, and Washington.

Small business development centers

This section contains a listing of all Small Business Development Centers, organized alphabetically by state/U.S. territory, then by city, then by agency name.

Alabama

Alabama SBDC

UNIVERSITY OF ALABAMA
2800 Milan Court Suite 124
Birmingham, AL 35211-6908
Phone: 205-943-6750
Fax: 205-943-6752
E-Mail: wcampbell@provost.uab.edu
Website: http://www.asbdc.org
Mr. William Campbell Jr, State Director

Alaska

Alaska SBDC

UNIVERSITY OF ALASKA - ANCHORAGE
430 West Seventh Avenue, Suite 110
Anchorage, AK 99501
Phone: 907-274 -7232
Fax: 907-272-0565
E-Mail: Isaac.Vanderburg@aksbdc.org
Website: http://www.aksbdc.org
Isaac Vanderburg, State Director

American Samoa

American Samoa SBDC

AMERICAN SAMOA COMMUNITY COLLEGE
P.O. Box 2609
Pago Pago, American Samoa 96799
Phone: 011-684-699-4830
Fax: 011-684-699-6132
E-Mail: hthweatt.sbdc@hotmail.com
Website: www.as-sbdc.org
Mr. Herbert Thweatt, Director

Arizona

Arizona SBDC

MARICOPA COUNTY COMMUNITY COLLEGE
2411 West 14th Street, Suite 114
Tempe, AZ 85281
Phone: 480-731-8720
Fax: 480-731-8729

E-Mail: janice.washington@domail
.maricopa.edu
Website: http://www.azsbdc.net
Janice Washington, State Director

Arkansas

Arkansas SBDC

UNIVERSITY OF ARKANSAS

2801 South University Avenue
Little Rock, AR 72204
Phone: 501-683-7700
Fax: 501-683-7720
E-Mail: jmroderick@ualr.edu
Website: http://asbtdc.org
Ms. Janet M. Roderick, State Director

California

California - Northern California Regional SBDC

Northern California SBDC

HUMBOLDT STATE UNIVERSITY

1 Harpst Street 2006A, 209 Siemens Hall
Arcata, CA, 95521
Phone: 707-826-3920
Fax: 707-826-3912
E-Mail: Kristin.Johnson@humboldt.edu
Website: https://www.norcalsbdc.org
Kristin Johnson, Regional Director

California - Northern California SBDC

CALIFORNIA STATE UNIVERSITY - CHICO

35 Main St., Rm 203rr
Chico, CA 95929-0765
Phone: 530-898-5443
Fax: 530-898-4734
E-Mail: dripke@csuchico.edu
Website: https://www.necsbdc.org
Mr. Dan Ripke, Interim Regional Director

California - San Diego and Imperial SBDC

SOUTHWESTERN COMMUNITY COLLEGE

880 National City Boulevard, Suite 103
National City, CA 91950
Phone: 619-216-6721
Fax: 619-216-6692
E-Mail: awilson@swccd.edu
Website: http://www.SBDCRegional
Network.org
Aleta Wilson, Regional Director

California - UC Merced SBDC

UC Merced Lead Center

UNIVERSITY OF CALIFORNIA - MERCED

550 East Shaw, Suite 105A
Fresno, CA 93710
Phone: 559-241-6590
Fax: 559-241-7422
E-Mail: dhowerton@ucmerced.edu
Website: http://sbdc.ucmerced.edu
Diane Howerton, State Director

California - Orange County/Inland Empire SBDC

Tri-County Lead SBDC

CALIFORNIA STATE UNIVERSITY - FULLERTON

800 North State College Boulevard,
SGMH 5313
Fullerton, CA 92834
Phone: 714-278-5168
Fax: 714-278-7101
E-Mail: kmpayne@fullerton.edu
Website: http://www.leadsbdc.org
Katrina Payne Smith, Lead Center Director

California - Los Angeles Region SBDC

LONG BEACH CITY COLLEGE

4900 E. Conant Street, Building 2
Long Beach, CA 90808
Phone: 562-938-5006
Fax: 562-938-5030
E-Mail: jtorres@lbcc.edu
Website: http://www.smallbizla.org
Jesse Torres, Lead Center Director

Colorado

Colorado SBDC

COLORADO SBDC

1625 Broadway, Suite 2700
Denver, CO 80202
Phone: 303-892-3864
Fax: 303-892-3848
E-Mail: Kelly.Manning@state.co.us
Website: http://
www.www.coloradosbdc.org
Ms. Kelly Manning, State Director

Connecticut

Connecticut SBDC

UNIVERSITY OF CONNECTICUT

2100 Hillside Road, Unit 1044
Storrs, CT 06269
Phone: 855-428-7232

E-Mail: ecarter@uconn.edu
Website: www.ctsbdc.com
Emily Carter, State Director

Delaware

Delaware SBDC

DELAWARE TECHNOLOGY PARK

1 Innovation Way, Suite 301
Newark, DE 19711
Phone: 302-831-4283
Fax: 302-831-1423
E-Mail: jmbowman@udel.edu
Website: http://www.delawaresbdc.org
Mike Bowman, State Director

District of Columbia

District of Columbia SBDC

HOWARD UNIVERSITY

2600 6th Street, NW Room 128
Washington, DC 20059
Phone: 202-806-1550
Fax: 202-806-1777
E-Mail: darrell.brown@howard.edu
Website: http://www.dcsbdc.com/
Darrell Brown, Executive Director

Florida

Florida SBDC

UNIVERSITY OF WEST FLORIDA

11000 University Parkway, Building 38
Pensacola, FL 32514
Phone: 850-473-7800
Fax: 850-473-7813
E-Mail: mmyhre@uwf.edu
Website: http://www.floridasbdc.com
Michael Myhre, State Director

Georgia

Georgia SBDC

UNIVERSITY OF GEORGIA

1180 East Broad Street
Athens, GA 30602
Phone: 706-542-6762
Fax: 706-542-7935
E-mail: aadams@georgiasbdc.org
Website: http://www.georgiasbdc.org
Mr. Allan Adams, State Director

Guam

Guam Small Business Development Center

UNIVERSITY OF GUAM

Pacific Islands SBDC
P.O. Box 5014 - U.O.G. Station

Mangilao, GU 96923
Phone: 671-735-2590
Fax: 671-734-2002
E-mail: casey@pacificsbdc.com
Website: http://www.uog.edu/sbdc
Mr. Casey Jeszenka, Director

Hawaii

Hawaii SBDC

UNIVERSITY OF HAWAII - HILO
200 W. Kawili Street, Suite 107
Hilo, HI 96720
Phone: 808-974-7515
Fax: 808-974-7683
E-Mail: cathy.wiltse@hisbdc.org
Website: http://www.hisbdc.org
Cathy Wiltse, State Director

Idaho

Idaho SBDC

BOISE STATE UNIVERSITY
1910 University Drive
Boise, ID 83725
Phone: 208-426-3838
Fax: 208-426-3877
E-mail: ksewell@boisestate.edu
Website: http://www.idahosbdc.org
Katie Sewell, State Director

Illinois

Illinois SBDC

DEPARTMENT OF COMMERCE AND ECONOMIC OPPORTUNITY
500 E. Monroe
Springfield, IL 62701
Phone: 217-524-5700
Fax: 217-524-0171
E-mail: mark.petrilli@illinois.gov
Website: http://www.ilsbdc.biz
Mr. Mark Petrilli, State Director

Indiana

Indiana SBDC

INDIANA ECONOMIC DEVELOPMENT CORPORATION
One North Capitol, Suite 700
Indianapolis, IN 46204
Phone: 317-232-8805
Fax: 317-232-8872
E-mail: JSchpok@iedc.in.gov
Website: http://www.isbdc.org
Jacob Schpok, State Director

Iowa

Iowa SBDC

IOWA STATE UNIVERSITY
2321 North Loop Drive, Suite 202
Ames, IA 50010
Phone: 515-294-2030
Fax: 515-294-6522
E-mail: lshimkat@iastate.edu
Website: http://www.iowasbdc.org
Lisa Shimkat, State Director

Kansas

Kansas SBDC

FORT HAYS STATE UNIVERSITY
214 SW Sixth Street, Suite 301
Topeka, KS 66603
Phone: 785-296-6514
Fax: 785-291-3261
E-mail: panichello@ksbdc.net
Website: http://www.fhsu.edu/ksbdc
Greg Panichello, State Director

Kentucky

Kentucky SBDC

UNIVERSITY OF KENTUCKY
One Quality Street
Lexington, KY 40507
Phone: 859-257-7668
Fax: 859-323-1907
E-mail: lrnaug0@uky.edu
Website: http://www.ksbdc.org
Becky Naugle, State Director

Louisiana

Louisiana SBDC

UNIVERSITY OF LOUISIANA - MONROE

College of Business Administration
700 University Avenue
Monroe, LA 71209
Phone: 318-342-5507
Fax: 318-342-5510
E-mail: rkessler@lsbdc.org
Website: http://www.lsbdc.org
Rande Kessler, State Director

Maine

Maine SBDC

UNIVERSITY OF SOUTHERN MAINE
96 Falmouth Street P.O. Box 9300
Portland, ME 04104
Phone: 207-780-4420
Fax: 207-780-4810

E-mail: mark.delisle@maine.edu
Website: http://www.mainesbdc.org
Mark Delisle, State Director

Maryland

Maryland SBDC

UNIVERSITY OF MARYLAND
7100 Baltimore Avenue, Suite 401
College Park, MD 20742
Phone: 301-403-8300
Fax: 301-403-8303
E-mail: rsprow@mdsbdc.umd.edu
Website: http://www.mdsbdc.umd.edu
Renee Sprow, State Director

Massachusetts

Massachusetts SBDC

UNIVERSITY OF MASSACHUSETTS
23 Tillson Farm Road
Amherst, MA 01003
Phone: 413-545-6301
Fax: 413-545-1273
E-mail: gparkin@msbdc.umass.edu
Website: http://www.www.msbdc.org
Georgianna Parkin, State Director

Michigan

Michigan SBTDC

GRAND VALLEY STATE UNIVERSITY
510 West Fulton Avenue
Grand Rapids, MI 49504
Phone: 616-331-7480
Fax: 616-331-7485
E-mail: boesen@gvsu.edu
Website: http://www.misbtdc.org
Nancy Boese, State Director

Minnesota

Minnesota SBDC

MINNESOTA SMALL BUSINESS DEVELOPMENT CENTER
1st National Bank Building
332 Minnesota Street, Suite E200
St. Paul, MN 55101-1349
Phone: 651-259-7420
Fax: 651-296-5287
E-mail: Bruce.Strong@state.mn.us
Website: http://www.mnsbdc.com
Bruce H. Strong, State Director

Mississippi

Mississippi SBDC

UNIVERSITY OF MISSISSIPPI
122 Jeanette Phillips Drive
P.O. Box 1848

University, MS 38677
Phone: 662-915-5001
Fax: 662-915-5650
E-mail: wgurley@olemiss.edu
Website: http://www.mssbdc.org
Doug Gurley, Jr., State Director

Missouri

Missouri SBDC

UNIVERSITY OF MISSOURI

410 South 6th Street, ?200 Engineering
North
Columbia, MO 65211
Phone: 573-882-9206
Fax: 573-884-4297
E-mail: bouchardc@missouri.edu
Website: http://
www.missouribusiness.net
Chris Bouchard, State Director

Montana

Montana SBDC

DEPARTMENT OF COMMERCE

301 S. Park Avenue, Room 114
Helena, MT 59601
Phone: 406-841-2746
Fax: 406-841-2728
E-mail: adesch@mt.gov
Website: http://www.sbdc.mt.gov
Ms. Ann Desch, State Director

Nebraska

Nebraska SBDC

UNIVERSITY OF NEBRASKA - OMAHA

200 Mammel Hall, 67th & Pine Streets
Omaha, NE 68182
Phone: 402-554-2521
Fax: 402-554-3473
E-mail: rbernier@unomaha.edu
Website: http://nbdc.unomaha.edu
Robert Bernier, State Director

Nevada

Nevada SBDC

UNIVERSITY OF NEVADA - RENO

Reno College of Business, Room 411
Reno, NV 89557-0100
Phone: 775-784-1717
Fax: 775-784-4337
E-mail: males@unr.edu
Website: http://www.nsbdc.org
Sam Males, State Director

New Hampshire

New Hampshire SBDC

UNIVERSITY OF NEW HAMPSHIRE

10 Garrison Avenue
Durham, NH 03824-3593
Phone: 603-862-2200
Fax: 603-862-4876
E-mail: Mary.Collins@unh.edu
Website: http://www.nhsbdc.org
Mary Collins, State Director

New Jersey

New Jersey SBDC

RUTGERS UNIVERSITY

1 Washington Park, 3rd Floor
Newark, NJ 07102
Phone: 973-353-1927
Fax: 973-353-1110
E-mail: bhopper@njsbdc.com
Website: http://www.njsbdc.com
Brenda Hopper, State Director

New Mexico

New Mexico SBDC

SANTA FE COMMUNITY COLLEGE

6401 Richards Avenue
Santa Fe, NM 87508
Phone: 505-428-1362
Fax: 505-428-1469
E-mail: russell.wyrick@sfcc.edu
Website: http://www.nmsbdc.org
Russell Wyrick, State Director

New York

New York SBDC

STATE UNIVERSITY OF NEW YORK

22 Corporate Woods, 3rd Floor
Albany, NY 12246
Phone: 518-443-5398
Fax: 518-443-5275
E-mail: j.king@nyssbdc.org
Website: http://www.nyssbdc.org
Jim King, State Director

North Carolina

North Carolina SBDTC

UNIVERSITY OF NORTH CAROLINA

5 West Hargett Street, Suite 600
Raleigh, NC 27601
Phone: 919-715-7272
Fax: 919-715-7777
E-mail: sdaugherty@sbtdc.org
Website: http://www.sbtdc.org
Scott Daugherty, State Director

North Dakota

North Dakota SBDC

UNIVERSITY OF NORTH DAKOTA

1200 Memorial Highway, PO Box 5509
Bismarck, ND 58506
Phone: 701-328-5375
Fax: 701-250-4304
E-mail: dkmartin@ndsbdc.org
Website: http://www.ndsbdc.org
David Martin, State Director

Ohio

Ohio SBDC

OHIO DEPARTMENT OF DEVELOPMENT

77 South High Street, 28th Floor
Columbus, OH 43216
Phone: 614-466-2711
Fax: 614-466-1789
E-mail: ezra.escudero@development
.ohio.gov
Website: http://www.ohiosbdc.org
Ezra Escudero, State Director

Oklahoma

Oklahoma SBDC

SOUTHEAST OKLAHOMA STATE UNIVERSITY

1405 N. 4th Avenue, PMB 2584
Durant, OK 74701
Phone: 580-745-2955
Fax: 580-745-7471
E-mail: wcarter@se.edu
Website: http://www.osbdc.org
Grady Pennington, State Director

Oregon

Oregon SBDC

LANE COMMUNITY COLLEGE

1445 Willamette Street, Suite 5
Eugene, OR 97401
Phone: 541-463-5250
Fax: 541-345-6006
E-mail: gregorym@lanecc.edu
Website: http://www.bizcenter.org
Mark Gregory, State Director

Pennsylvania

Pennsylvania SBDC

UNIVERSITY OF PENNSYLVANIA

The Wharton School
3819-33 Chestnut Street, Suite 325
Philadelphia, PA 19104

Organizations, Agencies, & Consultants

Phone: 215-898-1219
Fax: 215-573-2135
E-mail: cconroy@wharton.upenn.edu
Website: http://pasbdc.org
Christian Conroy, State Director

Puerto Rico

Puerto Rico SBDC

INTER-AMERICAN UNIVERSITY OF PUERTO RICO

416 Ponce de Leon Avenue, Union Plaza, Tenth Floor
Hato Rey, PR 00918
Phone: 787-763-6811
Fax: 787-763-6875
E-mail: cmarti@prsbdc.org
Website: http://www.prsbdc.org
Carmen Marti, Executive Director

Rhode Island

Rhode Island SBDC

UNIVERSITY OF RHODE ISLAND

75 Lower College Road, 2nd Floor
Kingston, RI 02881
Phone: 401-874-4576
E-mail: gsonnenfeld@uri.edu
Website: http://www.risbdc.org
Gerald Sonnenfeld, State Director

South Carolina

South Carolina SBDC

UNIVERSITY OF SOUTH CAROLINA

Moore School of Business
1014 Greene Street
Columbia, SC 29208
Phone: 803-777-0749
Fax: 803-777-6876
E-mail: michele.abraham@moore.sc.edu
Website: http://www.scsbdc.com
Michele Abraham, State Director

South Dakota

South Dakota SBDC

UNIVERSITY OF SOUTH DAKOTA

414 East Clark Street, Patterson Hall
Vermillion, SD 57069
Phone: 605-677-5103
Fax: 605-677-5427
E-mail: jeff.eckhoff@usd.edu
Website: http://www.usd.edu/sbdc
Jeff Eckhoff, State Director

Tennessee

Tennessee SBDC

MIDDLE TENNESSEE STATE UNIVERSITY

3050 Medical Center Parkway, Ste. 200
Nashville, TN 37129
Phone: 615-849-9999
Fax: 615-893-7089
E-mail: pgeho@tsbdc.org
Website: http://www.tsbdc.org
Patrick Geho, State Director

Texas

Texas-North SBDC

DALLAS COUNTY COMMUNITY COLLEGE

1402 Corinth Street
Dallas, TX 75215
Phone: 214-860-5832
Fax: 214-860-5813
E-mail: m.langford@dcccd.edu
Website: http://www.ntsbdc.org
Mark Langford, Region Director

Texas Gulf Coast SBDC

UNIVERSITY OF HOUSTON

2302 Fannin, Suite 200
Houston, TX 77002
Phone: 713-752-8444
Fax: 713-756-1500
E-mail: fyoung@uh.edu
Website: http://sbdcnetwork.uh.edu
Mike Young, Executive Director

Texas-NW SBDC

TEXAS TECH UNIVERSITY

2579 South Loop 289, Suite 114
Lubbock, TX 79423
Phone: 806-745-3973
Fax: 806-745-6207
E-mail: c.bean@nwtsbdc.org
Website: http://www.nwtsbdc.org
Craig Bean, Executive Director

Texas-South-West Texas Border Region SBDC

UNIVERSITY OF TEXAS - SAN ANTONIO

501 West Durango Boulevard
San Antonio, TX 78207-4415
Phone: 210-458-2480
Fax: 210-458-2425
E-mail: albert.salgado@utsa.edu
Website: https://www.txsbdc.org
Alberto Salgado, Region Director

Utah

Utah SBDC

SALT LAKE COMMUNITY COLLEGE

9750 South 300 West
Salt Lake City, UT 84070
Phone: 801-957-5384
Fax: 801-985-5300
E-mail: Sherm.Wilkinson@slcc.edu
Website: http://www.utahsbdc.org
Sherm Wilkinson, State Director

Vermont

Vermont SBDC

VERMONT TECHNICAL COLLEGE

PO Box 188, 1 Main Street
Randolph Center, VT 05061-0188
Phone: 802-728-9101
Fax: 802-728-3026
E-mail: lrossi@vtsbdc.org
Website: http://www.vtsbdc.org
Linda Rossi, State Director

Virgin Islands

Virgin Islands SBDC

UNIVERSITY OF THE VIRGIN ISLANDS

8000 Nisky Center, Suite 720
St. Thomas, VI 00802
Phone: 340-776-3206
Fax: 340-775-3756
E-mail: ldottin@uvi.edu
Website: http://www.sbdcvi.org
Leonor Dottin, State Director

Virginia

Virginia SBDC

GEORGE MASON UNIVERSITY

4031 University Drive, Suite100
Fairfax, VA 22030
Phone: 703-277-7727
Fax: 703-352-8518
E-mail: jkeenan@gmu.edu
Website: http://www.virginiasbdc.org
Jody Keenan, Director

Washington

Washington SBDC

WASHINGTON STATE UNIVERSITY

1235 N. Post Street, Suite 201
Spokane, WA 99201
Phone: 509-358-7765
Fax: 509-358-7764
E-mail: duane.fladland@wsbdc.org
Website: http://www.wsbdc.org
Duane Fladland, State Director

West Virginia

West Virginia SBDC

WEST VIRGINIA DEVELOPMENT OFFICE
Capital Complex, Building 6, Room 652
1900 Kanawha Boulevard
Charleston, WV 25305
Phone: 304-957-2087
Fax: 304-558-0127
E-mail: Kristina.J.Oliver@wv.gov
Website: http://www.wvsbdc.org
Mr. Conley Salyor, State Director

Wisconsin

Wisconsin SBDC

UNIVERSITY OF WISCONSIN
432 North Lake Street, Room 423
Madison, WI 53706
Phone: 608-263-7794
Fax: 608-263-7830
E-mail: bon.wikenheiser@uwex.edu
Website: http://www.uwex.edu/sbdc
Bon Wikenheiser, State Director

Wyoming

Wyoming SBDC

UNIVERSITY OF WYOMING
1000 E. University Ave., Dept. 3922
Laramie, WY 82071-3922
Phone: 307-766-3405
Fax: 307-766-3406
E-mail: jkline@uwyo.edu
Website: http://www.wyomingentre
preneur.biz
Jill Kline, Acting State Director

Service corps of retired executives (score) offices

This section contains a listing of all SCORE offices organized alphabetically by state/U.S. territory, then by city, then by agency name.

Alabama

SCORE Office (Northeast Alabama)
1400 Commerce Blvd., Northeast
Anniston, AL 36207
(256)241-6111

SCORE Office (North Alabama)
1731 1st Ave. North, Ste. 200
Birmingham, AL 35203
(205)264-8425
Fax: (205)934-0538

SCORE Office (Baldwin County)
327 Fairhope Avenue
Fairhope, AL 36532
(251)928-6387

SCORE Office (Mobile)
451 Government Street
Mobile, AL 36652
(251)431-8614
Fax: (251)431-8646

SCORE Office (Alabama Capitol City)
600 S. Court St.
Montgomery, AL 36104
(334)240-6868
Fax: (334)240-6869

SCORE Office (Tuscaloosa)
2200 University Blvd.
Tuscaloosa, AL 35402
(205)758-7588

Alaska

SCORE Office (Anchorage)
420 L St., Ste. 300
Anchorage, AK 99501
(907)271-4022
Fax: (907)271-4545

Arizona

SCORE Office (Greater Phoenix)
2828 N. Central Ave., Ste. 800
Phoenix, AZ 85004
(602)745-7250
Fax: (602)745-7210
E-mail: e-mail@SCORE-phoenix.org
Website: http://www.greaterphoenix
.score.org/

SCORE Office (Northern Arizona)
1228 Willow Creek Rd., Ste. 2
Prescott, AZ 86301
(928)778-7438
Fax: (928)778-0812
Website: http://www.northernarizona
.score.org/

SCORE Office (Southern Arizona)
1400 W Speedway Blvd.
Tucson, AZ 85745
(520)505-3636
Fax: (520)670-5011
Website: http://www.southernarizona
.score.org/

Arkansas

SCORE Office (South Central)
201 N. Jackson Ave.
El Dorado, AR 71730-5803
(870)863-6113
Fax: (870)863-6115

SCORE Office (Northwest Arkansas)
614 E. Emma St., Room M412
Springdale, AR 72764
(479)725-1809
Website: http://www.northwestarkansas
.score.org

SCORE Office (Little Rock)
2120 Riverfront Dr., Ste. 250
Little Rock, AR 72202-1747
(501)324-7379
Fax: (501)324-5199
Website: http://www.littlerock.score.org

SCORE Office (Southeast Arkansas)
P.O. Box 5069
Pine Bluff, AR 71611-5069
(870)535-0110
Fax: (870)535-1643

California

SCORE Office (Bakersfield)
P.O. Box 2426
Bakersfield, CA 93303
(661)861-9249
Fax: (661)395-4134
Website: http://www.bakersfield.score.org

SCORE Office (Santa Cruz County)
716 G Capitola Ave.
Capitola, CA 95010
(831)621-3735
Fax: (831)475-6530
Website: http://santacruzcounty
.score.org

SCORE Office (Greater Chico Area)
1324 Mangrove St., Ste. 114
Chico, CA 95926
(530)342-8932
Fax: (530)342-8932
Website: http://www.greaterchicoarea
.score.org

SCORE Office (El Centro)
1850 W. Main St, Ste. C
El Centro, CA 92243
(760)337-2692
Website: http://www.sandiego.score.org/

SCORE Office (Central Valley)
801 R St., Ste. 201
Fresno, CA 93721
(559)487-5605
Fax: (559)487-5636
Website: http://www.centralvalley.score
.org

SCORE Office (Los Angeles)
330 N. Brand Blvd., Ste. 190
Glendale, CA 91203-2304
(818)552-3206

Fax: (818)552-3323
Website: http://www.greaterlosangeles
.score.org

SCORE Office (Modesto Merced)
1880 W. Wardrobe Ave.
Merced, CA 95340
(209)725-2033
Fax: (209)577-2673
Website: http://www.modestomerced
.score.org

SCORE Office (Monterey Bay)
Monterey Chamber of Commerce
30 Ragsdale Dr.
Monterey, CA 93940
(831)648-5360
Website: http://
www.montereybay.score.org

SCORE Office (East Bay)
492 9th St., Ste. 350
Oakland, CA 94607
(510)273-6611
Fax: (510)273-6015
E-mail: webmaster@eastbayscore.org
Website: http://www.eastbay.score.org/

SCORE Office (Ventura County)
400 E. Esplanade Dr., Ste. 301
Oxnard, CA 93036
(805)204-6022
Fax: (805)650-1414
Website: http://www.ventura.score.org

SCORE Office (Coachella)
43100 Cook St., Ste. 104
Palm Desert, CA 92211
(760)773-6507
Fax: (760)773-6514
Website: http://www.coachellavalley
.score.org

SCORE Office (Antelope Valley)
1212 E. Avenue, S Ste. A3
Palmdale, CA 93550
(661)947-7679
Website: http://www.antelopevalley
.score.org/

SCORE Office (Inland Empire)
11801 Pierce St., 2nd Fl.
Riverside, CA 92505
(951)-652-4390
Fax: (951)929-8543
Website: http://www.inlandempire
.score.org/

SCORE Office (Sacramento)
4990 Stockton Blvd.
Sacramento, CA 95820
(916)635-9085

Fax: (916)635-9089
Website: http://www.sacramento
.score.org

SCORE Office (San Diego)
550 West C. St., Ste. 550
San Diego, CA 92101-3540
(619)557-7272
Website: http://www.sandiego
.score.org/

SCORE Office (San Francisco)
455 Market St., 6th Fl.
San Francisco, CA 94105
(415)744-6827
Fax: (415)744-6750
E-mail: sfscore@sfscore.
Website: http://www.sanfrancisco
.score.org/

SCORE Office (Silicon Valley)
234 E. Gish Rd., Ste. 100
San Jose, CA 95112
(408)453-6237
Fax: (408)494-0214
E-mail: info@svscore.org
Website: http://www.siliconvalley
.score.org/

SCORE Office (San Luis Obispo)
711 Tank Farm Rd., Ste. 210
San Luis Obispo, CA 93401
(805)547-0779
Website: http://www.sanluisobispo
.score.org

SCORE Office (Orange County)
200 W. Santa Anna Blvd., Ste. 700
Santa Ana, CA 92701
(714)550-7369
Fax: (714)550-0191
Website: http://www.orangecounty.score
.org

SCORE Office (Santa Barbara)
924 Anacapa St.
Santa Barbara, CA 93101
(805)563-0084
Website: http://www.santabarbara.score
.org/

SCORE Office (North Coast)
777 Sonoma Ave., Rm. 115E
Santa Rosa, CA 95404
(707)571-8342
Fax: (707)541-0331
Website: http://www.northcoast.score
.org

SCORE Office (Tuolumne County)
222 S. Shepherd St.
Sonora, CA 95370

(209)532-4316
Fax: (209)588-0673
Website: http://www.tuolumnecounty
.score.org/

Colorado

SCORE Office (Colorado Springs)
3595 E. Fountain Blvd., Ste. E-1
Colorado Springs, CO 80910
(719)636-3074
Fax: (719)635-1571
Website: http://www.coloradosprings
.score.org/

SCORE Office (Denver)
US Custom's House, 4th Fl.
721 19th St.
Denver, CO 80202
(303)844-3985
Fax: (303)844-6490
Website: http://www.denver.score.org/

SCORE Office (Tri-River)
1102 Grand Ave.
Glenwood Springs, CO 81601
(970)945-6589

SCORE Office (Grand Junction)
2591 B & 3/4 Rd.
Grand Junction, CO 81503
(970)243-5242

SCORE Office (Gunnison)
608 N. 11th
Gunnison, CO 81230
(303)641-4422

SCORE Office (Montrose)
1214 Peppertree Dr.
Montrose, CO 81401
(970)249-6080

SCORE Office (Pagosa Springs)
PO Box 4381
Pagosa Springs, CO 81157
(970)731-4890

SCORE Office (Rifle)
0854 W. Battlement Pky., Apt. C106
Parachute, CO 81635
(970)285-9390

SCORE Office (Pueblo)
302 N. Santa Fe
Pueblo, CO 81003
(719)542-1704
Fax: (719)542-1624
Website: http://www.pueblo.score.org

SCORE Office (Ridgway)
143 Poplar Pl.
Ridgway, CO 81432

SCORE Office (Silverton)
PO Box 480
Silverton, CO 81433
(303)387-5430

SCORE Office (Minturn)
PO Box 2066
Vail, CO 81658
(970)476-1224

Connecticut

SCORE Office (Greater Bridgeport)
230 Park Ave.
Bridgeport, CT 06604
(203)450-9484
Fax: (203)576-4388

SCORE Office (Western Connecticut)
155 Deer Hill Ave.
Danbury, CT 06010
(203)794-1404
Website: http://www.westernconnecticut
.score.org

SCORE Office (Greater Hartford County)
330 Main St., 2nd Fl.
Hartford, CT 06106
(860)240-4700
Fax: (860)240-4659
Website: http://www.greaterhartford.score.org

SCORE Office (Manchester)
20 Hartford Rd.
Manchester, CT 06040
(203)646-2223
Fax: (203)646-5871

SCORE Office (New Britain)
185 Main St., Ste. 431
New Britain, CT 06051
(203)827-4492
Fax: (203)827-4480

SCORE Office (New Haven)
60 Sargent Dr.
New Haven, CT 06511
(203)865-7645
Website: http://www.newhaven.score.org

SCORE Office (Fairfield County)
111 East Ave.
Norwalk, CT 06851
(203)847-7348
Fax: (203)849-9308
Website: http://www.fairfieldcounty
.score.org

SCORE Office (Southeastern Connecticut)
665 Boston Post Rd.
Old Saybrook, CT 06475

(860)388-9508
Website: http://www.southeastern
connecticut.score.org

SCORE Office (Northwest Connecticut)
333 Kennedy Dr.
Torrington, CT 06790
(560)482-6586
Website: http://www.northwest
connecticut.score.org

Delaware

SCORE Office (Dover)
Treadway Towers
PO Box 576
Dover, DE 19903
(302)678-0892
Fax: (302)678-0189

SCORE Office (Lewes)
PO Box 1
Lewes, DE 19958
(302)645-8073
Fax: (302)645-8412

SCORE Office (Milford)
204 NE Front St.
Milford, DE 19963
(302)422-3301

SCORE Office (Wilmington)
824 Market St., Ste. 610
Wilmington, DE 19801
(302)573-6652
Fax: (302)573-6092
Website: http://www.scoredelaware.com

District of Columbia

SCORE Office (George Mason University)
409 3rd St. SW, 4th Fl.
Washington, DC 20024
800-634-0245

SCORE Office (Washington DC)
1110 Vermont Ave. NW, 9th Fl.
Washington, DC 20043
(202)606-4000
Fax: (202)606-4225
E-mail: dcscore@hotmail.com
Website: http://www.scoredc.org/

Florida

SCORE Office (Desota County Chamber of Commerce)
16 South Velucia Ave.
Arcadia, FL 34266
(941)494-4033

SCORE Office (Suncoast/Pinellas)
Airport Business Ctr.
4707 - 140th Ave. N, No. 311
Clearwater, FL 33755
(813)532-6800
Fax: (813)532-6800

SCORE Office (DeLand)
336 N. Woodland Blvd.
DeLand, FL 32720
(904)734-4331
Fax: (904)734-4333

SCORE Office (South Palm Beach)
1050 S. Federal Hwy., Ste. 132
Delray Beach, FL 33483
(561)278-7752
Fax: (561)278-0288

SCORE Office (Ft. Lauderdale)
Federal Bldg., Ste. 123
299 E. Broward Blvd.
Ft. Lauderdale, FL 33301
(954)356-7263
Fax: (954)356-7145

SCORE Office (Southwest Florida)
The Renaissance
8695 College Pky., Ste. 345 & 346
Ft. Myers, FL 33919
(941)489-2935
Fax: (941)489-1170

SCORE Office (Treasure Coast)
Professional Center, Ste. 2
3220 S. US, No. 1
Ft. Pierce, FL 34982
(561)489-0548

SCORE Office (Gainesville)
101 SE 2nd Pl., Ste. 104
Gainesville, FL 32601
(904)375-8278

SCORE Office (Hialeah Dade Chamber)
59 W. 5th St.
Hialeah, FL 33010
(305)887-1515
Fax: (305)887-2453

SCORE Office (Daytona Beach)
921 Nova Rd., Ste. A
Holly Hills, FL 32117
(904)255-6889
Fax: (904)255-0229
E-mail: score87@dbeach.com

SCORE Office (South Broward)
3475 Sheridian St., Ste. 203
Hollywood, FL 33021
(305)966-8415

SCORE Office (Citrus County)
5 Poplar Ct.
Homosassa, FL 34446
(352)382-1037

SCORE Office (Jacksonville)
7825 Baymeadows Way, Ste. 100-B
Jacksonville, FL 32256
(904)443-1911
Fax: (904)443-1980
E-mail: scorejax@juno.com
Website: http://www.scorejax.org/

SCORE Office (Jacksonville Satellite)
3 Independent Dr.
Jacksonville, FL 32256
(904)366-6600
Fax: (904)632-0617

SCORE Office (Central Florida)
5410 S. Florida Ave., No. 3
Lakeland, FL 33801
(941)687-5783
Fax: (941)687-6225

SCORE Office (Lakeland)
100 Lake Morton Dr.
Lakeland, FL 33801
(941)686-2168

SCORE Office (St. Petersburg)
800 W. Bay Dr., Ste. 505
Largo, FL 33712
(813)585-4571

SCORE Office (Leesburg)
9501 US Hwy. 441
Leesburg, FL 34788-8751
(352)365-3556
Fax: (352)365-3501

SCORE Office (Cocoa)
1600 Farno Rd., Unit 205
Melbourne, FL 32935
(407)254-2288

SCORE Office (Melbourne)
Melbourne Professional Complex
1600 Sarno, Ste. 205
Melbourne, FL 32935
(407)254-2288
Fax: (407)245-2288

SCORE Office (Merritt Island)
1600 Sarno Rd., Ste. 205
Melbourne, FL 32935
(407)254-2288
Fax: (407)254-2288

SCORE Office (Space Coast)
Melbourn Professional Complex
1600 Sarno, Ste. 205
Melbourne, FL 32935
(407)254-2288
Fax: (407)254-2288

SCORE Office (Dade)
49 NW 5th St.
Miami, FL 33128
(305)371-6889
Fax: (305)374-1882
E-mail: score@netrox.net
Website: http://www.netrox.net/~score/

SCORE Office (Naples of Collier)
International College
2654 Tamiami Trl. E
Naples, FL 34112
(941)417-1280
Fax: (941)417-1281
E-mail: score@naples.net
Website: http://www.naples.net/clubs/
score/index.htm

SCORE Office (Pasco County)
6014 US Hwy. 19, Ste. 302
New Port Richey, FL 34652
(813)842-4638

SCORE Office (Southeast Volusia)
115 Canal St.
New Smyrna Beach, FL 32168
(904)428-2449
Fax: (904)423-3512

SCORE Office (Ocala)
110 E. Silver Springs Blvd.
Ocala, FL 34470
(352)629-5959

Clay County SCORE Office
Clay County Chamber of Commerce
1734 Kingsdey Ave.
PO Box 1441
Orange Park, FL 32073
(904)264-2651
Fax: (904)269-0363

SCORE Office (Orlando)
80 N. Hughey Ave.
Rm. 445 Federal Bldg.
Orlando, FL 32801
(407)648-6476
Fax: (407)648-6425

SCORE Office (Emerald Coast)
19 W. Garden St., No. 325
Pensacola, FL 32501
(904)444-2060
Fax: (904)444-2070

SCORE Office (Charlotte County)
201 W. Marion Ave., Ste. 211
Punta Gorda, FL 33950
(941)575-1818
E-mail: score@gls3c.com
Website: http://www.charlotte-florida
.com/business/scorepg01.htm

SCORE Office (St. Augustine)
1 Riberia St.
St. Augustine, FL 32084
(904)829-5681
Fax: (904)829-6477

SCORE Office (Bradenton)
2801 Fruitville, Ste. 280
Sarasota, FL 34237
(813)955-1029

SCORE Office (Manasota)
2801 Fruitville Rd., Ste. 280
Sarasota, FL 34237
(941)955-1029
Fax: (941)955-5581
E-mail: score116@gte.net
Website: http://www.score-suncoast.org/

SCORE Office (Tallahassee)
200 W. Park Ave.
Tallahassee, FL 32302
(850)487-2665

SCORE Office (Hillsborough)
4732 Dale Mabry Hwy. N, Ste. 400
Tampa, FL 33614-6509
(813)870-0125

SCORE Office (Lake Sumter)
122 E. Main St.
Tavares, FL 32778-3810
(352)365-3556

SCORE Office (Titusville)
2000 S. Washington Ave.
Titusville, FL 32780
(407)267-3036
Fax: (407)264-0127

SCORE Office (Venice)
257 N. Tamiami Trl.
Venice, FL 34285
(941)488-2236
Fax: (941)484-5903

SCORE Office (Palm Beach)
500 Australian Ave. S, Ste. 100
West Palm Beach, FL 33401
(561)833-1672
Fax: (561)833-1712

SCORE Office (Wildwood)
103 N. Webster St.
Wildwood, FL 34785

Georgia

SCORE Office (Atlanta)
Harris Tower, Suite 1900
233 Peachtree Rd., NE
Atlanta, GA 30309
(404)347-2442
Fax: (404)347-1227

SCORE Office (Augusta)
3126 Oxford Rd.
Augusta, GA 30909
(706)869-9100

SCORE Office (Columbus)
School Bldg.
PO Box 40
Columbus, GA 31901
(706)327-3654

SCORE Office (Dalton-Whitfield)
305 S. Thorton Ave.
Dalton, GA 30720
(706)279-3383

SCORE Office (Gainesville)
PO Box 374
Gainesville, GA 30503
(770)532-6206
Fax: (770)535-8419

SCORE Office (Macon)
711 Grand Bldg.
Macon, GA 31201
(912)751-6160

SCORE Office (Brunswick)
4 Glen Ave.
St. Simons Island, GA 31520
(912)265-0620
Fax: (912)265-0629

SCORE Office (Savannah)
111 E. Liberty St., Ste. 103
Savannah, GA 31401
(912)652-4335
Fax: (912)652-4184
E-mail: info@scoresav.org
Website: http://www.coastalempire.com/
score/index.htm

Guam

SCORE Office (Guam)
Pacific News Bldg., Rm. 103
238 Archbishop Flores St.
Agana, GU 96910-5100
(671)472-7308

Hawaii

SCORE Office (Hawaii, Inc.)
1111 Bishop St., Ste. 204
PO Box 50207
Honolulu, HI 96813
(808)522-8132
Fax: (808)522-8135
E-mail: hnlscore@juno.com

SCORE Office (Kahului)
250 Alamaha, Unit N16A
Kahului, HI 96732
(808)871-7711

SCORE Office (Maui, Inc.)
590 E. Lipoa Pkwy., Ste. 227
Kihei, HI 96753
(808)875-2380

Idaho

SCORE Office (Treasure Valley)
1020 Main St., No. 290
Boise, ID 83702
(208)334-1696
Fax: (208)334-9353

SCORE Office (Eastern Idaho)
2300 N. Yellowstone, Ste. 119
Idaho Falls, ID 83401
(208)523-1022
Fax: (208)528-7127

Illinois

SCORE Office (Fox Valley)
40 W. Downer Pl.
PO Box 277
Aurora, IL 60506
(630)897-9214
Fax: (630)897-7002

SCORE Office (Greater Belvidere)
419 S. State St.
Belvidere, IL 61008
(815)544-4357
Fax: (815)547-7654

SCORE Office (Bensenville)
1050 Busse Hwy. Suite 100
Bensenville, IL 60106
(708)350-2944
Fax: (708)350-2979

SCORE Office (Central Illinois)
402 N. Hershey Rd.
Bloomington, IL 61704
(309)644-0549
Fax: (309)663-8270
E-mail: webmaster@central-illinois-score
.org
Website: http://www.central-illinois-score
.org/

SCORE Office (Southern Illinois)
150 E. Pleasant Hill Rd.
Box 1
Carbondale, IL 62901
(618)453-6654
Fax: (618)453-5040

SCORE Office (Chicago)
Northwest Atrium Ctr.
500 W. Madison St., No. 1250
Chicago, IL 60661
(312)353-7724
Fax: (312)886-5688
Website: http://www.mcs.net/~bic/

SCORE Office (Chicago–Oliver Harvey College)
Pullman Bldg.
1000 E. 11th St., 7th Fl.
Chicago, IL 60628
Fax: (312)468-8086

SCORE Office (Danville)
28 W. N. Street
Danville, IL 61832
(217)442-7232
Fax: (217)442-6228

SCORE Office (Decatur)
Milliken University
1184 W. Main St.
Decatur, IL 62522
(217)424-6297
Fax: (217)424-3993
E-mail: charding@mail.millikin.edu
Website: http://www.millikin.edu/
academics/Tabor/score.html

SCORE Office (Downers Grove)
925 Curtis
Downers Grove, IL 60515
(708)968-4050
Fax: (708)968-8368

SCORE Office (Elgin)
24 E. Chicago, 3rd Fl.
PO Box 648
Elgin, IL 60120
(847)741-5660
Fax: (847)741-5677

SCORE Office (Freeport Area)
26 S. Galena Ave.
Freeport, IL 61032
(815)233-1350
Fax: (815)235-4038

SCORE Office (Galesburg)
292 E. Simmons St.
PO Box 749
Galesburg, IL 61401
(309)343-1194
Fax: (309)343-1195

SCORE Office (Glen Ellyn)
500 Pennsylvania
Glen Ellyn, IL 60137
(708)469-0907
Fax: (708)469-0426

SCORE Office (Greater Alton)
Alden Hall
5800 Godfrey Rd.
Godfrey, IL 62035-2466
(618)467-2280

Fax: (618)466-8289
Website: http://www.altonweb.com/score/

SCORE Office (Grayslake)
19351 W. Washington St.
Grayslake, IL 60030
(708)223-3633
Fax: (708)223-9371

SCORE Office (Harrisburg)
303 S. Commercial
Harrisburg, IL 62946-1528
(618)252-8528
Fax: (618)252-0210

SCORE Office (Joliet)
100 N. Chicago
Joliet, IL 60432
(815)727-5371
Fax: (815)727-5374

SCORE Office (Kankakee)
101 S. Schuyler Ave.
Kankakee, IL 60901
(815)933-0376
Fax: (815)933-0380

SCORE Office (Macomb)
216 Seal Hall, Rm. 214
Macomb, IL 61455
(309)298-1128
Fax: (309)298-2520

SCORE Office (Matteson)
210 Lincoln Mall
Matteson, IL 60443
(708)709-3750
Fax: (708)503-9322

SCORE Office (Mattoon)
1701 Wabash Ave.
Mattoon, IL 61938
(217)235-5661
Fax: (217)234-6544

SCORE Office (Quad Cities)
622 19th St.
Moline, IL 61265
(309)797-0082
Fax: (309)757-5435
E-mail: score@qconline.com
Website: http://www.qconline.com/
business/score/

SCORE Office (Naperville)
131 W. Jefferson Ave.
Naperville, IL 60540
(708)355-4141
Fax: (708)355-8355

SCORE Office (Northbrook)
2002 Walters Ave.
Northbrook, IL 60062

(847)498-5555
Fax: (847)498-5510

SCORE Office (Palos Hills)
10900 S. 88th Ave.
Palos Hills, IL 60465
(847)974-5468
Fax: (847)974-0078

SCORE Office (Peoria)
124 SW Adams, Ste. 300
Peoria, IL 61602
(309)676-0755
Fax: (309)676-7534

SCORE Office (Prospect Heights)
1375 Wolf Rd.
Prospect Heights, IL 60070
(847)537-8660
Fax: (847)537-7138

SCORE Office (Quincy Tri-State)
300 Civic Center Plz., Ste. 245
Quincy, IL 62301
(217)222-8093
Fax: (217)222-3033

SCORE Office (River Grove)
2000 5th Ave.
River Grove, IL 60171
(708)456-0300
Fax: (708)583-3121

SCORE Office (Northern Illinois)
515 N. Court St.
Rockford, IL 61103
(815)962-0122
Fax: (815)962-0122

SCORE Office (St. Charles)
103 N. 1st Ave.
St. Charles, IL 60174-1982
(847)584-8384
Fax: (847)584-6065

SCORE Office (Springfield)
511 W. Capitol Ave., Ste. 302
Springfield, IL 62704
(217)492-4416
Fax: (217)492-4867

SCORE Office (Sycamore)
112 Somunak St.
Sycamore, IL 60178
(815)895-3456
Fax: (815)895-0125

SCORE Office (University)
Hwy. 50 & Stuenkel Rd. Ste. C3305
University Park, IL 60466
(708)534-5000
Fax: (708)534-8457

Indiana

SCORE Office (Anderson)
205 W. 11th St.
Anderson, IN 46015
(317)642-0264

SCORE Office (Bloomington)
Star Center
216 W. Allen
Bloomington, IN 47403
(812)335-7334
E-mail: wtfische@indiana.edu
Website: http://www.brainfreezemedia
.com/score527/

SCORE Office (South East Indiana)
500 Franklin St.
Box 29
Columbus, IN 47201
(812)379-4457

SCORE Office (Corydon)
310 N. Elm St.
Corydon, IN 47112
(812)738-2137
Fax: (812)738-6438

SCORE Office (Crown Point)
Old Courthouse Sq. Ste. 206
PO Box 43
Crown Point, IN 46307
(219)663-1800

SCORE Office (Elkhart)
418 S. Main St.
Elkhart, IN 46515
(219)293-1531
Fax: (219)294-1859

SCORE Office (Evansville)
1100 W. Lloyd Expy., Ste. 105
Evansville, IN 47708
(812)426-6144

SCORE Office (Fort Wayne)
1300 S. Harrison St.
Ft. Wayne, IN 46802
(219)422-2601
Fax: (219)422-2601

SCORE Office (Gary)
973 W. 6th Ave., Rm. 326
Gary, IN 46402
(219)882-3918

SCORE Office (Hammond)
7034 Indianapolis Blvd.
Hammond, IN 46324
(219)931-1000
Fax: (219)845-9548

SCORE Office (Indianapolis)
429 N. Pennsylvania St., Ste. 100
Indianapolis, IN 46204-1873

(317)226-7264
Fax: (317)226-7259
E-mail: inscore@indy.net
Website: http://www.score-indianapolis
.org/

SCORE Office (Jasper)
PO Box 307
Jasper, IN 47547-0307
(812)482-6866

SCORE Office (Kokomo/Howard Counties)
106 N. Washington St.
Kokomo, IN 46901
(765)457-5301
Fax: (765)452-4564

SCORE Office (Logansport)
300 E. Broadway, Ste. 103
Logansport, IN 46947
(219)753-6388

SCORE Office (Madison)
301 E. Main St.
Madison, IN 47250
(812)265-3135
Fax: (812)265-2923

SCORE Office (Marengo)
Rt. 1 Box 224D
Marengo, IN 47140
Fax: (812)365-2793

SCORE Office (Marion/Grant Counties)
215 S. Adams
Marion, IN 46952
(765)664-5107

SCORE Office (Merrillville)
255 W. 80th Pl.
Merrillville, IN 46410
(219)769-8180
Fax: (219)736-6223

SCORE Office (Michigan City)
200 E. Michigan Blvd.
Michigan City, IN 46360
(219)874-6221
Fax: (219)873-1204

SCORE Office (South Central Indiana)
4100 Charleston Rd.
New Albany, IN 47150-9538
(812)945-0066

SCORE Office (Rensselaer)
104 W. Washington
Rensselaer, IN 47978

SCORE Office (Salem)
210 N. Main St.
Salem, IN 47167

(812)883-4303
Fax: (812)883-1467

SCORE Office (South Bend)
300 N. Michigan St.
South Bend, IN 46601
(219)282-4350
E-mail: chair@southbend-score.org
Website: http://www.southbend-score.org/

SCORE Office (Valparaiso)
150 Lincolnway
Valparaiso, IN 46383
(219)462-1105
Fax: (219)469-5710

SCORE Office (Vincennes)
27 N. 3rd
PO Box 553
Vincennes, IN 47591
(812)882-6440
Fax: (812)882-6441

SCORE Office (Wabash)
PO Box 371
Wabash, IN 46992
(219)563-1168
Fax: (219)563-6920

Iowa

SCORE Office (Burlington)
Federal Bldg.
300 N. Main St.
Burlington, IA 52601
(319)752-2967

SCORE Office (Cedar Rapids)
2750 1st Ave. NE, Ste 350
Cedar Rapids, IA 52401-1806
(319)362-6405
Fax: (319)362-7861
E:mail: score@scorecr.org
Website: http://www.scorecr.org

SCORE Office (Illowa)
333 4th Ave. S
Clinton, IA 52732
(319)242-5702

SCORE Office (Council Bluffs)
7 N. 6th St.
Council Bluffs, IA 51502
(712)325-1000

SCORE Office (Northeast Iowa)
3404 285th St.
Cresco, IA 52136
(319)547-3377

SCORE Office (Des Moines)
Federal Bldg., Rm. 749
210 Walnut St.

Des Moines, IA 50309-2186
(515)284-4760

SCORE Office (Ft. Dodge)
Federal Bldg., Rm. 436
205 S. 8th St.
Ft. Dodge, IA 50501
(515)955-2622

SCORE Office (Independence)
110 1st. St. east
Independence, IA 50644
(319)334-7178
Fax: (319)334-7179

SCORE Office (Iowa City)
210 Federal Bldg.
PO Box 1853
Iowa City, IA 52240-1853
(319)338-1662

SCORE Office (Keokuk)
401 Main St.
Pierce Bldg., No. 1
Keokuk, IA 52632
(319)524-5055

SCORE Office (Central Iowa)
Fisher Community College
709 S. Center
Marshalltown, IA 50158
(515)753-6645

SCORE Office (River City)
15 West State St.
Mason City, IA 50401
(515)423-5724

SCORE Office (South Central)
SBDC, Indian Hills Community College
525 Grandview Ave.
Ottumwa, IA 52501
(515)683-5127
Fax: (515)683-5263

SCORE Office (Dubuque)
10250 Sundown Rd.
Peosta, IA 52068
(319)556-5110

SCORE Office (Southwest Iowa)
614 W. Sheridan
Shenandoah, IA 51601
(712)246-3260

SCORE Office (Sioux City)
Federal Bldg.
320 6th St.
Sioux City, IA 51101
(712)277-2324
Fax: (712)277-2325

SCORE Office (Iowa Lakes)
122 W. 5th St.
Spencer, IA 51301
(712)262-3059

SCORE Office (Vista)
119 W. 6th St.
Storm Lake, IA 50588
(712)732-3780

SCORE Office (Waterloo)
215 E. 4th
Waterloo, IA 50703
(319)233-8431

Kansas

SCORE Office (Southwest Kansas)
501 W. Spruce
Dodge City, KS 67801
(316)227-3119

SCORE Office (Emporia)
811 Homewood
Emporia, KS 66801
(316)342-1600

SCORE Office (Golden Belt)
1307 Williams
Great Bend, KS 67530
(316)792-2401

SCORE Office (Hays)
PO Box 400
Hays, KS 67601
(913)625-6595

SCORE Office (Hutchinson)
1 E. 9th St.
Hutchinson, KS 67501
(316)665-8468
Fax: (316)665-7619

SCORE Office (Southeast Kansas)
404 Westminster Pl.
PO Box 886
Independence, KS 67301
(316)331-4741

SCORE Office (McPherson)
306 N. Main
PO Box 616
McPherson, KS 67460
(316)241-3303

SCORE Office (Salina)
120 Ash St.
Salina, KS 67401
(785)243-4290
Fax: (785)243-1833

SCORE Office (Topeka)
1700 College
Topeka, KS 66621
(785)231-1010

SCORE Office (Wichita)
100 E. English, Ste. 510
Wichita, KS 67202

(316)269-6273
Fax: (316)269-6499

SCORE Office (Ark Valley)
205 E. 9th St.
Winfield, KS 67156
(316)221-1617

Kentucky

SCORE Office (Ashland)
PO Box 830
Ashland, KY 41105
(606)329-8011
Fax: (606)325-4607

SCORE Office (Bowling Green)
812 State St.
PO Box 51
Bowling Green, KY 42101
(502)781-3200
Fax: (502)843-0458

SCORE Office (Tri-Lakes)
508 Barbee Way
Danville, KY 40422-1548
(606)231-9902

SCORE Office (Glasgow)
301 W. Main St.
Glasgow, KY 42141
(502)651-3161
Fax: (502)651-3122

SCORE Office (Hazard)
B & I Technical Center
100 Airport Gardens Rd.
Hazard, KY 41701
(606)439-5856
Fax: (606)439-1808

SCORE Office (Lexington)
410 W. Vine St., Ste. 290, Civic C
Lexington, KY 40507
(606)231-9902
Fax: (606)253-3190
E-mail: scorelex@uky.campus.mci.net

SCORE Office (Louisville)
188 Federal Office Bldg.
600 Dr. Martin L. King Jr. Pl.
Louisville, KY 40202
(502)582-5976

SCORE Office (Madisonville)
257 N. Main
Madisonville, KY 42431
(502)825-1399
Fax: (502)825-1396

SCORE Office (Paducah)
Federal Office Bldg.
501 Broadway, Rm. B-36

Paducah, KY 42001
(502)442-5685

Louisiana

SCORE Office (Central Louisiana)
802 3rd St.
Alexandria, LA 71309
(318)442-6671

SCORE Office (Baton Rouge)
564 Laurel St.
PO Box 3217
Baton Rouge, LA 70801
(504)381-7130
Fax: (504)336-4306

SCORE Office (North Shore)
2 W. Thomas
Hammond, LA 70401
(504)345-4457
Fax: (504)345-4749

SCORE Office (Lafayette)
804 St. Mary Blvd.
Lafayette, LA 70505-1307
(318)233-2705
Fax: (318)234-8671
E-mail: score302@aol.com

SCORE Office (Lake Charles)
120 W. Pujo St.
Lake Charles, LA 70601
(318)433-3632

SCORE Office (New Orleans)
365 Canal St., Ste. 3100
New Orleans, LA 70130
(504)589-2356
Fax: (504)589-2339

SCORE Office (Shreveport)
400 Edwards St.
Shreveport, LA 71101
(318)677-2536
Fax: (318)677-2541

Maine

SCORE Office (Augusta)
40 Western Ave.
Augusta, ME 04330
(207)622-8509

SCORE Office (Bangor)
Peabody Hall, Rm. 229
One College Cir.
Bangor, ME 04401
(207)941-9707

SCORE Office (Central & Northern Arroostock)
111 High St.
Caribou, ME 04736

(207)492-8010
Fax: (207)492-8010

SCORE Office (Penquis)
South St.
Dover Foxcroft, ME 04426
(207)564-7021

SCORE Office (Maine Coastal)
Mill Mall
Box 1105
Ellsworth, ME 04605-1105
(207)667-5800
E-mail: score@arcadia.net

SCORE Office (Lewiston-Auburn)
BIC of Maine-Bates Mill Complex
35 Canal St.
Lewiston, ME 04240-7764
(207)782-3708
Fax: (207)783-7745

SCORE Office (Portland)
66 Pearl St., Rm. 210
Portland, ME 04101
(207)772-1147
Fax: (207)772-5581
E-mail: Score53@score.maine.org
Website: http://www.score.maine.org/chapter53/

SCORE Office (Western Mountains)
255 River St.
PO Box 252
Rumford, ME 04257-0252
(207)369-9976

SCORE Office (Oxford Hills)
166 Main St.
South Paris, ME 04281
(207)743-0499

Maryland

SCORE Office (Southern Maryland)
2525 Riva Rd., Ste. 110
Annapolis, MD 21401
(410)266-9553
Fax: (410)573-0981
E-mail: score390@aol.com
Website: http://members.aol.com/score390/index.htm

SCORE Office (Baltimore)
The City Crescent Bldg., 6th Fl.
10 S. Howard St.
Baltimore, MD 21201
(410)962-2233
Fax: (410)962-1805

SCORE Office (Bel Air)
108 S. Bond St.
Bel Air, MD 21014

(410)838-2020
Fax: (410)893-4715

SCORE Office (Bethesda)
7910 Woodmont Ave., Ste. 1204
Bethesda, MD 20814
(301)652-4900
Fax: (301)657-1973

SCORE Office (Bowie)
6670 Race Track Rd.
Bowie, MD 20715
(301)262-0920
Fax: (301)262-0921

SCORE Office (Dorchester County)
203 Sunburst Hwy.
Cambridge, MD 21613
(410)228-3575

SCORE Office (Upper Shore)
210 Marlboro Ave.
Easton, MD 21601
(410)822-4606
Fax: (410)822-7922

SCORE Office (Frederick County)
43A S. Market St.
Frederick, MD 21701
(301)662-8723
Fax: (301)846-4427

SCORE Office (Gaithersburg)
9 Park Ave.
Gaithersburg, MD 20877
(301)840-1400
Fax: (301)963-3918

SCORE Office (Glen Burnie)
103 Crain Hwy. SE
Glen Burnie, MD 21061
(410)766-8282
Fax: (410)766-9722

SCORE Office (Hagerstown)
111 W. Washington St.
Hagerstown, MD 21740
(301)739-2015
Fax: (301)739-1278

SCORE Office (Laurel)
7901 Sandy Spring Rd. Ste. 501
Laurel, MD 20707
(301)725-4000
Fax: (301)725-0776

SCORE Office (Salisbury)
300 E. Main St.
Salisbury, MD 21801
(410)749-0185
Fax: (410)860-9925

Massachusetts

SCORE Office (NE Massachusetts)
100 Cummings Ctr., Ste. 101 K
Beverly, MA 01923
(978)922-9441
Website: http://www1.shore.net/~score/

SCORE Office (Boston)
10 Causeway St., Rm. 265
Boston, MA 02222-1093
(617)565-5591
Fax: (617)565-5598
E-mail: boston-score-20@worldnet.att.net
Website: http://www.scoreboston.org/

SCORE office (Bristol/Plymouth County)
53 N. 6th St., Federal Bldg.
Bristol, MA 02740
(508)994-5093

SCORE Office (SE Massachusetts)
60 School St.
Brockton, MA 02401
(508)587-2673
Fax: (508)587-1340
Website: http://www.metrosouthchamber.com/score.html

SCORE Office (North Adams)
820 N. State Rd.
Cheshire, MA 01225
(413)743-5100

SCORE Office (Clinton Satellite)
1 Green St.
Clinton, MA 01510
Fax: (508)368-7689

SCORE Office (Greenfield)
PO Box 898
Greenfield, MA 01302
(413)773-5463
Fax: (413)773-7008

SCORE Office (Haverhill)
87 Winter St.
Haverhill, MA 01830
(508)373-5663
Fax: (508)373-8060

SCORE Office (Hudson Satellite)
PO Box 578
Hudson, MA 01749
(508)568-0360
Fax: (508)568-0360

SCORE Office (Cape Cod)
Independence Pk., Ste. 5B
270 Communications Way
Hyannis, MA 02601

(508)775-4884
Fax: (508)790-2540

SCORE Office (Lawrence)
264 Essex St.
Lawrence, MA 01840
(508)686-0900
Fax: (508)794-9953

SCORE Office (Leominster Satellite)
110 Erdman Way
Leominster, MA 01453
(508)840-4300
Fax: (508)840-4896

SCORE Office (Bristol/Plymouth Counties)
53 N. 6th St., Federal Bldg.
New Bedford, MA 02740
(508)994-5093

SCORE Office (Newburyport)
29 State St.
Newburyport, MA 01950
(617)462-6680

SCORE Office (Pittsfield)
66 West St.
Pittsfield, MA 01201
(413)499-2485

SCORE Office (Haverhill-Salem)
32 Derby Sq.
Salem, MA 01970
(508)745-0330
Fax: (508)745-3855

SCORE Office (Springfield)
1350 Main St.
Federal Bldg.
Springfield, MA 01103
(413)785-0314

SCORE Office (Carver)
12 Taunton Green, Ste. 201
Taunton, MA 02780
(508)824-4068
Fax: (508)824-4069

SCORE Office (Worcester)
33 Waldo St.
Worcester, MA 01608
(508)753-2929
Fax: (508)754-8560

Michigan

SCORE Office (Allegan)
PO Box 338
Allegan, MI 49010
(616)673-2479

SCORE Office (Ann Arbor)
425 S. Main St., Ste. 103
Ann Arbor, MI 48104
(313)665-4433

SCORE Office (Battle Creek)
34 W. Jackson Ste. 4A
Battle Creek, MI 49017-3505
(616)962-4076
Fax: (616)962-6309

SCORE Office (Cadillac)
222 Lake St.
Cadillac, MI 49601
(616)775-9776
Fax: (616)768-4255

SCORE Office (Detroit)
477 Michigan Ave., Rm. 515
Detroit, MI 48226
(313)226-7947
Fax: (313)226-3448

SCORE Office (Flint)
708 Root Rd., Rm. 308
Flint, MI 48503
(810)233-6846

SCORE Office (Grand Rapids)
111 Pearl St. NW
Grand Rapids, MI 49503-2831
(616)771-0305
Fax: (616)771-0328
E-mail: scoreone@iserv.net
Website: http://www.iserv.net/
~scoreone/

SCORE Office (Holland)
480 State St.
Holland, MI 49423
(616)396-9472

SCORE Office (Jackson)
209 East Washington
PO Box 80
Jackson, MI 49204
(517)782-8221
Fax: (517)782-0061

SCORE Office (Kalamazoo)
345 W. Michigan Ave.
Kalamazoo, MI 49007
(616)381-5382
Fax: (616)384-0096
E-mail: score@nucleus.net

SCORE Office (Lansing)
117 E. Allegan
PO Box 14030
Lansing, MI 48901
(517)487-6340
Fax: (517)484-6910

SCORE Office (Livonia)
15401 Farmington Rd.
Livonia, MI 48154
(313)427-2122
Fax: (313)427-6055

SCORE Office (Madison Heights)
26345 John R
Madison Heights, MI 48071
(810)542-5010
Fax: (810)542-6821

SCORE Office (Monroe)
111 E. 1st
Monroe, MI 48161
(313)242-3366
Fax: (313)242-7253

SCORE Office (Mt. Clemens)
58 S/B Gratiot
Mt. Clemens, MI 48043
(810)463-1528
Fax: (810)463-6541

SCORE Office (Muskegon)
PO Box 1087
230 Terrace Plz.
Muskegon, MI 49443
(616)722-3751
Fax: (616)728-7251

SCORE Office (Petoskey)
401 E. Mitchell St.
Petoskey, MI 49770
(616)347-4150

SCORE Office (Pontiac)
Executive Office Bldg.
1200 N. Telegraph Rd.
Pontiac, MI 48341
(810)975-9555

SCORE Office (Pontiac)
PO Box 430025
Pontiac, MI 48343
(810)335-9600

SCORE Office (Port Huron)
920 Pinegrove Ave.
Port Huron, MI 48060
(810)985-7101

SCORE Office (Rochester)
71 Walnut Ste. 110
Rochester, MI 48307
(810)651-6700
Fax: (810)651-5270

SCORE Office (Saginaw)
901 S. Washington Ave.
Saginaw, MI 48601
(517)752-7161
Fax: (517)752-9055

SCORE Office (Upper Peninsula)
2581 I-75 Business Spur
Sault Ste. Marie, MI 49783
(906)632-3301

SCORE Office (Southfield)
21000 W. 10 Mile Rd.
Southfield, MI 48075
(810)204-3050
Fax: (810)204-3099

SCORE Office (Traverse City)
202 E. Grandview Pkwy.
PO Box 387
Traverse City, MI 49685
(616)947-5075
Fax: (616)946-2565

SCORE Office (Warren)
30500 Van Dyke, Ste. 118
Warren, MI 48093
(810)751-3939

Minnesota

SCORE Office (Aitkin)
Aitkin, MN 56431
(218)741-3906

SCORE Office (Albert Lea)
202 N. Broadway Ave.
Albert Lea, MN 56007
(507)373-7487

SCORE Office (Austin)
PO Box 864
Austin, MN 55912
(507)437-4561
Fax: (507)437-4869

SCORE Office (South Metro)
Ames Business Ctr.
2500 W. County Rd., No. 42
Burnsville, MN 55337
(612)898-5645
Fax: (612)435-6972
E-mail: southmetro@scoreminn.org
Website: http://www.scoreminn.org/
southmetro/

SCORE Office (Duluth)
1717 Minnesota Ave.
Duluth, MN 55802
(218)727-8286
Fax: (218)727-3113
E-mail: duluth@scoreminn.org
Website: http://www.scoreminn.org

SCORE Office (Fairmont)
PO Box 826
Fairmont, MN 56031
(507)235-5547
Fax: (507)235-8411

SCORE Office (Southwest Minnesota)
112 Riverfront St.
Box 999
Mankato, MN 56001

(507)345-4519
Fax: (507)345-4451
Website: http://www.scoreminn.org/

SCORE Office (Minneapolis)
North Plaza Bldg., Ste. 51
5217 Wayzata Blvd.
Minneapolis, MN 55416
(612)591-0539
Fax: (612)544-0436
Website: http://www.scoreminn.org/

SCORE Office (Owatonna)
PO Box 331
Owatonna, MN 55060
(507)451-7970
Fax: (507)451-7972

SCORE Office (Red Wing)
2000 W. Main St., Ste. 324
Red Wing, MN 55066
(612)388-4079

SCORE Office (Southeastern Minnesota)
220 S. Broadway, Ste. 100
Rochester, MN 55901
(507)288-1122
Fax: (507)282-8960
Website: http://www.scoreminn.org/

SCORE Office (Brainerd)
St. Cloud, MN 56301

SCORE Office (Central Area)
1527 Northway Dr.
St. Cloud, MN 56301
(320)240-1332
Fax: (320)255-9050
Website: http://www.scoreminn.org/

SCORE Office (St. Paul)
350 St. Peter St., No. 295
Lowry Professional Bldg.
St. Paul, MN 55102
(651)223-5010
Fax: (651)223-5048
Website: http://www.scoreminn.org/

SCORE Office (Winona)
Box 870
Winona, MN 55987
(507)452-2272
Fax: (507)454-8814

SCORE Office (Worthington)
1121 3rd Ave.
Worthington, MN 56187
(507)372-2919
Fax: (507)372-2827

Mississippi

SCORE Office (Delta)
915 Washington Ave.
PO Box 933
Greenville, MS 38701
(601)378-3141

SCORE Office (Gulfcoast)
1 Government Plaza
2909 13th St., Ste. 203
Gulfport, MS 39501
(228)863-0054

SCORE Office (Jackson)
1st Jackson Center, Ste. 400
101 W. Capitol St.
Jackson, MS 39201
(601)965-5533

SCORE Office (Meridian)
5220 16th Ave.
Meridian, MS 39305
(601)482-4412

Missouri

SCORE Office (Lake of the Ozark)
University Extension
113 Kansas St.
PO Box 1405
Camdenton, MO 65020
(573)346-2644
Fax: (573)346-2694
E-mail: score@cdoc.net
Website: http://sites.cdoc.net/score/

Chamber of Commerce (Cape Girardeau)
PO Box 98
Cape Girardeau, MO 63702-0098
(314)335-3312

SCORE Office (Mid-Missouri)
1705 Halstead Ct.
Columbia, MO 65203
(573)874-1132

SCORE Office (Ozark-Gateway)
1486 Glassy Rd.
Cuba, MO 65453-1640
(573)885-4954

SCORE Office (Kansas City)
323 W. 8th St., Ste. 104
Kansas City, MO 64105
(816)374-6675
Fax: (816)374-6692
E-mail: SCOREBIC@AOL.COM
Website: http://www.crn.org/score/

SCORE Office (Sedalia)
Lucas Place
323 W. 8th St., Ste.104

Kansas City, MO 64105
(816)374-6675

SCORE office (Tri-Lakes)
PO Box 1148
Kimberling, MO 65686
(417)739-3041

SCORE Office (Tri-Lakes)
HCRI Box 85
Lampe, MO 65681
(417)858-6798

SCORE Office (Mexico)
111 N. Washington St.
Mexico, MO 65265
(314)581-2765

SCORE Office (Southeast Missouri)
Rte. 1, Box 280
Neelyville, MO 63954
(573)989-3577

SCORE office (Poplar Bluff Area)
806 Emma St.
Poplar Bluff, MO 63901
(573)686-8892

SCORE Office (St. Joseph)
3003 Frederick Ave.
St. Joseph, MO 64506
(816)232-4461

SCORE Office (St. Louis)
815 Olive St., Rm. 242
St. Louis, MO 63101-1569
(314)539-6970
Fax: (314)539-3785
E-mail: info@stlscore.org
Website: http://www.stlscore.org/

SCORE Office (Lewis & Clark)
425 Spencer Rd.
St. Peters, MO 63376
(314)928-2900
Fax: (314)928-2900
E-mail: score01@mail.win.org

SCORE Office (Springfield)
620 S. Glenstone, Ste. 110
Springfield, MO 65802-3200
(417)864-7670
Fax: (417)864-4108

SCORE office (Southeast Kansas)
1206 W. First St.
Webb City, MO 64870
(417)673-3984

Montana

SCORE Office (Billings)
815 S. 27th St.
Billings, MT 59101
(406)245-4111

SCORE Office (Bozeman)
1205 E. Main St.
Bozeman, MT 59715
(406)586-5421

SCORE Office (Butte)
1000 George St.
Butte, MT 59701
(406)723-3177

SCORE Office (Great Falls)
710 First Ave. N
Great Falls, MT 59401
(406)761-4434
E-mail: scoregtf@in.tch.com

SCORE Office (Havre, Montana)
518 First St.
Havre, MT 59501
(406)265-4383

SCORE Office (Helena)
Federal Bldg.
301 S. Park
Helena, MT 59626-0054
(406)441-1081

SCORE Office (Kalispell)
2 Main St.
Kalispell, MT 59901
(406)756-5271
Fax: (406)752-6665

SCORE Office (Missoula)
723 Ronan
Missoula, MT 59806
(406)327-8806
E-mail: score@safeshop.com
Website: http://missoula.bigsky.net/
score/

Nebraska

SCORE Office (Columbus)
Columbus, NE 68601
(402)564-2769

SCORE Office (Fremont)
92 W. 5th St.
Fremont, NE 68025
(402)721-2641

SCORE Office (Hastings)
Hastings, NE 68901
(402)463-3447

SCORE Office (Lincoln)
8800 O St.
Lincoln, NE 68520
(402)437-2409

SCORE Office (Panhandle)
150549 CR 30
Minatare, NE 69356

(308)632-2133
Website: http://www.tandt.com/SCORE

SCORE Office (Norfolk)
3209 S. 48th Ave.
Norfolk, NE 68106
(402)564-2769

SCORE Office (North Platte)
3301 W. 2nd St.
North Platte, NE 69101
(308)532-4466

SCORE Office (Omaha)
11145 Mill Valley Rd.
Omaha, NE 68154
(402)221-3606
Fax: (402)221-3680
E-mail: infoctr@ne.uswest.net
Website: http://www.tandt.com/score/

Nevada

SCORE Office (Incline Village)
969 Tahoe Blvd.
Incline Village, NV 89451
(702)831-7327
Fax: (702)832-1605

SCORE Office (Carson City)
301 E. Stewart
PO Box 7527
Las Vegas, NV 89125
(702)388-6104

SCORE Office (Las Vegas)
300 Las Vegas Blvd. S, Ste. 1100
Las Vegas, NV 89101
(702)388-6104

SCORE Office (Northern Nevada)
SBDC, College of Business
Administration
Univ. of Nevada
Reno, NV 89557-0100
(702)784-4436
Fax: (702)784-4337

New Hampshire

SCORE Office (North Country)
PO Box 34
Berlin, NH 03570
(603)752-1090

SCORE Office (Concord)
143 N. Main St., Rm. 202A
PO Box 1258
Concord, NH 03301
(603)225-1400
Fax: (603)225-1409

SCORE Office (Dover)
299 Central Ave.
Dover, NH 03820

(603)742-2218
Fax: (603)749-6317

SCORE Office (Monadnock)
34 Mechanic St.
Keene, NH 03431-3421
(603)352-0320

SCORE Office (Lakes Region)
67 Water St., Ste. 105
Laconia, NH 03246
(603)524-9168

SCORE Office (Upper Valley)
Citizens Bank Bldg., Rm. 310
20 W. Park St.
Lebanon, NH 03766
(603)448-3491
Fax: (603)448-1908
E-mail: billt@valley.net
Website: http://www.valley.net/~score/

SCORE Office (Merrimack Valley)
275 Chestnut St., Rm. 618
Manchester, NH 03103
(603)666-7561
Fax: (603)666-7925

SCORE Office (Mt. Washington Valley)
PO Box 1066
North Conway, NH 03818
(603)383-0800

SCORE Office (Seacoast)
195 Commerce Way, Unit-A
Portsmouth, NH 03801-3251
(603)433-0575

New Jersey

SCORE Office (Somerset)
Paritan Valley Community College,
Rte. 28
Branchburg, NJ 08807
(908)218-8874
E-mail: nj-score@grizbiz.com.
Website: http://www.nj-score.org/

SCORE Office (Chester)
5 Old Mill Rd.
Chester, NJ 07930
(908)879-7080

SCORE Office (Greater Princeton)
4 A George Washington Dr.
Cranbury, NJ 08512
(609)520-1776

SCORE Office (Freehold)
36 W. Main St.
Freehold, NJ 07728
(908)462-3030
Fax: (908)462-2123

SCORE Office (North West)
Picantinny Innovation Ctr.
3159 Schrader Rd.
Hamburg, NJ 07419
(973)209-8525
Fax: (973)209-7252
E-mail: nj-score@grizbiz.com
Website: http://www.nj-score.org/

SCORE Office (Monmouth)
765 Newman Springs Rd.
Lincroft, NJ 07738
(908)224-2573
E-mail: nj-score@grizbiz.com
Website: http://www.nj-score.org/

SCORE Office (Manalapan)
125 Symmes Dr.
Manalapan, NJ 07726
(908)431-7220

SCORE Office (Jersey City)
2 Gateway Ctr., 4th Fl.
Newark, NJ 07102
(973)645-3982
Fax: (973)645-2375

SCORE Office (Newark)
2 Gateway Center, 15th Fl.
Newark, NJ 07102-5553
(973)645-3982
Fax: (973)645-2375
E-mail: nj-score@grizbiz.com
Website: http://www.nj-score.org

SCORE Office (Bergen County)
327 E. Ridgewood Ave.
Paramus, NJ 07652
(201)599-6090
E-mail: nj-score@grizbiz.com
Website: http://www.nj-score.org/

SCORE Office (Pennsauken)
4900 Rte. 70
Pennsauken, NJ 08109
(609)486-3421

SCORE Office (Southern New Jersey)
4900 Rte. 70
Pennsauken, NJ 08109
(609)486-3421
E-mail: nj-score@grizbiz.com
Website: http://www.nj-score.org/

SCORE Office (Greater Princeton)
216 Rockingham Row
Princeton Forrestal Village
Princeton, NJ 08540
(609)520-1776
Fax: (609)520-9107
E-mail: nj-score@grizbiz.com
Website: http://www.nj-score.org/

SCORE Office (Shrewsbury)
Hwy. 35
Shrewsbury, NJ 07702
(908)842-5995
Fax: (908)219-6140

SCORE Office (Ocean County)
33 Washington St.
Toms River, NJ 08754
(732)505-6033
E-mail: nj-score@grizbiz.com
Website: http://www.nj-score.org/

SCORE Office (Wall)
2700 Allaire Rd.
Wall, NJ 07719
(908)449-8877

SCORE Office (Wayne)
2055 Hamburg Tpke.
Wayne, NJ 07470
(201)831-7788
Fax: (201)831-9112

New Mexico

SCORE Office (Albuquerque)
525 Buena Vista, SE
Albuquerque, NM 87106
(505)272-7999
Fax: (505)272-7963

SCORE Office (Las Cruces)
Loretto Towne Center
505 S. Main St., Ste. 125
Las Cruces, NM 88001
(505)523-5627
Fax: (505)524-2101
E-mail: score.397@zianet.com

SCORE Office (Roswell)
Federal Bldg., Rm. 237
Roswell, NM 88201
(505)625-2112
Fax: (505)623-2545

SCORE Office (Santa Fe)
Montoya Federal Bldg.
120 Federal Place, Rm. 307
Santa Fe, NM 87501
(505)988-6302
Fax: (505)988-6300

New York

SCORE Office (Northeast)
1 Computer Dr. S
Albany, NY 12205
(518)446-1118
Fax: (518)446-1228

SCORE Office (Auburn)
30 South St.
PO Box 675

Auburn, NY 13021
(315)252-7291

SCORE Office (South Tier Binghamton)
Metro Center, 2nd Fl.
49 Court St.
PO Box 995
Binghamton, NY 13902
(607)772-8860

SCORE Office (Queens County City)
12055 Queens Blvd., Rm. 333
Borough Hall, NY 11424
(718)263-8961

SCORE Office (Buffalo)
Federal Bldg., Rm. 1311
111 W. Huron St.
Buffalo, NY 14202
(716)551-4301
Website: http://www2.pcom.net/score/
buf45.html

SCORE Office (Canandaigua)
Chamber of Commerce Bldg.
113 S. Main St.
Canandaigua, NY 14424
(716)394-4400
Fax: (716)394-4546

SCORE Office (Chemung)
333 E. Water St., 4th Fl.
Elmira, NY 14901
(607)734-3358

SCORE Office (Geneva)
Chamber of Commerce Bldg.
PO Box 587
Geneva, NY 14456
(315)789-1776
Fax: (315)789-3993

SCORE Office (Glens Falls)
84 Broad St.
Glens Falls, NY 12801
(518)798-8463
Fax: (518)745-1433

SCORE Office (Orange County)
40 Matthews St.
Goshen, NY 10924
(914)294-8080
Fax: (914)294-6121

SCORE Office (Huntington Area)
151 W. Carver St.
Huntington, NY 11743
(516)423-6100

SCORE Office (Tompkins County)
904 E. Shore Dr.
Ithaca, NY 14850
(607)273-7080

SCORE Office (Long Island City)
120-55 Queens Blvd.
Jamaica, NY 11424
(718)263-8961
Fax: (718)263-9032

SCORE Office (Chatauqua)
101 W. 5th St.
Jamestown, NY 14701
(716)484-1103

SCORE Office (Westchester)
2 Caradon Ln.
Katonah, NY 10536
(914)948-3907
Fax: (914)948-4645
E-mail: score@w-w-w.com
Website: http://w-w-w.com/score/

SCORE Office (Queens County)
Queens Borough Hall
120-55 Queens Blvd. Rm. 333
Kew Gardens, NY 11424
(718)263-8961
Fax: (718)263-9032

SCORE Office (Brookhaven)
3233 Rte. 112
Medford, NY 11763
(516)451-6563
Fax: (516)451-6925

SCORE Office (Melville)
35 Pinelawn Rd., Rm. 207-W
Melville, NY 11747
(516)454-0771

SCORE Office (Nassau County)
400 County Seat Dr., No. 140
Mineola, NY 11501
(516)571-3303
E-mail: Counse1998@aol.com
Website: http://members.aol.com/
Counse1998/Default.htm

SCORE Office (Mt. Vernon)
4 N. 7th Ave.
Mt. Vernon, NY 10550
(914)667-7500

SCORE Office (New York)
26 Federal Plz., Rm. 3100
New York, NY 10278
(212)264-4507
Fax: (212)264-4963
E-mail: score1000@erols.com
Website: http://users.erols.com/
score-nyc/

SCORE Office (Newburgh)
47 Grand St.
Newburgh, NY 12550
(914)562-5100

SCORE Office (Owego)
188 Front St.
Owego, NY 13827
(607)687-2020

SCORE Office (Peekskill)
1 S. Division St.
Peekskill, NY 10566
(914)737-3600
Fax: (914)737-0541

SCORE Office (Penn Yan)
2375 Rte. 14A
Penn Yan, NY 14527
(315)536-3111

SCORE Office (Dutchess)
110 Main St.
Poughkeepsie, NY 12601
(914)454-1700

SCORE Office (Rochester)
601 Keating Federal Bldg., Rm. 410
100 State St.
Rochester, NY 14614
(716)263-6473
Fax: (716)263-3146
Website: http://www.ggw.org/score/

SCORE Office (Saranac Lake)
30 Main St.
Saranac Lake, NY 12983
(315)448-0415

SCORE Office (Suffolk)
286 Main St.
Setauket, NY 11733
(516)751-3886

SCORE Office (Staten Island)
130 Bay St.
Staten Island, NY 10301
(718)727-1221

SCORE Office (Ulster)
Clinton Bldg., Rm. 107
Stone Ridge, NY 12484
(914)687-5035
Fax: (914)687-5015
Website: http://www.scoreulster.org/

SCORE Office (Syracuse)
401 S. Salina, 5th Fl.
Syracuse, NY 13202
(315)471-9393

SCORE Office (Utica)
SUNY Institute of Technology, Route 12
Utica, NY 13504-3050
(315)792-7553

SCORE Office (Watertown)
518 Davidson St.
Watertown, NY 13601

(315)788-1200
Fax: (315)788-8251

North Carolina

SCORE office (Asheboro)
317 E. Dixie Dr.
Asheboro, NC 27203
(336)626-2626
Fax: (336)626-7077

SCORE Office (Asheville)
Federal Bldg., Rm. 259
151 Patton
Asheville, NC 28801-5770
(828)271-4786
Fax: (828)271-4009

SCORE Office (Chapel Hill)
104 S. Estes Dr.
PO Box 2897
Chapel Hill, NC 27514
(919)967-7075

SCORE Office (Coastal Plains)
PO Box 2897
Chapel Hill, NC 27515
(919)967-7075
Fax: (919)968-6874

SCORE Office (Charlotte)
200 N. College St., Ste. A-2015
Charlotte, NC 28202
(704)344-6576
Fax: (704)344-6769
E-mail: CharlotteSCORE47@AOL.com
Website: http://www.charweb.org/
business/score/

SCORE Office (Durham)
411 W. Chapel Hill St.
Durham, NC 27707
(919)541-2171

SCORE Office (Gastonia)
PO Box 2168
Gastonia, NC 28053
(704)864-2621
Fax: (704)854-8723

SCORE Office (Greensboro)
400 W. Market St., Ste. 103
Greensboro, NC 27401-2241
(910)333-5399

SCORE Office (Henderson)
PO Box 917
Henderson, NC 27536
(919)492-2061
Fax: (919)430-0460

SCORE Office (Hendersonville)
Federal Bldg., Rm. 108
W. 4th Ave. & Church St.

Hendersonville, NC 28792
(828)693-8702
E-mail: score@circle.net
Website: http://www.wncguide.com/
score/Welcome.html

SCORE Office (Unifour)
PO Box 1828
Hickory, NC 28603
(704)328-6111

SCORE Office (High Point)
1101 N. Main St.
High Point, NC 27262
(336)882-8625
Fax: (336)889-9499

SCORE Office (Outer Banks)
Collington Rd. and Mustain
Kill Devil Hills, NC 27948
(252)441-8144

SCORE Office (Down East)
312 S. Front St., Ste. 6
New Bern, NC 28560
(252)633-6688
Fax: (252)633-9608

SCORE Office (Kinston)
PO Box 95
New Bern, NC 28561
(919)633-6688

SCORE Office (Raleigh)
Century Post Office Bldg., Ste. 306
300 Federal St. Mall
Raleigh, NC 27601
(919)856-4739
E-mail: jendres@ibm.net
Website: http://www.intrex.net/score96/
score96.htm

SCORE Office (Sanford)
1801 Nash St.
Sanford, NC 27330
(919)774-6442
Fax: (919)776-8739

SCORE Office (Sandhills Area)
1480 Hwy. 15-501
PO Box 458
Southern Pines, NC 28387
(910)692-3926

SCORE Office (Wilmington)
Corps of Engineers Bldg.
96 Darlington Ave., Ste. 207
Wilmington, NC 28403
(910)815-4576
Fax: (910)815-4658

North Dakota

SCORE Office (Bismarck-Mandan)
700 E. Main Ave., 2nd Fl.
PO Box 5509
Bismarck, ND 58506-5509
(701)250-4303

SCORE Office (Fargo)
657 2nd Ave., Rm. 225
Fargo, ND 58108-3083
(701)239-5677

SCORE Office (Upper Red River)
4275 Technology Dr., Rm. 156
Grand Forks, ND 58202-8372
(701)777-3051

SCORE Office (Minot)
100 1st St. SW
Minot, ND 58701-3846
(701)852-6883
Fax: (701)852-6905

Ohio

SCORE Office (Akron)
1 Cascade Plz., 7th Fl.
Akron, OH 44308
(330)379-3163
Fax: (330)379-3164

SCORE Office (Ashland)
Gill Center
47 W. Main St.
Ashland, OH 44805
(419)281-4584

SCORE Office (Canton)
116 Cleveland Ave. NW, Ste. 601
Canton, OH 44702-1720
(330)453-6047

SCORE Office (Chillicothe)
165 S. Paint St.
Chillicothe, OH 45601
(614)772-4530

SCORE Office (Cincinnati)
Ameritrust Bldg., Rm. 850
525 Vine St.
Cincinnati, OH 45202
(513)684-2812
Fax: (513)684-3251
Website: http://
www.score.chapter34.org/

SCORE Office (Cleveland)
Eaton Center, Ste. 620
1100 Superior Ave.
Cleveland, OH 44114-2507
(216)522-4194
Fax: (216)522-4844

SCORE Office (Columbus)
2 Nationwide Plz., Ste. 1400
Columbus, OH 43215-2542
(614)469-2357
Fax: (614)469-2391
E-mail: info@scorecolumbus.org
Website: http://www.scorecolumbus.org/

SCORE Office (Dayton)
Dayton Federal Bldg., Rm. 505
200 W. Second St.
Dayton, OH 45402-1430
(513)225-2887
Fax: (513)225-7667

SCORE Office (Defiance)
615 W. 3rd St.
PO Box 130
Defiance, OH 43512
(419)782-7946

SCORE Office (Findlay)
123 E. Main Cross St.
PO Box 923
Findlay, OH 45840
(419)422-3314

SCORE Office (Lima)
147 N. Main St.
Lima, OH 45801
(419)222-6045
Fax: (419)229-0266

SCORE Office (Mansfield)
55 N. Mulberry St.
Mansfield, OH 44902
(419)522-3211

SCORE Office (Marietta)
Thomas Hall
Marietta, OH 45750
(614)373-0268

SCORE Office (Medina)
County Administrative Bldg.
144 N. Broadway
Medina, OH 44256
(216)764-8650

SCORE Office (Licking County)
50 W. Locust St.
Newark, OH 43055
(614)345-7458

SCORE Office (Salem)
2491 State Rte. 45 S
Salem, OH 44460
(216)332-0361

SCORE Office (Tiffin)
62 S. Washington St.
Tiffin, OH 44883
(419)447-4141
Fax: (419)447-5141

SCORE Office (Toledo)
608 Madison Ave, Ste. 910
Toledo, OH 43624
(419)259-7598
Fax: (419)259-6460

SCORE Office (Heart of Ohio)
377 W. Liberty St.
Wooster, OH 44691
(330)262-5735
Fax: (330)262-5745

SCORE Office (Youngstown)
306 Williamson Hall
Youngstown, OH 44555
(330)746-2687

Oklahoma

SCORE Office (Anadarko)
PO Box 366
Anadarko, OK 73005
(405)247-6651

SCORE Office (Ardmore)
410 W. Main
Ardmore, OK 73401
(580)226-2620

SCORE Office (Northeast Oklahoma)
210 S. Main
Grove, OK 74344
(918)787-2796
Fax: (918)787-2796
E-mail: Score595@greencis.net

SCORE Office (Lawton)
4500 W. Lee Blvd., Bldg. 100, Ste. 107
Lawton, OK 73505
(580)353-8727
Fax: (580)250-5677

SCORE Office (Oklahoma City)
210 Park Ave., No. 1300
Oklahoma City, OK 73102
(405)231-5163
Fax: (405)231-4876
E-mail: score212@usa.net

SCORE Office (Stillwater)
439 S. Main
Stillwater, OK 74074
(405)372-5573
Fax: (405)372-4316

SCORE Office (Tulsa)
616 S. Boston, Ste. 406
Tulsa, OK 74119
(918)581-7462
Fax: (918)581-6908
Website: http://www.ionet.net/~tulscore/

Oregon

SCORE Office (Bend)
63085 N. Hwy. 97
Bend, OR 97701
(541)923-2849
Fax: (541)330-6900

SCORE Office (Willamette)
1401 Willamette St.
PO Box 1107
Eugene, OR 97401-4003
(541)465-6600
Fax: (541)484-4942

SCORE Office (Florence)
3149 Oak St.
Florence, OR 97439
(503)997-8444
Fax: (503)997-8448

SCORE Office (Southern Oregon)
33 N. Central Ave., Ste. 216
Medford, OR 97501
(541)776-4220
E-mail: pgr134f@prodigy.com

SCORE Office (Portland)
1515 SW 5th Ave., Ste. 1050
Portland, OR 97201
(503)326-3441
Fax: (503)326-2808
E-mail: gr134@prodigy.com

SCORE Office (Salem)
416 State St. (corner of Liberty)
Salem, OR 97301
(503)370-2896

Pennsylvania

SCORE Office (Altoona-Blair)
1212 12th Ave.
Altoona, PA 16601-3493
(814)943-8151

SCORE Office (Lehigh Valley)
Rauch Bldg. 37
Lehigh University
621 Taylor St.
Bethlehem, PA 18015
(610)758-4496
Fax: (610)758-5205

SCORE Office (Butler County)
100 N. Main St.
PO Box 1082
Butler, PA 16003
(412)283-2222
Fax: (412)283-0224

SCORE Office (Harrisburg)
4211 Trindle Rd.
Camp Hill, PA 17011

(717)761-4304
Fax: (717)761-4315

SCORE Office (Cumberland Valley)
75 S. 2nd St.
Chambersburg, PA 17201
(717)264-2935

SCORE Office (Monroe County-Stroudsburg)
556 Main St.
East Stroudsburg, PA 18301
(717)421-4433

SCORE Office (Erie)
120 W. 9th St.
Erie, PA 16501
(814)871-5650
Fax: (814)871-7530

SCORE Office (Bucks County)
409 Hood Blvd.
Fairless Hills, PA 19030
(215)943-8850
Fax: (215)943-7404

SCORE Office (Hanover)
146 Broadway
Hanover, PA 17331
(717)637-6130
Fax: (717)637-9127

SCORE Office (Harrisburg)
100 Chestnut, Ste. 309
Harrisburg, PA 17101
(717)782-3874

SCORE Office (East Montgomery County)
Baederwood Shopping Center
1653 The Fairways, Ste. 204
Jenkintown, PA 19046
(215)885-3027

SCORE Office (Kittanning)
2 Butler Rd.
Kittanning, PA 16201
(412)543-1305
Fax: (412)543-6206

SCORE Office (Lancaster)
118 W. Chestnut St.
Lancaster, PA 17603
(717)397-3092

SCORE Office (Westmoreland County)
300 Fraser Purchase Rd.
Latrobe, PA 15650-2690
(412)539-7505
Fax: (412)539-1850

SCORE Office (Lebanon)
252 N. 8th St.
PO Box 899

Lebanon, PA 17042-0899
(717)273-3727
Fax: (717)273-7940

SCORE Office (Lewistown)
3 W. Monument Sq., Ste. 204
Lewistown, PA 17044
(717)248-6713
Fax: (717)248-6714

SCORE Office (Delaware County)
602 E. Baltimore Pike
Media, PA 19063
(610)565-3677
Fax: (610)565-1606

SCORE Office (Milton Area)
112 S. Front St.
Milton, PA 17847
(717)742-7341
Fax: (717)792-2008

SCORE Office (Mon-Valley)
435 Donner Ave.
Monessen, PA 15062
(412)684-4277
Fax: (412)684-7688

SCORE Office (Monroeville)
William Penn Plaza
2790 Mosside Blvd., Ste. 295
Monroeville, PA 15146
(412)856-0622
Fax: (412)856-1030

SCORE Office (Airport Area)
986 Brodhead Rd.
Moon Township, PA 15108-2398
(412)264-6270
Fax: (412)264-1575

SCORE Office (Northeast)
8601 E. Roosevelt Blvd.
Philadelphia, PA 19152
(215)332-3400
Fax: (215)332-6050

SCORE Office (Philadelphia)
1315 Walnut St., Ste. 500
Philadelphia, PA 19107
(215)790-5050
Fax: (215)790-5057
E-mail: score46@bellatlantic.net
Website: http://www.pgweb.net/score46/

SCORE Office (Pittsburgh)
1000 Liberty Ave., Rm. 1122
Pittsburgh, PA 15222
(412)395-6560
Fax: (412)395-6562

SCORE Office (Tri-County)
801 N. Charlotte St.
Pottstown, PA 19464
(610)327-2673

SCORE Office (Reading)
601 Penn St.
Reading, PA 19601
(610)376-3497

SCORE Office (Scranton)
Oppenheim Bldg.
116 N. Washington Ave., Ste. 650
Scranton, PA 18503
(717)347-4611
Fax: (717)347-4611

SCORE Office (Central Pennsylvania)
200 Innovation Blvd., Ste. 242-B
State College, PA 16803
(814)234-9415
Fax: (814)238-9686
Website: http://countrystore.org/business/score.htm

SCORE Office (Monroe-Stroudsburg)
556 Main St.
Stroudsburg, PA 18360
(717)421-4433

SCORE Office (Uniontown)
Federal Bldg.
Pittsburg St.
PO Box 2065 DTS
Uniontown, PA 15401
(412)437-4222
E-mail: uniontownscore@lcsys.net

SCORE Office (Warren County)
315 2nd Ave.
Warren, PA 16365
(814)723-9017

SCORE Office (Waynesboro)
323 E. Main St.
Waynesboro, PA 17268
(717)762-7123
Fax: (717)962-7124

SCORE Office (Chester County)
Government Service Center, Ste. 281
601 Westtown Rd.
West Chester, PA 19382-4538
(610)344-6910
Fax: (610)344-6919
E-mail: score@locke.ccil.org

SCORE Office (Wilkes-Barre)
7 N. Wilkes-Barre Blvd.
Wilkes Barre, PA 18702-5241
(717)826-6502
Fax: (717)826-6287

SCORE Office (North Central Pennsylvania)
240 W. 3rd St., Rm. 227
PO Box 725
Williamsport, PA 17703

(717)322-3720
Fax: (717)322-1607
E-mail: score234@mail.csrlink.net
Website: http://www.lycoming.org/score/

SCORE Office (York)
Cyber Center
2101 Pennsylvania Ave.
York, PA 17404
(717)845-8830
Fax: (717)854-9333

Puerto Rico

SCORE Office (Puerto Rico & Virgin Islands)
PO Box 12383-96
San Juan, PR 00914-0383
(787)726-8040
Fax: (787)726-8135

Rhode Island

SCORE Office (Barrington)
281 County Rd.
Barrington, RI 02806
(401)247-1920
Fax: (401)247-3763

SCORE Office (Woonsocket)
640 Washington Hwy.
Lincoln, RI 02865
(401)334-1000
Fax: (401)334-1009

SCORE Office (Wickford)
8045 Post Rd.
North Kingstown, RI 02852
(401)295-5566
Fax: (401)295-8987

SCORE Office (J.G.E. Knight)
380 Westminster St.
Providence, RI 02903
(401)528-4571
Fax: (401)528-4539
Website: http://www.riscore.org

SCORE Office (Warwick)
3288 Post Rd.
Warwick, RI 02886
(401)732-1100
Fax: (401)732-1101

SCORE Office (Westerly)
74 Post Rd.
Westerly, RI 02891
(401)596-7761
800-732-7636
Fax: (401)596-2190

South Carolina

SCORE Office (Aiken)
PO Box 892
Aiken, SC 29802
(803)641-1111
800-542-4536
Fax: (803)641-4174

SCORE Office (Anderson)
Anderson Mall
3130 N. Main St.
Anderson, SC 29621
(864)224-0453

SCORE Office (Coastal)
284 King St.
Charleston, SC 29401
(803)727-4778
Fax: (803)853-2529

SCORE Office (Midlands)
Strom Thurmond Bldg., Rm. 358
1835 Assembly St., Rm 358
Columbia, SC 29201
(803)765-5131
Fax: (803)765-5962
Website: http://www.scoremidlands.org/

SCORE Office (Piedmont)
Federal Bldg., Rm. B-02
300 E. Washington St.
Greenville, SC 29601
(864)271-3638

SCORE Office (Greenwood)
PO Drawer 1467
Greenwood, SC 29648
(864)223-8357

SCORE Office (Hilton Head Island)
52 Savannah Trail
Hilton Head, SC 29926
(803)785-7107
Fax: (803)785-7110

SCORE Office (Grand Strand)
937 Broadway
Myrtle Beach, SC 29577
(803)918-1079
Fax: (803)918-1083
E-mail: score381@aol.com

SCORE Office (Spartanburg)
PO Box 1636
Spartanburg, SC 29304
(864)594-5000
Fax: (864)594-5055

South Dakota

SCORE Office (West River)
Rushmore Plz. Civic Ctr.
444 Mount Rushmore Rd., No. 209

Rapid City, SD 57701
(605)394-5311
E-mail: score@gwtc.net

SCORE Office (Sioux Falls)
First Financial Center
110 S. Phillips Ave., Ste. 200
Sioux Falls, SD 57104-6727
(605)330-4231
Fax: (605)330-4231

Tennessee

SCORE Office (Chattanooga)
Federal Bldg., Rm. 26
900 Georgia Ave.
Chattanooga, TN 37402
(423)752-5190
Fax: (423)752-5335

SCORE Office (Cleveland)
PO Box 2275
Cleveland, TN 37320
(423)472-6587
Fax: (423)472-2019

SCORE Office (Upper Cumberland Center)
1225 S. Willow Ave.
Cookeville, TN 38501
(615)432-4111
Fax: (615)432-6010

SCORE Office (Unicoi County)
PO Box 713
Erwin, TN 37650
(423)743-3000
Fax: (423)743-0942

SCORE Office (Greeneville)
115 Academy St.
Greeneville, TN 37743
(423)638-4111
Fax: (423)638-5345

SCORE Office (Jackson)
194 Auditorium St.
Jackson, TN 38301
(901)423-2200

SCORE Office (Northeast Tennessee)
1st Tennessee Bank Bldg.
2710 S. Roan St., Ste. 584
Johnson City, TN 37601
(423)929-7686
Fax: (423)461-8052

SCORE Office (Kingsport)
151 E. Main St.
Kingsport, TN 37662
(423)392-8805

SCORE Office (Greater Knoxville)
Farragot Bldg., Ste. 224
530 S. Gay St.
Knoxville, TN 37902
(423)545-4203
E-mail: scoreknox@ntown.com
Website: http://www.scoreknox.org/

SCORE Office (Maryville)
201 S. Washington St.
Maryville, TN 37804-5728
(423)983-2241
800-525-6834
Fax: (423)984-1386

SCORE Office (Memphis)
Federal Bldg., Ste. 390
167 N. Main St.
Memphis, TN 38103
(901)544-3588

SCORE Office (Nashville)
50 Vantage Way, Ste. 201
Nashville, TN 37228-1500
(615)736-7621

Texas

SCORE Office (Abilene)
2106 Federal Post Office and Court Bldg.
Abilene, TX 79601
(915)677-1857

SCORE Office (Austin)
2501 S. Congress
Austin, TX 78701
(512)442-7235
Fax: (512)442-7528

SCORE Office (Golden Triangle)
450 Boyd St.
Beaumont, TX 77704
(409)838-6581
Fax: (409)833-6718

SCORE Office (Brownsville)
3505 Boca Chica Blvd., Ste. 305
Brownsville, TX 78521
(210)541-4508

SCORE Office (Brazos Valley)
3000 Briarcrest, Ste. 302
Bryan, TX 77802
(409)776-8876
E-mail: 102633.2612@compuserve.com

SCORE Office (Cleburne)
Watergarden Pl., 9th Fl., Ste. 400
Cleburne, TX 76031
(817)871-6002

SCORE Office (Corpus Christi)
651 Upper North Broadway, Ste. 654
Corpus Christi, TX 78477

(512)888-4322
Fax: (512)888-3418

SCORE Office (Dallas)
6260 E. Mockingbird
Dallas, TX 75214-2619
(214)828-2471
Fax: (214)821-8033

SCORE Office (El Paso)
10 Civic Center Plaza
El Paso, TX 79901
(915)534-0541
Fax: (915)534-0513

SCORE Office (Bedford)
100 E. 15th St., Ste. 400
Ft. Worth, TX 76102
(817)871-6002

SCORE Office (Ft. Worth)
100 E. 15th St., No. 24
Ft. Worth, TX 76102
(817)871-6002
Fax: (817)871-6031
E-mail: fwbac@onramp.net

SCORE Office (Garland)
2734 W. Kingsley Rd.
Garland, TX 75041
(214)271-9224

SCORE Office (Granbury Chamber of Commerce)
416 S. Morgan
Granbury, TX 76048
(817)573-1622
Fax: (817)573-0805

SCORE Office (Lower Rio Grande Valley)
222 E. Van Buren, Ste. 500
Harlingen, TX 78550
(956)427-8533
Fax: (956)427-8537

SCORE Office (Houston)
9301 Southwest Fwy., Ste. 550
Houston, TX 77074
(713)773-6565
Fax: (713)773-6550

SCORE Office (Irving)
3333 N. MacArthur Blvd., Ste. 100
Irving, TX 75062
(214)252-8484
Fax: (214)252-6710

SCORE Office (Lubbock)
1205 Texas Ave., Rm. 411D
Lubbock, TX 79401
(806)472-7462
Fax: (806)472-7487

SCORE Office (Midland)
Post Office Annex
200 E. Wall St., Rm. P121
Midland, TX 79701
(915)687-2649

SCORE Office (Orange)
1012 Green Ave.
Orange, TX 77630-5620
(409)883-3536
800-528-4906
Fax: (409)886-3247

SCORE Office (Plano)
1200 E. 15th St.
PO Drawer 940287
Plano, TX 75094-0287
(214)424-7547
Fax: (214)422-5182

SCORE Office (Port Arthur)
4749 Twin City Hwy., Ste. 300
Port Arthur, TX 77642
(409)963-1107
Fax: (409)963-3322

SCORE Office (Richardson)
411 Belle Grove
Richardson, TX 75080
(214)234-4141
800-777-8001
Fax: (214)680-9103

SCORE Office (San Antonio)
Federal Bldg., Rm. A527
727 E. Durango
San Antonio, TX 78206
(210)472-5931
Fax: (210)472-5935

SCORE Office (Texarkana State College)
819 State Line Ave.
Texarkana, TX 75501
(903)792-7191
Fax: (903)793-4304

SCORE Office (East Texas)
RTDC
1530 SSW Loop 323, Ste. 100
Tyler, TX 75701
(903)510-2975
Fax: (903)510-2978

SCORE Office (Waco)
401 Franklin Ave.
Waco, TX 76701
(817)754-8898
Fax: (817)756-0776
Website: http://www.brc-waco.com/

SCORE Office (Wichita Falls)
Hamilton Bldg.
900 8th St.

Organizations, Agencies, & Consultants

Wichita Falls, TX 76307
(940)723-2741
Fax: (940)723-8773

Utah

SCORE Office (Northern Utah)
160 N. Main
Logan, UT 84321
(435)746-2269

SCORE Office (Ogden)
1701 E. Windsor Dr.
Ogden, UT 84604
(801)629-8613
E-mail: score158@netscape.net

SCORE Office (Central Utah)
1071 E. Windsor Dr.
Provo, UT 84604
(801)373-8660

SCORE Office (Southern Utah)
225 South 700 East
St. George, UT 84770
(435)652-7751

SCORE Office (Salt Lake)
310 S Main St.
Salt Lake City, UT 84101
(801)746-2269
Fax: (801)746-2273

Vermont

SCORE Office (Champlain Valley)
Winston Prouty Federal Bldg.
11 Lincoln St., Rm. 106
Essex Junction, VT 05452
(802)951-6762

SCORE Office (Montpelier)
87 State St., Rm. 205
PO Box 605
Montpelier, VT 05601
(802)828-4422
Fax: (802)828-4485

SCORE Office (Marble Valley)
256 N. Main St.
Rutland, VT 05701-2413
(802)773-9147

SCORE Office (Northeast Kingdom)
20 Main St.
PO Box 904
St. Johnsbury, VT 05819
(802)748-5101

Virgin Islands

SCORE Office (St. Croix)
United Plaza Shopping Center
PO Box 4010, Christiansted

St. Croix, VI 00822
(809)778-5380

SCORE Office (St. Thomas-St. John)
Federal Bldg., Rm. 21
Veterans Dr.
St. Thomas, VI 00801
(809)774-8530

Virginia

SCORE Office (Arlington)
2009 N. 14th St., Ste. 111
Arlington, VA 22201
(703)525-2400

SCORE Office (Blacksburg)
141 Jackson St.
Blacksburg, VA 24060
(540)552-4061

SCORE Office (Bristol)
20 Volunteer Pkwy.
Bristol, VA 24203
(540)989-4850

SCORE Office (Central Virginia)
1001 E. Market St., Ste. 101
Charlottesville, VA 22902
(804)295-6712
Fax: (804)295-7066

SCORE Office (Alleghany Satellite)
241 W. Main St.
Covington, VA 24426
(540)962-2178
Fax: (540)962-2179

SCORE Office (Central Fairfax)
3975 University Dr., Ste. 350
Fairfax, VA 22030
(703)591-2450

SCORE Office (Falls Church)
PO Box 491
Falls Church, VA 22040
(703)532-1050
Fax: (703)237-7904

SCORE Office (Glenns)
Glenns Campus
Box 287
Glenns, VA 23149
(804)693-9650

SCORE Office (Peninsula)
6 Manhattan Sq.
PO Box 7269
Hampton, VA 23666
(757)766-2000
Fax: (757)865-0339
E-mail: score100@seva.net

SCORE Office (Tri-Cities)
108 N. Main St.
Hopewell, VA 23860
(804)458-5536

SCORE Office (Lynchburg)
Federal Bldg.
1100 Main St.
Lynchburg, VA 24504-1714
(804)846-3235

SCORE Office (Greater Prince William)
8963 Center St
Manassas, VA 20110
(703)368-4813
Fax: (703)368-4733

SCORE Office (Martinsville)
115 Broad St.
Martinsville, VA 24112-0709
(540)632-6401
Fax: (540)632-5059

SCORE Office (Hampton Roads)
Federal Bldg., Rm. 737
200 Grandby St.
Norfolk, VA 23510
(757)441-3733
Fax: (757)441-3733
E-mail: scorehr60@juno.com

SCORE Office (Norfolk)
Federal Bldg., Rm. 737
200 Granby St.
Norfolk, VA 23510
(757)441-3733
Fax: (757)441-3733

SCORE Office (Virginia Beach)
Chamber of Commerce
200 Grandby St., Rm 737
Norfolk, VA 23510
(804)441-3733

SCORE Office (Radford)
1126 Norwood St.
Radford, VA 24141
(540)639-2202

SCORE Office (Richmond)
Federal Bldg.
400 N. 8th St., Ste. 1150
PO Box 10126
Richmond, VA 23240-0126
(804)771-2400
Fax: (804)771-8018
E-mail: scorechapter12@yahoo.com
Website: http://www.cvco.org/score/

SCORE Office (Roanoke)
Federal Bldg., Rm. 716
250 Franklin Rd.
Roanoke, VA 24011

(540)857-2834
Fax: (540)857-2043
E-mail: scorerva@juno.com
Website: http://hometown.aol.com/
scorerv/Index.html

SCORE Office (Fairfax)
8391 Old Courthouse Rd., Ste. 300
Vienna, VA 22182
(703)749-0400

SCORE Office (Greater Vienna)
513 Maple Ave. West
Vienna, VA 22180
(703)281-1333
Fax: (703)242-1482

SCORE Office (Shenandoah Valley)
301 W. Main St.
Waynesboro, VA 22980
(540)949-8203
Fax: (540)949-7740
E-mail: score427@intelos.net

SCORE Office (Williamsburg)
201 Penniman Rd.
Williamsburg, VA 23185
(757)229-6511
E-mail: wacc@williamsburgcc.com

SCORE Office (Northern Virginia)
1360 S. Pleasant Valley Rd.
Winchester, VA 22601
(540)662-4118

Washington

SCORE Office (Gray's Harbor)
506 Duffy St.
Aberdeen, WA 98520
(360)532-1924
Fax: (360)533-7945

SCORE Office (Bellingham)
101 E. Holly St.
Bellingham, WA 98225
(360)676-3307

SCORE Office (Everett)
2702 Hoyt Ave.
Everett, WA 98201-3556
(206)259-8000

SCORE Office (Gig Harbor)
3125 Judson St.
Gig Harbor, WA 98335
(206)851-6865

SCORE Office (Kennewick)
PO Box 6986
Kennewick, WA 99336
(509)736-0510

SCORE Office (Puyallup)
322 2nd St. SW
PO Box 1298
Puyallup, WA 98371
(206)845-6755
Fax: (206)848-6164

SCORE Office (Seattle)
1200 6th Ave., Ste. 1700
Seattle, WA 98101
(206)553-7320
Fax: (206)553-7044
E-mail: score55@aol.com
Website: http://www.scn.org/civic/score-
online/index55.html

SCORE Office (Spokane)
801 W. Riverside Ave., No. 240
Spokane, WA 99201
(509)353-2820
Fax: (509)353-2600
E-mail: score@dmi.net
Website: http://www.dmi.net/score/

SCORE Office (Clover Park)
PO Box 1933
Tacoma, WA 98401-1933
(206)627-2175

SCORE Office (Tacoma)
1101 Pacific Ave.
Tacoma, WA 98402
(253)274-1288
Fax: (253)274-1289

SCORE Office (Fort Vancouver)
1701 Broadway, S-1
Vancouver, WA 98663
(360)699-1079

SCORE Office (Walla Walla)
500 Tausick Way
Walla Walla, WA 99362
(509)527-4681

SCORE Office (Mid-Columbia)
1113 S. 14th Ave.
Yakima, WA 98907
(509)574-4944
Fax: (509)574-2943
Website: http://www.ellensburg.com/
~score/

West Virginia

SCORE Office (Charleston)
1116 Smith St.
Charleston, WV 25301
(304)347-5463
E-mail: score256@juno.com

SCORE Office (Virginia Street)
1116 Smith St., Ste. 302
Charleston, WV 25301
(304)347-5463

SCORE Office (Marion County)
PO Box 208
Fairmont, WV 26555-0208
(304)363-0486

SCORE Office (Upper Monongahela Valley)
1000 Technology Dr., Ste. 1111
Fairmont, WV 26555
(304)363-0486
E-mail: score537@hotmail.com

SCORE Office (Huntington)
1101 6th Ave., Ste. 220
Huntington, WV 25701-2309
(304)523-4092

SCORE Office (Wheeling)
1310 Market St.
Wheeling, WV 26003
(304)233-2575
Fax: (304)233-1320

Wisconsin

SCORE Office (Fox Cities)
227 S. Walnut St.
Appleton, WI 54913
(920)734-7101
Fax: (920)734-7161

SCORE Office (Beloit)
136 W. Grand Ave., Ste. 100
PO Box 717
Beloit, WI 53511
(608)365-8835
Fax: (608)365-9170

SCORE Office (Eau Claire)
Federal Bldg., Rm. B11
510 S. Barstow St.
Eau Claire, WI 54701
(715)834-1573
E-mail: score@ecol.net
Website: http://www.ecol.net/~score/

SCORE Office (Fond du Lac)
207 N. Main St.
Fond du Lac, WI 54935
(414)921-9500
Fax: (414)921-9559

SCORE Office (Green Bay)
835 Potts Ave.
Green Bay, WI 54304
(414)496-8930
Fax: (414)496-6009

SCORE Office (Janesville)
20 S. Main St., Ste. 11
PO Box 8008
Janesville, WI 53547
(608)757-3160
Fax: (608)757-3170

SCORE Office (La Crosse)
712 Main St.
La Crosse, WI 54602-0219
(608)784-4880

SCORE Office (Madison)
505 S. Rosa Rd.
Madison, WI 53719
(608)441-2820

SCORE Office (Manitowoc)
1515 Memorial Dr.
PO Box 903
Manitowoc, WI 54221-0903
(414)684-5575
Fax: (414)684-1915

**SCORE Office
(Milwaukee)**
310 W. Wisconsin Ave., Ste. 425
Milwaukee, WI 53203
(414)297-3942
Fax: (414)297-1377

**SCORE Office
(Central Wisconsin)**
1224 Lindbergh Ave.
Stevens Point, WI 54481
(715)344-7729

SCORE Office (Superior)
Superior Business Center Inc.
1423 N. 8th St.
Superior, WI 54880
(715)394-7388
Fax: (715)393-7414

SCORE Office (Waukesha)
223 Wisconsin Ave.
Waukesha, WI 53186-4926
(414)542-4249

SCORE Office (Wausau)
300 3rd St., Ste. 200
Wausau, WI 54402-6190
(715)845-6231

**SCORE Office
(Wisconsin Rapids)**
2240 Kingston Rd.
Wisconsin Rapids, WI 54494
(715)423-1830

Wyoming

SCORE Office (Casper)
Federal Bldg., No. 2215
100 East B St.
Casper, WY 82602
(307)261-6529
Fax: (307)261-6530

Venture capital & financing companies

*This section contains a listing of financing
and loan companies in the United States
and Canada. These listing are arranged
alphabetically by country, then by state or
province, then by city, then by organization
name.*

Canada

Alberta

Launchworks Inc.
1902J 11th St., S.E.
Calgary, AB, Canada T2G 3G2
(403)269-1119
Fax: (403)269-1141
Website: http://www.launchworks.com

Native Venture Capital Company, Inc.
21 Artist View Point, Box 7
Site 25, RR 12
Calgary, AB, Canada T3E 6W3
(903)208-5380

Miralta Capital Inc.
4445 Calgary Trail South
888 Terrace Plaza Alberta
Edmonton, AB, Canada T6H 5R7
(780)438-3535
Fax: (780)438-3129

Vencap Equities Alberta Ltd.
10180-101st St., Ste. 1980
Edmonton, AB, Canada T5J 3S4
(403)420-1171
Fax: (403)429-2541

British Columbia

Discovery Capital
5th Fl., 1199 West Hastings
Vancouver, BC, Canada V6E 3T5
(604)683-3000
Fax: (604)662-3457
E-mail: info@discoverycapital.com
Website: http://www.discoverycapital
.com

Greenstone Venture Partners
1177 West Hastings St.
Ste. 400
Vancouver, BC, Canada V6E 2K3
(604)717-1977
Fax: (604)717-1976
Website: http://www.greenstonevc.com

Growthworks Capital
2600-1055 West Georgia St.
Box 11170 Royal Centre

Vancouver, BC, Canada V6E 3R5
(604)895-7259
Fax: (604)669-7605
Website: http://www.wofund.com

MDS Discovery Venture Management, Inc.
555 W. Eighth Ave., Ste. 305
Vancouver, BC, Canada V5Z 1C6
(604)872-8464
Fax: (604)872-2977
E-mail: info@mds-ventures.com

Ventures West Management Inc.
1285 W. Pender St., Ste. 280
Vancouver, BC, Canada V6E 4B1
(604)688-9495
Fax: (604)687-2145
Website: http://www.ventureswest.com

Nova Scotia

ACF Equity Atlantic Inc.
Purdy's Wharf Tower II
Ste. 2106
Halifax, NS, Canada B3J 3R7
(902)421-1965
Fax: (902)421-1808

Montgomerie, Huck & Co.
146 Bluenose Dr.
PO Box 538
Lunenburg, NS, Canada B0J 2C0
(902)634-7125
Fax: (902)634-7130

Ontario

IPS Industrial Promotion Services Ltd.
60 Columbia Way, Ste. 720
Markham, ON, Canada L3R 0C9
(905)475-9400
Fax: (905)475-5003

Betwin Investments Inc.
Box 23110
Sault Ste. Marie, ON, Canada P6A 6W6
(705)253-0744
Fax: (705)253-0744

Bailey & Company, Inc.
594 Spadina Ave.
Toronto, ON, Canada M5S 2H4
(416)921-6930
Fax: (416)925-4670

BCE Capital
200 Bay St.
South Tower, Ste. 3120
Toronto, ON, Canada M5J 2J2
(416)815-0078
Fax: (416)941-1073
Website: http://www.bcecapital.com

Castlehill Ventures
55 University Ave., Ste. 500
Toronto, ON, Canada M5J 2H7
(416)862-8574
Fax: (416)862-8875

CCFL Mezzanine Partners of Canada
70 University Ave.
Ste. 1450
Toronto, ON, Canada M5J 2M4
(416)977-1450
Fax: (416)977-6764
E-mail: info@ccfl.com
Website: http://www.ccfl.com

Celtic House International
100 Simcoe St., Ste. 100
Toronto, ON, Canada M5H 3G2
(416)542-2436
Fax: (416)542-2435
Website: http://www.celtic-house.com

Clairvest Group Inc.
22 St. Clair Ave. East
Ste. 1700
Toronto, ON, Canada M4T 2S3
(416)925-9270
Fax: (416)925-5753

Crosbie & Co., Inc.
One First Canadian Place
9th Fl.
PO Box 116
Toronto, ON, Canada M5X 1A4
(416)362-7726
Fax: (416)362-3447
E-mail: info@crosbieco.com
Website: http://www.crosbieco.com

Drug Royalty Corp.
Eight King St. East
Ste. 202
Toronto, ON, Canada M5C 1B5
(416)863-1865
Fax: (416)863-5161

Grieve, Horner, Brown & Asculai
8 King St. E, Ste. 1704
Toronto, ON, Canada M5C 1B5
(416)362-7668
Fax: (416)362-7660

Jefferson Partners
77 King St. West
Ste. 4010
PO Box 136
Toronto, ON, Canada M5K 1H1
(416)367-1533
Fax: (416)367-5827
Website: http://www.jefferson.com

J.L. Albright Venture Partners
Canada Trust Tower, 161 Bay St.
Ste. 4440
PO Box 215
Toronto, ON, Canada M5J 2S1
(416)367-2440
Fax: (416)367-4604
Website: http://www.jlaventures.com

McLean Watson Capital Inc.
One First Canadian Place
Ste. 1410
PO Box 129
Toronto, ON, Canada M5X 1A4
(416)363-2000
Fax: (416)363-2010
Website: http://www.mcleanwatson.com

Middlefield Capital Fund
One First Canadian Place
85th Fl.
PO Box 192
Toronto, ON, Canada M5X 1A6
(416)362-0714
Fax: (416)362-7925
Website: http://www.middlefield.com

Mosaic Venture Partners
24 Duncan St.
Ste. 300
Toronto, ON, Canada M5V 3M6
(416)597-8889
Fax: (416)597-2345

Onex Corp.
161 Bay St.
PO Box 700
Toronto, ON, Canada M5J 2S1
(416)362-7711
Fax: (416)362-5765

Penfund Partners Inc.
145 King St. West
Ste. 1920
Toronto, ON, Canada M5H 1J8
(416)865-0300
Fax: (416)364-6912
Website: http://www.penfund.com

Primaxis Technology Ventures Inc.
1 Richmond St. West, 8th Fl.
Toronto, ON, Canada M5H 3W4
(416)313-5210
Fax: (416)313-5218
Website: http://www.primaxis.com

Priveq Capital Funds
240 Duncan Mill Rd., Ste. 602
Toronto, ON, Canada M3B 3P1
(416)447-3330
Fax: (416)447-3331
E-mail: priveq@sympatico.ca

Roynat Ventures
40 King St. West, 26th Fl.
Toronto, ON, Canada M5H 1H1
(416)933-2667
Fax: (416)933-2783
Website: http://www.roynatcapital.com

Tera Capital Corp.
366 Adelaide St. East, Ste. 337
Toronto, ON, Canada M5A 3X9
(416)368-1024
Fax: (416)368-1427

Working Ventures Canadian Fund Inc.
250 Bloor St. East, Ste. 1600
Toronto, ON, Canada M4W 1E6
(416)934-7718
Fax: (416)929-0901
Website: http://www.workingventures.ca

Quebec

Altamira Capital Corp.
202 University
Niveau de Maisoneuve, Bur. 201
Montreal, QC, Canada H3A 2A5
(514)499-1656
Fax: (514)499-9570

Federal Business Development Bank
Venture Capital Division
Five Place Ville Marie, Ste. 600
Montreal, QC, Canada H3B 5E7
(514)283-1896
Fax: (514)283-5455

Hydro-Quebec Capitech Inc.
75 Boul, Rene Levesque Quest
Montreal, QC, Canada H2Z 1A4
(514)289-4783
Fax: (514)289-5420
Website: http://www.hqcapitech.com

Investissement Desjardins
2 complexe Desjardins
C.P. 760
Montreal, QC, Canada H5B 1B8
(514)281-7131
Fax: (514)281-7808
Website: http://www.desjardins.com/id

Marleau Lemire Inc.
One Place Ville-Marie, Ste. 3601
Montreal, QC, Canada H3B 3P2
(514)877-3800
Fax: (514)875-6415

Speirs Consultants Inc.
365 Stanstead
Montreal, QC, Canada H3R 1X5
(514)342-3858
Fax: (514)342-1977

Tecnocap Inc.
4028 Marlowe
Montreal, QC, Canada H4A 3M2
(514)483-6009
Fax: (514)483-6045
Website: http://www.technocap.com

Telsoft Ventures
1000, Rue de la Gauchetiere
Quest, 25eme Etage
Montreal, QC, Canada H3B 4W5
(514)397-8450
Fax: (514)397-8451

Saskatchewan

Saskatchewan Government Growth Fund
1801 Hamilton St., Ste. 1210
Canada Trust Tower
Regina, SK, Canada S4P 4B4
(306)787-2994
Fax: (306)787-2086

United states

Alabama

FHL Capital Corp.
600 20th Street North
Suite 350
Birmingham, AL 35203
(205)328-3098
Fax: (205)323-0001

Harbert Management Corp.
One Riverchase Pkwy. South
Birmingham, AL 35244
(205)987-5500
Fax: (205)987-5707
Website: http://www.harbert.net

Jefferson Capital Fund
PO Box 13129
Birmingham, AL 35213
(205)324-7709

Private Capital Corp.
100 Brookwood Pl., 4th Fl.
Birmingham, AL 35209
(205)879-2722
Fax: (205)879-5121

21st Century Health Ventures
One Health South Pkwy.
Birmingham, AL 35243
(256)268-6250
Fax: (256)970-8928

FJC Growth Capital Corp.
200 W. Side Sq., Ste. 340
Huntsville, AL 35801
(256)922-2918
Fax: (256)922-2909

Hickory Venture Capital Corp.
301 Washington St. NW
Suite 301
Huntsville, AL 35801
(256)539-1931
Fax: (256)539-5130
E-mail: hvcc@hvcc.com
Website: http://www.hvcc.com

Southeastern Technology Fund
7910 South Memorial Pkwy., Ste. F
Huntsville, AL 35802
(256)883-8711
Fax: (256)883-8558

Cordova Ventures
4121 Carmichael Rd., Ste. 301
Montgomery, AL 36106
(334)271-6011
Fax: (334)260-0120
Website: http://
www.cordovaventures.com

Small Business Clinic of Alabama/AG Bartholomew & Associates
PO Box 231074
Montgomery, AL 36123-1074
(334)284-3640

Arizona

Miller Capital Corp.
4909 E. McDowell Rd.
Phoenix, AZ 85008
(602)225-0504
Fax: (602)225-9024
Website: http://www.themillergroup.com

The Columbine Venture Funds
9449 North 90th St., Ste. 200
Scottsdale, AZ 85258
(602)661-9222
Fax: (602)661-6262

Koch Ventures
17767 N. Perimeter Dr., Ste. 101
Scottsdale, AZ 85255
(480)419-3600
Fax: (480)419-3606
Website: http://www.kochventures.com

McKee & Co.
7702 E. Doubletree Ranch Rd.
Suite 230
Scottsdale, AZ 85258
(480)368-0333
Fax: (480)607-7446

Merita Capital Ltd.
7350 E. Stetson Dr., Ste. 108-A
Scottsdale, AZ 85251
(480)947-8700
Fax: (480)947-8766

Valley Ventures / Arizona Growth Partners L.P.
6720 N. Scottsdale Rd., Ste. 208
Scottsdale, AZ 85253
(480)661-6600
Fax: (480)661-6262

Estreetcapital.com
660 South Mill Ave., Ste. 315
Tempe, AZ 85281
(480)968-8400
Fax: (480)968-8480
Website: http://www.estreetcapital.com

Coronado Venture Fund
PO Box 65420
Tucson, AZ 85728-5420
(520)577-3764
Fax: (520)299-8491

Arkansas

Arkansas Capital Corp.
225 South Pulaski St.
Little Rock, AR 72201
(501)374-9247
Fax: (501)374-9425
Website: http://www.arcapital.com

California

Sundance Venture Partners, L.P.
100 Clocktower Place, Ste. 130
Carmel, CA 93923
(831)625-6500
Fax: (831)625-6590

Westar Capital (Costa Mesa)
949 South Coast Dr., Ste. 650
Costa Mesa, CA 92626
(714)481-5160
Fax: (714)481-5166
E-mail: mailbox@westarcapital.com
Website: http://www.westarcapital.com

Alpine Technology Ventures
20300 Stevens Creek Boulevard, Ste. 495
Cupertino, CA 95014
(408)725-1810
Fax: (408)725-1207
Website: http://www.alpineventures.com

Bay Partners
10600 N. De Anza Blvd.
Cupertino, CA 95014-2031
(408)725-2444
Fax: (408)446-4502
Website: http://www.baypartners.com

Novus Ventures
20111 Stevens Creek Blvd., Ste. 130
Cupertino, CA 95014
(408)252-3900

Fax: (408)252-1713
Website: http://www.novusventures.com

Triune Capital
19925 Stevens Creek Blvd., Ste. 200
Cupertino, CA 95014
(310)284-6800
Fax: (310)284-3290

Acorn Ventures
268 Bush St., Ste. 2829
Daly City, CA 94014
(650)994-7801
Fax: (650)994-3305
Website: http://www.acornventures.com

Digital Media Campus
2221 Park Place
El Segundo, CA 90245
(310)426-8000
Fax: (310)426-8010
E-mail: info@thecampus.com
Website: http://
www.digitalmediacampus.com

BankAmerica Ventures / BA Venture Partners
950 Tower Ln., Ste. 700
Foster City, CA 94404
(650)378-6000
Fax: (650)378-6040
Website: http://www.baventurepartners.com

Starting Point Partners
666 Portofino Lane
Foster City, CA 94404
(650)722-1035
Website: http://
www.startingpointpartners.com

Opportunity Capital Partners
2201 Walnut Ave., Ste. 210
Fremont, CA 94538
(510)795-7000
Fax: (510)494-5439
Website: http://www.ocpcapital.com

Imperial Ventures Inc.
9920 S. La Cienega Boulevar, 14th Fl.
Inglewood, CA 90301
(310)417-5409
Fax: (310)338-6115

Ventana Global (Irvine)
18881 Von Karman Ave., Ste. 1150
Irvine, CA 92612
(949)476-2204
Fax: (949)752-0223
Website: http://www.ventanaglobal.com

Integrated Consortium Inc.
50 Ridgecrest Rd.
Kentfield, CA 94904

(415)925-0386
Fax: (415)461-2726

Enterprise Partners
979 Ivanhoe Ave., Ste. 550
La Jolla, CA 92037
(858)454-8833
Fax: (858)454-2489
Website: http://www.epvc.com

Domain Associates
28202 Cabot Rd., Ste. 200
Laguna Niguel, CA 92677
(949)347-2446
Fax: (949)347-9720
Website: http://www.domainvc.com

Cascade Communications Ventures
60 E. Sir Francis Drake Blvd., Ste. 300
Larkspur, CA 94939
(415)925-6500
Fax: (415)925-6501

Allegis Capital
One First St., Ste. Two
Los Altos, CA 94022
(650)917-5900
Fax: (650)917-5901
Website: http://www.allegiscapital.com

Aspen Ventures
1000 Fremont Ave., Ste. 200
Los Altos, CA 94024
(650)917-5670
Fax: (650)917-5677
Website: http://www.aspenventures.com

AVI Capital L.P.
1 First St., Ste. 2
Los Altos, CA 94022
(650)949-9862
Fax: (650)949-8510
Website: http://www.avicapital.com

Bastion Capital Corp.
1999 Avenue of the Stars, Ste. 2960
Los Angeles, CA 90067
(310)788-5700
Fax: (310)277-7582
E-mail: ga@bastioncapital.com
Website: http://www.bastioncapital.com

Davis Group
PO Box 69953
Los Angeles, CA 90069-0953
(310)659-6327
Fax: (310)659-6337

Developers Equity Corp.
1880 Century Park East, Ste. 211
Los Angeles, CA 90067
(213)277-0300

Far East Capital Corp.
350 S. Grand Ave., Ste. 4100
Los Angeles, CA 90071
(213)687-1361
Fax: (213)617-7939
E-mail: free@fareastnationalbank.com

Kline Hawkes & Co.
11726 San Vicente Blvd., Ste. 300
Los Angeles, CA 90049
(310)442-4700
Fax: (310)442-4707
Website: http://www.klinehawkes.com

Lawrence Financial Group
701 Teakwood
PO Box 491773
Los Angeles, CA 90049
(310)471-4060
Fax: (310)472-3155

Riordan Lewis & Haden
300 S. Grand Ave., 29th Fl.
Los Angeles, CA 90071
(213)229-8500
Fax: (213)229-8597

Union Venture Corp.
445 S. Figueroa St., 9th Fl.
Los Angeles, CA 90071
(213)236-4092
Fax: (213)236-6329

Wedbush Capital Partners
1000 Wilshire Blvd.
Los Angeles, CA 90017
(213)688-4545
Fax: (213)688-6642
Website: http://www.wedbush.com

Advent International Corp.
2180 Sand Hill Rd., Ste. 420
Menlo Park, CA 94025
(650)233-7500
Fax: (650)233-7515
Website: http://www.adventinternational.com

Altos Ventures
2882 Sand Hill Rd., Ste. 100
Menlo Park, CA 94025
(650)234-9771
Fax: (650)233-9821
Website: http://www.altosvc.com

Applied Technology
1010 El Camino Real, Ste. 300
Menlo Park, CA 94025
(415)326-8622
Fax: (415)326-8163

APV Technology Partners
535 Middlefield, Ste. 150
Menlo Park, CA 94025

(650)327-7871
Fax: (650)327-7631
Website: http://www.apvtp.com

August Capital Management
2480 Sand Hill Rd., Ste. 101
Menlo Park, CA 94025
(650)234-9900
Fax: (650)234-9910
Website: http://www.augustcap.com

Baccharis Capital Inc.
2420 Sand Hill Rd., Ste. 100
Menlo Park, CA 94025
(650)324-6844
Fax: (650)854-3025

Benchmark Capital
2480 Sand Hill Rd., Ste. 200
Menlo Park, CA 94025
(650)854-8180
Fax: (650)854-8183
E-mail: info@benchmark.com
Website: http://www.benchmark.com

Bessemer Venture Partners (Menlo Park)
535 Middlefield Rd., Ste. 245
Menlo Park, CA 94025
(650)853-7000
Fax: (650)853-7001
Website: http://www.bvp.com

The Cambria Group
1600 El Camino Real Rd., Ste. 155
Menlo Park, CA 94025
(650)329-8600
Fax: (650)329-8601
Website: http://www.cambriagroup.com

Canaan Partners
2884 Sand Hill Rd., Ste. 115
Menlo Park, CA 94025
(650)854-8092
Fax: (650)854-8127
Website: http://www.canaan.com

Capstone Ventures
3000 Sand Hill Rd., Bldg. One, Ste. 290
Menlo Park, CA 94025
(650)854-2523
Fax: (650)854-9010
Website: http://www.capstonevc.com

Comdisco Venture Group (Silicon Valley)
3000 Sand Hill Rd., Bldg. 1, Ste. 155
Menlo Park, CA 94025
(650)854-9484
Fax: (650)854-4026

Commtech International
535 Middlefield Rd., Ste. 200
Menlo Park, CA 94025

(650)328-0190
Fax: (650)328-6442

Compass Technology Partners
1550 El Camino Real, Ste. 275
Menlo Park, CA 94025-4111
(650)322-7595
Fax: (650)322-0588
Website: http://www.compasstechpartners.com

Convergence Partners
3000 Sand Hill Rd., Ste. 235
Menlo Park, CA 94025
(650)854-3010
Fax: (650)854-3015
Website: http://www.convergencepartners.com

The Dakota Group
PO Box 1025
Menlo Park, CA 94025
(650)853-0600
Fax: (650)851-4899
E-mail: info@dakota.com

Delphi Ventures
3000 Sand Hill Rd.
Bldg. One, Ste. 135
Menlo Park, CA 94025
(650)854-9650
Fax: (650)854-2961
Website: http://www.delphiventures.com

El Dorado Ventures
2884 Sand Hill Rd., Ste. 121
Menlo Park, CA 94025
(650)854-1200
Fax: (650)854-1202
Website: http://www.eldoradoventures.com

Glynn Ventures
3000 Sand Hill Rd., Bldg. 4, Ste. 235
Menlo Park, CA 94025
(650)854-2215

Indosuez Ventures
2180 Sand Hill Rd., Ste. 450
Menlo Park, CA 94025
(650)854-0587
Fax: (650)323-5561
Website: http://www.indosuezventures.com

Institutional Venture Partners
3000 Sand Hill Rd., Bldg. 2, Ste. 290
Menlo Park, CA 94025
(650)854-0132
Fax: (650)854-5762
Website: http://www.ivp.com

Interwest Partners (Menlo Park)
3000 Sand Hill Rd., Bldg. 3, Ste. 255
Menlo Park, CA 94025-7112
(650)854-8585
Fax: (650)854-4706
Website: http://www.interwest.com

Kleiner Perkins Caufield & Byers (Menlo Park)
2750 Sand Hill Rd.
Menlo Park, CA 94025
(650)233-2750
Fax: (650)233-0300
Website: http://www.kpcb.com

Magic Venture Capital LLC
1010 El Camino Real, Ste. 300
Menlo Park, CA 94025
(650)325-4149

Matrix Partners
2500 Sand Hill Rd., Ste. 113
Menlo Park, CA 94025
(650)854-3131
Fax: (650)854-3296
Website: http://www.matrixpartners.com

Mayfield Fund
2800 Sand Hill Rd.
Menlo Park, CA 94025
(650)854-5560
Fax: (650)854-5712
Website: http://www.mayfield.com

McCown De Leeuw and Co. (Menlo Park)
3000 Sand Hill Rd., Bldg. 3, Ste. 290
Menlo Park, CA 94025-7111
(650)854-6000
Fax: (650)854-0853
Website: http://www.mdcpartners.com

Menlo Ventures
3000 Sand Hill Rd., Bldg. 4, Ste. 100
Menlo Park, CA 94025
(650)854-8540
Fax: (650)854-7059
Website: http://www.menloventures.com

Merrill Pickard Anderson & Eyre
2480 Sand Hill Rd., Ste. 200
Menlo Park, CA 94025
(650)854-8600
Fax: (650)854-0345

New Enterprise Associates (Menlo Park)
2490 Sand Hill Rd.
Menlo Park, CA 94025
(650)854-9499
Fax: (650)854-9397
Website: http://www.nea.com

Onset Ventures
2400 Sand Hill Rd., Ste. 150
Menlo Park, CA 94025
(650)529-0700
Fax: (650)529-0777
Website: http://www.onset.com

Paragon Venture Partners
3000 Sand Hill Rd., Bldg. 1, Ste. 275
Menlo Park, CA 94025
(650)854-8000
Fax: (650)854-7260

Pathfinder Venture Capital Funds (Menlo Park)
3000 Sand Hill Rd., Bldg. 3, Ste. 255
Menlo Park, CA 94025
(650)854-0650
Fax: (650)854-4706

Rocket Ventures
3000 Sandhill Rd., Bldg. 1, Ste. 170
Menlo Park, CA 94025
(650)561-9100
Fax: (650)561-9183
Website: http://www.rocketventures.com

Sequoia Capital
3000 Sand Hill Rd., Bldg. 4, Ste. 280
Menlo Park, CA 94025
(650)854-3927
Fax: (650)854-2977
E-mail: sequoia@sequioacap.com
Website: http://www.sequoiacap.com

Sierra Ventures
3000 Sand Hill Rd., Bldg. 4, Ste. 210
Menlo Park, CA 94025
(650)854-1000
Fax: (650)854-5593
Website: http://www.sierraventures.com

Sigma Partners
2884 Sand Hill Rd., Ste. 121
Menlo Park, CA 94025-7022
(650)853-1700
Fax: (650)853-1717
E-mail: info@sigmapartners.com
Website: http://www.sigmapartners.com

Sprout Group (Menlo Park)
3000 Sand Hill Rd.
Bldg. 3, Ste. 170
Menlo Park, CA 94025
(650)234-2700
Fax: (650)234-2779
Website: http://www.sproutgroup.com

TA Associates (Menlo Park)
70 Willow Rd., Ste. 100
Menlo Park, CA 94025
(650)328-1210

Fax: (650)326-4933
Website: http://www.ta.com

Thompson Clive & Partners Ltd.
3000 Sand Hill Rd., Bldg. 1, Ste. 185
Menlo Park, CA 94025-7102
(650)854-0314
Fax: (650)854-0670
E-mail: mail@tcvc.com
Website: http://www.tcvc.com

Trinity Ventures Ltd.
3000 Sand Hill Rd., Bldg. 1, Ste. 240
Menlo Park, CA 94025
(650)854-9500
Fax: (650)854-9501
Website: http://www.trinityventures.com

U.S. Venture Partners
2180 Sand Hill Rd., Ste. 300
Menlo Park, CA 94025
(650)854-9080
Fax: (650)854-3018
Website: http://www.usvp.com

USVP-Schlein Marketing Fund
2180 Sand Hill Rd., Ste. 300
Menlo Park, CA 94025
(415)854-9080
Fax: (415)854-3018
Website: http://www.usvp.com

Venrock Associates
2494 Sand Hill Rd., Ste. 200
Menlo Park, CA 94025
(650)561-9580
Fax: (650)561-9180
Website: http://www.venrock.com

Brad Peery Capital Inc.
145 Chapel Pkwy.
Mill Valley, CA 94941
(415)389-0625
Fax: (415)389-1336

Dot Edu Ventures
650 Castro St., Ste. 270
Mountain View, CA 94041
(650)575-5638
Fax: (650)325-5247
Website: http://www.doteduventures.com

Forrest, Binkley & Brown
840 Newport Ctr. Dr., Ste. 480
Newport Beach, CA 92660
(949)729-3222
Fax: (949)729-3226
Website: http://www.fbbvc.com

Marwit Capital LLC
180 Newport Center Dr., Ste. 200
Newport Beach, CA 92660
(949)640-6234

Fax: (949)720-8077
Website: http://www.marwit.com

Kaiser Permanente / National Venture Development
1800 Harrison St., 22nd Fl.
Oakland, CA 94612
(510)267-4010
Fax: (510)267-4036
Website: http://www.kpventures.com

Nu Capital Access Group, Ltd.
7677 Oakport St., Ste. 105
Oakland, CA 94621
(510)635-7345
Fax: (510)635-7068

Inman and Bowman
4 Orinda Way, Bldg. D, Ste. 150
Orinda, CA 94563
(510)253-1611
Fax: (510)253-9037

Accel Partners (San Francisco)
428 University Ave.
Palo Alto, CA 94301
(650)614-4800
Fax: (650)614-4880
Website: http://www.accel.com

Advanced Technology Ventures
485 Ramona St., Ste. 200
Palo Alto, CA 94301
(650)321-8601
Fax: (650)321-0934
Website: http://www.atvcapital.com

Anila Fund
400 Channing Ave.
Palo Alto, CA 94301
(650)833-5790
Fax: (650)833-0590
Website: http://www.anila.com

Asset Management Company Venture Capital
2275 E. Bayshore, Ste. 150
Palo Alto, CA 94303
(650)494-7400
Fax: (650)856-1826
E-mail: postmaster@assetman.com
Website: http://www.assetman.com

BancBoston Capital / BancBoston Ventures
435 Tasso St., Ste. 250
Palo Alto, CA 94305
(650)470-4100
Fax: (650)853-1425
Website: http://www.bancbostoncapita
.com

Charter Ventures
525 University Ave., Ste. 1400
Palo Alto, CA 94301
(650)325-6953
Fax: (650)325-4762
Website: http://
www.charterventures.com

Communications Ventures
505 Hamilton Avenue, Ste. 305
Palo Alto, CA 94301
(650)325-9600
Fax: (650)325-9608
Website: http://www.comven.com

HMS Group
2468 Embarcadero Way
Palo Alto, CA 94303-3313
(650)856-9862
Fax: (650)856-9864

Jafco America Ventures, Inc.
505 Hamilton Ste. 310
Palto Alto, CA 94301
(650)463-8800
Fax: (650)463-8801
Website: http://www.jafco.com

New Vista Capital
540 Cowper St., Ste. 200
Palo Alto, CA 94301
(650)329-9333
Fax: (650)328-9434
E-mail: fgreene@nvcap.com
Website: http://www.nvcap.com

Norwest Equity Partners (Palo Alto)
245 Lytton Ave., Ste. 250
Palo Alto, CA 94301-1426
(650)321-8000
Fax: (650)321-8010
Website: http://www.norwestvp.com

Oak Investment Partners
525 University Ave., Ste. 1300
Palo Alto, CA 94301
(650)614-3700
Fax: (650)328-6345
Website: http://www.oakinv.com

Patricof & Co. Ventures, Inc. (Palo Alto)
2100 Geng Rd., Ste. 150
Palo Alto, CA 94303
(650)494-9944
Fax: (650)494-6751
Website: http://www.patricof.com

RWI Group
835 Page Mill Rd.
Palo Alto, CA 94304
(650)251-1800

Fax: (650)213-8660
Website: http://www.rwigroup.com

Summit Partners (Palo Alto)
499 Hamilton Ave., Ste. 200
Palo Alto, CA 94301
(650)321-1166
Fax: (650)321-1188
Website: http://www.summitpartners.com

Sutter Hill Ventures
755 Page Mill Rd., Ste. A-200
Palo Alto, CA 94304
(650)493-5600
Fax: (650)858-1854
E-mail: shv@shv.com

Vanguard Venture Partners
525 University Ave., Ste. 600
Palo Alto, CA 94301
(650)321-2900
Fax: (650)321-2902
Website: http://
www.vanguardventures.com

Venture Growth Associates
2479 East Bayshore St., Ste. 710
Palo Alto, CA 94303
(650)855-9100
Fax: (650)855-9104

Worldview Technology Partners
435 Tasso St., Ste. 120
Palo Alto, CA 94301
(650)322-3800
Fax: (650)322-3880
Website: http://www.worldview.com

Draper, Fisher, Jurvetson / Draper Associates
400 Seaport Ct., Ste.250
Redwood City, CA 94063
(415)599-9000
Fax: (415)599-9726
Website: http://www.dfj.com

Gabriel Venture Partners
350 Marine Pkwy., Ste. 200
Redwood Shores, CA 94065
(650)551-5000
Fax: (650)551-5001
Website: http://www.gabrielvp.com

Hallador Venture Partners, L.L.C.
740 University Ave., Ste. 110
Sacramento, CA 95825-6710
(916)920-0191
Fax: (916)920-5188
E-mail: chris@hallador.com

Emerald Venture Group
12396 World Trade Dr., Ste. 116
San Diego, CA 92128

(858)451-1001
Fax: (858)451-1003
Website: http://
www.emeraldventure.com

Forward Ventures
9255 Towne Centre Dr.
San Diego, CA 92121
(858)677-6077
Fax: (858)452-8799
E-mail: info@forwardventure.com
Website: http://
www.forwardventure.com

Idanta Partners Ltd.
4660 La Jolla Village Dr., Ste. 850
San Diego, CA 92122
(619)452-9690
Fax: (619)452-2013
Website: http://www.idanta.com

Kingsbury Associates
3655 Nobel Dr., Ste. 490
San Diego, CA 92122
(858)677-0600
Fax: (858)677-0800

Kyocera International Inc.
Corporate Development
8611 Balboa Ave.
San Diego, CA 92123
(858)576-2600
Fax: (858)492-1456

Sorrento Associates, Inc.
4370 LaJolla Village Dr., Ste. 1040
San Diego, CA 92122
(619)452-3100
Fax: (619)452-7607
Website: http://www.sorrentoventures
.com

Western States Investment Group
9191 Towne Ctr. Dr., Ste. 310
San Diego, CA 92122
(619)678-0800
Fax: (619)678-0900

Aberdare Ventures
One Embarcadero Center, Ste. 4000
San Francisco, CA 94111
(415)392-7442
Fax: (415)392-4264
Website: http://www.aberdare.com

Acacia Venture Partners
101 California St., Ste. 3160
San Francisco, CA 94111
(415)433-4200
Fax: (415)433-4250
Website: http://www.acaciavp.com

Access Venture Partners
319 Laidley St.
San Francisco, CA 94131
(415)586-0132
Fax: (415)392-6310
Website: http://
www.accessventurepartners.com

Alta Partners
One Embarcadero Center, Ste. 4050
San Francisco, CA 94111
(415)362-4022
Fax: (415)362-6178
E-mail: alta@altapartners.com
Website: http://www.altapartners.com

Bangert Dawes Reade Davis & Thom
220 Montgomery St., Ste. 424
San Francisco, CA 94104
(415)954-9900
Fax: (415)954-9901
E-mail: bdrdt@pacbell.net

Berkeley International Capital Corp.
650 California St., Ste. 2800
San Francisco, CA 94108-2609
(415)249-0450
Fax: (415)392-3929
Website: http://www.berkeleyvc.com

Blueprint Ventures LLC
456 Montgomery St., 22nd Fl.
San Francisco, CA 94104
(415)901-4000
Fax: (415)901-4035
Website: http://www.blueprintventures.com

Blumberg Capital Ventures
580 Howard St., Ste. 401
San Francisco, CA 94105
(415)905-5007
Fax: (415)357-5027
Website: http://www.blumberg-capital.com

Burr, Egan, Deleage, and Co. (San Francisco)
1 Embarcadero Center, Ste. 4050
San Francisco, CA 94111
(415)362-4022
Fax: (415)362-6178

Burrill & Company
120 Montgomery St., Ste. 1370
San Francisco, CA 94104
(415)743-3160
Fax: (415)743-3161
Website: http://www.burrillandco.com

CMEA Ventures
235 Montgomery St., Ste. 920
San Francisco, CA 94401
(415)352-1520
Fax: (415)352-1524
Website: http://www.cmeaventures.com

Crocker Capital
1 Post St., Ste. 2500
San Francisco, CA 94101
(415)956-5250
Fax: (415)959-5710

Dominion Ventures, Inc.
44 Montgomery St., Ste. 4200
San Francisco, CA 94104
(415)362-4890
Fax: (415)394-9245

Dorset Capital
Pier 1
Bay 2
San Francisco, CA 94111
(415)398-7101
Fax: (415)398-7141
Website: http://www.dorsetcapital
.com

Gatx Capital
Four Embarcadero Center, Ste. 2200
San Francisco, CA 94904
(415)955-3200
Fax: (415)955-3449

IMinds
135 Main St., Ste. 1350
San Francisco, CA 94105
(415)547-0000
Fax: (415)227-0300
Website: http://www.iminds.com

LF International Inc.
360 Post St., Ste. 705
San Francisco, CA 94108
(415)399-0110
Fax: (415)399-9222
Website: http://www.lfvc.com

Newbury Ventures
535 Pacific Ave., 2nd Fl.
San Francisco, CA 94133
(415)296-7408
Fax: (415)296-7416
Website: http://www.newburyven
.com

Quest Ventures (San Francisco)
333 Bush St., Ste. 1750
San Francisco, CA 94104
(415)782-1414
Fax: (415)782-1415

Robertson-Stephens Co.
555 California St., Ste. 2600
San Francisco, CA 94104
(415)781-9700
Fax: (415)781-2556
Website: http://
www.omegaadventures.com

Rosewood Capital, L.P.
One Maritime Plaza, Ste. 1330
San Francisco, CA 94111-3503
(415)362-5526
Fax: (415)362-1192
Website: http://www.rosewoodvc.com

Ticonderoga Capital Inc.
555 California St., No. 4950
San Francisco, CA 94104
(415)296-7900
Fax: (415)296-8956

21st Century Internet Venture Partners
Two South Park
2nd Floor
San Francisco, CA 94107
(415)512-1221
Fax: (415)512-2650
Website: http://www.21vc.com

VK Ventures
600 California St., Ste.1700
San Francisco, CA 94111
(415)391-5600
Fax: (415)397-2744

Walden Group of Venture Capital Funds
750 Battery St., Seventh Floor
San Francisco, CA 94111
(415)391-7225
Fax: (415)391-7262

Acer Technology Ventures
2641 Orchard Pkwy.
San Jose, CA 95134
(408)433-4945
Fax: (408)433-5230

Authosis
226 Airport Pkwy., Ste. 405
San Jose, CA 95110
(650)814-3603
Website: http://www.authosis.com

Western Technology Investment
2010 N. First St., Ste. 310
San Jose, CA 95131
(408)436-8577
Fax: (408)436-8625
E-mail: mktg@westerntech.com

Drysdale Enterprises
177 Bovet Rd., Ste. 600
San Mateo, CA 94402
(650)341-6336
Fax: (650)341-1329
E-mail: drysdale@aol.com

Greylock
2929 Campus Dr., Ste. 400
San Mateo, CA 94401
(650)493-5525
Fax: (650)493-5575
Website: http://www.greylock.com

Technology Funding
2000 Alameda de las Pulgas, Ste. 250
San Mateo, CA 94403
(415)345-2200
Fax: (415)345-1797

2M Invest Inc.
1875 S. Grant St.
Suite 750
San Mateo, CA 94402
(650)655-3765
Fax: (650)372-9107
E-mail: 2minfo@2minvest.com
Website: http://www.2minvest.com

Phoenix Growth Capital Corp.
2401 Kerner Blvd.
San Rafael, CA 94901
(415)485-4569
Fax: (415)485-4663

NextGen Partners LLC
1705 East Valley Rd.
Santa Barbara, CA 93108
(805)969-8540
Fax: (805)969-8542
Website: http://
www.nextgenpartners.com

Denali Venture Capital
1925 Woodland Ave.
Santa Clara, CA 95050
(408)690-4838
Fax: (408)247-6979
E-mail: wael@denaliventurecapital.com
Website: http://www.denaliventurecapital
.com

Dotcom Ventures LP
3945 Freedom Circle, Ste. 740
Santa Clara, CA 95045
(408)919-9855
Fax: (408)919-9857
Website: http://
www.dotcomventuresatl.com

Silicon Valley Bank
3003 Tasman
Santa Clara, CA 95054
(408)654-7400
Fax: (408)727-8728

Al Shugart International
920 41st Ave.
Santa Cruz, CA 95062

(831)479-7852
Fax: (831)479-7852
Website: http://www.alshugart.com

Leonard Mautner Associates
1434 Sixth St.
Santa Monica, CA 90401
(213)393-9788
Fax: (310)459-9918

Palomar Ventures
100 Wilshire Blvd., Ste. 450
Santa Monica, CA 90401
(310)260-6050
Fax: (310)656-4150
Website: http://
www.palomarventures.com

Medicus Venture Partners
12930 Saratoga Ave., Ste. D8
Saratoga, CA 95070
(408)447-8600
Fax: (408)447-8599
Website: http://www.medicusvc.com

Redleaf Venture Management
14395 Saratoga Ave., Ste. 130
Saratoga, CA 95070
(408)868-0800
Fax: (408)868-0810
E-mail: nancy@redleaf.com
Website: http://www.redleaf.com

Artemis Ventures
207 Second St., Ste. E
3rd Fl.
Sausalito, CA 94965
(415)289-2500
Fax: (415)289-1789
Website: http://
www.artemisventures.com

Deucalion Venture Partners
19501 Brooklime
Sonoma, CA 95476
(707)938-4974
Fax: (707)938-8921

Windward Ventures
PO Box 7688
Thousand Oaks, CA 91359-7688
(805)497-3332
Fax: (805)497-9331

National Investment Management, Inc.
2601 Airport Dr., Ste.210
Torrance, CA 90505
(310)784-7600
Fax: (310)784-7605

Southern California Ventures
406 Amapola Ave. Ste. 125
Torrance, CA 90501

(310)787-4381
Fax: (310)787-4382

Sandton Financial Group
21550 Oxnard St., Ste. 300
Woodland Hills, CA 91367
(818)702-9283

Woodside Fund
850 Woodside Dr.
Woodside, CA 94062
(650)368-5545
Fax: (650)368-2416
Website: http://www.woodsidefund.com

Colorado

Colorado Venture Management
Ste. 300
Boulder, CO 80301
(303)440-4055
Fax: (303)440-4636

Dean & Associates
4362 Apple Way
Boulder, CO 80301
Fax: (303)473-9900

Roser Ventures LLC
1105 Spruce St.
Boulder, CO 80302
(303)443-6436
Fax: (303)443-1885
Website: http://www.roserventures.com

Sequel Venture Partners
4430 Arapahoe Ave., Ste. 220
Boulder, CO 80303
(303)546-0400
Fax: (303)546-9728
E-mail: tom@sequelvc.com
Website: http://www.sequelvc.com

New Venture Resources
445C E. Cheyenne Mtn. Blvd.
Colorado Springs, CO 80906-4570
(719)598-9272
Fax: (719)598-9272

The Centennial Funds
1428 15th St.
Denver, CO 80202-1318
(303)405-7500
Fax: (303)405-7575
Website: http://www.centennial.com

Rocky Mountain Capital Partners
1125 17th St., Ste. 2260
Denver, CO 80202
(303)291-5200
Fax: (303)291-5327

Sandlot Capital LLC
600 South Cherry St., Ste. 525
Denver, CO 80246
(303)893-3400
Fax: (303)893-3403
Website: http://www.sandlotcapital.com

Wolf Ventures
50 South Steele St., Ste. 777
Denver, CO 80209
(303)321-4800
Fax: (303)321-4848
E-mail: businessplan@wolfventures.com
Website: http://www.wolfventures.com

The Columbine Venture Funds
5460 S. Quebec St., Ste. 270
Englewood, CO 80111
(303)694-3222
Fax: (303)694-9007

Investment Securities of Colorado, Inc.
4605 Denice Dr.
Englewood, CO 80111
(303)796-9192

Kinship Partners
6300 S. Syracuse Way, Ste. 484
Englewood, CO 80111
(303)694-0268
Fax: (303)694-1707
E-mail: block@vailsys.com

Boranco Management, L.L.C.
1528 Hillside Dr.
Fort Collins, CO 80524-1969
(970)221-2297
Fax: (970)221-4787

Aweida Ventures
890 West Cherry St., Ste. 220
Louisville, CO 80027
(303)664-9520
Fax: (303)664-9530
Website: http://www.aweida.com

Access Venture Partners
8787 Turnpike Dr., Ste. 260
Westminster, CO 80030
(303)426-8899
Fax: (303)426-8828

Connecticut

Medmax Ventures, LP
1 Northwestern Dr., Ste. 203
Bloomfield, CT 06002
(860)286-2960
Fax: (860)286-9960

James B. Kobak & Co.
Four Mansfield Place
Darien, CT 06820

(203)656-3471
Fax: (203)655-2905

Orien Ventures
1 Post Rd.
Fairfield, CT 06430
(203)259-9933
Fax: (203)259-5288

ABP Acquisition Corporation
115 Maple Ave.
Greenwich, CT 06830
(203)625-8287
Fax: (203)447-6187

Catterton Partners
9 Greenwich Office Park
Greenwich, CT 06830
(203)629-4901
Fax: (203)629-4903
Website: http://www.cpequity.com

Consumer Venture Partners
3 Pickwick Plz.
Greenwich, CT 06830
(203)629-8800
Fax: (203)629-2019

Insurance Venture Partners
31 Brookside Dr., Ste. 211
Greenwich, CT 06830
(203)861-0030
Fax: (203)861-2745

The NTC Group
Three Pickwick Plaza
Ste. 200
Greenwich, CT 06830
(203)862-2800
Fax: (203)622-6538

Regulus International Capital Co., Inc.
140 Greenwich Ave.
Greenwich, CT 06830
(203)625-9700
Fax: (203)625-9706

Axiom Venture Partners
City Place II
185 Asylum St., 17th Fl.
Hartford, CT 06103
(860)548-7799
Fax: (860)548-7797
Website: http://www.axiomventures.com

Conning Capital Partners
City Place II
185 Asylum St.
Hartford, CT 06103-4105
(860)520-1289
Fax: (860)520-1299
E-mail: pe@conning.com
Website: http://www.conning.com

First New England Capital L.P.
100 Pearl St.
Hartford, CT 06103
(860)293-3333
Fax: (860)293-3338
E-mail: info@firstnewenglandcapital.com
Website: http://www.firstnewenglandcapital
.com

Northeast Ventures
One State St., Ste. 1720
Hartford, CT 06103
(860)547-1414
Fax: (860)246-8755

Windward Holdings
38 Sylvan Rd.
Madison, CT 06443
(203)245-6870
Fax: (203)245-6865

Advanced Materials Partners, Inc.
45 Pine St.
PO Box 1022
New Canaan, CT 06840
(203)966-6415
Fax: (203)966-8448
E-mail: wkb@amplink.com

RFE Investment Partners
36 Grove St.
New Canaan, CT 06840
(203)966-2800
Fax: (203)966-3109
Website: http://www.rfeip.com

Connecticut Innovations, Inc.
999 West St.
Rocky Hill, CT 06067
(860)563-5851
Fax: (860)563-4877
E-mail: pamela.hartley@ctinnovations.com
Website: http://www.ctinnovations.com

Canaan Partners
105 Rowayton Ave.
Rowayton, CT 06853
(203)855-0400
Fax: (203)854-9117
Website: http://www.canaan.com

Landmark Partners, Inc.
10 Mill Pond Ln.
Simsbury, CT 06070
(860)651-9760
Fax: (860)651-8890
Website: http://www.landmarkpartners.com

Sweeney & Company
PO Box 567
Southport, CT 06490
(203)255-0220
Fax: (203)255-0220
E-mail: sweeney@connix.com

Baxter Associates, Inc.
PO Box 1333
Stamford, CT 06904
(203)323-3143
Fax: (203)348-0622

Beacon Partners Inc.
6 Landmark Sq., 4th Fl.
Stamford, CT 06901-2792
(203)359-5776
Fax: (203)359-5876

Collinson, Howe, and Lennox, LLC
1055 Washington Blvd., 5th Fl.
Stamford, CT 06901
(203)324-7700
Fax: (203)324-3636
E-mail: info@chlmedical.com
Website: http://www.chlmedical.com

Prime Capital Management Co.
550 West Ave.
Stamford, CT 06902
(203)964-0642
Fax: (203)964-0862

Saugatuck Capital Co.
1 Canterbury Green
Stamford, CT 06901
(203)348-6669
Fax: (203)324-6995
Website: http://www.saugatuckcapital
.com

Soundview Financial Group Inc.
22 Gatehouse Rd.
Stamford, CT 06902
(203)462-7200
Fax: (203)462-7350
Website: http://www.sndv.com

TSG Ventures, L.L.C.
177 Broad St., 12th Fl.
Stamford, CT 06901
(203)406-1500
Fax: (203)406-1590

Whitney & Company
177 Broad St.
Stamford, CT 06901
(203)973-1400
Fax: (203)973-1422
Website: http://www.jhwhitney.com

Cullinane & Donnelly Venture Partners L.P.
970 Farmington Ave.
West Hartford, CT 06107
(860)521-7811

The Crestview Investment and Financial Group
431 Post Rd. E, Ste. 1

Westport, CT 06880-4403
(203)222-0333
Fax: (203)222-0000

Marketcorp Venture Associates, L.P. (MCV)
274 Riverside Ave.
Westport, CT 06880
(203)222-3030
Fax: (203)222-3033

Oak Investment Partners (Westport)
1 Gorham Island
Westport, CT 06880
(203)226-8346
Fax: (203)227-0372
Website: http://www.oakinv.com

Oxford Bioscience Partners
315 Post Rd. W
Westport, CT 06880-5200
(203)341-3300
Fax: (203)341-3309
Website: http://www.oxbio.com

Prince Ventures (Westport)
25 Ford Rd.
Westport, CT 06880
(203)227-8332
Fax: (203)226-5302

LTI Venture Leasing Corp.
221 Danbury Rd.
Wilton, CT 06897
(203)563-1100
Fax: (203)563-1111
Website: http://www.ltileasing.com

Delaware

Blue Rock Capital
5803 Kennett Pike, Ste. A
Wilmington, DE 19807
(302)426-0981
Fax: (302)426-0982
Website: http://
www.bluerockcapital.com

District of Columbia

Allied Capital Corp.
1919 Pennsylvania Ave. NW
Washington, DC 20006-3434
(202)331-2444
Fax: (202)659-2053
Website: http://www.alliedcapital.com

Atlantic Coastal Ventures, L.P.
3101 South St. NW
Washington, DC 20007
(202)293-1166
Fax: (202)293-1181
Website: http://www.atlanticcv.com

Columbia Capital Group, Inc.
1660 L St. NW, Ste. 308
Washington, DC 20036
(202)775-8815
Fax: (202)223-0544

Core Capital Partners
901 15th St., NW
9th Fl.
Washington, DC 20005
(202)589-0090
Fax: (202)589-0091
Website: http://www.core-capital.com

Next Point Partners
701 Pennsylvania Ave. NW, Ste. 900
Washington, DC 20004
(202)661-8703
Fax: (202)434-7400
E-mail: mf@nextpoint.vc
Website: http://www.nextpointvc.com

Telecommunications Development Fund
2020 K. St. NW
Ste. 375
Washington, DC 20006
(202)293-8840
Fax: (202)293-8850
Website: http://www.tdfund.com

Wachtel & Co., Inc.
1101 4th St. NW
Washington, DC 20005-5680
(202)898-1144

Winslow Partners LLC
1300 Connecticut Ave. NW
Washington, DC 20036-1703
(202)530-5000
Fax: (202)530-5010
E-mail: winslow@winslowpartners.com

Women's Growth Capital Fund
1054 31st St., NW
Ste. 110
Washington, DC 20007
(202)342-1431
Fax: (202)341-1203
Website: http://www.wgcf.com

Florida

Sigma Capital Corp.
22668 Caravelle Circle
Boca Raton, FL 33433
(561)368-9783

North American Business Development Co., L.L.C.
111 East Las Olas Blvd.
Ft. Lauderdale, FL 33301
(305)463-0681

Fax: (305)527-0904
Website: http://
www.northamericanfund.com

Chartwell Capital Management Co. Inc.
1 Independent Dr., Ste. 3120
Jacksonville, FL 32202
(904)355-3519
Fax: (904)353-5833
E-mail: info@chartwellcap.com

CEO Advisors
1061 Maitland Center Commons
Ste. 209
Maitland, FL 32751
(407)660-9327
Fax: (407)660-2109

Henry & Co.
8201 Peters Rd., Ste. 1000
Plantation, FL 33324
(954)797-7400

Avery Business Development Services
2506 St. Michel Ct.
Ponte Vedra, FL 32082
(904)285-6033

New South Ventures
5053 Ocean Blvd.
Sarasota, FL 34242
(941)358-6000
Fax: (941)358-6078
Website: http://
www.newsouthventures.com

Venture Capital Management Corp.
PO Box 2626
Satellite Beach, FL 32937
(407)777-1969

Florida Capital Venture Ltd.
325 Florida Bank Plaza
100 W. Kennedy Blvd.
Tampa, FL 33602
(813)229-2294
Fax: (813)229-2028

Quantum Capital Partners
339 South Plant Ave.
Tampa, FL 33606
(813)250-1999
Fax: (813)250-1998
Website: http://
www.quantumcapitalpartners.com

South Atlantic Venture Fund
614 W. Bay St.
Tampa, FL 33606-2704
(813)253-2500
Fax: (813)253-2360
E-mail: venture@southatlantic.com
Website: http://www.southatlantic.com

LM Capital Corp.
120 S. Olive, Ste. 400
West Palm Beach, FL 33401
(561)833-9700
Fax: (561)655-6587
Website: http://www.lmcapitalsecurities
.com

Georgia

Venture First Associates
4811 Thornwood Dr.
Acworth, GA 30102
(770)928-3733
Fax: (770)928-6455

Alliance Technology Ventures
8995 Westside Pkwy., Ste. 200
Alpharetta, GA 30004
(678)336-2000
Fax: (678)336-2001
E-mail: info@atv.com
Website: http://www.atv.com

Cordova Ventures
2500 North Winds Pkwy., Ste. 475
Alpharetta, GA 30004
(678)942-0300
Fax: (678)942-0301
Website: http://www.cordovaventures
.com

Advanced Technology Development Fund
1000 Abernathy, Ste. 1420
Atlanta, GA 30328-5614
(404)668-2333
Fax: (404)668-2333

CGW Southeast Partners
12 Piedmont Center, Ste. 210
Atlanta, GA 30305
(404)816-3255
Fax: (404)816-3258
Website: http://www.cgwlp.com

Cyberstarts
1900 Emery St., NW
3rd Fl.
Atlanta, GA 30318
(404)267-5000
Fax: (404)267-5200
Website: http://www.cyberstarts.com

EGL Holdings, Inc.
10 Piedmont Center, Ste. 412
Atlanta, GA 30305
(404)949-8300
Fax: (404)949-8311

Equity South
1790 The Lenox Bldg.
3399 Peachtree Rd. NE

Atlanta, GA 30326
(404)237-6222
Fax: (404)261-1578

Five Paces
3400 Peachtree Rd., Ste. 200
Atlanta, GA 30326
(404)439-8300
Fax: (404)439-8301
Website: http://www.fivepaces.com

Frontline Capital, Inc.
3475 Lenox Rd., Ste. 400
Atlanta, GA 30326
(404)240-7280
Fax: (404)240-7281

Fuqua Ventures LLC
1201 W. Peachtree St. NW, Ste. 5000
Atlanta, GA 30309
(404)815-4500
Fax: (404)815-4528
Website: http://www.fuquaventures.com

Noro-Moseley Partners
4200 Northside Pkwy., Bldg. 9
Atlanta, GA 30327
(404)233-1966
Fax: (404)239-9280
Website: http://www.noro-moseley.com

Renaissance Capital Corp.
34 Peachtree St. NW, Ste. 2230
Atlanta, GA 30303
(404)658-9061
Fax: (404)658-9064

River Capital, Inc.
Two Midtown Plaza
1360 Peachtree St. NE, Ste. 1430
Atlanta, GA 30309
(404)873-2166
Fax: (404)873-2158

State Street Bank & Trust Co.
3414 Peachtree Rd. NE, Ste. 1010
Atlanta, GA 30326
(404)364-9500
Fax: (404)261-4469

UPS Strategic Enterprise Fund
55 Glenlake Pkwy. NE
Atlanta, GA 30328
(404)828-8814
Fax: (404)828-8088
E-mail: jcacyce@ups.com
Website: http://www.ups.com/sef/
sef_home

Wachovia
191 Peachtree St. NE, 26th Fl.
Atlanta, GA 30303
(404)332-1000

Fax: (404)332-1392
Website: http://www.wachovia.com/wca

Brainworks Ventures
4243 Dunwoody Club Dr.
Chamblee, GA 30341
(770)239-7447

First Growth Capital Inc.
Best Western Plaza, Ste. 105
PO Box 815
Forsyth, GA 31029
(912)781-7131

Financial Capital Resources, Inc.
21 Eastbrook Bend, Ste. 116
Peachtree City, GA 30269
(404)487-6650

Hawaii

HMS Hawaii Management Partners
Davies Pacific Center
841 Bishop St., Ste. 860
Honolulu, HI 96813
(808)545-3755
Fax: (808)531-2611

Idaho

Sun Valley Ventures
160 Second St.
Ketchum, ID 83340
(208)726-5005
Fax: (208)726-5094

Illinois

Open Prairie Ventures
115 N. Neil St., Ste. 209
Champaign, IL 61820
(217)351-7000
Fax: (217)351-7051
E-mail: inquire@openprairie.com
Website: http://www.openprairie.com

ABN AMRO Private Equity
208 S. La Salle St., 10th Fl.
Chicago, IL 60604
(312)855-7079
Fax: (312)553-6648
Website: http://www.abnequity.com

Alpha Capital Partners, Ltd.
122 S. Michigan Ave., Ste. 1700
Chicago, IL 60603
(312)322-9800
Fax: (312)322-9808
E-mail: acp@alphacapital.com

Ameritech Development Corp.
30 S. Wacker Dr., 37th Fl.
Chicago, IL 60606

(312)750-5083
Fax: (312)609-0244

Apex Investment Partners
225 W. Washington, Ste. 1450
Chicago, IL 60606
(312)857-2800
Fax: (312)857-1800
E-mail: apex@apexvc.com
Website: http://www.apexvc.com

Arch Venture Partners
8725 W. Higgins Rd., Ste. 290
Chicago, IL 60631
(773)380-6600
Fax: (773)380-6606
Website: http://www.archventure.com

The Bank Funds
208 South LaSalle St., Ste. 1680
Chicago, IL 60604
(312)855-6020
Fax: (312)855-8910

Batterson Venture Partners
303 W. Madison St., Ste. 1110
Chicago, IL 60606-3309
(312)269-0300
Fax: (312)269-0021
Website: http://www.battersonvp.com

William Blair Capital Partners, L.L.C.
222 W. Adams St., Ste. 1300
Chicago, IL 60606
(312)364-8250
Fax: (312)236-1042
E-mail: privateequity@wmblair.com
Website: http://www.wmblair.com

Bluestar Ventures
208 South LaSalle St., Ste. 1020
Chicago, IL 60604
(312)384-5000
Fax: (312)384-5005
Website: http://www.bluestarventures.com

The Capital Strategy Management Co.
233 S. Wacker Dr.
Box 06334
Chicago, IL 60606
(312)444-1170

DN Partners
77 West Wacker Dr., Ste. 4550
Chicago, IL 60601
(312)332-7960
Fax: (312)332-7979

Dresner Capital Inc.
29 South LaSalle St., Ste. 310
Chicago, IL 60603
(312)726-3600
Fax: (312)726-7448

Eblast Ventures LLC
11 South LaSalle St., 5th Fl.
Chicago, IL 60603
(312)372-2600
Fax: (312)372-5621
Website: http://www.eblastventures.com

Essex Woodlands Health Ventures, L.P.
190 S. LaSalle St., Ste. 2800
Chicago, IL 60603
(312)444-6040
Fax: (312)444-6034
Website: http://www.essexwoodlands.com

First Analysis Venture Capital
233 S. Wacker Dr., Ste. 9500
Chicago, IL 60606
(312)258-1400
Fax: (312)258-0334
Website: http://www.firstanalysis.com

Frontenac Co.
135 S. LaSalle St., Ste.3800
Chicago, IL 60603
(312)368-0044
Fax: (312)368-9520
Website: http://www.frontenac.com

GTCR Golder Rauner, LLC
6100 Sears Tower
Chicago, IL 60606
(312)382-2200
Fax: (312)382-2201
Website: http://www.gtcr.com

High Street Capital LLC
311 South Wacker Dr., Ste. 4550
Chicago, IL 60606
(312)697-4990
Fax: (312)697-4994
Website: http://www.highstr.com

IEG Venture Management, Inc.
70 West Madison
Chicago, IL 60602
(312)644-0890
Fax: (312)454-0369
Website: http://www.iegventure.com

JK&B Capital
180 North Stetson, Ste. 4500
Chicago, IL 60601
(312)946-1200
Fax: (312)946-1103
E-mail: gspencer@jkbcapital.com
Website: http://www.jkbcapital.com

Kettle Partners L.P.
350 W. Hubbard, Ste. 350
Chicago, IL 60610
(312)329-9300

Fax: (312)527-4519
Website: http://www.kettlevc.com

Lake Shore Capital Partners
20 N. Wacker Dr., Ste. 2807
Chicago, IL 60606
(312)803-3536
Fax: (312)803-3534

LaSalle Capital Group Inc.
70 W. Madison St., Ste. 5710
Chicago, IL 60602
(312)236-7041
Fax: (312)236-0720

Linc Capital, Inc.
303 E. Wacker Pkwy., Ste. 1000
Chicago, IL 60601
(312)946-2670
Fax: (312)938-4290
E-mail: bdemars@linccap.com

Madison Dearborn Partners, Inc.
3 First National Plz., Ste. 3800
Chicago, IL 60602
(312)895-1000
Fax: (312)895-1001
E-mail: invest@mdcp.com
Website: http://www.mdcp.com

Mesirow Private Equity Investments Inc.
350 N. Clark St.
Chicago, IL 60610
(312)595-6950
Fax: (312)595-6211
Website: http://
www.meisrowfinancial.com

Mosaix Ventures LLC
1822 North Mohawk
Chicago, IL 60614
(312)274-0988
Fax: (312)274-0989
Website: http://www.mosaixventures
.com

Nesbitt Burns
111 West Monroe St.
Chicago, IL 60603
(312)416-3855
Fax: (312)765-8000
Website: http://www.harrisbank.com

Polestar Capital, Inc.
180 N. Michigan Ave., Ste. 1905
Chicago, IL 60601
(312)984-9090
Fax: (312)984-9877
E-mail: wl@polestarvc.com
Website: http://www.polestarvc.com

Prince Ventures (Chicago)
10 S. Wacker Dr., Ste. 2575
Chicago, IL 60606-7407
(312)454-1408
Fax: (312)454-9125

Prism Capital
444 N. Michigan Ave.
Chicago, IL 60611
(312)464-7900
Fax: (312)464-7915
Website: http://www.prismfund.com

Third Coast Capital
900 N. Franklin St., Ste. 700
Chicago, IL 60610
(312)337-3303
Fax: (312)337-2567
E-mail: manic@earthlink.com
Website: http://
www.thirdcoastcapital.com

Thoma Cressey Equity Partners
4460 Sears Tower, 92nd Fl.
233 S. Wacker Dr.
Chicago, IL 60606
(312)777-4444
Fax: (312)777-4445
Website: http://www.thomacressey.com

Tribune Ventures
435 N. Michigan Ave., Ste. 600
Chicago, IL 60611
(312)527-8797
Fax: (312)222-5993
Website: http://
www.tribuneventures.com

Wind Point Partners (Chicago)
676 N. Michigan Ave., Ste. 330
Chicago, IL 60611
(312)649-4000
Website: http://www.wppartners.com

Marquette Venture Partners
520 Lake Cook Rd., Ste. 450
Deerfield, IL 60015
(847)940-1700
Fax: (847)940-1724
Website: http://
www.marquetteventures.com

Duchossois Investments Limited, LLC
845 Larch Ave.
Elmhurst, IL 60126
(630)530-6105
Fax: (630)993-8644
Website: http://www.duchtec.com

Evanston Business Investment Corp.
1840 Oak Ave.
Evanston, IL 60201

(847)866-1840
Fax: (847)866-1808
E-mail: t-parkinson@nwu.com
Website: http://www.ebic.com

Inroads Capital Partners L.P.
1603 Orrington Ave., Ste. 2050
Evanston, IL 60201-3841
(847)864-2000
Fax: (847)864-9692

The Cerulean Fund/WGC Enterprises
1701 E. Lake Ave., Ste. 170
Glenview, IL 60025
(847)657-8002
Fax: (847)657-8168

Ventana Financial Resources, Inc.
249 Market Sq.
Lake Forest, IL 60045
(847)234-3434

Beecken, Petty & Co.
901 Warrenville Rd., Ste. 205
Lisle, IL 60532
(630)435-0300
Fax: (630)435-0370
E-mail: hep@bpcompany.com
Website: http://www.bpcompany.com

Allstate Private Equity
3075 Sanders Rd., Ste. G5D
Northbrook, IL 60062-7127
(847)402-8247
Fax: (847)402-0880

KB Partners
1101 Skokie Blvd., Ste. 260
Northbrook, IL 60062-2856
(847)714-0444
Fax: (847)714-0445
E-mail: keith@kbpartners.com
Website: http://www.kbpartners.com

Transcap Associates Inc.
900 Skokie Blvd., Ste. 210
Northbrook, IL 60062
(847)753-9600
Fax: (847)753-9090

Graystone Venture Partners, L.L.C. / Portage Venture Partners
One Northfield Plaza, Ste. 530
Northfield, IL 60093
(847)446-9460
Fax: (847)446-9470
Website: http://
www.portageventures.com

Motorola Inc.
1303 E. Algonquin Rd.
Schaumburg, IL 60196-1065
(847)576-4929

Fax: (847)538-2250
Website: http://www.mot.com/mne

Indiana

Irwin Ventures LLC
500 Washington St.
Columbus, IN 47202
(812)373-1434
Fax: (812)376-1709
Website: http://www.irwinventures.com

Cambridge Venture Partners
4181 East 96th St., Ste. 200
Indianapolis, IN 46240
(317)814-6192
Fax: (317)944-9815

CID Equity Partners
One American Square, Ste. 2850
Box 82074
Indianapolis, IN 46282
(317)269-2350
Fax: (317)269-2355
Website: http://www.cidequity.com

Gazelle Techventures
6325 Digital Way, Ste. 460
Indianapolis, IN 46278
(317)275-6800
Fax: (317)275-1101
Website: http://www.gazellevc.com

Monument Advisors Inc.
Bank One Center/Circle
111 Monument Circle, Ste. 600
Indianapolis, IN 46204-5172
(317)656-5065
Fax: (317)656-5060
Website: http://www.monumentadv.com

MWV Capital Partners
201 N. Illinois St., Ste. 300
Indianapolis, IN 46204
(317)237-2323
Fax: (317)237-2325
Website: http://www.mwvcapital.com

First Source Capital Corp.
100 North Michigan St.
PO Box 1602
South Bend, IN 46601
(219)235-2180
Fax: (219)235-2227

Iowa

Allsop Venture Partners
118 Third Ave. SE, Ste. 837
Cedar Rapids, IA 52401
(319)368-6675
Fax: (319)363-9515

InvestAmerica Investment Advisors, Inc.
101 2nd St. SE, Ste. 800
Cedar Rapids, IA 52401
(319)363-8249
Fax: (319)363-9683

Pappajohn Capital Resources
2116 Financial Center
Des Moines, IA 50309
(515)244-5746
Fax: (515)244-2346
Website: http://www.pappajohn.com

Berthel Fisher & Company Planning Inc.
701 Tama St.
PO Box 609
Marion, IA 52302
(319)497-5700
Fax: (319)497-4244

Kansas

Enterprise Merchant Bank
7400 West 110th St., Ste. 560
Overland Park, KS 66210
(913)327-8500
Fax: (913)327-8505

Kansas Venture Capital, Inc. (Overland Park)
6700 Antioch Plz., Ste. 460
Overland Park, KS 66204
(913)262-7117
Fax: (913)262-3509
E-mail: jdalton@kvci.com

Child Health Investment Corp.
6803 W. 64th St., Ste. 208
Shawnee Mission, KS 66202
(913)262-1436
Fax: (913)262-1575
Website: http://www.chca.com

Kansas Technology Enterprise Corp.
214 SW 6th, 1st Fl.
Topeka, KS 66603-3719
(785)296-5272
Fax: (785)296-1160
E-mail: ktec@ktec.com
Website: http://www.ktec.com

Kentucky

Kentucky Highlands Investment Corp.
362 Old Whitley Rd.
London, KY 40741
(606)864-5175
Fax: (606)864-5194
Website: http://www.khic.org

Chrysalis Ventures, L.L.C.
1850 National City Tower
Louisville, KY 40202
(502)583-7644
Fax: (502)583-7648
E-mail: bobsany@chrysalisventures.com
Website: http://www.chrysalisventures
.com

Humana Venture Capital
500 West Main St.
Louisville, KY 40202
(502)580-3922
Fax: (502)580-2051
E-mail: gemont@humana.com
George Emont, Director

Summit Capital Group, Inc.
6510 Glenridge Park Pl., Ste. 8
Louisville, KY 40222
(502)332-2700

Louisiana

Bank One Equity Investors, Inc.
451 Florida St.
Baton Rouge, LA 70801
(504)332-4421
Fax: (504)332-7377

Advantage Capital Partners
LLE Tower
909 Poydras St., Ste. 2230
New Orleans, LA 70112
(504)522-4850
Fax: (504)522-4950
Website: http://www.advantagecap.com

Maine

CEI Ventures / Coastal Ventures LP
2 Portland Fish Pier, Ste. 201
Portland, ME 04101
(207)772-5356
Fax: (207)772-5503
Website: http://www.ceiventures.com

Commwealth Bioventures, Inc.
4 Milk St.
Portland, ME 04101
(207)780-0904
Fax: (207)780-0913

Maryland

Annapolis Ventures LLC
151 West St., Ste. 302
Annapolis, MD 21401
(443)482-9555
Fax: (443)482-9565
Website: http://www.annapolisventures
.com

Delmag Ventures
220 Wardour Dr.
Annapolis, MD 21401
(410)267-8196
Fax: (410)267-8017
Website: http://www.delmagventures.com

Abell Venture Fund
111 S. Calvert St., Ste. 2300
Baltimore, MD 21202
(410)547-1300
Fax: (410)539-6579
Website: http://www.abell.org

ABS Ventures (Baltimore)
1 South St., Ste. 2150
Baltimore, MD 21202
(410)895-3895
Fax: (410)895-3899
Website: http://www.absventures.com

Anthem Capital, L.P.
16 S. Calvert St., Ste. 800
Baltimore, MD 21202-1305
(410)625-1510
Fax: (410)625-1735
Website: http://www.anthemcapital.com

Catalyst Ventures
1119 St. Paul St.
Baltimore, MD 21202
(410)244-0123
Fax: (410)752-7721

Maryland Venture Capital Trust
217 E. Redwood St., Ste. 2200
Baltimore, MD 21202
(410)767-6361
Fax: (410)333-6931

New Enterprise Associates (Baltimore)
1119 St. Paul St.
Baltimore, MD 21202
(410)244-0115
Fax: (410)752-7721
Website: http://www.nea.com

T. Rowe Price Threshold Partnerships
100 E. Pratt St., 8th Fl.
Baltimore, MD 21202
(410)345-2000
Fax: (410)345-2800

Spring Capital Partners
16 W. Madison St.
Baltimore, MD 21201
(410)685-8000
Fax: (410)727-1436
E-mail: mailbox@springcap.com

Arete Corporation
3 Bethesda Metro Ctr., Ste. 770
Bethesda, MD 20814

(301)657-6268
Fax: (301)657-6254
Website: http://www.arete-microgen.com

Embryon Capital
7903 Sleaford Place
Bethesda, MD 20814
(301)656-6837
Fax: (301)656-8056

Potomac Ventures
7920 Norfolk Ave., Ste. 1100
Bethesda, MD 20814
(301)215-9240
Website: http://
www.potomacventures.com

Toucan Capital Corp.
3 Bethesda Metro Center, Ste. 700
Bethesda, MD 20814
(301)961-1970
Fax: (301)961-1969
Website: http://www.toucancapital.com

Kinetic Ventures LLC
2 Wisconsin Cir., Ste. 620
Chevy Chase, MD 20815
(301)652-8066
Fax: (301)652-8310
Website: http://
www.kineticventures.com

Boulder Ventures Ltd.
4750 Owings Mills Blvd.
Owings Mills, MD 21117
(410)998-3114
Fax: (410)356-5492
Website: http://
www.boulderventures.com

Grotech Capital Group
9690 Deereco Rd., Ste. 800
Timonium, MD 21093
(410)560-2000
Fax: (410)560-1910
Website: http://www.grotech.com

Massachusetts

Adams, Harkness & Hill, Inc.
60 State St.
Boston, MA 02109
(617)371-3900

Advent International
75 State St., 29th Fl.
Boston, MA 02109
(617)951-9400
Fax: (617)951-0566
Website: http://www.adventinernational
.com

American Research and Development
30 Federal St.
Boston, MA 02110-2508
(617)423-7500
Fax: (617)423-9655

Ascent Venture Partners
255 State St., 5th Fl.
Boston, MA 02109
(617)270-9400
Fax: (617)270-9401
E-mail: info@ascentvp.com
Website: http://www.ascentvp.com

Atlas Venture
222 Berkeley St.
Boston, MA 02116
(617)488-2200
Fax: (617)859-9292
Website: http://www.atlasventure.com

Axxon Capital
28 State St., 37th Fl.
Boston, MA 02109
(617)722-0980
Fax: (617)557-6014
Website: http://www.axxoncapital.com

BancBoston Capital/BancBoston Ventures
175 Federal St., 10th Fl.
Boston, MA 02110
(617)434-2509
Fax: (617)434-6175
Website: http://
www.bancbostoncapital.com

Boston Capital Ventures
Old City Hall
45 School St.
Boston, MA 02108
(617)227-6550
Fax: (617)227-3847
E-mail: info@bcv.com
Website: http://www.bcv.com

Boston Financial & Equity Corp.
20 Overland St.
PO Box 15071
Boston, MA 02215
(617)267-2900
Fax: (617)437-7601
E-mail: debbie@bfec.com

Boston Millennia Partners
30 Rowes Wharf
Boston, MA 02110
(617)428-5150
Fax: (617)428-5160
Website: http://www.millenniapartners
.com

Bristol Investment Trust
842A Beacon St.
Boston, MA 02215-3199
(617)566-5212
Fax: (617)267-0932

Brook Venture Management LLC
50 Federal St., 5th Fl.
Boston, MA 02110
(617)451-8989
Fax: (617)451-2369
Website: http://www.brookventure.com

Burr, Egan, Deleage, and Co. (Boston)
200 Clarendon St., Ste. 3800
Boston, MA 02116
(617)262-7770
Fax: (617)262-9779

Cambridge/Samsung Partners
One Exeter Plaza
Ninth Fl.
Boston, MA 02116
(617)262-4440
Fax: (617)262-5562

Chestnut Street Partners, Inc.
75 State St., Ste. 2500
Boston, MA 02109
(617)345-7220
Fax: (617)345-7201
E-mail: chestnut@chestnutp.com

Claflin Capital Management, Inc.
10 Liberty Sq., Ste. 300
Boston, MA 02109
(617)426-6505
Fax: (617)482-0016
Website: http://www.claflincapital.com

Copley Venture Partners
99 Summer St., Ste. 1720
Boston, MA 02110
(617)737-1253
Fax: (617)439-0699

Corning Capital / Corning Technology Ventures
121 High Street, Ste. 400
Boston, MA 02110
(617)338-2656
Fax: (617)261-3864
Website: http://www.corningventures.com

Downer & Co.
211 Congress St.
Boston, MA 02110
(617)482-6200
Fax: (617)482-6201
E-mail: cdowner@downer.com
Website: http://www.downer.com

Fidelity Ventures
82 Devonshire St.
Boston, MA 02109
(617)563-6370
Fax: (617)476-9023
Website: http://www.fidelityventures.com

Greylock Management Corp. (Boston)
1 Federal St.
Boston, MA 02110-2065
(617)423-5525
Fax: (617)482-0059

Gryphon Ventures
222 Berkeley St., Ste.1600
Boston, MA 02116
(617)267-9191
Fax: (617)267-4293
E-mail: all@gryphoninc.com

Halpern, Denny & Co.
500 Boylston St.
Boston, MA 02116
(617)536-6602
Fax: (617)536-8535

Harbourvest Partners, LLC
1 Financial Center, 44th Fl.
Boston, MA 02111
(617)348-3707
Fax: (617)350-0305
Website: http://www.hvpllc.com

Highland Capital Partners
2 International Pl.
Boston, MA 02110
(617)981-1500
Fax: (617)531-1550
E-mail: info@hcp.com
Website: http://www.hcp.com

Lee Munder Venture Partners
John Hancock Tower T-53
200 Clarendon St.
Boston, MA 02103
(617)380-5600
Fax: (617)380-5601
Website: http://www.leemunder.com

M/C Venture Partners
75 State St., Ste. 2500
Boston, MA 02109
(617)345-7200
Fax: (617)345-7201
Website: http://www.mcventurepartners
.com

Massachusetts Capital Resources Co.
420 Boylston St.
Boston, MA 02116
(617)536-3900
Fax: (617)536-7930

Massachusetts Technology Development Corp. (MTDC)
148 State St.
Boston, MA 02109
(617)723-4920
Fax: (617)723-5983
E-mail: jhodgman@mtdc.com
Website: http://www.mtdc.com

New England Partners
One Boston Place, Ste. 2100
Boston, MA 02108
(617)624-8400
Fax: (617)624-8999
Website: http://www.nepartners.com

North Hill Ventures
Ten Post Office Square
11th Fl.
Boston, MA 02109
(617)788-2112
Fax: (617)788-2152
Website: http://www.northhillventures
.com

OneLiberty Ventures
150 Cambridge Park Dr.
Boston, MA 02140
(617)492-7280
Fax: (617)492-7290
Website: http://www.oneliberty.com

Schroder Ventures
Life Sciences
60 State St., Ste. 3650
Boston, MA 02109
(617)367-8100
Fax: (617)367-1590
Website: http://www.shroderventures.com

Shawmut Capital Partners
75 Federal St., 18th Fl.
Boston, MA 02110
(617)368-4900
Fax: (617)368-4910
Website: http://www.shawmutcapital.com

Solstice Capital LLC
15 Broad St., 3rd Fl.
Boston, MA 02109
(617)523-7733
Fax: (617)523-5827
E-mail: solticecapital@solcap.com

Spectrum Equity Investors
One International Pl., 29th Fl.
Boston, MA 02110
(617)464-4600
Fax: (617)464-4601
Website: http://www.spectrumequity.com

Spray Venture Partners
One Walnut St.
Boston, MA 02108
(617)305-4140
Fax: (617)305-4144
Website: http://www.sprayventure.com

The Still River Fund
100 Federal St., 29th Fl.
Boston, MA 02110
(617)348-2327
Fax: (617)348-2371
Website: http://www.stillriverfund.com

Summit Partners
600 Atlantic Ave., Ste. 2800
Boston, MA 02210-2227
(617)824-1000
Fax: (617)824-1159
Website: http://www.summitpartners.com

TA Associates, Inc. (Boston)
High Street Tower
125 High St., Ste. 2500
Boston, MA 02110
(617)574-6700
Fax: (617)574-6728
Website: http://www.ta.com

TVM Techno Venture Management
101 Arch St., Ste. 1950
Boston, MA 02110
(617)345-9320
Fax: (617)345-9377
E-mail: info@tvmvc.com
Website: http://www.tvmvc.com

UNC Ventures
64 Burough St.
Boston, MA 02130-4017
(617)482-7070
Fax: (617)522-2176

**Venture Investment Management
Company (VIMAC)**
177 Milk St.
Boston, MA 02190-3410
(617)292-3300
Fax: (617)292-7979
E-mail: bzeisig@vimac.com
Website: http://www.vimac.com

MDT Advisers, Inc.
125 Cambridge Park Dr.
Cambridge, MA 02140-2314
(617)234-2200
Fax: (617)234-2210
Website: http://www.mdtai.com

TTC Ventures
One Main St., 6th Fl.
Cambridge, MA 02142

(617)528-3137
Fax: (617)577-1715
E-mail: info@ttcventures.com

Zero Stage Capital Co. Inc.
101 Main St., 17th Fl.
Cambridge, MA 02142
(617)876-5355
Fax: (617)876-1248
Website: http://www.zerostage.com

Atlantic Capital
164 Cushing Hwy.
Cohasset, MA 02025
(617)383-9449
Fax: (617)383-6040
E-mail: info@atlanticcap.com
Website: http://www.atlanticcap.com

Seacoast Capital Partners
55 Ferncroft Rd.
Danvers, MA 01923
(978)750-1300
Fax: (978)750-1301
E-mail: gdeli@seacoastcapital.com
Website: http://www.seacoastcapital.com

Sage Management Group
44 South Street
PO Box 2026
East Dennis, MA 02641
(508)385-7172
Fax: (508)385-7272
E-mail: sagemgt@capecod.net

Applied Technology
1 Cranberry Hill
Lexington, MA 02421-7397
(617)862-8622
Fax: (617)862-8367

Royalty Capital Management
5 Downing Rd.
Lexington, MA 02421-6918
(781)861-8490

Argo Global Capital
210 Broadway, Ste. 101
Lynnfield, MA 01940
(781)592-5250
Fax: (781)592-5230
Website: http://www.gsmcapital.com

Industry Ventures
6 Bayne Lane
Newburyport, MA 01950
(978)499-7606
Fax: (978)499-0686
Website: http://www.industryventures.com

Softbank Capital Partners
10 Langley Rd., Ste. 202
Newton Center, MA 02459

(617)928-9300
Fax: (617)928-9305
E-mail: clax@bvc.com

**Advanced Technology Ventures
(Boston)**
281 Winter St., Ste. 350
Waltham, MA 02451
(781)290-0707
Fax: (781)684-0045
E-mail: info@atvcapital.com
Website: http://www.atvcapital.com

Castile Ventures
890 Winter St., Ste. 140
Waltham, MA 02451
(781)890-0060
Fax: (781)890-0065
Website: http://www.castileventures.com

Charles River Ventures
1000 Winter St., Ste. 3300
Waltham, MA 02451
(781)487-7060
Fax: (781)487-7065
Website: http://www.crv.com

Comdisco Venture Group (Waltham)
Totton Pond Office Center
400-1 Totten Pond Rd.
Waltham, MA 02451
(617)672-0250
Fax: (617)398-8099

Marconi Ventures
890 Winter St., Ste. 310
Waltham, MA 02451
(781)839-7177
Fax: (781)522-7477
Website: http://www.marconi.com

Matrix Partners
Bay Colony Corporate Center
1000 Winter St., Ste.4500
Waltham, MA 02451
(781)890-2244
Fax: (781)890-2288
Website: http://www.matrixpartners.com

North Bridge Venture Partners
950 Winter St. Ste. 4600
Waltham, MA 02451
(781)290-0004
Fax: (781)290-0999
E-mail: eta@nbvp.com

Polaris Venture Partners
Bay Colony Corporate Ctr.
1000 Winter St., Ste. 3500
Waltham, MA 02451
(781)290-0770
Fax: (781)290-0880

E-mail: partners@polarisventures.com
Website: http://www.polarisventures.com

Seaflower Ventures
Bay Colony Corporate Ctr.
1000 Winter St. Ste. 1000
Waltham, MA 02451
(781)466-9552
Fax: (781)466-9553
E-mail: moot@seaflower.com
Website: http://www.seaflower.com

Ampersand Ventures
55 William St., Ste. 240
Wellesley, MA 02481
(617)239-0700
Fax: (617)239-0824
E-mail: info@ampersandventures.com
Website: http://www.ampersandventures
.com

Battery Ventures (Boston)
20 William St., Ste. 200
Wellesley, MA 02481
(781)577-1000
Fax: (781)577-1001
Website: http://www.battery.com

Commonwealth Capital Ventures, L.P.
20 William St., Ste.225
Wellesley, MA 02481
(781)237-7373
Fax: (781)235-8627
Website: http://www.ccvlp.com

Fowler, Anthony & Company
20 Walnut St.
Wellesley, MA 02481
(781)237-4201
Fax: (781)237-7718

Gemini Investors
20 William St.
Wellesley, MA 02481
(781)237-7001
Fax: (781)237-7233

Grove Street Advisors Inc.
20 William St., Ste. 230
Wellesley, MA 02481
(781)263-6100
Fax: (781)263-6101
Website: http://
www.grovestreetadvisors.com

Mees Pierson Investeringsmaat B.V.
20 William St., Ste. 210
Wellesley, MA 02482
(781)239-7600
Fax: (781)239-0377

Norwest Equity Partners
40 William St., Ste. 305

Wellesley, MA 02481-3902
(781)237-5870
Fax: (781)237-6270
Website: http://www.norwestvp.com

Bessemer Venture Partners (Wellesley Hills)
83 Walnut St.
Wellesley Hills, MA 02481
(781)237-6050
Fax: (781)235-7576
E-mail: travis@bvpny.com
Website: http://www.bvp.com

Venture Capital Fund of New England
20 Walnut St., Ste. 120
Wellesley Hills, MA 02481-2175
(781)239-8262
Fax: (781)239-8263

Prism Venture Partners
100 Lowder Brook Dr., Ste. 2500
Westwood, MA 02090
(781)302-4000
Fax: (781)302-4040
E-mail: dwbaum@prismventure.com

Palmer Partners LP
200 Unicorn Park Dr.
Woburn, MA 01801
(781)933-5445
Fax: (781)933-0698

Michigan

Arbor Partners, L.L.C.
130 South First St.
Ann Arbor, MI 48104
(734)668-9000
Fax: (734)669-4195
Website: http://www.arborpartners.com

EDF Ventures
425 N. Main St.
Ann Arbor, MI 48104
(734)663-3213
Fax: (734)663-7358
E-mail: edf@edfvc.com
Website: http://www.edfvc.com

White Pines Management, L.L.C.
2401 Plymouth Rd., Ste. B
Ann Arbor, MI 48105
(734)747-9401
Fax: (734)747-9704
E-mail: ibund@whitepines.com
Website: http://www.whitepines.com

Wellmax, Inc.
3541 Bendway Blvd., Ste. 100
Bloomfield Hills, MI 48301
(248)646-3554
Fax: (248)646-6220

Venture Funding, Ltd.
Fisher Bldg.
3011 West Grand Blvd., Ste. 321
Detroit, MI 48202
(313)871-3606
Fax: (313)873-4935

Investcare Partners L.P. / GMA Capital LLC
32330 W. Twelve Mile Rd.
Farmington Hills, MI 48334
(248)489-9000
Fax: (248)489-8819
E-mail: gma@gmacapital.com
Website: http://www.gmacapital.com

Liberty Bidco Investment Corp.
30833 Northwestern Highway, Ste. 211
Farmington Hills, MI 48334
(248)626-6070
Fax: (248)626-6072

Seaflower Ventures
5170 Nicholson Rd.
PO Box 474
Fowlerville, MI 48836
(517)223-3335
Fax: (517)223-3337
E-mail: gibbons@seaflower.com
Website: http://www.seaflower.com

Ralph Wilson Equity Fund LLC
15400 E. Jefferson Ave.
Gross Pointe Park, MI 48230
(313)821-9122
Fax: (313)821-9101
Website: http://www.RalphWilsonEquity
Fund.com
J. Skip Simms, President

Minnesota

Development Corp. of Austin
1900 Eighth Ave., NW
Austin, MN 55912
(507)433-0346
Fax: (507)433-0361
E-mail: dca@smig.net
Website: http://www.spamtownusa.com

Northeast Ventures Corp.
802 Alworth Bldg.
Duluth, MN 55802
(218)722-9915
Fax: (218)722-9871

Medical Innovation Partners, Inc.
6450 City West Pkwy.
Eden Prairie, MN 55344-3245
(612)828-9616
Fax: (612)828-9596

St. Paul Venture Capital, Inc.
10400 Vicking Dr., Ste. 550
Eden Prairie, MN 55344
(612)995-7474
Fax: (612)995-7475
Website: http://www.stpaulvc.com

Cherry Tree Investments, Inc.
7601 France Ave. S, Ste. 150
Edina, MN 55435
(612)893-9012
Fax: (612)893-9036
Website: http://www.cherrytree.com

Shared Ventures, Inc.
6550 York Ave. S
Edina, MN 55435
(612)925-3411

Sherpa Partners LLC
5050 Lincoln Dr., Ste. 490
Edina, MN 55436
(952)942-1070
Fax: (952)942-1071
Website: http://www.sherpapartners.com

Affinity Capital Management
901 Marquette Ave., Ste. 1810
Minneapolis, MN 55402
(612)252-9900
Fax: (612)252-9911
Website: http://www.affinitycapital.com

Artesian Capital
1700 Foshay Tower
821 Marquette Ave.
Minneapolis, MN 55402
(612)334-5600
Fax: (612)334-5601
E-mail: artesian@artesian.com

Coral Ventures
60 S. 6th St., Ste. 3510
Minneapolis, MN 55402
(612)335-8666
Fax: (612)335-8668
Website: http://www.coralventures.com

Crescendo Venture Management, L.L.C.
800 LaSalle Ave., Ste. 2250
Minneapolis, MN 55402
(612)607-2800
Fax: (612)607-2801
Website: http://www.crescendoventures
.com

Gideon Hixon Venture
1900 Foshay Tower
821 Marquette Ave.
Minneapolis, MN 55402
(612)904-2314
Fax: (612)204-0913

Norwest Equity Partners
3600 IDS Center
80 S. 8th St.
Minneapolis, MN 55402
(612)215-1600
Fax: (612)215-1601
Website: http://www.norwestvp.com

Oak Investment Partners (Minneapolis)
4550 Norwest Center
90 S. 7th St.
Minneapolis, MN 55402
(612)339-9322
Fax: (612)337-8017
Website: http://www.oakinv.com

Pathfinder Venture Capital Funds (Minneapolis)
7300 Metro Blvd., Ste. 585
Minneapolis, MN 55439
(612)835-1121
Fax: (612)835-8389
E-mail: jahrens620@aol.com

U.S. Bancorp Piper Jaffray Ventures, Inc.
800 Nicollet Mall, Ste. 800
Minneapolis, MN 55402
(612)303-5686
Fax: (612)303-1350
Website: http://www.paperjaffrey
ventures.com

The Food Fund, Ltd. Partnership
5720 Smatana Dr., Ste. 300
Minnetonka, MN 55343
(612)939-3950
Fax: (612)939-8106

Mayo Medical Ventures
200 First St. SW
Rochester, MN 55905
(507)266-4586
Fax: (507)284-5410
Website: http://www.mayo.edu

Missouri

Bankers Capital Corp.
3100 Gillham Rd.
Kansas City, MO 64109
(816)531-1600
Fax: (816)531-1334

Capital for Business, Inc. (Kansas City)
1000 Walnut St., 18th Fl.
Kansas City, MO 64106
(816)234-2357
Fax: (816)234-2952
Website: http://www.capitalforbusiness
.com

De Vries & Co. Inc.
800 West 47th St.
Kansas City, MO 64112
(816)756-0055
Fax: (816)756-0061

InvestAmerica Venture Group Inc. (Kansas City)
Commerce Tower
911 Main St., Ste. 2424
Kansas City, MO 64105
(816)842-0114
Fax: (816)471-7339

Kansas City Equity Partners
233 W. 47th St.
Kansas City, MO 64112
(816)960-1771
Fax: (816)960-1777
Website: http://www.kcep.com

Bome Investors, Inc.
8000 Maryland Ave., Ste. 1190
St. Louis, MO 63105
(314)721-5707
Fax: (314)721-5135
Website: http://www.gatewayventures.com

Capital for Business, Inc. (St. Louis)
11 S. Meramac St., Ste. 1430
St. Louis, MO 63105
(314)746-7427
Fax: (314)746-8739
Website: http://www.capitalforbusiness.com

Crown Capital Corp.
540 Maryville Centre Dr., Ste. 120
Saint Louis, MO 63141
(314)576-1201
Fax: (314)576-1525
Website: http://www.crown-cap.com

Gateway Associates L.P.
8000 Maryland Ave., Ste. 1190
St. Louis, MO 63105
(314)721-5707
Fax: (314)721-5135

Harbison Corp.
8112 Maryland Ave., Ste. 250
Saint Louis, MO 63105
(314)727-8200
Fax: (314)727-0249

Nebraska

Heartland Capital Fund, Ltd.
PO Box 642117
Omaha, NE 68154
(402)778-5124
Fax: (402)445-2370
Website: http://www.heartlandcapitalfund
.com

Odin Capital Group
1625 Farnam St., Ste. 700
Omaha, NE 68102
(402)346-6200
Fax: (402)342-9311
Website: http://www.odincapital.com

Nevada

Edge Capital Investment Co. LLC
1350 E. Flamingo Rd., Ste. 3000
Las Vegas, NV 89119
(702)438-3343
E-mail: info@edgecapital.net
Website: http://www.edgecapital.net

The Benefit Capital Companies Inc.
PO Box 542
Logandale, NV 89021
(702)398-3222
Fax: (702)398-3700

Millennium Three Venture Group LLC
6880 South McCarran Blvd., Ste. A-11
Reno, NV 89509
(775)954-2020
Fax: (775)954-2023
Website: http://www.m3vg.com

New Jersey

Alan I. Goldman & Associates
497 Ridgewood Ave.
Glen Ridge, NJ 07028
(973)857-5680
Fax: (973)509-8856

CS Capital Partners LLC
328 Second St., Ste. 200
Lakewood, NJ 08701
(732)901-1111
Fax: (212)202-5071
Website: http://www.cs-capital.com

Edison Venture Fund
1009 Lenox Dr., Ste. 4
Lawrenceville, NJ 08648
(609)896-1900
Fax: (609)896-0066
E-mail: info@edisonventure.com
Website: http://www.edisonventure.com

Tappan Zee Capital Corp. (New Jersey)
201 Lower Notch Rd.
PO Box 416
Little Falls, NJ 07424
(973)256-8280
Fax: (973)256-2841

The CIT Group/Venture Capital, Inc.
650 CIT Dr.
Livingston, NJ 07039
(973)740-5429

Fax: (973)740-5555
Website: http://www.cit.com

Capital Express, L.L.C.
1100 Valleybrook Ave.
Lyndhurst, NJ 07071
(201)438-8228
Fax: (201)438-5131
E-mail: niles@capitalexpress.com
Website: http://www.capitalexpress.com

Westford Technology Ventures, L.P.
17 Academy St.
Newark, NJ 07102
(973)624-2131
Fax: (973)624-2008

Accel Partners
1 Palmer Sq.
Princeton, NJ 08542
(609)683-4500
Fax: (609)683-4880
Website: http://www.accel.com

Cardinal Partners
221 Nassau St.
Princeton, NJ 08542
(609)924-6452
Fax: (609)683-0174
Website: http://www.cardinalhealth
partners.com

Domain Associates L.L.C.
One Palmer Sq., Ste. 515
Princeton, NJ 08542
(609)683-5656
Fax: (609)683-9789
Website: http://www.domainvc.com

Johnston Associates, Inc.
181 Cherry Valley Rd.
Princeton, NJ 08540
(609)924-3131
Fax: (609)683-7524
E-mail: jaincorp@aol.com

Kemper Ventures
Princeton Forrestal Village
155 Village Blvd.
Princeton, NJ 08540
(609)936-3035
Fax: (609)936-3051

Penny Lane Parnters
One Palmer Sq., Ste. 309
Princeton, NJ 08542
(609)497-4646
Fax: (609)497-0611

Early Stage Enterprises L.P.
995 Route 518
Skillman, NJ 08558
(609)921-8896

Fax: (609)921-8703
Website: http://www.esevc.com

MBW Management Inc.
1 Springfield Ave.
Summit, NJ 07901
(908)273-4060
Fax: (908)273-4430

BCI Advisors, Inc.
Glenpointe Center W.
Teaneck, NJ 07666
(201)836-3900
Fax: (201)836-6368
E-mail: info@bciadvisors.com
Website: http://www.bcipartners.com

Demuth, Folger & Wetherill / DFW Capital Partners
Glenpointe Center E., 5th Fl.
300 Frank W. Burr Blvd.
Teaneck, NJ 07666
(201)836-2233
Fax: (201)836-5666
Website: http://www.dfwcapital.com

First Princeton Capital Corp.
189 Berdan Ave., No. 131
Wayne, NJ 07470-3233
(973)278-3233
Fax: (973)278-4290
Website: http://www.lytellcatt.net

Edelson Technology Partners
300 Tice Blvd.
Woodcliff Lake, NJ 07675
(201)930-9898
Fax: (201)930-8899
Website: http://www.edelsontech.com

New Mexico

Bruce F. Glaspell & Associates
10400 Academy Rd. NE, Ste. 313
Albuquerque, NM 87111
(505)292-4505
Fax: (505)292-4258

High Desert Ventures, Inc.
6101 Imparata St. NE, Ste. 1721
Albuquerque, NM 87111
(505)797-3330
Fax: (505)338-5147

New Business Capital Fund, Ltd.
5805 Torreon NE
Albuquerque, NM 87109
(505)822-8445

SBC Ventures
10400 Academy Rd. NE, Ste. 313
Albuquerque, NM 87111

(505)292-4505
Fax: (505)292-4528

Technology Ventures Corp.
1155 University Blvd. SE
Albuquerque, NM 87106
(505)246-2882
Fax: (505)246-2891

New York

Small Business Technology Investment Fund
99 Washington Ave., Ste. 1731
Albany, NY 12210
(518)473-9741
Fax: (518)473-6876

Rand Capital Corp.
2200 Rand Bldg.
Buffalo, NY 14203
(716)853-0802
Fax: (716)854-8480
Website: http://www.randcapital.com

Seed Capital Partners
620 Main St.
Buffalo, NY 14202
(716)845-7520
Fax: (716)845-7539
Website: http://www.seedcp.com

Coleman Venture Group
5909 Northern Blvd.
PO Box 224
East Norwich, NY 11732
(516)626-3642
Fax: (516)626-9722

Vega Capital Corp.
45 Knollwood Rd.
Elmsford, NY 10523
(914)345-9500
Fax: (914)345-9505

Herbert Young Securities, Inc.
98 Cuttermill Rd.
Great Neck, NY 11021
(516)487-8300
Fax: (516)487-8319

Sterling/Carl Marks Capital, Inc.
175 Great Neck Rd., Ste. 408
Great Neck, NY 11021
(516)482-7374
Fax: (516)487-0781
E-mail: stercrlmar@aol.com
Website: http://www.serlingcarlmarks.com

Impex Venture Management Co.
PO Box 1570
Green Island, NY 12183
(518)271-8008
Fax: (518)271-910i

Corporate Venture Partners L.P.
200 Sunset Park
Ithaca, NY 14850
(607)257-6323
Fax: (607)257-6128

Arthur P. Gould & Co.
One Wilshire Dr.
Lake Success, NY 11020
(516)773-3000
Fax: (516)773-3289

Dauphin Capital Partners
108 Forest Ave.
Locust Valley, NY 11560
(516)759-3339
Fax: (516)759-3322
Website: http://www.dauphincapital.com

550 Digital Media Ventures
555 Madison Ave., 10th Fl.
New York, NY 10022
Website: http://www.550dmv.com

Aberlyn Capital Management Co., Inc.
500 Fifth Ave.
New York, NY 10110
(212)391-7750
Fax: (212)391-7762

Adler & Company
342 Madison Ave., Ste. 807
New York, NY 10173
(212)599-2535
Fax: (212)599-2526

Alimansky Capital Group, Inc.
605 Madison Ave., Ste. 300
New York, NY 10022-1901
(212)832-7300
Fax: (212)832-7338

Allegra Partners
515 Madison Ave., 29th Fl.
New York, NY 10022
(212)826-9080
Fax: (212)759-2561

The Argentum Group
The Chyrsler Bldg.
405 Lexington Ave.
New York, NY 10174
(212)949-6262
Fax: (212)949-8294
Website: http://www.argentumgroup.com

Axavision Inc.
14 Wall St., 26th Fl.
New York, NY 10005
(212)619-4000
Fax: (212)619-7202

Bedford Capital Corp.
18 East 48th St., Ste. 1800
New York, NY 10017
(212)688-5700
Fax: (212)754-4699
E-mail: info@bedfordnyc.com
Website: http://www.bedfordnyc.com

Bloom & Co.
950 Third Ave.
New York, NY 10022
(212)838-1858
Fax: (212)838-1843

Bristol Capital Management
300 Park Ave., 17th Fl.
New York, NY 10022
(212)572-6306
Fax: (212)705-4292

Citicorp Venture Capital Ltd. (New York City)
399 Park Ave., 14th Fl.
Zone 4
New York, NY 10043
(212)559-1127
Fax: (212)888-2940

CM Equity Partners
135 E. 57th St.
New York, NY 10022
(212)909-8428
Fax: (212)980-2630

Cohen & Co., L.L.C.
800 Third Ave.
New York, NY 10022
(212)317-2250
Fax: (212)317-2255
E-mail: nlcohen@aol.com

Cornerstone Equity Investors, L.L.C.
717 5th Ave., Ste. 1100
New York, NY 10022
(212)753-0901
Fax: (212)826-6798
Website: http://www.cornerstone-equity.com

CW Group, Inc.
1041 3rd Ave., 2nd fl.
New York, NY 10021
(212)308-5266
Fax: (212)644-0354
Website: http://www.cwventures.com

DH Blair Investment Banking Corp.
44 Wall St., 2nd Fl.
New York, NY 10005
(212)495-5000
Fax: (212)269-1438

Dresdner Kleinwort Capital
75 Wall St.
New York, NY 10005
(212)429-3131
Fax: (212)429-3139
Website: http://www.dresdnerkb.com

East River Ventures, L.P.
645 Madison Ave., 22nd Fl.
New York, NY 10022
(212)644-2322
Fax: (212)644-5498

Easton Hunt Capital Partners
641 Lexington Ave., 21st Fl.
New York, NY 10017
(212)702-0950
Fax: (212)702-0952
Website: http://www.eastoncapital.com

Elk Associates Funding Corp.
747 3rd Ave., Ste. 4C
New York, NY 10017
(212)355-2449
Fax: (212)759-3338

EOS Partners, L.P.
320 Park Ave., 22nd Fl.
New York, NY 10022
(212)832-5800
Fax: (212)832-5815
E-mail: mfirst@eospartners.com
Website: http://www.eospartners.com

Euclid Partners
45 Rockefeller Plaza, Ste. 3240
New York, NY 10111
(212)218-6880
Fax: (212)218-6877
E-mail: graham@euclidpartners.com
Website: http://www.euclidpartners.com

Evergreen Capital Partners, Inc.
150 East 58th St.
New York, NY 10155
(212)813-0758
Fax: (212)813-0754

Exeter Capital L.P.
10 E. 53rd St.
New York, NY 10022
(212)872-1172
Fax: (212)872-1198
E-mail: exeter@usa.net

Financial Technology Research Corp.
518 Broadway
Penthouse
New York, NY 10012
(212)625-9100
Fax: (212)431-0300
E-mail: fintek@financier.com

4C Ventures
237 Park Ave., Ste. 801
New York, NY 10017
(212)692-3680
Fax: (212)692-3685
Website: http://www.4cventures.com

Fusient Ventures
99 Park Ave., 20th Fl.
New York, NY 10016
(212)972-8999
Fax: (212)972-9876
E-mail: info@fusient.com
Website: http://www.fusient.com

Generation Capital Partners
551 Fifth Ave., Ste. 3100
New York, NY 10176
(212)450-8507
Fax: (212)450-8550
Website: http://www.genpartners.com

Golub Associates, Inc.
555 Madison Ave.
New York, NY 10022
(212)750-6060
Fax: (212)750-5505

Hambro America Biosciences Inc.
650 Madison Ave., 21st Floor
New York, NY 10022
(212)223-7400
Fax: (212)223-0305

Hanover Capital Corp.
505 Park Ave., 15th Fl.
New York, NY 10022
(212)755-1222
Fax: (212)935-1787

Harvest Partners, Inc.
280 Park Ave, 33rd Fl.
New York, NY 10017
(212)559-6300
Fax: (212)812-0100
Website: http://www.harvpart.com

Holding Capital Group, Inc.
10 E. 53rd St., 30th Fl.
New York, NY 10022
(212)486-6670
Fax: (212)486-0843

Hudson Venture Partners
660 Madison Ave., 14th Fl.
New York, NY 10021-8405
(212)644-9797
Fax: (212)644-7430
Website: http://www.hudsonptr.com

IBJS Capital Corp.
1 State St., 9th Fl.
New York, NY 10004

(212)858-2018
Fax: (212)858-2768

InterEquity Capital Partners, L.P.
220 5th Ave.
New York, NY 10001
(212)779-2022
Fax: (212)779-2103
Website: http://www.interequity-capital.com

The Jordan Edmiston Group Inc.
150 East 52nd St., 18th Fl.
New York, NY 10022
(212)754-0710
Fax: (212)754-0337

Josephberg, Grosz and Co., Inc.
633 3rd Ave., 13th Fl.
New York, NY 10017
(212)974-9926
Fax: (212)397-5832

J.P. Morgan Capital Corp.
60 Wall St.
New York, NY 10260-0060
(212)648-9000
Fax: (212)648-5002
Website: http://www.jpmorgan.com

The Lambda Funds
380 Lexington Ave., 54th Fl.
New York, NY 10168
(212)682-3454
Fax: (212)682-9231

Lepercq Capital Management Inc.
1675 Broadway
New York, NY 10019
(212)698-0795
Fax: (212)262-0155

Loeb Partners Corp.
61 Broadway, Ste. 2400
New York, NY 10006
(212)483-7000
Fax: (212)574-2001

Madison Investment Partners
660 Madison Ave.
New York, NY 10021
(212)223-2600
Fax: (212)223-8208

MC Capital Inc.
520 Madison Ave., 16th Fl.
New York, NY 10022
(212)644-0841
Fax: (212)644-2926

McCown, De Leeuw and Co. (New York)
65 E. 55th St., 36th Fl.
New York, NY 10022

(212)355-5500
Fax: (212)355-6283
Website: http://www.mdcpartners.com

Morgan Stanley Venture Partners
1221 Avenue of the Americas, 33rd Fl.
New York, NY 10020
(212)762-7900
Fax: (212)762-8424
E-mail: msventures@ms.com
Website: http://www.msvp.com

Nazem and Co.
645 Madison Ave., 12th Fl.
New York, NY 10022
(212)371-7900
Fax: (212)371-2150

Needham Capital Management, L.L.C.
445 Park Ave.
New York, NY 10022
(212)371-8300
Fax: (212)705-0299
Website: http://www.needhamco.com

Norwood Venture Corp.
1430 Broadway, Ste. 1607
New York, NY 10018
(212)869-5075
Fax: (212)869-5331
E-mail: nvc@mail.idt.net
Website: http://www.norven.com

Noveltek Venture Corp.
521 Fifth Ave., Ste. 1700
New York, NY 10175
(212)286-1963

Paribas Principal, Inc.
787 7th Ave.
New York, NY 10019
(212)841-2005
Fax: (212)841-3558

**Patricof & Co. Ventures, Inc.
(New York)**
445 Park Ave.
New York, NY 10022
(212)753-6300
Fax: (212)319-6155
Website: http://www.patricof.com

The Platinum Group, Inc.
350 Fifth Ave, Ste. 7113
New York, NY 10118
(212)736-4300
Fax: (212)736-6086
Website: http://www.platinumgroup.com

Pomona Capital
780 Third Ave., 28th Fl.
New York, NY 10017
(212)593-3639

Fax: (212)593-3987
Website: http://www.pomonacapital.com

Prospect Street Ventures
10 East 40th St., 44th Fl.
New York, NY 10016
(212)448-0702
Fax: (212)448-9652
E-mail: wkohler@prospectstreet.com
Website: http://www.prospectstreet.com

Regent Capital Management
505 Park Ave., Ste. 1700
New York, NY 10022
(212)735-9900
Fax: (212)735-9908

Rothschild Ventures, Inc.
1251 Avenue of the Americas, 51st Fl.
New York, NY 10020
(212)403-3500
Fax: (212)403-3652
Website: http://www.nmrothschild.com

Sandler Capital Management
767 Fifth Ave., 45th Fl.
New York, NY 10153
(212)754-8100
Fax: (212)826-0280

Siguler Guff & Company
630 Fifth Ave., 16th Fl.
New York, NY 10111
(212)332-5100
Fax: (212)332-5120

Spencer Trask Ventures Inc.
535 Madison Ave.
New York, NY 10022
(212)355-5565
Fax: (212)751-3362
Website: http://www.spencertrask.com

Sprout Group (New York City)
277 Park Ave.
New York, NY 10172
(212)892-3600
Fax: (212)892-3444
E-mail: info@sproutgroup.com
Website: http://www.sproutgroup.com

US Trust Private Equity
114 W.47th St.
New York, NY 10036
(212)852-3949
Fax: (212)852-3759
Website: http://www.ustrust.com/
privateequity

Vencon Management Inc.
301 West 53rd St., Ste. 10F
New York, NY 10019
(212)581-8787

Fax: (212)397-4126
Website: http://www.venconinc.com

Venrock Associates
30 Rockefeller Plaza, Ste. 5508
New York, NY 10112
(212)649-5600
Fax: (212)649-5788
Website: http://www.venrock.com

Venture Capital Fund of America, Inc.
509 Madison Ave., Ste. 812
New York, NY 10022
(212)838-5577
Fax: (212)838-7614
E-mail: mail@vcfa.com
Website: http://www.vcfa.com

Venture Opportunities Corp.
150 E. 58th St.
New York, NY 10155
(212)832-3737
Fax: (212)980-6603

Warburg Pincus Ventures, Inc.
466 Lexington Ave., 11th Fl.
New York, NY 10017
(212)878-9309
Fax: (212)878-9200
Website: http://www.warburgpincus.com

Wasserstein, Perella & Co. Inc.
31 W. 52nd St., 27th Fl.
New York, NY 10019
(212)702-5691
Fax: (212)969-7879

Welsh, Carson, Anderson, & Stowe
320 Park Ave., Ste. 2500
New York, NY 10022-6815
(212)893-9500
Fax: (212)893-9575

Whitney and Co. (New York)
630 Fifth Ave. Ste. 3225
New York, NY 10111
(212)332-2400
Fax: (212)332-2422
Website: http://www.jhwitney.com

Winthrop Ventures
74 Trinity Place, Ste. 600
New York, NY 10006
(212)422-0100

The Pittsford Group
8 Lodge Pole Rd.
Pittsford, NY 14534
(716)223-3523

Genesee Funding
70 Linden Oaks, 3rd Fl.
Rochester, NY 14625

(716)383-5550
Fax: (716)383-5305

Gabelli Multimedia Partners
One Corporate Center
Rye, NY 10580
(914)921-5395
Fax: (914)921-5031

Stamford Financial
108 Main St.
Stamford, NY 12167
(607)652-3311
Fax: (607)652-6301
Website: http://www.stamfordfinancial.
com

Northwood Ventures LLC
485 Underhill Blvd., Ste. 205
Syosset, NY 11791
(516)364-5544
Fax: (516)364-0879
E-mail: northwood@northwood.com
Website: http://www.northwood
ventures.com

Exponential Business Development Co.
216 Walton St.
Syracuse, NY 13202-1227
(315)474-4500
Fax: (315)474-4682
E-mail: dirksonn@aol.com
Website: http://www.exponential-ny.com

Onondaga Venture Capital Fund Inc.
714 State Tower Bldg.
Syracuse, NY 13202
(315)478-0157
Fax: (315)478-0158

Bessemer Venture Partners (Westbury)
1400 Old Country Rd., Ste. 109
Westbury, NY 11590
(516)997-2300
Fax: (516)997-2371
E-mail: bob@bvpny.com
Website: http://www.bvp.com

Ovation Capital Partners
120 Bloomingdale Rd., 4th Fl.
White Plains, NY 10605
(914)258-0011
Fax: (914)684-0848
Website: http://www.ovationcapital.com

North Carolina

Carolinas Capital Investment Corp.
1408 Biltmore Dr.
Charlotte, NC 28207
(704)375-3888
Fax: (704)375-6226

First Union Capital Partners
1st Union Center, 12th Fl.
301 S. College St.
Charlotte, NC 28288-0732
(704)383-0000
Fax: (704)374-6711
Website: http://www.fucp.com

Frontier Capital LLC
525 North Tryon St., Ste. 1700
Charlotte, NC 28202
(704)414-2880
Fax: (704)414-2881
Website: http://www.frontierfunds.com

Kitty Hawk Capital
2700 Coltsgate Rd., Ste. 202
Charlotte, NC 28211
(704)362-3909
Fax: (704)362-2774
Website: http://www.kittyhawk
capital.com

Piedmont Venture Partners
One Morrocroft Centre
6805 Morisson Blvd., Ste. 380
Charlotte, NC 28211
(704)731-5200
Fax: (704)365-9733
Website: http://www.piedmontvp.com

Ruddick Investment Co.
1800 Two First Union Center
Charlotte, NC 28282
(704)372-5404
Fax: (704)372-6409

The Shelton Companies Inc.
3600 One First Union Center
301 S. College St.
Charlotte, NC 28202
(704)348-2200
Fax: (704)348-2260

Wakefield Group
1110 E. Morehead St.
PO Box 36329
Charlotte, NC 28236
(704)372-0355
Fax: (704)372-8216
Website: http://www.wakefieldgroup.com

Aurora Funds, Inc.
2525 Meridian Pkwy., Ste. 220
Durham, NC 27713
(919)484-0400
Fax: (919)484-0444
Website: http://www.aurorafunds.com

Intersouth Partners
3211 Shannon Rd., Ste. 610
Durham, NC 27707

(919)493-6640
Fax: (919)493-6649
E-mail: info@intersouth.com
Website: http://www.intersouth.com

Geneva Merchant Banking Partners
PO Box 21962
Greensboro, NC 27420
(336)275-7002
Fax: (336)275-9155
Website: http://www.genevamer
chantbank.com

**The North Carolina Enterprise Fund,
L.P.**
3600 Glenwood Ave., Ste. 107
Raleigh, NC 27612
(919)781-2691
Fax: (919)783-9195
Website: http://www.ncef.com

Ohio

Senmend Medical Ventures
4445 Lake Forest Dr., Ste. 600
Cincinnati, OH 45242
(513)563-3264
Fax: (513)563-3261

The Walnut Group
312 Walnut St., Ste. 1151
Cincinnati, OH 45202
(513)651-3300
Fax: (513)929-4441
Website: http://www.thewalnutgroup.
com

Brantley Venture Partners
20600 Chagrin Blvd., Ste. 1150
Cleveland, OH 44122
(216)283-4800
Fax: (216)283-5324

Clarion Capital Corp.
1801 E. 9th St., Ste. 1120
Cleveland, OH 44114
(216)687-1096
Fax: (216)694-3545

Crystal Internet Venture Fund, L.P.
1120 Chester Ave., Ste. 418
Cleveland, OH 44114
(216)263-5515
Fax: (216)263-5518
E-mail: jf@crystalventure.com
Website: http://www.crystalventure.com

Key Equity Capital Corp.
127 Public Sq., 28th Fl.
Cleveland, OH 44114
(216)689-3000
Fax: (216)689-3204
Website: http://www.keybank.com

Morgenthaler Ventures
Terminal Tower
50 Public Square, Ste. 2700
Cleveland, OH 44113
(216)416-7500
Fax: (216)416-7501
Website: http://www.morgenthaler.com

National City Equity Partners Inc.
1965 E. 6th St.
Cleveland, OH 44114
(216)575-2491
Fax: (216)575-9965
E-mail: nccap@aol.com
Website: http://www.nccapital.com

Primus Venture Partners, Inc.
5900 LanderBrook Dr., Ste. 2000
Cleveland, OH 44124-4020
(440)684-7300
Fax: (440)684-7342
E-mail: info@primusventure.com
Website: http://www.primusventure.com

Banc One Capital Partners (Columbus)
150 East Gay St., 24th Fl.
Columbus, OH 43215
(614)217-1100
Fax: (614)217-1217

Battelle Venture Partners
505 King Ave.
Columbus, OH 43201
(614)424-7005
Fax: (614)424-4874

Ohio Partners
62 E. Board St., 3rd Fl.
Columbus, OH 43215
(614)621-1210
Fax: (614)621-1240

Capital Technology Group, L.L.C.
400 Metro Place North, Ste. 300
Dublin, OH 43017
(614)792-6066
Fax: (614)792-6036
E-mail: info@capitaltech.com
Website: http://www.capitaltech.com

Northwest Ohio Venture Fund
4159 Holland-Sylvania R., Ste. 202
Toledo, OH 43623
(419)824-8144
Fax: (419)882-2035
E-mail: bwalsh@novf.com

Oklahoma

Moore & Associates
1000 W. Wilshire Blvd., Ste. 370
Oklahoma City, OK 73116
(405)842-3660
Fax: (405)842-3763

Chisholm Private Capital Partners
100 West 5th St., Ste. 805
Tulsa, OK 74103
(918)584-0440
Fax: (918)584-0441
Website: http://www.chisholmvc.com

Davis, Tuttle Venture Partners (Tulsa)
320 S. Boston, Ste. 1000
Tulsa, OK 74103-3703
(918)584-7272
Fax: (918)582-3404
Website: http://www.davistuttle.com

RBC Ventures
2627 E. 21st St.
Tulsa, OK 74114
(918)744-5607
Fax: (918)743-8630

Oregon

Utah Ventures II LP
10700 SW Beaverton-Hillsdale Hwy., Ste. 548
Beaverton, OR 97005
(503)574-4125
E-mail: adishlip@uven.com
Website: http://www.uven.com

Orien Ventures
14523 SW Westlake Dr.
Lake Oswego, OR 97035
(503)699-1680
Fax: (503)699-1681

OVP Venture Partners (Lake Oswego)
340 Oswego Pointe Dr., Ste. 200
Lake Oswego, OR 97034
(503)697-8766
Fax: (503)697-8863
E-mail: info@ovp.com
Website: http://www.ovp.com

Oregon Resource and Technology Development Fund
4370 NE Halsey St., Ste. 233
Portland, OR 97213-1566
(503)282-4462
Fax: (503)282-2976

Shaw Venture Partners
400 SW 6th Ave., Ste. 1100
Portland, OR 97204-1636
(503)228-4884
Fax: (503)227-2471
Website: http://www.shawventures.com

Pennsylvania

Mid-Atlantic Venture Funds
125 Goodman Dr.
Bethlehem, PA 18015

(610)865-6550
Fax: (610)865-6427
Website: http://www.mavf.com

Newspring Ventures
100 W. Elm St., Ste. 101
Conshohocken, PA 19428
(610)567-2380
Fax: (610)567-2388
Website: http://www.newsprintventures.com

Patricof & Co. Ventures, Inc.
455 S. Gulph Rd., Ste. 410
King of Prussia, PA 19406
(610)265-0286
Fax: (610)265-4959
Website: http://www.patricof.com

Loyalhanna Venture Fund
527 Cedar Way, Ste. 104
Oakmont, PA 15139
(412)820-7035
Fax: (412)820-7036

Innovest Group Inc.
2000 Market St., Ste. 1400
Philadelphia, PA 19103
(215)564-3960
Fax: (215)569-3272

Keystone Venture Capital Management Co.
1601 Market St., Ste. 2500
Philadelphia, PA 19103
(215)241-1200
Fax: (215)241-1211
Website: http://www.keystonevc.com

Liberty Venture Partners
2005 Market St., Ste. 200
Philadelphia, PA 19103
(215)282-4484
Fax: (215)282-4485
E-mail: info@libertyvp.com
Website: http://www.libertyvp.com

Penn Janney Fund, Inc.
1801 Market St., 11th Fl.
Philadelphia, PA 19103
(215)665-4447
Fax: (215)557-0820

Philadelphia Ventures, Inc.
The Bellevue
200 S. Broad St.
Philadelphia, PA 19102
(215)732-4445
Fax: (215)732-4644

Birchmere Ventures Inc.
2000 Technology Dr.
Pittsburgh, PA 15219-3109

(412)803-8000
Fax: (412)687-8139
Website: http://www.birchmerevc.com

CEO Venture Fund
2000 Technology Dr., Ste. 160
Pittsburgh, PA 15219-3109
(412)687-3451
Fax: (412)687-8139
E-mail: ceofund@aol.com
Website: http://
www.ceoventurefund.com

Innovation Works Inc.
2000 Technology Dr., Ste. 250
Pittsburgh, PA 15219
(412)681-1520
Fax: (412)681-2625
Website: http://www.innovationworks.org

Keystone Minority Capital Fund L.P.
1801 Centre Ave., Ste. 201
Williams Sq.
Pittsburgh, PA 15219
(412)338-2230
Fax: (412)338-2224

Mellon Ventures, Inc.
One Mellon Bank Ctr., Rm. 3500
Pittsburgh, PA 15258
(412)236-3594
Fax: (412)236-3593
Website: http://www.mellonventures.com

Pennsylvania Growth Fund
5850 Ellsworth Ave., Ste. 303
Pittsburgh, PA 15232
(412)661-1000
Fax: (412)361-0676

Point Venture Partners
The Century Bldg.
130 Seventh St., 7th Fl.
Pittsburgh, PA 15222
(412)261-1966
Fax: (412)261-1718

Cross Atlantic Capital Partners
5 Radnor Corporate Center, Ste. 555
Radnor, PA 19087
(610)995-2650
Fax: (610)971-2062
Website: http://www.xacp.com

Meridian Venture Partners (Radnor)
The Radnor Court Bldg., Ste. 140
259 Radnor-Chester Rd.
Radnor, PA 19087
(610)254-2999
Fax: (610)254-2996
E-mail: mvpart@ix.netcom.com

TDH
919 Conestoga Rd., Bldg. 1, Ste. 301
Rosemont, PA 19010
(610)526-9970
Fax: (610)526-9971

Adams Capital Management
500 Blackburn Ave.
Sewickley, PA 15143
(412)749-9454
Fax: (412)749-9459
Website: http://www.acm.com

S.R. One, Ltd.
Four Tower Bridge
200 Barr Harbor Dr., Ste. 250
W. Conshohocken, PA 19428
(610)567-1000
Fax: (610)567-1039

Greater Philadelphia Venture Capital Corp.
351 East Conestoga Rd.
Wayne, PA 19087
(610)688-6829
Fax: (610)254-8958

PA Early Stage
435 Devon Park Dr., Bldg. 500, Ste. 510
Wayne, PA 19087
(610)293-4075
Fax: (610)254-4240
Website: http://www.paearlystage.com

The Sandhurst Venture Fund, L.P.
351 E. Constoga Rd.
Wayne, PA 19087
(610)254-8900
Fax: (610)254-8958

TL Ventures
700 Bldg.
435 Devon Park Dr.
Wayne, PA 19087-1990
(610)975-3765
Fax: (610)254-4210
Website: http://www.tlventures.com

Rockhill Ventures, Inc.
100 Front St., Ste. 1350
West Conshohocken, PA 19428
(610)940-0300
Fax: (610)940-0301

Puerto Rico

Advent-Morro Equity Partners
Banco Popular Bldg.
206 Tetuan St., Ste. 903
San Juan, PR 00902
(787)725-5285
Fax: (787)721-1735

North America Investment Corp.
Mercantil Plaza, Ste. 813
PO Box 191831
San Juan, PR 00919
(787)754-6178
Fax: (787)754-6181

Rhode Island

Manchester Humphreys, Inc.
40 Westminster St., Ste. 900
Providence, RI 02903
(401)454-0400
Fax: (401)454-0403

Navis Partners
50 Kennedy Plaza, 12th Fl.
Providence, RI 02903
(401)278-6770
Fax: (401)278-6387
Website: http://www.navispartners.com

South Carolina

Capital Insights, L.L.C.
PO Box 27162
Greenville, SC 29616-2162
(864)242-6832
Fax: (864)242-6755
E-mail: jwarner@capitalinsights.com
Website: http://www.capitalinsights.com

Transamerica Mezzanine Financing
7 N. Laurens St., Ste. 603
Greenville, SC 29601
(864)232-6198
Fax: (864)241-4444

Tennessee

Valley Capital Corp.
Krystal Bldg.
100 W. Martin Luther King Blvd., Ste. 212
Chattanooga, TN 37402
(423)265-1557
Fax: (423)265-1588

Coleman Swenson Booth Inc.
237 2nd Ave. S
Franklin, TN 37064-2649
(615)791-9462
Fax: (615)791-9636
Website: http://www.colemanswenson.com

Capital Services & Resources, Inc.
5159 Wheelis Dr., Ste. 106
Memphis, TN 38117
(901)761-2156
Fax: (907)767-0060

Paradigm Capital Partners LLC
6410 Poplar Ave., Ste. 395
Memphis, TN 38119

(901)682-6060
Fax: (901)328-3061

SSM Ventures
845 Crossover Ln., Ste. 140
Memphis, TN 38117
(901)767-1131
Fax: (901)767-1135
Website: http://www.ssmventures.com

Capital Across America L.P.
501 Union St., Ste. 201
Nashville, TN 37219
(615)254-1414
Fax: (615)254-1856
Website: http://www.capitalacrossamerica.com

Equitas L.P.
2000 Glen Echo Rd., Ste. 101
PO Box 158838
Nashville, TN 37215-8838
(615)383-8673
Fax: (615)383-8693

Massey Burch Capital Corp.
One Burton Hills Blvd., Ste. 350
Nashville, TN 37215
(615)665-3221
Fax: (615)665-3240
E-mail: tcalton@masseyburch.com
Website: http://www.masseyburch.com

Nelson Capital Corp.
3401 West End Ave., Ste. 300
Nashville, TN 37203
(615)292-8787
Fax: (615)385-3150

Texas

Phillips-Smith Specialty Retail Group
5080 Spectrum Dr., Ste. 805 W
Addison, TX 75001
(972)387-0725
Fax: (972)458-2560
E-mail: pssrg@aol.com
Website: http://www.phillips-smith.com

Austin Ventures, L.P.
701 Brazos St., Ste. 1400
Austin, TX 78701
(512)485-1900
Fax: (512)476-3952
E-mail: info@ausven.com
Website: http://www.austinventures.com

The Capital Network
3925 West Braker Lane, Ste. 406
Austin, TX 78759-5321
(512)305-0826
Fax: (512)305-0836

Techxas Ventures LLC
5000 Plaza on the Lake
Austin, TX 78746
(512)343-0118
Fax: (512)343-1879
E-mail: bruce@techxas.com
Website: http://www.techxas.com

Alliance Financial of Houston
218 Heather Ln.
Conroe, TX 77385-9013
(936)447-3300
Fax: (936)447-4222

Amerimark Capital Corp.
1111 W. Mockingbird, Ste. 1111
Dallas, TX 75247
(214)638-7878
Fax: (214)638-7612
E-mail: amerimark@amcapital.com
Website: http://www.amcapital.com

AMT Venture Partners / AMT Capital Ltd.
5220 Spring Valley Rd., Ste. 600
Dallas, TX 75240
(214)905-9757
Fax: (214)905-9761
Website: http://www.amtcapital.com

Arkoma Venture Partners
5950 Berkshire Lane, Ste. 1400
Dallas, TX 75225
(214)739-3515
Fax: (214)739-3572
E-mail: joelf@arkomavp.com

Capital Southwest Corp.
12900 Preston Rd., Ste. 700
Dallas, TX 75230
(972)233-8242
Fax: (972)233-7362
Website: http://www.capitalsouthwest.com

Dali, Hook Partners
One Lincoln Center, Ste. 1550
5400 LBJ Freeway
Dallas, TX 75240
(972)991-5457
Fax: (972)991-5458
E-mail: dhook@hookpartners.com
Website: http://www.hookpartners.com

HO2 Partners
Two Galleria Tower
13455 Noel Rd., Ste. 1670
Dallas, TX 75240
(972)702-1144
Fax: (972)702-8234
Website: http://www.ho2.com

Interwest Partners (Dallas)
2 Galleria Tower
13455 Noel Rd., Ste. 1670
Dallas, TX 75240
(972)392-7279
Fax: (972)490-6348
Website: http://www.interwest.com

Kahala Investments, Inc.
8214 Westchester Dr., Ste. 715
Dallas, TX 75225
(214)987-0077
Fax: (214)987-2332

MESBIC Ventures Holding Co.
2435 North Central Expressway, Ste. 200
Dallas, TX 75080
(972)991-1597
Fax: (972)991-4770
Website: http://www.mvhc.com

North Texas MESBIC, Inc.
9500 Forest Lane, Ste. 430
Dallas, TX 75243
(214)221-3565
Fax: (214)221-3566

Richard Jaffe & Company, Inc,
7318 Royal Cir.
Dallas, TX 75230
(214)265-9397
Fax: (214)739-1845

Sevin Rosen Management Co.
13455 Noel Rd., Ste. 1670
Dallas, TX 75240
(972)702-1100
Fax: (972)702-1103
E-mail: info@srfunds.com
Website: http://www.srfunds.com

Stratford Capital Partners, L.P.
300 Crescent Ct., Ste. 500
Dallas, TX 75201
(214)740-7377
Fax: (214)720-7393
E-mail: stratcap@hmtf.com

Sunwestern Investment Group
12221 Merit Dr., Ste. 935
Dallas, TX 75251
(972)239-5650
Fax: (972)701-0024

Wingate Partners
750 N. St. Paul St., Ste. 1200
Dallas, TX 75201
(214)720-1313
Fax: (214)871-8799

Buena Venture Associates
201 Main St., 32nd Fl.
Fort Worth, TX 76102

(817)339-7400
Fax: (817)390-8408
Website: http://www.buenaventure.com

The Catalyst Group
3 Riverway, Ste. 770
Houston, TX 77056
(713)623-8133
Fax: (713)623-0473
E-mail: herman@thecatalystgroup.net
Website: http://www.thecatalystgroup.net

Cureton & Co., Inc.
1100 Louisiana, Ste. 3250
Houston, TX 77002
(713)658-9806
Fax: (713)658-0476

Davis, Tuttle Venture Partners (Dallas)
8 Greenway Plaza, Ste. 1020
Houston, TX 77046
(713)993-0440
Fax: (713)621-2297
Website: http://www.davistuttle.com

Houston Partners
401 Louisiana, 8th Fl.
Houston, TX 77002
(713)222-8600
Fax: (713)222-8932

Southwest Venture Group
10878 Westheimer, Ste. 178
Houston, TX 77042
(713)827-8947
(713)461-1470

AM Fund
4600 Post Oak Place, Ste. 100
Houston, TX 77027
(713)627-9111
Fax: (713)627-9119

Ventex Management, Inc.
3417 Milam St.
Houston, TX 77002-9531
(713)659-7870
Fax: (713)659-7855

MBA Venture Group
1004 Olde Town Rd., Ste. 102
Irving, TX 75061
(972)986-6703

First Capital Group Management Co.
750 East Mulberry St., Ste. 305
PO Box 15616
San Antonio, TX 78212
(210)736-4233
Fax: (210)736-5449

The Southwest Venture Partnerships
16414 San Pedro, Ste. 345
San Antonio, TX 78232

(210)402-1200
Fax: (210)402-1221
E-mail: swvp@aol.com

Medtech International Inc.
1742 Carriageway
Sugarland, TX 77478
(713)980-8474
Fax: (713)980-6343

Utah

First Security Business Investment Corp.
15 East 100 South, Ste. 100
Salt Lake City, UT 84111
(801)246-5737
Fax: (801)246-5740

Utah Ventures II, L.P.
423 Wakara Way, Ste. 206
Salt Lake City, UT 84108
(801)583-5922
Fax: (801)583-4105
Website: http://www.uven.com

Wasatch Venture Corp.
1 S. Main St., Ste. 1400
Salt Lake City, UT 84133
(801)524-8939
Fax: (801)524-8941
E-mail: mail@wasatchvc.com

Vermont

North Atlantic Capital Corp.
76 Saint Paul St., Ste. 600
Burlington, VT 05401
(802)658-7820
Fax: (802)658-5757
Website: http://
www.northatlanticcapital.com

Green Mountain Advisors Inc.
PO Box 1230
Quechee, VT 05059
(802)296-7800
Fax: (802)296-6012
Website: http://www.gmtcap.com

Virginia

Oxford Financial Services Corp.
Alexandria, VA 22314
(703)519-4900
Fax: (703)519-4910
E-mail: oxford133@aol.com

Continental SBIC
4141 N. Henderson Rd.
Arlington, VA 22203
(703)527-5200
Fax: (703)527-3700

Novak Biddle Venture Partners
1750 Tysons Blvd., Ste. 1190
McLean, VA 22102
(703)847-3770
Fax: (703)847-3771
E-mail: roger@novakbiddle.com
Website: http://www.novakbiddle.com

Spacevest
11911 Freedom Dr., Ste. 500
Reston, VA 20190
(703)904-9800
Fax: (703)904-0571
E-mail: spacevest@spacevest.com
Website: http://www.spacevest.com

Virginia Capital
1801 Libbie Ave., Ste. 201
Richmond, VA 23226
(804)648-4802
Fax: (804)648-4809
E-mail: webmaster@vacapital.com
Website: http://www.vacapital.com

Calvert Social Venture Partners
402 Maple Ave. W
Vienna, VA 22180
(703)255-4930
Fax: (703)255-4931
E-mail: calven2000@aol.com

Fairfax Partners
8000 Towers Crescent Dr., Ste. 940
Vienna, VA 22182
(703)847-9486
Fax: (703)847-0911

Global Internet Ventures
8150 Leesburg Pike, Ste. 1210
Vienna, VA 22182
(703)442-3300
Fax: (703)442-3388
Website: http://www.givinc.com

Walnut Capital Corp. (Vienna)
8000 Towers Crescent Dr., Ste. 1070
Vienna, VA 22182
(703)448-3771
Fax: (703)448-7751

Washington

Encompass Ventures
777 108th Ave. NE, Ste. 2300
Bellevue, WA 98004
(425)486-3900
Fax: (425)486-3901
E-mail: info@evpartners.com
Website: http://www.encompass
ventures.com

Fluke Venture Partners
11400 SE Sixth St., Ste. 230

Bellevue, WA 98004
(425)453-4590
Fax: (425)453-4675
E-mail: gabelein@flukeventures.com
Website: http://www.flukeventures.com

Pacific Northwest Partners SBIC, L.P.
15352 SE 53rd St.
Bellevue, WA 98006
(425)455-9967
Fax: (425)455-9404

Materia Venture Associates, L.P.
3435 Carillon Pointe
Kirkland, WA 98033-7354
(425)822-4100
Fax: (425)827-4086

OVP Venture Partners (Kirkland)
2420 Carillon Pt.
Kirkland, WA 98033
(425)889-9192
Fax: (425)889-0152
E-mail: info@ovp.com
Website: http://www.ovp.com

Digital Partners
999 3rd Ave., Ste. 1610
Seattle, WA 98104
(206)405-3607
Fax: (206)405-3617
Website: http://www.digitalpartners.com

Frazier & Company
601 Union St., Ste. 3300
Seattle, WA 98101

(206)621-7200
Fax: (206)621-1848
E-mail: jon@frazierco.com

Kirlan Venture Capital, Inc.
221 First Ave. W, Ste. 108
Seattle, WA 98119-4223
(206)281-8610
Fax: (206)285-3451
Website: http://www.kirlanventure.com

Phoenix Partners
1000 2nd Ave., Ste. 3600
Seattle, WA 98104
(206)624-8968
Fax: (206)624-1907

Voyager Capital
800 5th St., Ste. 4100
Seattle, WA 98103
(206)470-1180
Fax: (206)470-1185
E-mail: info@voyagercap.com
Website: http://www.voyagercap.com

Northwest Venture Associates
221 N. Wall St., Ste. 628
Spokane, WA 99201
(509)747-0728
Fax: (509)747-0758
Website: http://www.nwva.com

Wisconsin

Venture Investors Management, L.L.C.
University Research Park

505 S. Rosa Rd.
Madison, WI 53719
(608)441-2700
Fax: (608)441-2727
E-mail: roger@ventureinvestors.com
Website: //www.ventureinvesters.com

Capital Investments, Inc.
1009 West Glen Oaks Lane,
Ste. 103
Mequon, WI 53092
(414)241-0303
Fax: (414)241-8451
Website: http://www.capitalinvest
mentsinc.com

Future Value Venture, Inc.
2745 N. Martin Luther King Dr.,
Ste. 204
Milwaukee, WI 53212-2300
(414)264-2252
Fax: (414)264-2253
E-mail: fvventures@aol.com
William Beckett, President

Lubar and Co., Inc.
700 N. Water St., Ste. 1200
Milwaukee, WI 53202
(414)291-9000
Fax: (414)291-9061

GCI
20875 Crossroads Cir., Ste. 100
Waukesha, WI 53186
(262)798-5080
Fax: (262)798-5087

Glossary of Small Business Terms

Absolute liability
Liability that is incurred due to product defects or negligent actions. Manufacturers or retail establishments are held responsible, even though the defect or action may not have been intentional or negligent.

ACE
See Active Corps of Executives

Accident and health benefits
Benefits offered to employees and their families in order to offset the costs associated with accidental death, accidental injury, or sickness.

Account statement
A record of transactions, including payments, new debt, and deposits, incurred during a defined period of time.

Accounting system
System capturing the costs of all employees and/or machinery included in business expenses.

Accounts payable
See Trade credit

Accounts receivable
Unpaid accounts which arise from unsettled claims and transactions from the sale of a company's products or services to its customers.

Active Corps of Executives (ACE)
A group of volunteers for a management assistance program of the U.S. Small Business Administration; volunteers provide one-on-one counseling and teach workshops and seminars for small firms.

ADA
See Americans with Disabilities Act

Adaptation
The process whereby an invention is modified to meet the needs of users.

Adaptive engineering
The process whereby an invention is modified to meet the manufacturing and commercial requirements of a targeted market.

Adverse selection
The tendency for higher-risk individuals to purchase health care and more comprehensive plans, resulting in increased costs.

Advertising
A marketing tool used to capture public attention and influence purchasing decisions for a product or service. Utilizes various forms of media to generate consumer response, such as flyers, magazines, newspapers, radio, and television.

Age discrimination
The denial of the rights and privileges of employment based solely on the age of an individual.

Agency costs
Costs incurred to insure that the lender or investor maintains control over assets while allowing the borrower or entrepreneur to use them. Monitoring and information costs are the two major types of agency costs.

Agribusiness
The production and sale of commodities and products from the commercial farming industry.

Americans with Disabilities Act (ADA)
Law designed to ensure equal access and opportunity to handicapped persons.

Annual report
Yearly financial report prepared by a business that adheres to the requirements set forth by the Securities and Exchange Commission (SEC).

Antitrust immunity
Exemption from prosecution under antitrust laws. In the transportation industry, firms with antitrust immunity are permitted under certain conditions to set schedules and sometimes prices for the public benefit.

Applied research
Scientific study targeted for use in a product or process.

Assets
Anything of value owned by a company.

Audit
The verification of accounting records and business procedures conducted by an outside accounting service.

Average cost
Total production costs divided by the quantity produced.

Balance Sheet
A financial statement listing the total assets and liabilities of a company at a given time.

Bankruptcy
The condition in which a business cannot meet its debt obligations and petitions a federal district court either for reorganization of its debts (Chapter 11) or for liquidation of its assets (Chapter 7).

Basket clause
A provision specifying the amount of public pension funds that may be placed in investments not included on a state's legal list (see separate citation).

BDC
See Business development corporation

Benefit
Various services, such as health care, flextime, day care, insurance, and vacation, offered to employees as part of a hiring package. Typically subsidized in whole or in part by the business.

BIDCO
See Business and industrial development company

Billing cycle
A system designed to evenly distribute customer billing throughout the month, preventing clerical backlogs.

Blue chip security
A low-risk, low-yield security representing an interest in a very stable company.

Blue sky laws
A general term that denotes various states' laws regulating securities.

Bond
A written instrument executed by a bidder or contractor (the principal) and a second party (the surety or sureties) to assure fulfillment of the principal's obligations to a third party (the obligee or government) identified in the bond. If the principal's obligations are not met, the bond assures payment to the extent stipulated of any loss sustained by the obligee.

Bonding requirements
Terms contained in a bond (see separate citation).

Bonus
An amount of money paid to an employee as a reward for achieving certain business goals or objectives.

Brainstorming
A group session where employees contribute their ideas for solving a problem or meeting a company objective without fear of retribution or ridicule.

Brand name
The part of a brand, trademark, or service mark that can be spoken. It can be a word, letter, or group of words or letters.

Bridge financing
A short-term loan made in expectation of intermediateterm or long-term financing. Can be used when a company plans to go public in the near future.

Broker
One who matches resources available for innovation with those who need them.

Budget
An estimate of the spending necessary to complete a project or offer a service in comparison to cash-on-hand and expected earnings for the coming year, with an emphasis on cost control.

Business and industrial development company (BIDCO)

A private, for-profit financing corporation chartered by the state to provide both equity and long-term debt capital to small business owners (see separate citations for equity and debt capital).

Business birth

The formation of a new establishment or enterprise. The appearance of a new establishment or enterprise in the Small Business Data Base (see separate citation).

Business conditions

Outside factors that can affect the financial performance of a business.

Business contractions

The number of establishments that have decreased in employment during a specified time.

Business cycle

A period of economic recession and recovery. These cycles vary in duration.

Business death

The voluntary or involuntary closure of a firm or establishment. The disappearance of an establishment or enterprise from the Small Business Data Base (see separate citation).

Business development corporation (BDC)

A business financing agency, usually composed of the financial institutions in an area or state, organized to assist in financing businesses unable to obtain assistance through normal channels; the risk is spread among various members of the business development corporation, and interest rates may vary somewhat from those charged by member institutions.

A venture capital firm in which shares of ownership are publicly held and to which the Investment Act of 1940 applies.

Business dissolution

For enumeration purposes, the absence of a business that was present in the prior time period from any current record.

Business entry

See Business birth

Business ethics

Moral values and principles espoused by members of the business community as a guide to fair and honest business practices.

Business exit

See Business death

Business expansions

The number of establishments that added employees during a specified time.

Business failure

Closure of a business causing a loss to at least one creditor.

Business format franchising

The purchase of the name, trademark, and an ongoing business plan of the parent corporation or franchisor by the franchisee.

Business license

A legal authorization issued by municipal and state governments and required for business operations.

Business name

Enterprises must register their business names with local governments usually on a "doing business as" (DBA) form. (This name is sometimes referred to as a "fictional name.") The procedure is part of the business licensing process and prevents any other business from using that same name for a similar business in the same locality.

Business norms

See Financial ratios

Business permit

See Business license

Business plan

A document that spells out a company's expected course of action for a specified period, usually including a detailed listing and analysis of risks and uncertainties. For the small business, it should examine the proposed products, the market, the industry, the management policies, the marketing policies, production needs, and financial needs. Frequently, it is used as a prospectus for potential investors and lenders.

Business proposal
See Business plan

Business service firm
An establishment primarily engaged in rendering services to other business organizations on a fee or contract basis.

Business start
For enumeration purposes, a business with a name or similar designation that did not exist in a prior time period.

Cafeteria plan
See Flexible benefit plan

Capacity
Level of a firm's, industry's, or nation's output corresponding to full practical utilization of available resources.

Capital
Assets less liabilities, representing the ownership interest in a business. A stock of accumulated goods, especially at a specified time and in contrast to income received during a specified time period. Accumulated goods devoted to production. Accumulated possessions calculated to bring income.

Capital expenditure
Expenses incurred by a business for improvements that will depreciate over time.

Capital gain
The monetary difference between the purchase price and the selling price of capital. Capital gains are taxed at a rate of 28% by the federal government.

Capital intensity
The relative importance of capital in the production process, usually expressed as the ratio of capital to labor but also sometimes as the ratio of capital to output.

Capital resource
The equipment, facilities and labor used to create products and services.

Catastrophic care
Medical and other services for acute and long-term illnesses that cost more than insurance coverage limits or that cost the amount most families may be expected to pay with their own resources.

CDC
See Certified development corporation

Certified development corporation (CDC)
A local area or statewide corporation or authority (for profit or nonprofit) that packages U.S. Small Business Administration (SBA), bank, state, and/or private money into financial assistance for existing business capital improvements. The SBA holds the second lien on its maximum share of 40 percent involvement. Each state has at least one certified development corporation. This program is called the SBA 504 Program.

Certified lenders
Banks that participate in the SBA guaranteed loan program (see separate citation). Such banks must have a good track record with the U.S. Small Business Administration (SBA) and must agree to certain conditions set forth by the agency. In return, the SBA agrees to process any guaranteed loan application within three business days.

Channel of distribution
The means used to transport merchandise from the manufacturer to the consumer.

Chapter 7 of the 1978 Bankruptcy Act
Provides for a court-appointed trustee who is responsible for liquidating a company's assets in order to settle outstanding debts.

Chapter 11 of the 1978 Bankruptcy Act
Allows the business owners to retain control of the company while working with their creditors to reorganize their finances and establish better business practices to prevent liquidation of assets.

Closely held corporation
A corporation in which the shares are held by a few persons, usually officers, employees, or others close to the management; these shares are rarely offered to the public.

Code of Federal Regulations
Codification of general and permanent rules of the federal government published in the Federal Register.

Code sharing
See Computer code sharing

Coinsurance
Upon meeting the deductible payment, health insurance participants may be required to make additional health care cost-sharing payments. Coinsurance is a payment of a fixed percentage of the cost of each service; copayment is usually a fixed amount to be paid with each service.

Collateral
Securities, evidence of deposit, or other property pledged by a borrower to secure repayment of a loan.

Collective ratemaking
The establishment of uniform charges for services by a group of businesses in the same industry.

Commercial insurance plan
See Underwriting

Commercial loans
Short-term renewable loans used to finance specific capital needs of a business.

Commercialization
The final stage of the innovation process, including production and distribution.

Common stock
The most frequently used instrument for purchasing ownership in private or public companies. Common stock generally carries the right to vote on certain corporate actions and may pay dividends, although it rarely does in venture investments. In liquidation, common stockholders are the last to share in the proceeds from the sale of a corporation's assets; bondholders and preferred shareholders have priority. Common stock is often used in firstround start-up financing.

Community development corporation
A corporation established to develop economic programs for a community and, in most cases, to provide financial support for such development.

Competitor
A business whose product or service is marketed for the same purpose/use and to the same consumer group as the product or service of another.

Consignment
A merchandising agreement, usually referring to secondhand shops, where the dealer pays the owner of an item a percentage of the profit when the item is sold.

Consortium
A coalition of organizations such as banks and corporations for ventures requiring large capital resources.

Consultant
An individual that is paid by a business to provide advice and expertise in a particular area.

Consumer price index
A measure of the fluctuation in prices between two points in time.

Consumer research
Research conducted by a business to obtain information about existing or potential consumer markets.

Continuation coverage
Health coverage offered for a specified period of time to employees who leave their jobs and to their widows, divorced spouses, or dependents.

Contractions
See Business contractions

Convertible preferred stock
A class of stock that pays a reasonable dividend and is convertible into common stock (see separate citation). Generally the convertible feature may only be exercised after being held for a stated period of time. This arrangement is usually considered second-round financing when a company needs equity to maintain its cash flow.

Convertible securities
A feature of certain bonds, debentures, or preferred stocks that allows them to be exchanged by the owner for another class of securities at a future date and in accordance with any other terms of the issue.

Copayment
See Coinsurance

Copyright
A legal form of protection available to creators and authors to safeguard their works from unlawful use or

claim of ownership by others. Copyrights may be acquired for works of art, sculpture, music, and published or unpublished manuscripts. All copyrights should be registered at the Copyright Office of the Library of Congress.

Corporate financial ratios
The relationship between key figures found in a company's financial statement expressed as a numeric value. Used to evaluate risk and company performance. Also known as Financial averages, Operating ratios, and Business ratios.

Corporation
A legal entity, chartered by a state or the federal government, recognized as a separate entity having its own rights, privileges, and liabilities distinct from those of its members.

Cost containment
Actions taken by employers and insurers to curtail rising health care costs; for example, increasing employee cost sharing (see separate citation), requiring second opinions, or preadmission screening.

Cost sharing
The requirement that health care consumers contribute to their own medical care costs through deductibles and coinsurance (see separate citations). Cost sharing does not include the amounts paid in premiums. It is used to control utilization of services; for example, requiring a fixed amount to be paid with each health care service.

Cottage industry
Businesses based in the home in which the family members are the labor force and family-owned equipment is used to process the goods.

Credit Rating
A letter or number calculated by an organization (such as Dun & Bradstreet) to represent the ability and disposition of a business to meet its financial obligations.

Customer service
Various techniques used to ensure the satisfaction of a customer.

Cyclical peak
The upper turning point in a business cycle.

Cyclical trough
The lower turning point in a business cycle.

DBA (Doing business as)
See Business name

Death
See Business death

Debenture
A certificate given as acknowledgment of a debt (see separate citation) secured by the general credit of the issuing corporation. A bond, usually without security, issued by a corporation and sometimes convertible to common stock.

Debt
Something owed by one person to another. Financing in which a company receives capital that must be repaid; no ownership is transferred.

Debt capital
Business financing that normally requires periodic interest payments and repayment of the principal within a specified time.

Debt financing
See Debt capital

Debt securities
Loans such as bonds and notes that provide a specified rate of return for a specified period of time.

Deductible
A set amount that an individual must pay before any benefits are received.

Demand shock absorbers
A term used to describe the role that some small firms play by expanding their output levels to accommodate a transient surge in demand.

Demographics
Statistics on various markets, including age, income, and education, used to target specific products or services to appropriate consumer groups.

Demonstration
Showing that a product or process has been modified sufficiently to meet the needs of users.

Deregulation
The lifting of government restrictions; for example, the lifting of government restrictions on the entry of new businesses, the expansion of services, and the setting of prices in particular industries.

Disaster loans
Various types of physical and economic assistance available to individuals and businesses through the U.S. Small Business Administration (SBA). This is the only SBA loan program available for residential purposes.

Discrimination
The denial of the rights and privileges of employment based on factors such as age, race, religion, or gender.

Diseconomies of scale
The condition in which the costs of production increase faster than the volume of production.

Dissolution
See Business dissolution

Distribution
Delivering a product or process to the user.

Distributor
One who delivers merchandise to the user.

Diversified company
A company whose products and services are used by several different markets.

Doing business as (DBA)
See Business name

Dow Jones
An information services company that publishes the Wall Street Journal and other sources of financial information.

Dow Jones Industrial Average
An indicator of stock market performance.

Earned income
A tax term that refers to wages and salaries earned by the recipient, as opposed to monies earned through interest and dividends.

Economic efficiency
The use of productive resources to the fullest practical extent in the provision of the set of goods and services that is most preferred by purchasers in the economy.

Economic indicators
Statistics used to express the state of the economy. These include the length of the average work week, the rate of unemployment, and stock prices.

Economically disadvantaged
See Socially and economically disadvantaged

Economies of scale
See Scale economies

EEOC
See Equal Employment Opportunity Commission

8(a) Program
A program authorized by the Small Business Act that directs federal contracts to small businesses owned and operated by socially and economically disadvantaged individuals.

Electronic mail (e-mail)
The electronic transmission of mail via phone lines.

E-mail
See Electronic mail

Employee leasing
A contract by which employers arrange to have their workers hired by a leasing company and then leased back to them for a management fee. The leasing company typically assumes the administrative burden of payroll and provides a benefit package to the workers.

Employee tenure
The length of time an employee works for a particular employer.

Employer identification number
The business equivalent of a social security number. Assigned by the U.S. Internal Revenue Service.

Enterprise
An aggregation of all establishments owned by a parent company. An enterprise may consist of a single, independent establishment or include subsidiaries and other branches under the same ownership and control.

Enterprise zone
A designated area, usually found in inner cities and other areas with significant unemployment, where businesses receive tax credits and other incentives to entice them to establish operations there.

Entrepreneur
A person who takes the risk of organizing and operating a new business venture.

Entry
See Business entry

Equal Employment Opportunity Commission (EEOC)
A federal agency that ensures nondiscrimination in the hiring and firing practices of a business.

Equal opportunity employer
An employer who adheres to the standards set by the Equal Employment Opportunity Commission (see separate citation).

Equity
The ownership interest. Financing in which partial or total ownership of a company is surrendered in exchange for capital. An investor's financial return comes from dividend payments and from growth in the net worth of the business.

Equity capital
See Equity; Equity midrisk venture capital

Equity financing
See Equity; Equity midrisk venture capital

Equity midrisk venture capital
An unsecured investment in a company. Usually a purchase of ownership interest in a company that occurs in the later stages of a company's development.

Equity partnership
A limited partnership arrangement for providing start-up and seed capital to businesses.

Equity securities
See Equity

Equity-type
Debt financing subordinated to conventional debt.

Establishment
A single-location business unit that may be independent (a single-establishment enterprise) or owned by a parent enterprise.

Establishment and Enterprise Microdata File
See U.S. Establishment and Enterprise Microdata File

Establishment birth
See Business birth

Establishment Longitudinal Microdata File
See U.S. Establishment Longitudinal Microdata File

Ethics
See Business ethics

Evaluation
Determining the potential success of translating an invention into a product or process.

Exit
See Business exit

Experience rating
See Underwriting

Export
A product sold outside of the country.

Export license
A general or specific license granted by the U.S. Department of Commerce required of anyone wishing to export goods. Some restricted articles need approval from the U.S. Departments of State, Defense, or Energy.

Failure
See Business failure

Fair share agreement
An agreement reached between a franchisor and a minority business organization to extend business ownership to minorities by either reducing the amount of capital required or by setting aside certain marketing areas for minority business owners.

Feasibility study
A study to determine the likelihood that a proposed product or development will fulfill the objectives of a particular investor.

Federal Trade Commission (FTC)
Federal agency that promotes free enterprise and competition within the U.S.

Federal Trade Mark Act of 1946
See Lanham Act

Fictional name
See Business name

Fiduciary
An individual or group that hold assets in trust for a beneficiary.

Financial analysis
The techniques used to determine money needs in a business. Techniques include ratio analysis, calculation of return on investment, guides for measuring profitability, and break-even analysis to determine ultimate success.

Financial intermediary
A financial institution that acts as the intermediary between borrowers and lenders. Banks, savings and loan associations, finance companies, and venture capital companies are major financial intermediaries in the United States.

Financial ratios
See Corporate financial ratios; Industry financial ratios

Financial statement
A written record of business finances, including balance sheets and profit and loss statements.

Financing
See First-stage financing; Second-stage financing; Thirdstage financing

First-stage financing
Financing provided to companies that have expended their initial capital, and require funds to start full-scale manufacturing and sales. Also known as First-round financing.

Fiscal year
Any twelve-month period used by businesses for accounting purposes.

504 Program
See Certified development corporation

Flexible benefit plan
A plan that offers a choice among cash and/or qualified benefits such as group term life insurance, accident and health insurance, group legal services, dependent care assistance, and vacations.

FOB
See Free on board

Format franchising
See Business format franchising; Franchising

401(k) plan
A financial plan where employees contribute a percentage of their earnings to a fund that is invested in stocks, bonds, or money markets for the purpose of saving money for retirement.

Four Ps
Marketing terms referring to Product, Price, Place, and Promotion.

Franchising
A form of licensing by which the owner-the franchisor- distributes or markets a product, method, or service through affiliated dealers called franchisees. The product, method, or service being marketed is identified by a brand name, and the franchisor maintains control over the marketing methods employed. The franchisee is often given exclusive access to a defined geographic area.

Free on board (FOB)
A pricing term indicating that the quoted price includes the cost of loading goods into transport vessels at a specified place.

Frictional unemployment
See Unemployment

FTC
See Federal Trade Commission

Fulfillment
The systems necessary for accurate delivery of an ordered item, including subscriptions and direct marketing.

Full-time workers
Generally, those who work a regular schedule of more than 35 hours per week.

Garment registration number
A number that must appear on every garment sold in the U.S. to indicate the manufacturer of the garment, which may or may not be the same as the label under which the garment is sold. The U.S. Federal Trade

Commission assigns and regulates garment registration numbers.

Gatekeeper
A key contact point for entry into a network.

GDP
See Gross domestic product

General obligation bond
A municipal bond secured by the taxing power of the municipality. The Tax Reform Act of 1986 limits the purposes for which such bonds may be issued and establishes volume limits on the extent of their issuance.

GNP
See Gross national product

Good Housekeeping Seal
Seal appearing on products that signifies the fulfillment of the standards set by the Good Housekeeping Institute to protect consumer interests.

Goods sector
All businesses producing tangible goods, including agriculture, mining, construction, and manufacturing businesses.

GPO
See Gross product originating

Gross domestic product (GDP)
The part of the nation's gross national product (see separate citation) generated by private business using resources from within the country.

Gross national product (GNP)
The most comprehensive single measure of aggregate economic output. Represents the market value of the total output of goods and services produced by a nation's economy.

Gross product originating (GPO)
A measure of business output estimated from the income or production side using employee compensation, profit income, net interest, capital consumption, and indirect business taxes.

HAL
See Handicapped assistance loan program

Handicapped assistance loan program (HAL)
Low-interest direct loan program through the U.S. Small Business Administration (SBA) for handicapped persons. The SBA requires that these persons demonstrate that their disability is such that it is impossible for them to secure employment, thus making it necessary to go into their own business to make a living.

Health maintenance organization (HMO)
Organization of physicians and other health care professionals that provides health services to subscribers and their dependents on a prepaid basis.

Health provider
An individual or institution that gives medical care. Under Medicare, an institutional provider is a hospital, skilled nursing facility, home health agency, or provider of certain physical therapy services.

Hispanic
A person of Cuban, Mexican, Puerto Rican, Latin American (Central or South American), European Spanish, or other Spanish-speaking origin or ancestry.

HMO
See Health maintenance organization

Home-based business
A business with an operating address that is also a residential address (usually the residential address of the proprietor).

Hub-and-spoke system
A system in which flights of an airline from many different cities (the spokes) converge at a single airport (the hub). After allowing passengers sufficient time to make connections, planes then depart for different cities.

Human Resources Management
A business program designed to oversee recruiting, pay, benefits, and other issues related to the company's work force, including planning to determine the optimal use of labor to increase production, thereby increasing profit.

Idea
An original concept for a new product or process.

Import
Products produced outside the country in which they are consumed.

Income
Money or its equivalent, earned or accrued, resulting from the sale of goods and services.

Income statement
A financial statement that lists the profits and losses of a company at a given time.

Incorporation
The filing of a certificate of incorporation with a state's secretary of state, thereby limiting the business owner's liability.

Incubator
A facility designed to encourage entrepreneurship and minimize obstacles to new business formation and growth, particularly for high-technology firms, by housing a number of fledgling enterprises that share an array of services, such as meeting areas, secretarial services, accounting, research library, on-site financial and management counseling, and word processing facilities.

Independent contractor
An individual considered self-employed (see separate citation) and responsible for paying Social Security taxes and income taxes on earnings.

Indirect health coverage
Health insurance obtained through another individual's health care plan; for example, a spouse's employersponsored plan.

Industrial development authority
The financial arm of a state or other political subdivision established for the purpose of financing economic development in an area, usually through loans to nonprofit organizations, which in turn provide facilities for manufacturing and other industrial operations.

Industry financial ratios
Corporate financial ratios averaged for a specified industry. These are used for comparison purposes and reveal industry trends and identify differences between the performance of a specific company and the performance of its industry. Also known as Industrial averages, Industry ratios, Financial averages, and Business or Industrial norms.

Inflation
Increases in volume of currency and credit, generally resulting in a sharp and continuing rise in price levels.

Informal capital
Financing from informal, unorganized sources; includes informal debt capital such as trade credit or loans from friends and relatives and equity capital from informal investors.

Initial public offering (IPO)
A corporation's first offering of stock to the public.

Innovation
The introduction of a new idea into the marketplace in the form of a new product or service or an improvement in organization or process.

Intellectual property
Any idea or work that can be considered proprietary in nature and is thus protected from infringement by others.

Internal capital
Debt or equity financing obtained from the owner or through retained business earnings.

Internet
A government-designed computer network that contains large amounts of information and is accessible through various vendors for a fee.

Intrapreneurship
The state of employing entrepreneurial principles to nonentrepreneurial situations.

Invention
The tangible form of a technological idea, which could include a laboratory prototype, drawings, formulas, etc.

IPO
See Initial public offering

Job description
The duties and responsibilities required in a particular position.

Job tenure
A period of time during which an individual is continuously employed in the same job.

Joint marketing agreements
Agreements between regional and major airlines, often involving the coordination of flight schedules, fares, and baggage transfer. These agreements help regional carriers operate at lower cost.

Joint venture
Venture in which two or more people combine efforts in a particular business enterprise, usually a single transaction or a limited activity, and agree to share the profits and losses jointly or in proportion to their contributions.

Keogh plan
Designed for self-employed persons and unincorporated businesses as a tax-deferred pension account.

Labor force
Civilians considered eligible for employment who are also willing and able to work.

Labor force participation rate
The civilian labor force as a percentage of the civilian population.

Labor intensity
The relative importance of labor in the production process, usually measured as the capital-labor ratio; i.e., the ratio of units of capital (typically, dollars of tangible assets) to the number of employees. The higher the capital-labor ratio exhibited by a firm or industry, the lower the capital intensity of that firm or industry is said to be.

Labor surplus area
An area in which there exists a high unemployment rate. In procurement (see separate citation), extra points are given to firms in counties that are designated a labor surplus area; this information is requested on procurement bid sheets.

Labor union
An organization of similarly-skilled workers who collectively bargain with management over the conditions of employment.

Laboratory prototype
See Prototype

LAN
See Local Area Network

Lanham Act
Refers to the Federal Trade Mark Act of 1946. Protects registered trademarks, trade names, and other service marks used in commerce.

Large business-dominated industry
Industry in which a minimum of 60 percent of employment or sales is in firms with more than 500 workers.

LBO
See Leveraged buy-out

Leader pricing
A reduction in the price of a good or service in order to generate more sales of that good or service.

Legal list
A list of securities selected by a state in which certain institutions and fiduciaries (such as pension funds, insurance companies, and banks) may invest. Securities not on the list are not eligible for investment. Legal lists typically restrict investments to high quality securities meeting certain specifications. Generally, investment is limited to U.S. securities and investment-grade blue chip securities (see separate citation).

Leveraged buy-out (LBO)
The purchase of a business or a division of a corporation through a highly leveraged financing package.

Liability
An obligation or duty to perform a service or an act. Also defined as money owed.

License
A legal agreement granting to another the right to use a technological innovation.

Limited Liability Company
A hybrid type of legal structure that provides the limited liability features of a corporation and the tax efficiencies and operational flexibility of a partnership.

Depending on the state, the members can consist of a single individual (one owner), two or more individuals, corporations or other LLCs.

Limited liability partnerships

A business organization that allows limited partners to enjoy limited personal liability while general partners have unlimited personal liability

Liquidity

The ability to convert a security into cash promptly.

Loans

See Commercial loans; Disaster loans; SBA direct loans; SBA guaranteed loans; SBA special lending institution categories Local Area Network (LAN) Computer networks contained within a single building or small area; used to facilitate the sharing of information.

Local development corporation

An organization, usually made up of local citizens of a community, designed to improve the economy of the area by inducing business and industry to locate and expand there. A local development corporation establishes a capability to finance local growth.

Long-haul rates

Rates charged by a transporter in which the distance traveled is more than 800 miles.

Long-term debt

An obligation that matures in a period that exceeds five years.

Low-grade bond

A corporate bond that is rated below investment grade by the major rating agencies (Standard and Poor's, Moody's).

Macro-efficiency

Efficiency as it pertains to the operation of markets and market systems.

Managed care

A cost-effective health care program initiated by employers whereby low-cost health care is made available to the employees in return for exclusive patronage to program doctors.

Management Assistance Programs

See SBA Management Assistance Programs

Management and technical assistance

A term used by many programs to mean business (as opposed to technological) assistance.

Mandated benefits

Specific treatments, providers, or individuals required by law to be included in commercial health plans.

Market evaluation

The use of market information to determine the sales potential of a specific product or process.

Market failure

The situation in which the workings of a competitive market do not produce the best results from the point of view of the entire society.

Market information

Data of any type that can be used for market evaluation, which could include demographic data, technology forecasting, regulatory changes, etc.

Market research

A systematic collection, analysis, and reporting of data about the market and its preferences, opinions, trends, and plans; used for corporate decision-making.

Market share

In a particular market, the percentage of sales of a specific product.

Marketing

Promotion of goods or services through various media.

Master Establishment List (MEL)

A list of firms in the United States developed by the U.S. Small Business Administration; firms can be selected by industry, region, state, standard metropolitan statistical area (see separate citation), county, and zip code.

Maturity

The date upon which the principal or stated value of a bond or other indebtedness becomes due and payable.

Medicaid (Title XIX)

A federally aided, state-operated and administered program that provides medical benefits for certain low

Glossary

income persons in need of health and medical care who are eligible for one of the government's welfare cash payment programs, including the aged, the blind, the disabled, and members of families with dependent children where one parent is absent, incapacitated, or unemployed.

Medicare (Title XVIII)
A nationwide health insurance program for disabled and aged persons. Health insurance is available to insured persons without regard to income. Monies from payroll taxes cover hospital insurance and monies from general revenues and beneficiary premiums pay for supplementary medical insurance.

MEL
See Master Establishment List

Merchant Status
The relationship between a company and a bank or credit card company allowing the company to accept credit card payments

MESBIC
See Minority enterprise small business investment corporation

MET
See Multiple employer trust

Metropolitan statistical area (MSA)
A means used by the government to define large population centers that may transverse different governmental jurisdictions. For example, the Washington, D.C. MSA includes the District of Columbia and contiguous parts of Maryland and Virginia because all of these geopolitical areas comprise one population and economic operating unit.

Mezzanine financing
See Third-stage financing

Micro-efficiency
Efficiency as it pertains to the operation of individual firms.

Microdata
Information on the characteristics of an individual business firm.

Microloan
An SBA loan program that helps entrepreneurs obtain loans from less than $100 to $25,000.

Mid-term debt
An obligation that matures within one to five years.

Midrisk venture capital
See Equity midrisk venture capital

Minimum premium plan
A combination approach to funding an insurance plan aimed primarily at premium tax savings. The employer self-funds a fixed percentage of estimated monthly claims and the insurance company insures the excess.

Minimum wage
The lowest hourly wage allowed by the federal government.

Minority Business Development Agency
Contracts with private firms throughout the nation to sponsor Minority Business Development Centers which provide minority firms with advice and technical assistance on a fee basis.

Minority Enterprise Small Business Investment Corporation (MESBIC)
A federally funded private venture capital firm licensed by the U.S. Small Business Administration to provide capital to minority-owned businesses (see separate citation).

Minority-owned business
Businesses owned by those who are socially or economically disadvantaged (see separate citation).

Mission statement
A short statement describing a company's function, markets and competitive advantages.

Mom and Pop business
A small store or enterprise having limited capital, principally employing family members.

Multi-employer plan
A health plan to which more than one employer is required to contribute and that may be maintained through a collective bargaining agreement and required to meet standards prescribed by the U.S. Department of Labor.

Multi-level marketing
A system of selling in which you sign up other people to assist you and they, in turn, recruit others to help them. Some entrepreneurs have built successful companies on this concept because the main focus of their activities is their product and product sales.

Multiple employer trust (MET)
A self-funded benefit plan generally geared toward small employers sharing a common interest.

NASDAQ
See National Association of Securities Dealers Automated Quotations

National Association of Securities Dealers Automated Quotations
Provides price quotes on over-the-counter securities as well as securities listed on the New York Stock Exchange.

National income
Aggregate earnings of labor and property arising from the production of goods and services in a nation's economy.

Net assets
See Net worth

Net income
The amount remaining from earnings and profits after all expenses and costs have been met or deducted. Also known as Net earnings.

Net profit
Money earned after production and overhead expenses (see separate citations) have been deducted.

Net worth
The difference between a company's total assets and its total liabilities.

Network
A chain of interconnected individuals or organizations sharing information and/or services.

New York Stock Exchange (NYSE)
The oldest stock exchange in the U.S. Allows for trading in stocks, bonds, warrants, options, and rights that meet listing requirements.

Niche
A career or business for which a person is well-suited. Also, a product which fulfills one need of a particular market segment, often with little or no competition.

Nodes
One workstation in a network, either local area or wide area (see separate citations).

Nonbank bank
A bank that either accepts deposits or makes loans, but not both. Used to create many new branch banks.

Noncompetitive awards
A method of contracting whereby the federal government negotiates with only one contractor to supply a product or service.

Nonmember bank
A state-regulated bank that does not belong to the federal bank system.

Nonprofit
An organization that has no shareholders, does not distribute profits, and is without federal and state tax liabilities.

Norms
See Financial ratios

North American Free Trade Agreement (NAFTA)
Passed in 1993, NAFTA eliminates trade barriers among businesses in the U.S., Canada, and Mexico.

NYSE
See New York Stock Exchange

Occupational Safety & Health Administration (OSHA)
Federal agency that regulates health and safety standards within the workplace.

Operating Expenses
Business expenditures not directly associated with the production of goods or services.

Optimal firm size
The business size at which the production cost per unit of output (average cost) is, in the long run, at its minimum.

Organizational chart
A hierarchical chart tracking the chain of command within an organization.

OSHA
See Occupational Safety & Health Administration

Overhead
Expenses, such as employee benefits and building utilities, incurred by a business that are unrelated to the actual product or service sold.

Owner's capital
Debt or equity funds provided by the owner(s) of a business; sources of owner's capital are personal savings, sales of assets, or loans from financial institutions.

P & L
See Profit and loss statement

Part-time workers
Normally, those who work less than 35 hours per week. The Tax Reform Act indicated that part-time workers who work less than 17.5 hours per week may be excluded from health plans for purposes of complying with federal nondiscrimination rules.

Part-year workers
Those who work less than 50 weeks per year.

Partnership
Two or more parties who enter into a legal relationship to conduct business for profit. Defined by the U.S. Internal Revenue Code as joint ventures, syndicates, groups, pools, and other associations of two or more persons organized for profit that are not specifically classified in the IRS code as corporations or proprietorships.

Patent
A grant made by the government assuring an inventor the sole right to make, use, and sell an invention for a period of 17 years.

PC
See Professional corporation

Peak
See Cyclical peak

Pension
A series of payments made monthly, semiannually, annually, or at other specified intervals during the lifetime of the pensioner for distribution upon retirement. The term is sometimes used to denote the portion of the retirement allowance financed by the employer's contributions.

Pension fund
A fund established to provide for the payment of pension benefits; the collective contributions made by all of the parties to the pension plan.

Performance appraisal
An established set of objective criteria, based on job description and requirements, that is used to evaluate the performance of an employee in a specific job.

Permit
See Business license

Plan
See Business plan

Pooling
An arrangement for employers to achieve efficiencies and lower health costs by joining together to purchase group health insurance or self-insurance.

PPO
See Preferred provider organization

Preferred lenders program
See SBA special lending institution categories

Preferred provider organization (PPO)
A contractual arrangement with a health care services organization that agrees to discount its health care rates in return for faster payment and/or a patient base.

Premiums
The amount of money paid to an insurer for health insurance under a policy. The premium is generally paid periodically (e.g., monthly), and often is split between the employer and the employee. Unlike deductibles and coinsurance or copayments, premiums are paid for coverage whether or not benefits are actually used.

Prime-age workers
Employees 25 to 54 years of age.

Prime contract
A contract awarded directly by the U.S. Federal Government.

Private company
See Closely held corporation

Private placement
A method of raising capital by offering for sale an investment or business to a small group of investors (generally avoiding registration with the Securities and Exchange Commission or state securities registration agencies). Also known as Private financing or Private offering.

Pro forma
The use of hypothetical figures in financial statements to represent future expenditures, debts, and other potential financial expenses.

Proactive
Taking the initiative to solve problems and anticipate future events before they happen, instead of reacting to an already existing problem or waiting for a difficult situation to occur.

Procurement
A contract from an agency of the federal government for goods or services from a small business.

Product development
The stage of the innovation process where research is translated into a product or process through evaluation, adaptation, and demonstration.

Product franchising
An arrangement for a franchisee to use the name and to produce the product line of the franchisor or parent corporation.

Production
The manufacture of a product.

Production prototype
See Prototype

Productivity
A measurement of the number of goods produced during a specific amount of time.

Professional corporation (PC)
Organized by members of a profession such as medicine, dentistry, or law for the purpose of conducting their professional activities as a corporation. Liability of a member or shareholder is limited in the same manner as in a business corporation.

Profit and loss statement (P & L)
The summary of the incomes (total revenues) and costs of a company's operation during a specific period of time. Also known as Income and expense statement.

Proposal
See Business plan

Proprietorship
The most common legal form of business ownership; about 85 percent of all small businesses are proprietorships. The liability of the owner is unlimited in this form of ownership.

Prospective payment system
A cost-containment measure included in the Social Security Amendments of 1983 whereby Medicare payments to hospitals are based on established prices, rather than on cost reimbursement.

Prototype
A model that demonstrates the validity of the concept of an invention (laboratory prototype); a model that meets the needs of the manufacturing process and the user (production prototype).

Prudent investor rule or standard
A legal doctrine that requires fiduciaries to make investments using the prudence, diligence, and intelligence that would be used by a prudent person in making similar investments. Because fiduciaries make investments on behalf of third-party beneficiaries, the standard results in very conservative investments. Until recently, most state regulations required the fiduciary to apply this standard to each investment. Newer, more progressive regulations permit fiduciaries to apply this standard to the portfolio taken as a whole, thereby allowing a fiduciary to balance a portfolio with higher-yield, higher-risk investments. In states with more progressive regulations, practically every type of security is eligible for inclusion in the portfolio of investments made by a fiduciary, provided that the portfolio investments, in their totality, are those of a prudent person.

Public equity markets
Organized markets for trading in equity shares such as common stocks, preferred stocks, and warrants. Includes markets for both regularly traded and nonregularly traded securities.

Public offering
General solicitation for participation in an investment opportunity. Interstate public offerings are supervised by the U.S. Securities and Exchange Commission (see separate citation).

Quality control
The process by which a product is checked and tested to ensure consistent standards of high quality.

Rate of return
The yield obtained on a security or other investment based on its purchase price or its current market price. The total rate of return is current income plus or minus capital appreciation or depreciation.

Real property
Includes the land and all that is contained on it.

Realignment
See Resource realignment

Recession
Contraction of economic activity occurring between the peak and trough (see separate citations) of a business cycle.

Regulated market
A market in which the government controls the forces of supply and demand, such as who may enter and what price may be charged.

Regulation D
A vehicle by which small businesses make small offerings and private placements of securities with limited disclosure requirements. It was designed to ease the burdens imposed on small businesses utilizing this method of capital formation.

Regulatory Flexibility Act
An act requiring federal agencies to evaluate the impact of their regulations on small businesses before the regulations are issued and to consider less burdensome alternatives.

Research
The initial stage of the innovation process, which includes idea generation and invention.

Research and development financing
A tax-advantaged partnership set up to finance product development for start-ups as well as more mature companies.

Resource mobility
The ease with which labor and capital move from firm to firm or from industry to industry.

Resource realignment
The adjustment of productive resources to interindustry changes in demand.

Resources
The sources of support or help in the innovation process, including sources of financing, technical evaluation, market evaluation, management and business assistance, etc.

Retained business earnings
Business profits that are retained by the business rather than being distributed to the shareholders as dividends.

Return on investment
A profitability measure that evaluates the performance of a business by dividing net profit by net worth.

Revolving credit
An agreement with a lending institution for an amount of money, which cannot exceed a set maximum, over a specified period of time. Each time the borrower repays a portion of the loan, the amount of the repayment may be borrowed yet again.

Risk capital
See Venture capital

Risk management
The act of identifying potential sources of financial loss and taking action to minimize their negative impact.

Routing
The sequence of steps necessary to complete a product during production.

S corporations
See Sub chapter S corporations

SBA
See Small Business Administration

SBA direct loans
Loans made directly by the U.S. Small Business Administration (SBA); monies come from funds appropriated specifically for this purpose. In general, SBA direct loans carry interest rates slightly lower than those in the private financial markets and are available only to applicants unable to secure private financing or an SBA guaranteed loan.

SBA 504 Program
See Certified development corporation

SBA guaranteed loans
Loans made by lending institutions in which the U.S. Small Business Administration (SBA) will pay a prior agreed-upon percentage of the outstanding principal in the event the borrower of the loan defaults. The terms of the loan and the interest rate are negotiated between theborrower and the lending institution, within set parameters.

SBA loans
See Disaster loans; SBA direct loans; SBA guaranteed loans; SBA special lending institution categories

SBA Management Assistance Programs
Classes, workshops, counseling, and publications offered by the U.S. Small Business Administration.

SBA special lending institution categories
U.S. Small Business Administration (SBA) loan program in which the SBA promises certified banks a 72-hour turnaround period in giving its approval for a loan, and in which preferred lenders in a pilot program are allowed to write SBA loans without seeking prior SBA approval.

SBDB
See Small Business Data Base

SBDC
See Small business development centers

SBI
See Small business institutes program

SBIC
See Small business investment corporation

SBIR Program
See Small Business Innovation Development Act of 1982

Scale economies
The decline of the production cost per unit of output (average cost) as the volume of output increases.

Scale efficiency
The reduction in unit cost available to a firm when producing at a higher output volume.

SCORE
See Service Corps of Retired Executives

SEC
See Securities and Exchange Commission

SECA
See Self-Employment Contributions Act

Second-stage financing
Working capital for the initial expansion of a company that is producing, shipping, and has growing accounts receivable and inventories. Also known as Second-round financing.

Secondary market
A market established for the purchase and sale of outstanding securities following their initial distribution.

Secondary worker
Any worker in a family other than the person who is the primary source of income for the family.

Secondhand capital
Previously used and subsequently resold capital equipment (e.g., buildings and machinery).

Securities and Exchange Commission (SEC)
Federal agency charged with regulating the trade of securities to prevent unethical practices in the investor market.

Securitized debt
A marketing technique that converts long-term loans to marketable securities.

Seed capital
Venture financing provided in the early stages of the innovation process, usually during product development.

Self-employed person
One who works for a profit or fees in his or her own business, profession, or trade, or who operates a farm.

Self-Employment Contributions Act (SECA)
Federal law that governs the self-employment tax (see separate citation).

Self-employment income
Income covered by Social Security if a business earns a net income of at least $400.00 during the year. Taxes are paid on earnings that exceed $400.00.

Self-employment retirement plan
See Keogh plan

Self-employment tax
Required tax imposed on self-employed individuals for the provision of Social Security and Medicare. The tax must be paid quarterly with estimated income tax statements.

Self-funding
A health benefit plan in which a firm uses its own funds to pay claims, rather than transferring the financial risks of paying claims to an outside insurer in exchange for premium payments.

Service Corps of Retired Executives (SCORE)
Volunteers for the SBA Management Assistance Program who provide one-on-one counseling and teach workshops and seminars for small firms.

Service firm
See Business service firm

Service sector
Broadly defined, all U.S. industries that produce intangibles, including the five major industry divisions of transportation, communications, and utilities; wholesale trade; retail trade; finance, insurance, and real estate; and services.

Set asides
See Small business set asides

Short-haul service
A type of transportation service in which the transporter supplies service between cities where the maximum distance is no more than 200 miles.

Short-term debt
An obligation that matures in one year.

SIC codes
See Standard Industrial Classification codes

Single-establishment enterprise
See Establishment

Small business
An enterprise that is independently owned and operated, is not dominant in its field, and employs fewer than 500 people. For SBA purposes, the U.S. Small Business Administration (SBA) considers various other factors (such as gross annual sales) in determining size of a business.

Small Business Administration (SBA)
An independent federal agency that provides assistance with loans, management, and advocating interests before other federal agencies.

Small Business Data Base
A collection of microdata (see separate citation) files on individual firms developed and maintained by the U.S. Small Business Administration.

Small business development centers (SBDC)
Centers that provide support services to small businesses, such as individual counseling, SBA advice, seminars and conferences, and other learning center activities. Most services are free of charge, or available at minimal cost.

Small business development corporation
See Certified development corporation

Small business-dominated industry
Industry in which a minimum of 60 percent of employment or sales is in firms with fewer than 500 employees.

Small Business Innovation Development Act of 1982
Federal statute requiring federal agencies with large extramural research and development budgets to allocate a certain percentage of these funds to small research and development firms. The program, called the Small Business Innovation Research (SBIR) Program, is designed to stimulate technological innovation and make greater use of small businesses in meeting national innovation needs.

Small business institutes (SBI) program
Cooperative arrangements made by U.S. Small Business Administration district offices and local colleges and universities to provide small business firms with graduate students to counsel them without charge.

Small business investment corporation (SBIC)
A privately owned company licensed and funded through the U.S. Small Business Administration and private sector sources to provide equity or debt capital to small businesses.

Small business set asides
Procurement (see separate citation) opportunities required by law to be on all contracts under $10,000 or a certain percentage of an agency's total procurement expenditure.

Smaller firms
For U.S. Department of Commerce purposes, those firms not included in the Fortune 1000.

SMSA
See Metropolitan statistical area

Socially and economically disadvantaged
Individuals who have been subjected to racial or ethnic prejudice or cultural bias without regard to their qualities as individuals, and whose abilities to compete are impaired because of diminished opportunities to obtain capital and credit.

Sole proprietorship
An unincorporated, one-owner business, farm, or professional practice.

Special lending institution categories
See SBA special lending institution categories

Standard Industrial Classification (SIC) codes
Four-digit codes established by the U.S. Federal Government to categorize businesses by type of economic activity; the first two digits correspond to major groups such as construction and manufacturing, while the last two digits correspond to subgroups such as home construction or highway construction.

Start-up
A new business, at the earliest stages of development and financing.

Start-up costs
Costs incurred before a business can commence operations.

Start-up financing
Financing provided to companies that have either completed product development and initial marketing or have been in business for less than one year but have not yet sold their product commercially.

Stock
A certificate of equity ownership in a business.

Stop-loss coverage
Insurance for a self-insured plan that reimburses the company for any losses it might incur in its health claims beyond a specified amount.

Strategic planning
Projected growth and development of a business to establish a guiding direction for the future. Also used to determine which market segments to explore for optimal sales of products or services.

Structural unemployment
See Unemployment

Sub chapter S corporations
Corporations that are considered noncorporate for tax purposes but legally remain corporations.

Subcontract
A contract between a prime contractor and a subcontractor, or between subcontractors, to furnish supplies or services for performance of a prime contract (see separate citation) or a subcontract.

Surety bonds
Bonds providing reimbursement to an individual, company, or the government if a firm fails to complete a contract. The U.S. Small Business Administration guarantees surety bonds in a program much like the SBA guaranteed loan program (see separate citation).

Swing loan
See Bridge financing

Target market
The clients or customers sought for a business' product or service.

Targeted Jobs Tax Credit
Federal legislation enacted in 1978 that provides a tax credit to an employer who hires structurally unemployed individuals.

Tax number
A number assigned to a business by a state revenue department that enables the business to buy goods without paying sales tax.

Taxable bonds
An interest-bearing certificate of public or private indebtedness. Bonds are issued by public agencies to finance economic development.

Technical assistance
See Management and technical assistance

Technical evaluation
Assessment of technological feasibility.

Technology
The method in which a firm combines and utilizes labor and capital resources to produce goods or services; the application of science for commercial or industrial purposes.

Technology transfer
The movement of information about a technology or intellectual property from one party to another for use.

Tenure
See Employee tenure

Term
The length of time for which a loan is made.

Terms of a note
The conditions or limits of a note; includes the interest rate per annum, the due date, and transferability and convertibility features, if any.

Third-party administrator
An outside company responsible for handling claims and performing administrative tasks associated with health insurance plan maintenance.

Third-stage financing
Financing provided for the major expansion of a company whose sales volume is increasing and that is breaking even or profitable. These funds are used for

further plant expansion, marketing, working capital, or development of an improved product. Also known as Third-round or Mezzanine financing.

Time management
Skills and scheduling techniques used to maximize productivity.

Trade credit
Credit extended by suppliers of raw materials or finished products. In an accounting statement, trade credit is referred to as "accounts payable."

Trade name
The name under which a company conducts business, or by which its business, goods, or services are identified. It may or may not be registered as a trademark.

Trade periodical
A publication with a specific focus on one or more aspects of business and industry.

Trade secret
Competitive advantage gained by a business through the use of a unique manufacturing process or formula.

Trade show
An exhibition of goods or services used in a particular industry. Typically held in exhibition centers where exhibitors rent space to display their merchandise.

Trademark
A graphic symbol, device, or slogan that identifies a business. A business has property rights to its trademark from the inception of its use, but it is still prudent to register all trademarks with the Trademark Office of the U.S. Department of Commerce.

Trend
A statistical measurement used to track changes that occur over time.

Trough
See Cyclical trough

UCC
See Uniform Commercial Code

UL
See Underwriters Laboratories

Glossary

Underwriters Laboratories (UL)
One of several private firms that tests products and processes to determine their safety. Although various firms can provide this kind of testing service, many local and insurance codes specify UL certification.

Underwriting
A process by which an insurer determines whether or not and on what basis it will accept an application for insurance. In an experience-rated plan, premiums are based on a firm's or group's past claims; factors other than prior claims are used for community-rated or manually rated plans.

Unfair competition
Refers to business practices, usually unethical, such as using unlicensed products, pirating merchandise, or misleading the public through false advertising, which give the offending business an unequitable advantage over others.

Unfunded accrued liability
The excess of total liabilities, both present and prospective, over present and prospective assets.

Unemployment
The joblessness of individuals who are willing to work, who are legally and physically able to work, and who are seeking work. Unemployment may represent the temporary joblessness of a worker between jobs (frictional unemployment) or the joblessness of a worker whose skills are not suitable for jobs available in the labor market (structural unemployment).

Uniform Commercial Code (UCC)
A code of laws governing commercial transactions across the U.S., except Louisiana. Their purpose is to bring uniformity to financial transactions.

Uniform product code (UPC symbol)
A computer-readable label comprised of ten digits and stripes that encodes what a product is and how much it costs. The first five digits are assigned by the Uniform Product Code Council, and the last five digits by the individual manufacturer.

Unit cost
See Average cost

UPC symbol
See Uniform product code

U.S. Establishment and Enterprise Microdata (USEEM) File
A cross-sectional database containing information on employment, sales, and location for individual enterprises and establishments with employees that have a Dun & Bradstreet credit rating.

U.S. Establishment Longitudinal Microdata (USELM) File
A database containing longitudinally linked sample microdata on establishments drawn from the U.S. Establishment and Enterprise Microdata file (see separate citation).

U.S. Small Business Administration 504 Program
See Certified development corporation

USEEM
See U.S. Establishment and Enterprise Microdata File

USELM
See U.S. Establishment Longitudinal Microdata File

VCN
See Venture capital network

Venture capital
Money used to support new or unusual business ventures that exhibit above-average growth rates, significant potential for market expansion, and are in need of additional financing to sustain growth or further research and development; equity or equity-type financing traditionally provided at the commercialization stage, increasingly available prior to commercialization.

Venture capital company
A company organized to provide seed capital to a business in its formation stage, or in its first or second stage of expansion. Funding is obtained through public or private pension funds, commercial banks and bank holding companies, small business investment corporations licensed by the U.S. Small Business Administration, private venture capital firms, insurance companies, investment management companies, bank trust departments, industrial companies seeking to diversify their investment, and

investment bankers acting as intermediaries for other investors or directly investing on their own behalf.

Venture capital limited partnerships
Designed for business development, these partnerships are an institutional mechanism for providing capital for young, technology-oriented businesses. The investors' money is pooled and invested in money market assets until venture investments have been selected. The general partners are experienced investment managers who select and invest the equity and debt securities of firms with high growth potential and the ability to go public in the near future.

Venture capital network (VCN)
A computer database that matches investors with entrepreneurs.

WAN
See Wide Area Network

Wide Area Network (WAN)
Computer networks linking systems throughout a state or around the world in order to facilitate the sharing of information.

Withholding
Federal, state, social security, and unemployment taxes withheld by the employer from employees' wages; employers are liable for these taxes and the corporate umbrella and bankruptcy will not exonerate an employer from paying back payroll withholding. Employers should escrow these funds in a separate account and disperse them quarterly to withholding authorities.

Workers' compensation
A state-mandated form of insurance covering workers injured in job-related accidents. In some states, the state is the insurer; in other states, insurance must be acquired from commercial insurance firms. Insurance rates are based on a number of factors, including salaries, firm history, and risk of occupation.

Working capital
Refers to a firm's short-term investment of current assets, including cash, short-term securities, accounts receivable, and inventories.

Yield
The rate of income returned on an investment, expressed as a percentage. Income yield is obtained by dividing the current dollar income by the current market price of the security. Net yield or yield to maturity is the current income yield minus any premium above par or plus any discount from par in purchase price, with the adjustment spread over the period from the date of purchase to the date of maturity.

Index

Listings in this index are arranged alphabetically by business plan type, then alphabetically by business plan name. Users are provided with the volume number in which the plan appears.

Index

Index

Index

Index

Index